HERO/ANTI-HERO

HERO/ANTI-HERO

Edited by
Roger B. Rollin

WEBSTER DIVISION McGRAW-HILL BOOK COMPANY

New York   St. Louis   Dallas
San Francisco   Atlanta

Library of Congress Cataloging in Publication Data

Rollin, Roger B   comp.
    Hero/anti-hero.

    (Patterns in literary art series, no. 11)
    Bibliography: p.
    1.   Heroes—Literary collections.
I.   Title.
PN6071.H4R6   1973   808.8'0352   73-3484
ISBN 0-07-053568-X

Editorial Development, Susan Gelles; Editing and Styling, Linda Epstein and Vickie Woodruff; Design, John Keithley and Cathy Gallagher; Production, Peter Guilmette

For Bruce and Lisa Rollin

For their helpful suggestions and personal support I would like to thank Professors Robert Russell, Angela Jeannet, Gordon Wickstrom, and Mr. Thomas Cervasio—all of Franklin and Marshall College, as well as Professors Frederick Garber and George Wellwarth of the State University of New York at Binghamton.

CONTENTS

General Introduction   **xiii**

CHAPTER ONE   THE QUEST FOR
              HONOR AND GLORY   **1**

SHORT STORIES
Hero or Fool?   **2**
    A Son of the Gods   Ambrose Bierce   **3**
    Run, Run, Run, Run   A. J. Liebling   **8**
    The Greatest Man in the World   James Thurber   **21**

POETRY
Above All, Honor   **27**
    To Sir Henry Cary   Ben Jonson   **27**
    To Lucasta, Going to the Wars   Richard Lovelace   **28**
Ulysses: Hero, Villain, or Victim?   **28**
    Ulysses and the Siren   Samuel Daniel   **29**
    Ulysses   Alfred, Lord Tennyson   **31**
    Odysseus   W. S. Merwin   **33**
    Ulysses   John Ciardi   **34**
Home and the Hero   **36**
    Sir Patrick Spens   Anonymous   **36**
    Oh stay at home, my lad, and plough
                             A. E. Housman   **38**
The Athlete as Hero   **38**
    To an Athlete Dying Young   A. E. Housman   **39**
    Ex-Basketball Player   John Updike   **40**
    Autumn Begins in Martin's Ferry, Ohio
                             James Wright   **41**

Two American Heroes: Studies in Black and White   **42**
  John Henry   Anonymous   **42**
  Buffalo Bill's   e. e. cummings   **44**
The Hero as Memory   **45**
  I Think Continually of Those Who Were
    Truly Great   Stephen Spender   **45**

DRAMA
  King Henry the Fourth, Part One
    William Shakespeare   **48**

CHAPTER TWO   THE QUEST FOR VICTORY   **127**

SHORT STORIES
  The Ironies of Victory   **128**
    David and Goliath   Old Testament   **130**
    David   Josephine Miles   **133**
    David and Goliath   Don Geiger   **134**
    A Mystery of Heroism   Stephen Crane   **135**
    Buddies   Giovanni Verga   **142**
    War   Luigi Pirandello   **150**

POETRY
  The Hero in Peace and War   **153**
    Beat! Beat! Drums!   Walt Whitman   **154**
    The March into Virginia   Ending in the
      First Manassas   Herman Melville   **155**
    Christmas Eve Under Hooker's Statue
      Robert Lowell   **156**

Initiation   **157**
   Unarmed Combat   Henry Reed   **157**
   Losses   Randall Jarrell   **159**
   Base Details   Siegfried Sassoon   **160**
   Dulce et Decorum Est   Wilfred Owen **160**
Pro Patria Mori   **161**
   The Death of the Ball Turret Gunner

                             Randall Jarrell **162**
   The Death of a Soldier   Wallace Stevens **162**
   A Hell of a Day   Tim Reynolds   **162**
   My Triumph Lasted   Emily Dickinson   **163**
   Disabled   Wilfred Owen   **163**
   The Heroes   Louis Simpson   **165**
In Memoriam   **165**
   Concord Hymn   Ralph Waldo Emerson   **166**
   Grass   Carl Sandburg   **166**

DRAMA
   The Straw Man   Antonio Martínez Ballesteros   **168**

**CHAPTER THREE   THE QUEST FOR
                        SOCIAL ORDER**   **181**

SHORT STORIES
   The Hero and Society   **183**
     Fire and Cloud   Richard Wright   **184**
     The Patriot   Sean O'Faolain   **228**

POETRY

O Brave New World   **244**

   To the Virginian Voyage   Michael Drayton   **244**

   Bermudas   Andrew Marvell   **247**

   The Gift Outright   Robert Frost   **248**

   For the Grave of Daniel Boone   William Stafford   **248**

One Nation Indivisible   **249**

   October 16   Langston Hughes   **250**

   Frederick Douglass   Robert Hayden   **251**

I Have a Dream...   **251**

   Malcolm Spoke/who listened?   Don L. Lee   **252**

   Medgar Evers   Gwendolyn Brooks   **253**

   next to of course god america i   e. e. cummings   **254**

DRAMA

   The Devil in the Dark   Gene Coon   **256**

CHAPTER FOUR   THE QUEST FOR LOVE   **285**

SHORT STORIES

The Power of Love: Heroism in Everyday Life   **286**

   The Kiss   Anton Chekhov   **287**

   A & P   John Updike   **301**

   The Magic Barrel   Bernard Malamud   **306**

POETRY

The Hero as Lover   **320**

   The Squire   From "The General Prologue" to

     The Canterbury Tales   Geoffrey Chaucer   **321**

   Sonnet 41   Sir Philip Sidney   **322**

x

The Lady as Hero and Heroine   **323**
    The White Goddess   Robert Graves   **324**
    The Sleeping Beauty   E. L. Mayo   **325**
    Her Triumph   William Butler Yeats   **325**
    No Second Troy   William Butler Yeats   **326**
    Ariadne   Thomas Merton   **326**
    Sonnet 130   William Shakespeare   **327**
    Love Poem   John Frederick Nims   **328**
    Men marry what they need. I marry you
                                 John Ciardi   **329**
    The Ballad of Sue Ellen Westerfield
                            Robert Hayden   **330**
Lovers as Heroes   **331**
    Meeting   Josephine Miles   **332**
    Crossing the Frontier   A. D. Hope   **332**
    The Sun Rising   John Donne   **333**
Love and Loss   **334**
    Whoso List To Hunt   Sir Thomas Wyatt   **335**
    They Flee from Me   Sir Thomas Wyatt   **336**
    The Lost Music   Robert Hillyer   **336**
Anyone as Hero   **337**
    After The Lone Ranger Died   R. G. Vliet   **338**
    anyone lived in a pretty how town
                           e. e. cummings   **338**

DRAMA
    Marty   Paddy Chayefsky   **340**

Acknowledgments   **371**

Bibliography   **374**

GENERAL INTRODUCTION

The American hero lives in all of us ... and if we are not all heroes, we are all hero-ridden. Descendents of a legend, we persist in identifying with it.

Milton Caniff

When it comes to heroes, Milton Caniff is something of an expert. For almost forty years millions of Americans have avidly followed the adventures of the fictional heroes he has created in his comic strips, *Terry and the Pirates* and *Steve Canyon.* But is Caniff's claim that we Americans are "hero-ridden" really valid?

Certainly it is difficult to deny that we seem to be fond of naming our cities, our streets, and even our schools after heroes, both male and female. And it is also true that in school heroes are often the subjects of our study. Outside of school Americans do seem to pay a good deal of attention to sports and entertainment heroes, to the fictional heroes of movies and television, and to the real-life heroes offered to us by the news media.

Though we may not always be aware of it, then, wherever we turn we seem to encounter figures who remind us of our legendary past— or who are in the process of making the legends of the future out of the present. Heroes, in short, seem to form a rather important part of our experience.

I

In this book the term "hero" will be applied to female as well as male characters. The term "heroine"—at least in discussions of literature—has become associated with the type of character who often is merely a complement to the male, who functions in the story mainly as his "romantic interest." Such a term seems unsuitable for a Joan of Arc, for example, who is the hero of George Bernard Shaw's play, *St. Joan,* not its heroine.

All of us begin to acquire heroes quite early in life. Whether they wish it or not, parents, other relatives, older children, teachers, and others often become heroes to the very young. As they mature, children become intrigued by real-life heroes, ranging from the fireman at the nearby station to the star of the high school football team. Finally, although most people are as adults less inclined toward overt hero-worship, there are very few individuals who have not enshrined at least one or two heroes in their personal Valhallas. Thus, if all of us may not be "hero-ridden" exactly, most of us are at least quite "hero-conscious." The intriguing question is—"Why?"

The hero is something more than our conscious ideal. He is also our sometimes conscious, sometimes unconscious, dream. He represents not only what we value in the external world, the world beyond ourselves, but what we value in ourselves, in that inner world of our minds or psyches. For in our dreams and in our daydreams all of us are heroes at least some of the time.

Psychologists tell us that dreaming is valuable for our mental health, that it provides us with a way of getting rid of the frustrations that inevitably occur in our daily lives. Whenever we identify with heroes, whether real or fictitious, we are in effect daydreaming. Whatever power or success we achieve in such daydreams is characteristically possessed by hero figures. By their deeds, then, they act out our wishes for us and this provides us with a form of gratification.

On the other hand, as the hero represents what we desire, the forces arrayed against him represent what we consciously or unconsciously fear. This fear—of various kinds of limitation imposed upon us, of pain, or even of death—is projected onto the human, super-human, or animalistic figures which we identify by such terms as "the enemy" or "the Monster." In his struggles against such figures the hero acts in our behalf. His victory is our victory, as individuals or as members of a group. Even the "tragic hero," who goes down to defeat before his antagonists, provides us with a form of gratification. He demonstrates that though our anxieties or fears are indeed real (and are likely beyond our remedy), our wishes and values are also real and are capable of surviving mere physical defeat. In one way or another, then, the hero transforms nightmare into daydream, negative thoughts and feelings into positive ones. Life-affirming, he combats whatever seems to be life-denying. Creative—even though he is often, paradoxically, a killer—he opposes himself to destruction. It is no wonder then that we value our heroes, that we may well *need* them.

The satisfaction of this need may be one important reason why we continually turn from life to literature. Literature in fact is not necessary to life. Some people apparently can get along without it. How then to explain why most of us seek out literature in *some* form—in books, plays, films, or television dramas? The answer, according to one theory, lies in the previously mentioned analogy between literature and dream. Both, it is thought, give us pleasure by "managing" or controlling in some manner our deepest feelings.

The surface resemblance at least between literature and dream is most obvious in those works that approach closest to fantasy—fairy tales and some types of science fiction, for example. It is much less obvious that other types of literature, even the most realistic novels or films, also bear some resemblance to dream. For like dreams, all types of literature in effect create their own "worlds." The "world" of each literary work is distinctive, bearing its own unique relationship to external reality. When, as readers, we enter into that "world," we experience things, receive varying kinds of satisfaction from that experience, and then return to external reality somehow better off than before we began to read (if we "liked" the work). We seem more able to cope with everyday life. The literary hero helps us to do so because in him we are able to see what we are and what we might become. It is not surprising then that literary heroes can sometimes seem more "real" to us than some of the real people we meet in everyday life.

II

The hero is less important to us as an individual human being than he is as an embodiment and focal point of our emotions. We perceive in him things that we deeply feel. The feelings we project onto the hero are positive ones, and while some of them may be instinctive (like aggressiveness), they may also have their "philosophical" aspects, having to do with our values (such as love of country). Whatever we value in the way of human qualities—courage, strength, high-mindedness, dynamism—is embodied in our heroes or in our images of them. Whether they actually possess such qualities may be less important to us, at least on the emotional level, than our *belief* that they possess them.

This is not to suggest that the hero is merely an image of our own creation, without any real substance. He may be, but most "public" heroes have achieved that status through some visible action. We are what we do, not what we think. The hero, then, must be someone who has *done something,* something special, which others feel has positive value and meaning.

The circumstances amid which the hero does his significant deed are frequently physical, violent, and potentially fatal. It is seldom amid the seats of learning and art, in lovely cities and temperate climes, on sunshine days, or in physical safety that the hero fulfills himself. "Cultural heroes" do exist, of course—individuals like

Leonardo da Vinci or Shakespeare or Einstein—who win admiration for their artistic or intellectual achievements. But for the most part the term "hero" is associated in our minds with one whose struggle has been more external than internal, who has triumphed physically as well as intellectually and spiritually. All heroes are "born" (and sometimes die) amid tension, but usually implicit in our notion of the hero is that, to have become what he is, he has to have risked what he was.

III

Though conflict is the making of the hero, his mission is ultimately to put an end to it. But *how* he does so is all-important. Whether a hero succeeds or fails, neither his success nor his failure can be achieved at *any* price. For, while lesser individuals may act out of mere instinct, the hero is supposed to act out of his commitment to some system of values, whether that system be religious, moral, political, or all three. Nor can that system of values be merely personal. Normally it has to have been sanctified by the group of which he is a member—his tribe, society, or nation. The hero then is supposed to act out of belief and his act engenders belief—in himself and in that value system which has through him been put to the test and which has in effect been proved valid and viable as a guide to conduct. Since most moral values tend to be supported by some religion (in that term's most general sense), the success of the traditional hero is often taken as an affirmation of that "religion." The hero, in short, seems to prove that what we most believe in, and must believe in, is right.

One result of his function as a kind of religio-ethical representative is that the hero is usually an "establishment figure." In a society dominated by a single value system, the hero, in his embodiment and justification of that system, is a force for public solidarity. Invariably then he becomes associated with those for whom such solidarity is right or particularly advantageous or both—society's leaders. A large and complex society (such as ours) can contain more than one important value system, and such systems (and the heroes who embody them) can conflict. When such clashes occur within a society or between two distinct societies (such as nations), the terms "hero" and "villain" tend to be designated according to one's perspective. The "hero" of Society A becomes the "villain" of Society B and vice versa. It is not often that the hero is a hero to his enemies.

In literature "villain" and "anti-hero," it should be stressed, are terms which take on quite different meanings. For the purposes of this discussion the anti-hero can be defined as a literary character who does not conspicuously embody any value system except his own private one (which is frequently in conflict with that of his society). Thus the anti-hero normally is an "anti-establishment" figure. As such he could be regarded as a "villain," but he is usually of too little consequence to merit such status. For example, Yossarian, the main character of Joseph Heller's novel *Catch-22,* a mere captain in the Air Force, is too unimportant for the military establishment to bother itself much about him. Most of the time he is ignored, even though, like other anti-heroes, his personal value system conflicts with that of the powers that be and implies its impoverishment or irrelevance. At his most active, the anti-hero may be something of a rebel, but a rebel without much of a cause other than his own self-interest. A hero's acts are sanctified by his society, an anti-hero's by himself. In an age such as ours, however, in which the retreat into the self has become understandable to many and approved by some, an anti-hero such as Yossarian need not be a contemptible figure.

IV

Heroes, as we have seen, are unifying figures. They provide links between us and our society, between our personal values and those of the public realm, between our dreams and our realities, and among literary works of all kinds—from those we encounter in school to those we seek out for sheer entertainment.

The variety of heroes to be encountered in literature seems almost infinite, but Northrop Frye in *Anatomy of Criticism* has suggested a way in which they can be conveniently grouped into five essential types—not on the basis of their moral stature but by their "power of action," which "may be greater than ours, less, or roughly the same." In this system hero types are classified according to the extent to which they are able to control the natural and human worlds in which they operate.

The first type of hero is the Super Man, who is "superior in *kind*" to ordinary mortals. He is not only much "greater" than we are; he is also significantly "different" from us. It is as if he were of another species than *homo sapiens.* This feeling is reinforced by the fact that the Super Man hero can control his world in ways we cannot control ours. He can, for example, defy "natural law." In this respect he is very like a god, whether he is a character like Prince Arthur in Edmund Spenser's epic poem, *The Faerie Queene,* or like "Superman" of the comics. To *identify* with such great heroes is possible only in our most extreme fantasies. To try to *aspire* to their status might be ennobling but also frustrating. Hence Super Man heroes probably gratify us on the conscious level as exemplars of our highest values and on the unconscious level as agents who transform our deepest anxieties into our most profound wishes. In a sense then they are "Messiah figures" who, it is implied, will appear upon the scene to solve those problems which are so grave that mere mortals can no longer cope with them.

The Supreme Man is the second hero type. Although he is "superior in *degree*" to other human beings, this hero is (or appears to be) human. But he is so much more powerful than we are that it seems as if he could not only control us but our world as well, even though he may not actually be able to do so. Thus, though he is not a god, the Supreme Man hero has a godlike aura about him. The title figure of the great Anglo-Saxon poem *Beowulf* is such a hero; a hero known to every American child, the comic book character "Batman," is another. Both are, like the rest of us, capable of making mistakes (but seldom do), physically vulnerable (but are seldom really hurt), and ultimately mortal (though one sometimes *feels* that they are immortal). The Supreme Man hero can no more defy natural law than we can, yet he may *seem* to.

The third type of hero is the Leader. He is a figure with whom we can identify and toward whom we can aspire because what he is and what he represents are (at least theoretically) within our grasp. He is unmistakably human, not a god or even godlike. He is capable of error, even of sin. He is vulnerable to the assaults of other humans and of the natural world. Though far from weak, he *is* mortal. Milton Caniff's "Steve Canyon," for example, may possess more skills than most of us, but at least some of those skills—such as being able to fly an airplane expertly—could be mastered by us. A hero like the title figure of Shakespeare's history-play *Henry V* may have more power than we have, but we could conceivably become quite powerful governors or senators. The Leader heroes then are of this world and subject to its laws, but they also happen to be about the best this world can produce.

It is with the fourth type of hero, the Common Man hero, that we approach a paradox. In our century it has been the custom of some, chiefly politicians, to flatter ordinary mortals by representing them as the really important members of the human race. Politicians and others have announced that we live in the Age of the Common Man— the true hero of our time. Even though he has been told this time and time again, the Common Man commonly takes the Uncommon Man as *his* hero. Sometimes, of course, it does happen, in life as well as in literature, that ordinary mortals become heroes—but they do so, usually, by fulfilling the traditional standards of heroism. The Common Man hero, therefore, possesses no more power than we do and no more virtue or skill. He is just an ordinary person who happens to rise to an extraordinary occasion, and in doing so he becomes extraordinary, a hero. Sydney Carton, of Charles Dickens' *A Tale of Two Cities,* does one "far, far better thing" than he has ever done, and in so doing he dooms himself to a hero's death. But the Common Man hero may also be a basically ordinary human being who continually becomes involved in extraordinary adventures, such as the youthful police heroes of the television series, *Mod Squad.* Such characters are in a sense "heroes of the moment" rather than "heroes by inheritance." That is, they have not been endowed by nature with special powers but rather have managed under pressure to call upon all of their natural resources.

The hero as Lowly Man is the fifth type of hero. Because he is at best inept and at worst disreputable, this figure is clearly not one toward whom we aspire. Indeed, we may be able to identify with him only during our most self-deprecating moods or in his moments of transcendence. For example, George, of John Steinbeck's novel *Of Mice and Men,* is a migrant farm worker, impoverished, and without any special talents. He could be a hero only to someone like Lennie, his big, half-witted friend. Yet when a series of fatal circumstances finally forces George into taking action, he manages to transcend himself and his lowly situation. Lowly Man heroes are, however, more likely to be encountered in literature in a lighter vein. In the television series *Gomer Pyle,* for example, the title figure is a grown man serving in the Marines, but he manages to be more innocent, more childlike, than most of his younger viewers. Although this naiveté would seem to render him ill-suited for living in this world, it is matched by so much innate virtue that he invariably triumphs over more sophisticated and less high-minded characters. Thus in each episode Gomer blunders into some comic form of heroism.

Worth remembering is the fact that the Common Man Hero and the Lowly Man Hero are most often to be found in comedy, satire, and realistic fiction—that is, in literary works which generally deal with everyday life. Super Man heroes, on the other hand, are more likely to be encountered in works of a "mythic" character. *It is important to note here that in this book the term "myth" and its derivatives will be used in their primary sense—as denoting stories about gods or godlike heroes.* "Myth" is often—and incorrectly—used as just another word for a mere falsehood—as in the exclamation, "Oh, that's only a myth!" But in this book the term "myth" will denote a story whose *truth* about human life is of more importance than its adherence to mere *facts.* In the purest form of myth we (and the hero) encounter a world where the supernatural seems almost commonplace, where the battle between Good and Evil is clearly defined and normally is resolved in a decisive victory for the former. The world of the epic poem is often like this, and the world of the "superhero" comic book is almost always like this.

Supreme Man heroes are also to be found in such literary worlds. More frequently, however, they appear in fictions whose settings suggest a somewhat simplified and somewhat idealized version of the world as we know it. The medieval England of some of Tennyson's poems and the wild West of the more romanticized cowboy films have these qualities in common. The generic term for this kind of high adventure in a half-historical, half-legendary world is "romance."

The Leader heroes can appear in works which seem "realistic" but which, upon closer examination, are highly romanticized. The "Waverly" novels of Sir Walter Scott exemplify this tendency, as do the "James Bond" novels of Ian Fleming. The Leader Hero can, however, also be found in works which appear to be romanticized but which in fact are not at all remote from actual history. *A Man for All Seasons*, Robert Bolt's play about Sir Thomas More, is like this, and so is the film about the invasion of France during World War II, *The Longest Day*.

Because different hero types tend to be thus associated with different kinds of literature, anyone who is able to classify the heroes of the fictions he reads or views has a head start at understanding the nature of such works and how they operate. Such understanding can significantly increase the possibilities for enjoying a wide variety of literature. And increased enjoyment, in the end, is what the study of literature is mainly about.

V

To facilitate the study of the works in this anthology, its plays, poems, and short stories have been grouped under four headings based upon the metaphor of the *quest*. For every hero has his quest, his vital mission. That quest may involve an actual journey to some distant place or an inner journey to the outermost reaches of the hero's mind. But whether that journey is physical or mental, long or short, it invariably will be arduous, perilous, and necessary, for at its end is something of great value to the hero or to those who depend upon him. As the four main divisions of this book suggest, that "something" may be in the form of *Honor and Glory*, of *Victory*, of some kind of *Social Order*, or of *Love*.

But whatever his goal, the hero must be a seeker. To decline the quest is to lose his opportunity to become a hero. To decline the quest is to be less than himself. For, in a sense, any quest is a search for oneself, for one's identity. The hero may or may not triumph. He may win Honor and Glory, Victory, Social Order, or Love—or he may see them slip from his grasp. But whatever the outcome, he *will* find himself. What he is, what he could be, can be determined in the end only by what he does or tries to do.

The quest then can be a metaphor for life itself, the "journey" that every human being must make. That journey will inevitably be one of self-discovery to a greater or lesser degree, but it will also entail a process of self-creation. Whether hero, nonhero, or anti-hero, every individual becomes what he experiences. Literature, then, among all the things it can do for us, is important not only because it gives us pleasure, but also because it can reveal to us the possibilities and the limitations, the dangers and the rewards, of being—and becoming. Literature may not be able to transform us into heroes, but it may help us to become more human. And there may, in the last analysis, be something heroic in that.

The Quest for Honor and Glory

CHAPTER ONE

"Honor" is the code the traditional hero lives by. It is that set of values which finds its highest expression in the hero's deeds. Everyone, of course, has such a code, but the hero's is comprised of the highest possible standards, standards to which he must, if he is an ideal hero, measure up.

The hero's need to satisfy his honor often is what motivates his quest. Whatever challenge he faces is a threat not only to his person, but to his principles. To decline such a challenge would be to risk compromising not only his honor, but those religious or philosophical premises upon which his code is based. When a knight of King Arthur's Round Table does battle with an enemy knight, he is not only defending his personal code of honor, but also the code of honor of King Arthur's court and of chivalry itself. Similarly, when the Western hero faces the gunfighter-villain in the traditional showdown, he is defending not only his personal code of honor but also the "Code of the West." Both the knight and the Western hero are defending "Good" itself, however that "Good" may be interpreted.

The traditional hero must fulfill his honor and he can do that only through action. For besides his principles, the hero must also have the will and the physical ability to act upon those principles when they are threatened.

Glory—fame, renown, reputation—is in one sense only a by-product of heroism; yet the hero is seldom unaware of it. While he may sense that the true value of his deeds lies in their affirmation of religious or philosophical truth and in the benefits they bestow upon society, the hero would be less than human if he did not expect some recognition for his sacrifices and his success. "Fame," John Milton wrote, "is the spur that the clear spirit doth raise," but he went on to observe that the desire for fame is "that last infirmity of noble mind"—a weakness in heroes, perhaps, but truly a weakness of heroes.

Glory is granted to the hero only if he is known to have retained his honor in the accomplishment of his mission. The fact that the hero not only performs great deeds but performs them out of great principles is what raises such deeds from mere actions to the stuff of which legends or myths are made. Paradoxically, this transformation is accomplished by those who are themselves less worthy than the hero. His glory is granted him by nonheroes, by those who affirm his code of honor but who are less able to live up to it. The hero then exists in the splendid isolation of his spiritual, moral, and physical superiority, but one of his rewards is to endure in the splendid isolation of his own myth.

SHORT STORIES

Hero or Fool?

A common fate of the hero is that he is not always recognized as such. Indeed he is often regarded as a fool by those around him, at least initially. Thus the nameless young officer of Ambrose Bierce's Civil War story "A Son of the Gods" is rudely mocked by the ordinary soldiers when they first see him. Paradoxically, it is these same men, steeped in the cynicism and common sense of the ordinary soldier, who are inspired to act gallantly when the young officer proves himself to be, not a fool, but a hero. For one brief moment these nonheroes are transformed into heroes (or fools) themselves.

"A Son of the Gods" could be subtitled "Birth of a Hero." So too could the World War II story "Run, Run, Run, Run" by A. J. Liebling— but only in an ironic sense. For Meecham, the story's main character, is a very ordinary human being with very ordinary and mixed motives for setting out on his quest for honor and glory. As a war correspondent he is supposed to experience combat. And as a human being he has aspirations toward becoming a hero—or at least toward *appearing* to be a hero. Yet he is intensely aware of the risks—risks which he sees being taken every day by many other ordinary men. Are they heroes or fools? Meecham himself doubts that glory is worth such risks, and as for honor, to him it ranks a poor second to survival. Yet Meecham finally elects to go on a bombing mission over France. Is he motivated to go out of a sense of guilt, out of a selfish need to overcome his feelings of cowardice, out of some mixed-up sense of honor—or out of all of these? Faced with the opportunity for heroic behavior, how is one to understand his own motives?

The motives of the main character of James Thurber's fable "The Greatest Man in the World" are clear enough. The trouble is that they

2

are not "acceptable" motives, at least to society. Out of this comic clash of views emerges the significant and serious truth that society has a very high stake in its heroes. Thurber's character is unheroically named Jack Smurch, but he has performed an authentically heroic deed (or an authentically foolish one). Jack, however, is a hero without honor. He is arrogant rather than humble, materialistic rather than idealistic, immoral rather than virtuous. This "daring aviator" is a comic definition of the anti-hero. But since society will grant glory only to those who conform, or appear to conform, to its own sense of what honor is, it is Jack's fate to be suddenly and drastically transformed into a conventional hero in spite of himself.

A Son of the Gods

A Study in the Present Tense

Ambrose Bierce

A breezy day and a sunny landscape. An open country to right and left and forward; behind, a wood. In the edge of this wood, facing the open but not venturing into it, long lines of troops, halted. The wood is alive with them, and full of confused noises—the occasional rattle of wheels as a battery of artillery goes into position to cover the advance; the hum and murmur of the soldiers talking; a sound of innumerable feet in the dry leaves that strew the interspaces among the trees; hoarse commands of officers. Detached groups of horsemen are well in front—not altogether exposed—many of them intently regarding the crest of a hill a mile away in the direction of the interrupted advance. For this powerful army, moving in battle order through a forest, has met with a formidable obstacle—the open country. The crest of that gentle hill a mile away has a sinister look; it says, Beware! Along it runs a stone wall extending to left and right a great distance. Behind the wall is a hedge; behind the hedge are seen the tops of trees in rather straggling order. Among the trees—what? It is necessary to know.

Yesterday, and for many days and nights previously, we were fighting somewhere; always there was cannonading, with occasional keen rattlings of musketry, mingled with cheers, our own or the enemy's, we seldom knew, attesting some temporary advantage. This morning at daybreak the enemy was gone. We have moved forward across his earthworks, across which we have so often vainly attempted to move before, through the debris of his abandoned camps, among the graves of his fallen, into the woods beyond.

How curiously we had regarded everything! how odd it all had seemed! Nothing had appeared quite familiar; the most commonplace objects—an old saddle, a splintered wheel, a forgotten canteen—everything had related something of the mysterious personality of those strange men who had been killing us. The soldier never becomes wholly familiar with the conception of his foes as men like himself; he cannot divest himself of the feeling that they are another order of beings, differently conditioned, in an environment not altogether of the earth. The smallest vestiges of them rivet his attention and engage his interest. He thinks of them as inaccessible; and, catching an unexpected glimpse of them, they appear farther away, and therefore larger, than they really are—like objects in a fog. He is somewhat in awe of them.

From the edge of the wood leading up the acclivity are the tracks of horses and wheels—the wheels of cannon. The yellow grass is beaten down by the feet of infantry. Clearly they have passed this way in thousands; they have not withdrawn by the country roads. This is significant —it is the difference between retiring and retreating.

That group of horsemen is our commander, his staff and escort. He is facing the distant crest, holding his field glass against his eyes with both hands, his elbows needlessly elevated. It is a fashion; it seems to dignify the act; we are all addicted to it. Suddenly he lowers the glass and says a few words to those about him. Two or three aides detach themselves from the group and canter away into the woods, along the lines in each direction. We did not hear his words, but we know them: "Tell General X. to send forward the skirmish line." Those of us who have been out of place resume our positions; the men resting at ease straighten themselves and the ranks are re-formed without a command. Some of us staff officers dismount and look at our saddle girths; those already on the ground remount.

Galloping rapidly along in the edge of the open ground comes a young officer on a snow-white horse. His saddle blanket is scarlet. What a fool! No one who has ever been in action but remembers how naturally every rifle turns toward the man on a white horse; no one but has observed how a bit of red enrages the bull of battle. That such colors are fashionable in military life must be accepted as the most astonishing of all the phenomena of human vanity. They would seem to have been devised to increase the death rate.

This young officer is in full uniform, as if on parade. He is all agleam with bullion—a blue and gold edition of the Poetry of War. A wave of derisive laughter runs abreast of him all along the line. But how handsome he is!—with what careless grace he sits his horse!

He reins up within a respectful distance of the corps commander and salutes. The old soldier nods familiarly; he evidently knows him. A brief colloquy between them is going on; the young man seems to be preferring some request which the elder one is indisposed to grant. Let us ride a little nearer. Ah! too late—it is ended. The young officer salutes again, wheels his horse, and rides straight toward the crest of the hill!

A thin line of skirmishers, the men deployed at six paces or so apart, now pushes from the wood into the open. The commander speaks to his bugler, who claps his instrument to his lips. *Tra-la-la! Tra-la-la!* The skirmishers halt in their tracks.

Meantime the young horseman has advanced a hundred yards. He is riding at a walk, straight up the long slope, with never a turn of the head. How glorious! Gods! what would we not give to be in his place—with his soul! He does not draw his sabre; his right hand hangs easily at his side. The breeze catches the plume in his hat and flutters it smartly. The sunshine rests upon his shoulder straps, lovingly, like a visible benediction. Straight on he rides. Ten thousand pairs of eyes are fixed upon him with an intensity that he can hardly fail to feel; ten thousand hearts keep quick time to the inaudible hoofbeats of his snowy steed. He is not alone—he draws all souls after him. But we remember that we laughed! On and on, straight for the hedge-lined wall, he rides. Not a look backward. O, if he would but turn—if he could but see the love, the adoration, the atonement!

Not a word is spoken; the populous depths of the forest still murmur with their unseen and unseeing swarm, but all along the fringe is silence. The burly commander is an equestrian statue of himself. The mounted staff officers, their field glasses up, are motionless all. The line of battle in the edge of the wood stands at a new kind of "attention," each man in the attitude in which he was caught by the consciousness of what is going on. All these hardened and impenitent man-killers, to whom death in its awfulest forms is a fact familiar to their everyday observation; who sleep on hills trembling with the thunder of great guns, dine in the midst of streaming missiles, and play at cards among the dead faces of their dearest friends—all are watching with suspended breath and beating hearts the outcome of an act involving the life of one man. Such is the magnetism of courage and devotion.

If now you should turn your head you would see a simultaneous movement among the spectators—a start, as if they had received an electric shock—and looking forward again to the now distant horseman you would see that he has in that instant altered his direction and is riding at an angle to his former course. The spectators suppose the sudden deflection to be caused by a shot, perhaps a wound; but take this field glass and you will observe that he is riding toward a break in the wall and hedge. He means, if not killed, to ride through and overlook the country beyond.

You are not to forget the nature of this man's act; it is not permitted to you to think of it as an instance of bravado, nor, on the other hand, a needless sacrifice of self. If the enemy has not retreated he is in force on that ridge. The investigator will encounter nothing less than a line of battle; there is no need of pickets, videttes,[1] skirmishers, to give warning of our approach; our attacking lines will be visible, conspicuous, exposed to an artillery fire that will shave the ground the moment they break from cover, and for half the distance to a sheet of rifle bullets in which nothing can live. In short, if the enemy is there, it would be madness to attack him in front; he must be maneuvered out by the immemorial plan of threatening his line of communication, as necessary to his existence as to the diver at the bottom of the sea his air tube. But how ascertain if the enemy is there? There is but one way,—somebody must go and see. The natural and customary thing to do is to send forward a line of skirmishers. But in this case they will answer in the affirmative with all their lives; the enemy, crouching in double ranks behind the stone wall and in cover of the hedge, will wait until it is possible to count each assailant's teeth. At the first volley a half of the questioning line will fall, the other half before it can accomplish the predestined retreat. What a price to pay for gratified curiosity! At what a dear rate an army must sometimes purchase knowledge! "Let me pay all," says this gallant man—this military Christ!

There is no hope except the hope against hope that the crest is clear. True, he might prefer capture to death. So long as he advances, the line will not fire—why should it? He can safely ride into the hostile ranks and become a prisoner of war. But this would defeat his object. It would not answer our question; it is necessary either that he return unharmed or be shot to death before our eyes. Only so shall we know how to act. If captured—why, that might have been done by a half-dozen stragglers.

Now begins an extraordinary contest of intellect between a man and an army. Our horseman, now within a quarter of a mile of the crest, suddenly wheels to the left and gallops in a direction parallel to it. He has caught sight of his antagonist; he knows all. Some slight advantage of ground has enabled him to overlook a part of the line. If he were here he could tell us in words. But that is now hopeless; he must make the best use of the few minutes of life remaining to him, by compelling the enemy himself to tell us as much and as plainly as possible—which, naturally, that discreet power is reluctant to do. Not a rifleman in those crouching ranks, not a cannoneer at those masked and shotted guns, but knows the needs of the situation, the imperative duty of forbearance.

1. *videttes* (a variation of vedettes) Mounted sentinels stationed in advance of pickets.

Besides, there has been time enough to forbid them all to fire. True, a single rifle shot might drop him and be no great disclosure. But firing is infectious—and see how rapidly he moves, with never a pause except as he whirls his horse about to take a new direction, never directly backward toward us, never directly forward toward his executioners. All this is visible through the glass; it seems occurring within pistol shot; we see all but the enemy, whose presence, whose thoughts, whose motives we infer. To the unaided eye there is nothing but a black figure on a white horse, tracing slow zigzags against the slope of a distant hill—so slowly they seem almost to creep.

Now—the glass again—he has tired of his failure, or sees his error, or has gone mad; he is dashing directly forward at the wall, as if to take it at a leap, hedge and all! One moment only and he wheels right about and is speeding like the wind straight down the slope—toward his friends, toward his death! Instantly the wall is topped with a fierce roll of smoke for a distance of hundreds of yards to right and left. This is as instantly dissipated by the wind, and before the rattle of the rifles reaches us he is down. No, he recovers his seat; he has but pulled his horse upon its haunches. They are up and away! A tremendous cheer bursts from our ranks, relieving the insupportable tension of our feelings. And the horse and its rider? Yes, they are up and away. Away, indeed—they are making directly to our left, parallel to the now steadily blazing and smoking wall. The rattle of the musketry is continuous, and every bullet's target is that courageous heart.

Suddenly a great bank of white smoke pushes upward from behind the wall. Another and another—a dozen roll up before the thunder of the explosions and the humming of the missiles reach our ears and the missiles themselves come bounding through clouds of dust into our covert, knocking over here and there a man and causing a temporary distraction, a passing thought of self.

The dust drifts away. Incredible!—that enchanted horse and rider have passed a ravine and are climbing another slope to unveil another conspiracy of silence, to thwart the will of another armed host. Another moment and that crest too is in eruption. The horse rears and strikes the air with its forefeet. They are down at last. But look again—the man has detached himself from the dead animal. He stands erect, motionless, holding his sabre in his right hand straight above his head. His face is toward us. Now he lowers his hand to a level with his face and moves it outward, the blade of the sabre describing a downward curve. It is a sign to us, to the world, to posterity. It is a hero's salute to death and history.

Again the spell is broken; our men attempt to cheer; they are choking with emotion; they utter hoarse, discordant cries; they clutch their weapons and press tumultuously forward into the open. The skirmishers, without orders, against orders, are going forward at a keen run, like hounds unleashed. Our cannon speak and the enemy's now open in full chorus; to right and left as far as we can see, the distant crest, seeming now so near, erects its towers of cloud and the great shot pitch roaring down among our moving masses. Flag after flag of ours emerges from the wood, line after line sweeps forth, catching the sunlight on its burnished arms. The rear battalions alone are in obedience; they preserve their proper distance from the insurgent front.

The commander has not moved. He now removes his field glass from his eyes and glances to the right and left. He sees the human current flowing on either side of him and his huddled escort, like tide waves parted by a rock. Not a sign of feeling in his face; he is thinking. Again he directs his eyes forward; they slowly traverse that malign and awful crest. He addresses a calm word to his bugler. *Tra-la-la! Tra-la-la!* The injunction has an imperiousness which enforces it. It is repeated by all the bugles of all the subordinate commanders; the sharp metallic notes assert themselves above the hum of the advance and penetrate the sound of the cannon. To halt is to withdraw. The colors move slowly back; the lines face about and sullenly follow, bearing their wounded; the skirmishers return, gathering up the dead.

Ah, those many, many needless dead! That great soul whose beautiful body is lying over yonder, so conspicuous against the sere hillside—could it not have been spared the bitter consciousness of a vain devotion? Would one exception have marred too much the pitiless perfection of the divine, eternal plan?

Run, Run, Run, Run

A. J. Liebling

When Allardyce Meecham heard that the boys were dead, he felt that he should have flown with them. Meecham was a war correspondent, but he had not yet had a chance to see much of the war. He had come to England in February, 1944, straight from the Hotel Algonquin, where he had had only four or five days to wear his uniform in the lobby, and he did not feel natural wearing it even after a fortnight in London. His nearest approach to action so far had been a visit to an American bomber station in Essex, where he had arranged to go on a bombing mission with a Marauder crew. Now he felt guilty because he had not gone. If he had he would have been dead, too, and that had not been part of his plan, but he felt somehow that this was an ignoble consideration. At the field, a squadron intelligence officer named Kobold had told him the mediums had been having very small losses, an average of one in two hundred sorties. "I wanted to fly one mission and write a story about it, and pretend to myself that I was a big man," Meecham thought self-accusingly, "but if I had expected they would be killed I wouldn't have gone with them." This may or may not have been true. There was no way now of proving it. But Meecham never gave himself the benefit of the doubt because he was afraid that if he did it once he would take advantage of the precedent. "What could you have done, anyway," he asked himself, "if you had known they were going to be killed? Would you have made some excuse and left? Or would you have tried to get them not to go? They would have wanted to know how you could be sure. They would have said you were crazy. They would have gone anyway." But he continued to feel as if he had done something wrong. Meecham had left the airfield because he had tired of hanging about waiting for flying weather. Three days' missions had been washed out and there was no sign it would open up, and he had a date with a British woman officer in London for Friday evening.

This was Sunday. Meecham was standing at the bar of his hotel in Piccadilly, and next to him was Kobold, the intelligence officer he had met at the bomber base. Kobold had come into London on a weekend pass, and he had just told Meecham the bad news. "I wasn't frightened," Meecham thought. "I really wasn't. I told them I was coming back to fly with them next week. They expected to be there. They had flown forty missions. They didn't think the weather would clear off during the weekend. They said I would be a sucker to stay." The weather had cleared on Friday afternoon, after he had left. Saturday morning the bomber crew had been killed. At what precise minute, Meecham wondered, but he felt almost sure he knew. It was March, and dawn came medium late. They would not have been fairly on their way before eight. Over Beauvais, in the north of France, at nine, nine-thirty, maybe. Perhaps at the moment he had picked up the telephone by his bed to order breakfast. "Two teas, sausage and tomato. Darling, do you want sausage and tomato or sausage and mushroom? There's bacon, but it's usually like eating a candle." That must have been the minute. "Two sausage and tomato, then. And lots of toast. Thank you."

"They had all their bombs aboard," Kobold was saying. He was an oldish lieutenant who felt that he should have been a captain months ago. "One big hell of a cloud of smoke, and then parts of the plane falling out of it. No chutes—no time for them. The other boys brought back wonderful pictures of it. Poor bastards." The intelligence officer talked loudly, a little truculently, because he wanted a couple of B-17 pilots at the other end of the bar to hear him. The heavy-bomber people sometimes talked as if they had all the losses; the lieutenant wanted to impress this pair. He never flew on operations himself.

Meecham stood just six feet in shoes, but because of his thin, long legs and short, beanlike torso he seemed longer than that when he stood up and shorter than that when he sat down. He had a white face, wide at the cheekbones and covered with faint, rusty blotches, and carroty hair that for the last five years had just failed to cover the top of his head. People seeing him at a bar thought of him as tall and red-headed, but others, who had looked at him seated at a restaurant table, remembered him as bald and middle-sized. His eyelashes were almost white. In New York he was a dramatic critic, but as the war entered its fifth year and all his acquaintances—book reviewers, editorial writers, political columnists, racing handicappers, and publishers' assistants—became war correspondents and went overseas, he had felt lonely. There must be something in the war that none of these people were fine enough to perceive, he had told his wife, who had a responsible job in the promotion department of a woman's magazine and always referred to herself as a "gal." She had agreed with him. She was a good gal. "Besides," she had said, "I think it would be a professional disadvantage for a dramatic critic after the war not to have been a war correspondent. No one would want to hear you lecture." She was having an affair with a Rumanian fashion photographer, who worked her for assignments. Meecham had been disappointed that even his own wife misread his motives. But, fighting down this disappointment, he had gone to his managing editor and asked to be sent to Europe. The editor had sent him because he rather thought there would be a lull before the invasion of the Continent. Meecham would spell one of the paper's regular correspondents accredited to the Army, who would come home for a short vacation before the big show began. "But, of course, if it should start suddenly, you'll be there," the editor had said. "Yes, sir," Meecham had said in a voice from which he had tried to exclude excitement. He had felt exalted as he walked over to Abercrombie & Fitch to be measured for his uniform. But, as he now reflected, he had not thought that he really might be killed. "I wanted something for nothing," he thought unmercifully. He was on the point of admiring how hard on himself he could be, and then he remembered that that would constitute self-approval, so he stopped.

Meecham remembered the interior of the Nissen hut he had slept in at the Marauder field. There had been cots and a table and a stove, hooks on the walls to hang clothes on, and even coat hangers, but to him it had been a Spartan place, where he had been more conscious of the war than in his room in London, which contained a good deal of inlaid furniture and a double bed with a yellow damask cover. There were electric-light bulbs in the hut, but they were not shaded, and you had to go outdoors to get to the latrine. There were six cots in the hut. A Marauder carries a complement of three officers and three enlisted men; the hut accommodated the officers of two planes. One set of three had gone to town on pass; men who flew together took their passes at the same time. This gave Meecham his choice of three cots. The boys of the other Marauder crew had just come back from forty-eight hours in London. Meecham found them in the hut when Kobold brought him there in the evening. He had stayed at the officers' club drinking gin and Italian vermouth with the C.O. and a couple of non-flying intelligence officers until the bar closed, at ten o'clock. Then Kobold had guided him to the hut. It would have been hard to find in the blackout if he had been alone. Kobold had introduced Meecham to the three crewmates. One of them, a large, hairy, blond young man, was in bed already. He was Captain Barry, the pilot. Barry was smoking a last cigarette before going to sleep. One bare, powerful arm lay outside the blankets as he puffed. A B-26, romantically known as a Marauder, is not an easy plane to fly, and old pilots get big forearms and biceps. Barry reached out a big hand to shake Meecham's. "Make yourself at home," he said. Brownlea, the copilot, a wiry young man with a crew haircut, sat at the table with his back to the stove, reading what Meecham observed wonderingly was a book by Robert Briffault, an author Meecham associated vaguely with Granville Hicks and Ouida. "I hope you don't mind loud noises," Brownlea said. "Barry is about to go to sleep. Luckily they have radar here or somebody would have shot him down before this. When he snores he sounds exactly like a four-motor job. He has the Air Force sack medal with so many clusters it looks like a bunch of grapes." "Brownlea is an intellectual," Barry said. "He is a wizard intellectual, they would say in the R.A.F. He is very cheesed with life. He thinks life is a ruddy pantomime. Someday when he is at the controls he will be thinking of an ideology and he will prang the crate. A wizard prang." Elkan, the bombardier-navigator, was sitting on a cot, looking over a set of shiny photographer's prints; he had interrupted the examination only long enough to nod at Meecham when Kobold introduced them. He was a thin young man who in civilian clothes could have been mistaken for a high-school junior. He could not weigh more than a hundred and fifteen pounds and he had a long, pointed nose and large ears. He was still wearing the Class A uniform blouse and pinks in which he had come back from London, and the garrison cap was still on his head. The left breast of his blouse was pretty well loaded with ribbons—even Meecham could recognize the Silver Star, the Distinguished Flying Cross, the Air Medal nutmegged with oak-leaf clusters, the E.T.O. ribbon dotted with stars, and a couple of the innocuous red and yellow ones that make good background even though they don't mean anything much.

Kobold went away and Meecham settled down on a cot. "I'm glad to have you here, sir," Brownlea said to Meecham. "Barry and Elkan are good joes, but Elkan is emotional and Barry is inclined to pure escapism. I have been wanting a chance to talk to someone who has really been around a lot."

Meecham was ashamed to tell him that his travels, until this trip, had been limited to a tourist-class vacation in France when he was in college and four trips to the Central City, Colorado, annual dramatic festivals, so he said nothing.

"Don't give Brownlea any encouragement, sir," Elkan said, "or he will read you the first ten chapters of his book."

"I wouldn't think of it," Brownlea said. "Anyway, they're only in a kind of outline form. I really don't know anything about writing. What I want to know is what you think of the Russians."

Meecham considered himself an untrammelled liberal—during the Spanish Civil War he had attended several cocktail parties for the benefit of the Loyalists—but he had heard talk at home about the Fascist mind of the Air Corps, so he was careful in answering. He liked these boys so much already that he didn't want to alarm or antagonize them. He said merely, "I know the Russians are our Allies. I mean, I believe they're sincere, and they're certainly fighting hard."

"Is that all?" Brownlea said. "Why, they're absolutely wonderful. They're the only hope I see for civilization. Surely, sir, you don't think capitalist society can survive all this? Say, have you ever read this man Briffault?"

"Brownie got a brushoff from a society dame at a bottle club in London," Barry said. "She said she was going to spend a penny and she never came back. He's been a militant proletarian ever since."

Meecham said that, of course, the role Russia would be called upon to play in the future should not be underestimated.

"Well, I don't worry much about that," Barry said, "although I still have a card in the typographical union, so it burns me when I read in the *Reader's Digest* that organized labor is to blame for about everything that gets screwed up. I worked my way through the University of California that way, setting type at night on a paper in Oakland. Where the hell does the *Reader's Digest* think I am, and where is the bird who is writing that stuff? Sitting on his can, I bet. But being from the Coast, I mean, I don't think very much about this war. I'd like to be out smacking those Japs around. I haven't got anything too much against the Germans, except Hitler is a son of a bitch."

"I have," Elkan said. "I'm a Jew, and they've been killing millions of Jews who didn't do a goddam thing to them. I hate the bastards. I like to think of what the bombs will do to them when we make our run."

"You see?" Brownlea said. "Pure emotion. Barry and Elkan don't know anything about the economic bases of imperialism. They reduce everything to personal relationships."

"She said she had to spend a penny," Barry said to nobody in particular. "Brownie offered to lend her a shilling. She gave him a look that said, 'Anybody that dumb . . .' And the brush."

Elkan said, "To change the subject, which of these pictures do you like the best?"

"Are they of a broad?" Barry asked.

"No, you wolf—me," Elkan answered severely. "I went down to see the Tower of London yesterday, and then I walked around and had some pictures taken at a photographer's. I want to pick out the best one and have some copies made from it to send home. I want to send them to my mother and my girl and people like that." Meecham had already learned that Elkan's parents lived in Bayonne, New Jersey, where his father had a dry-cleaning store. He had gone two years to Rutgers but hadn't had enough money to continue, and for a year or so before he enlisted he had helped in the store. He hadn't as much assurance as some of the bigger, louder boys, who gave the impression that the whole Air Force came from Texas, but the fellows in his squadron had a lot of respect for him. Barry, Brownlea, and Meecham began passing the photographer's proofs from one to another. Meecham could see that the two pilots were considering them very seriously. In all but one of the proofs, Elkan had the visor of his cap pulled well down and was scowling and puffing out his chest. The photographer had got a good, clear picture of the ribbons. But the thin, triangular face and the frail, bony neck still looked like a little boy's. Only one of the proofs showed Elkan smiling. The wide smile made him look younger and more ingenuous than ever, but the picture was the only one of the lot that wasn't absurd. All three of the consultants agreed it was the best.

"That's the only one that looks like the real Ernie," Barry said.

"That's the one your mother would like to have," said Brownlea.

And Meecham said, "That's the best." He could sense that Ernie was disappointed and that if he had not been there the little bombardier-navigator might have tried to argue with the others.

But Elkan accepted the reinforced verdict. "Christ," he said sadly, "I guess I'll never look like a hero." Meecham could see that he was worrying about his girl back home.

They had talked a while longer and then turned in. Meecham had felt unexpectedly ashamed because his body looked so white and old compared to theirs. He was forty-three and the last exercise he could remember had been a fight with the juvenile of a show he had panned in 1937, but the bartender and the home and garden editor had stopped it after the first swing, when the juvenile's pince-nez fell on the floor.

There had been no mission the next morning, on account of the weather. Meecham had got up at seven and gone dutifully to mess, but the boys had chosen to sleep until nearly noon.

"It must be awfully slow for you here, sir," Barry had said the next time Meecham saw him. "I suppose you wanted to go over with us and see some fun."

"It isn't dull at all," Meecham had said, and meant it. "It's very interesting." He had not added, "It's all new to me," because he felt a childish reluctance to let the boys know he was so green. He hadn't really thought of flying a mission on his first visit to the field, either. But Barry looked so competent and unworried that Meecham had found himself saying, "I sure would like to go with you. Do you think the C.O. would let me?"

Barry had grinned and said, "Sure. We've flew lots of correspondents in our ship. It breaks the monotony." And they had shaken hands on it.

Meecham had slept in the hut a second and third night and each had been followed by a day of bad weather. Even in this brief time he had begun to think of himself as a member of the crew of the Typographical Error, the name Barry had given his B-26. He had gone through the preliminary processes of a Marauder mission, which at that time he had thought piquant rather than grim. The squadron intelligence officer had told him what to do if he had to bail out over France. He was to hide his parachute and then take cover and lie still until somebody found him. The French underground people would be pretty sure to find him, the intelligence officer said, and they would smuggle him across France and into a neutral country, although it might take months. The prospect had sounded alluring as the intelligence officer described it, and Meecham had been unable to stop daydreaming about adventures with admiring and sympathetic Frenchwomen. The one thing the officer had not said anything about was what to do if you were dead. So Meecham had not thought about it.

On the third bad morning he had begun to feel bored and had remembered the date with the woman officer in London. There was a train at noon and he had decided to leave by it. When he began packing his bag the boys were still in bed, and when he finished he went around to each cot and shook hands before he started for the jeep that was to take him to the railway station. Meecham could remember Barry's strong grip and Elkan's slender hand and Brownlea grinning and waving his clenched left fist. Brownlea's father, Meecham had learned, was president of a savings bank in Boston.

Remembering, Meecham felt that the date with them was more binding than if they had survived and that he could never be pleased with himself if he did not fly a mission now. But there was no exhilaration in the thought. He returned to Essex three days later. He found it easy to arrange, at Ninth Air Force Headquarters, for permission to go along on a bombardment. "The story has been done a lot of times before," a public relations officer warned him. "There's nothing much to it." Meecham explained that he just wanted to see what it was like. He didn't say anything about the crew of the Typographical Error. It seemed to him for a moment, after they had said he could go, that he was doing a causeless thing. It isn't being brave, he told himself, because the mathematical chance of getting hurt is no greater now than it was last week, and then it was very small. Barry and his ship just had bad luck. And there won't be any story in it either. But he was afraid, and that was precisely what he could not afford to admit to himself. Nobody at the field seemed astonished that he wanted to do it. The boys at the officers' club made him welcome with gin and Italian vermouth, and he was introduced to the officers he was now assigned to fly with. Their ship was named the Roll Me Over, and they were nice boys enough, Meecham thought, but it was like a widower's marriage; he could not get as interested in them as in the dead crew. Schifferdecker, the pilot, was a squat, broad-shouldered boy who had played football at Cornell, where he had taken a course in hotel management. He kept telling Meecham that after the war the British would have to build modern hotels all over England if they expected any Americans ever to come back there. Thurman, the copilot, a tall, handsome young man from someplace in Wisconsin, did not have much to say for himself. He had a girl in a show in London, his crewmates said, and he considered every hour he had to spend at the field time wasted. "Missions are the only chance he has to catch up on his sleep," Schifferdecker said. Muldowney, the bombardier-navigator, was a pale, gray-eyed young man who looked like a very youthful Franchot Tone and knew it, and who had played in a dance band in St. Paul before enlisting in the Air Corps. "It's a good deal, having a correspondent along," he told Meecham. "We'll be in a soft spot, right in the center of one of the middle elements, where nothing ever happens. Those flak gunners loose off at the first ships, and then, when the first elements drop their bombs, the gunners run like hell. We'll have a breeze. Same thing for fighters. We haven't been getting much fighter opposition. The Heinies keep most of that in Germany to use against the heavy bombers.

But what we have been getting usually lays for the rear element, on the way home, hoping to knock off stragglers. We lost a ship that way yesterday. The boys in the middle have a soft touch." Muldowney had a wide, white grin. "An easy one is always all right with me," he went on. "I've had twenty-eight missions so far, and every easy one means that much better a chance to finish the fifty."

There was no cot for Meecham in the hutment where the Roll Me Overs slept, so he spent the night in a hut in another part of the field, about half a mile from the mess hall. The men in the hut with him were armament and engineering officers. Only two were in bed when Meecham got there. The rest were up most of the night preparing planes for the takeoff. They got in so late that they had just begun to snore when an orderly turned on the lights before dawn next morning. They stayed in bed, the blankets over their heads, while Meecham and the two men who had been in bed early began to dress. Meecham hated to get up early in the morning for any reason at all, and on this particular day he felt worse than usual. He dressed fast, for him, but he was not yet familiar with lace boots, and he had to fumble around in his musette bag to find toothpaste and a towel. Then he felt colicky and went out to look for a latrine. By the time he returned the two other men had gone to the mess hall, and he began to fear that he would lose his way in the dark. The buildings were, of course, blacked out, so he would have no lighted windows to guide him. It would sound like an implausible excuse for missing the raid. He went out of the hut and saw the silhouette of a jeep moving up the road past the hut. There were at least a dozen men on it, some sitting on the hood. He yelled, "Going up to mess?" Someone shouted to him to jump on. Awkwardly he ran along beside the slowly moving jeep, not knowing quite how to get aboard without knocking some other rider off his perch. The jeep stopped and somebody said, "Come along, Pop. You can sit in the back." One of the youngsters in the back seat scrambled out and found a few inches of space on a mudguard, and half a dozen hands grabbed Meecham and hoisted him into the place just vacated. He rode along to the mess hall oblivious of everything except his humiliation. At table he found Schifferdecker and Thurman. Muldowney came along a couple of minutes later, carrying a shiny brown quilted flying suit which he had drawn for Meecham. The breakfast was poor—an omelet badly made of powdered egg and bacon that was all rind and grease. The fruit juice was all gone and the coffee tasted metallic. He wondered if the breakfast was really that bad or if he was frightened. "This is poor chow," Thurman said, and Meecham was reassured. The men in the mess hall straggled out in little groups, crewmates and fellows who knew each other, and climbed into weapons carriers for the ride out to the dispersal building for the briefing. Meecham, of course, rode with the Roll Me Overs.

The briefing reminded him of a lecture in a compulsory course at college. The hall was filled with fellows in flying gear who talked to each other and did not seem too attentive. The intelligence officer stood on a dais at one end of the hall and waved a pointer at various spots on a large map that was projected on a screen behind him. Meecham learned later that all the fliers had been to these particular targets several times and that the lecture had about the same interest for them as an explanation of how to reach New Rochelle. "Our primary target today will be the Montdidier airfield," the officer said. "There is a battery of six mediums on the approach to the Montdidier field. Six mediums." Somebody whistled. "All of you can go now except the bombardiers. Bombardiers stay a minute after the others leave."

Meecham went out with Schifferdecker and Thurman and three sergeants who had joined them in the briefing hall. The sergeants were the rest of the Roll Me Over's crew—radio gunner, flight engineer, and tail gunner. They were named Mickiewicz, Klopstock, and Leopardi. Muldowney had to stay to get his detailed bombing map. When he came out they all got into a weapons carrier with perhaps twenty other fliers. The carrier rolled along on the cinder path that circled the field, stopping at each plane to let off the men who were going to fly in it. So Meecham found himself eventually standing under the shadow of the Roll Me Over. It was daylight now, but the sky was still pink with the embers of dawn. In the truck the boys had been singing a song of which Meecham had been able to distinguish only the first line, "How's your love life?"

He put on the flying suit over his G.I. pants, his sweater, and his combat jacket. Muldowney was brisk and happy, although cold. He rubbed his gloved hands together furiously and stamped about in his flying boots. Schifferdecker was serious and conscientious, conferring with the sergeants. Thurman leaned against the fuselage and Meecham noticed that he looked sleepy. He wondered if Thurman could have got down to London on a late train and back in time to fly. Meecham nodded toward the ship and asked Muldowney if it was all right to get aboard. Muldowney said sure, and went ahead to show the way. This was a moment Meecham had anticipated with distaste, because he didn't know how to get into a B-26 and had a feeling it might call for some display of acrobacy. It was not so hard as he had feared. There were two metal stirrups, no higher than those on an English saddle, and when you got one foot up you reached up with your hands and caught two metal handles in the interior of the plane. Then you swung yourself up and in. He could see that it would be easy to get out when they returned—he would only have to swing himself out by the handles and drop. Somehow this was a major satisfaction. Muldowney motioned him into a compartment behind the nose of the plane. There was no need to kneel or crawl. "There's a hell of a lot of room in these things," Muldowney said. "More than in a Fort. You just sit over there at the side on that pile of chutes." The others came aboard one by one. Schifferdecker and Thurman went past Meecham and into the pilots' compartment, in the nose. The sergeants joined Meecham and Muldowney in the compartment behind the pilots' because Schifferdecker would want their weight up forward for the take-off. "This is a place for the navigator to work," Muldowney told Meecham, "but there isn't any real navigating to do when we follow the leader in a big formation like today. Of course, if we got crippled or had to beat it off by ourselves for any reason, it would be different. I just wander around the ship when we get going, sometimes here and some-times in the bomb bay. We're carrying frag bombs today, by the way. Thirty one-hundred-pound frag bombs. We drop them on the runway and dispersal area to take care of planes and personnel. Sometimes we carry a couple of big ones, but today frags." The motors were turning over. Other planes taxied by them on their way to the runway. Then the Roll Me Over began to roll, too. The motors made such a noise that conversation became impractical, although it was still possible to under-stand a shouted monosyllable. The compartment in which Meecham rode was comfortable, but there was only a view straight out to either side. There was nothing to see in either direction except other B-26s. The plane was swaying and slipping about and he could see Thurman turn and swear. Schifferdecker was running the ship. The pilots sat next to each other. The backs of their seats were armor-plated, as a pro-tection against pieces of flak. Meecham could see there was room for a man to crouch behind them, and he looked forward enviously because there was more to see from the nose of the plane. Thurman, as if reading his thoughts, waved to him to come forward, and he did, scrunching his torso and hams down behind Thurman's seat, while his legs extended over behind Schifferdecker's.

Now the sky was as blue as the Bay of Naples on the wall of a spa-ghetti joint, and it was full of B-26s. They flew in "loose fives," their favorite formation. Meecham started to count all those in sight; he made it sixty-seven, including the planes on the Roll Me Over's wings, but more appeared constantly and he stopped counting. He deduced that the B-26s were just circling while the groups assembled and that the serious part of the expedition had not begun yet. Then the course began to seem to him more purposeful. Almost before he was sure of this, Thurman was plucking at his elbow, waving an arm downward. They were over the coast, heading out over the Channel, which looked not blue but had, at its English edge, the color of a puddle of rain water glistening in sun-light. Then it became lead color. Meecham noticed for the first time that the motors were saying words. They were saying words, groaning, rather, "No, no, no, no." He had ridden in planes before but he had never recognized the words. When they got over the French coast, he thought, "I should be curious. I haven't seen France in twenty years." He looked and it seemed quite like England. He leaned close to Thur-man's ear and shouted, "How long to over target?" Thurman howled back, "Twenty minutes." Meeham went back to the pile of parachutes in the navigator's cabin and Muldowney appeared, probably from the bomb bay, and seemed to be saying something about "fighters." Meecham re-turned to his place behind the pilots and looked down. He saw a midget plane far below them. It was a Spitfire, but he did not know it; he could not tell Allied fighters from Germans. All the attention began to embar-rass Meecham. He felt that Muldowney was treating him like a grand-father on a Sunday auto ride. Muldowney reached through the doorway to the pilots' compartment and tapped Meecham on the shoulder. He wanted to show him something dead ahead, a series of specks in the sky. Then Muldowney grinned and started back to the bomb bay. The specks were not fighters, Meecham saw as the plane drew up on them, but puffs of black smoke. They multiplied, as he watched, and hung in the air, little black balls of grime. He knew what they were from his sporadic attendance at newsreel theaters. The planes of the forward elements were flying through them now. The flak was at very nearly the right altitude, and Meecham began to hear a new sound over the motors—a sharp "Pak!" like a champagne cork popping and then "S-s-s" like half the wine in the bottle fizzing out. The "Pak!" was the shell bursting, and the fizz was the flight of the fragments. Once Thurman threw up a hand in front of his face and flattened himself against the back of his seat, but nothing happened. Meecham wondered if it had been a close one or if Thurman was just jumpy from too much tomcatting. The copilot was waving his hand now and Meecham, following his gesture, could see the bombs falling away from the planes up ahead of them, like chewing gum nuggets out of a vending machine. Then there were no more puffs in the sky. He felt Muldowney's hand on his shoulder again. The boy had been away only an instant, it seemed. Muldowney was laughing and waving his hands palm upward. Thurman took off his earphones and put them on Meecham, so Meecham could listen to the intercom. Schifferdecker said to Meecham through the intercom, "How'd you like it?" Meecham tried to smile, and for all he knew succeeded. Then Schifferdecker made Thurman take the ship. Meecham understood from that that they were on the way home. He gave Thurman the earphones again. The motors said now, "Run, run, run, run." He said to himself,

"I am not making this up, that is what they are saying." He listened again and they were indeed saying, "Run, run," instead of "No, no." Meecham looked at the air-speed indicator and it said "330," which pleased him. Then he went back to Muldowney's compartment and relaxed on the parachutes. Muldowney was grinning and waving his hands and shouting into Meecham's ear, and finally Meecham could understand what he was saying: "I told you that flak would stop as soon as the first planes got their bombs away!" Meecham succeeded in asking whether *he* had got his bombs away and Muldowney joined a thumb and forefinger in a circle to show he had put his bombs right on the bull's-eye. Sergeant Mickiewicz, a bulky blond with a red face, appeared in the compartment and grinned at Meecham. Nothing happened on the way back, but it seemed five times as long as it had going out.

When they got out of the plane, Schifferdecker started swearing. "The goddam wash nearly made me airsick," he said. "Those goddam cowboys in the ships on our wings must think they're driving taxicabs. Whoever checked them out in a bomber ought to have his head examined. What a rat race. . . ."

Thurman said, "If they don't keep us too long at the goddam interrogation I can catch the twelve-o'clock train to London."

Muldowney said, "Twenty-nine down and twenty-one to go. I hope they send us a correspondent on every trip! I wonder if any of those leading planes got flak in them."

Meecham felt unreasonably exalted. After all, he told himself reprovingly, he had only escaped from a danger that he had got himself into. And not a great danger, either, he thought. I didn't see one plane shot down. Still, he couldn't help thinking, pretty good for a dramatic critic. He had forgotten Barry and Elkan and Brownlea.

Meecham was still in the midst of his euphoria when he boarded the London train at Chelmsford in midafternoon. He had not been in as much haste to get away as Thurman, and had remained to eat a pretty good lunch of pork chops and canned pineapple at the field. The train was crowded, and although he had a first-class ticket, he had to stand in the corridor outside a compartment filled with American enlisted men who had got on further up the line. When they saw his war-correspondent shoulder flash they tapped on the glass and asked him in. They were all Fortress men who, it appeared, had been on dozens of twelve-hour missions over Germany, from almost all of which they had returned with their ships aflame and three engines out. Meecham was ashamed to tell them he had been only as far as France that morning. By the time the train arrived at Liverpool Street station his exuberance was waning. Coming out into Broad street, he felt hungry again. He had had what for him was a phenomenally long day. He stopped in at a place called Gow's, a combination fishmonger's and restaurant, and ordered a dozen oysters at the counter. He ordered a second dozen, but the man behind the counter said that the Ministry of Food did not allow them to sell more than eight bob worth to a customer and he had had it. Meecham felt a certain resentment; he had half a mind to tell the man where he had been that morning. That would show him. But perhaps the man had a son in the R.A.F., so he would not be impressed. Or three R.A.F. sons, all killed in the Battle of Britain, so he would be pained by any reference to flying. The thought recalled Barry and Brownlea and Elkan for the first time that day. Meecham wondered why it had seemed essential that, because of them, he go on a mission after they were dead. He paid for his oysters and went out into the street to look for a taxi. He hoped his girl was in town and had no date for the evening. After all, this ought to impress her.

The Greatest Man in the World

James Thurber

Looking back on it now, from the vantage point of 1950, one can only marvel that it hadn't happened long before it did. The United States of America had been, ever since Kitty Hawk, blindly constructing the elaborate petard by which, sooner or later, it must be hoist. It was inevitable that some day there would come roaring out of the skies a national hero of insufficient intelligence, background, and character successfully to endure the mounting orgies of glory prepared for aviators who stayed up a long time or flew a great distance. Both Lindbergh and Byrd, fortunately for national decorum and international amity, had been gentlemen; so had our other famous aviators. They wore their laurels gracefully, withstood the awful weather of publicity, married excellent women, usually of fine family, and quietly retired to private life and the enjoyment of their varying fortunes. No untoward incidents, on a worldwide scale, marred the perfection of their conduct on the perilous heights of fame. The exception to the rule was, however, bound to occur and it did, in July, 1937, when Jack ("Pal") Smurch, erstwhile mechanic's helper in a small garage in Westfield, Iowa, flew a secondhand, single-motored Bresthaven Dragon-Fly III monoplane all the way around the world, without stopping.

Never before in the history of aviation had such a flight as Smurch's ever been dreamed of. No one had even taken seriously the weird floating auxiliary gas tanks, invention of the mad New Hampshire professor of astronomy, Dr. Charles Lewis Gresham, upon which Smurch placed full reliance. When the garage worker, a slightly built, surly, unprepossessing young man of twenty-two, appeared at Roosevelt Field in early July, 1937, slowly chewing a great quid of scrap tobacco, and announced, "Nobody ain't seen no flyin' yet," the newspapers touched briefly and satirically upon his projected twenty-five-thousand-mile flight. Aeronautical and automotive experts dismissed the idea curtly, implying that it was a hoax, a publicity stunt. The rusty, battered, secondhand plane wouldn't go. The Gresham auxiliary tanks wouldn't work. It was simply a cheap joke.

Smurch, however, after calling on a girl in Brooklyn who worked in the flap-folding department of a large paper-box factory, a girl whom he later described as his "sweet patootie," climbed nonchalantly into his ridiculous plane at dawn of the memorable seventh of July, 1937, spit a curve of tobacco juice into the still air, and took off, carrying with him only a gallon of bootleg gin and six pounds of salami.

When the garage boy thundered out over the ocean the papers were forced to record, in all seriousness, that a mad, unknown young man—his name was variously misspelled—had actually set out upon a preposterous attempt to span the world in a rickety, one-engined contraption, trusting to the long-distance refueling device of a crazy schoolmaster. When, nine days later, without having stopped once, the tiny plane appeared above San Francisco Bay, headed for New York, sputtering and choking, to be sure, but still magnificently and miraculously aloft, the headlines, which long since had crowded everything else off the front page—even the shooting of the Governor of Illinois by the Vileti gang—swelled to unprecedented size, and the news stories began to run to twenty-five and thirty columns. It was noticeable, however, that the accounts of the epoch-making flight touched rather lightly upon the aviator himself. This was not because facts about the hero as a man were too meager, but because they were too complete.

Reporters, who had been rushed out to Iowa when Smurch's plane was first sighted over the little French coast town of Serly-le-Mer, to dig up the story of the great man's life, had promptly discovered that the story of his life could not be printed. His mother, a sullen short-order cook in a shack restaurant on the edge of a tourists' camping ground near Westfield, met all inquiries as to her son with an angry "Ah, the hell with him; I hope he drowns." His father appeared to be in jail somewhere for stealing spotlights and laprobes from tourists' automobiles; his young brother, a weak-minded lad, had but recently escaped from the Preston, Iowa,

Reformatory and was already wanted in several Western towns for the theft of money order blanks from post offices. These alarming discoveries were still piling up at the very time that Pal Smurch, the greatest hero of the twentieth century, blear-eyed, dead for sleep, half-starved, and piloting his crazy junk heap high above the region in which the lamentable story of his private life was being unearthed, headed for New York and a greater glory than any man of his time had ever known.

The necessity for printing some account in the papers of the young man's career and personality had led to a remarkable predicament. It was of course impossible to reveal the facts, for a tremendous popular feeling in favor of the young hero had sprung up, like a grass fire, when he was halfway across Europe on his flight around the globe. He was, therefore, described as a modest chap, taciturn, blond, popular with his friends, popular with girls. The only available snapshot of Smurch, taken at the wheel of a phony automobile in a cheap photo studio at an amusement park, was touched up so that the little vulgarian looked quite handsome. His twisted leer was smoothed into a pleasant smile. The truth was, in this way, kept from the youth's ecstatic compatriots; they did not dream that the Smurch family was despised and feared by its neighbors in the obscure Iowa town, nor that the hero himself, because of numerous unsavory exploits, had come to be regarded in Westfield as a nuisance and a menace. He had, the reporters discovered, once knifed the principal of his high school—not mortally, to be sure, but he had knifed him; and on another occasion, surprised in the act of stealing an altar cloth from a church, he had bashed the sacristan over the head with a pot of Easter lilies; for each of these offences he had served a sentence in the reformatory.

Inwardly, the authorities, both in New York and in Washington, prayed that an understanding Providence might, however awful such a thing seemed, bring disaster to the rusty, battered plane and its illustrious pilot, whose unheard-of flight had aroused the civilized world to hosannas of hysterical praise. The authorities were convinced that the character of the renowned aviator was such that the limelight of adulation was bound to reveal him to all the world as a congenital hooligan mentally and morally unequipped to cope with his own prodigious fame. "I trust," said the Secretary of State, at one of many secret Cabinet meetings called to consider the national dilemma, "I trust that his mother's prayer will be answered," by which he referred to Mrs. Emma Smurch's wish that her son might be drowned. It was, however, too late for that—Smurch had leaped the Atlantic and then the Pacific as if they were millponds. At three minutes after two o'clock on the afternoon of July 17, 1937, the garage boy brought his idiotic plane into Roosevelt Field for a perfect three-point landing.

It had, of course, been out of the question to arrange a modest little reception for the greatest flier in the history of the world. He was received at Roosevelt Field with such elaborate and pretentious ceremonies as rocked the world. Fortunately, however, the worn and spent hero promptly swooned, had to be removed bodily from his plane, and was spirited from the field without having opened his mouth once. Thus he did not jeopardize the dignity of this first reception, a reception illumined by the presence of the Secretaries of War and the Navy, Mayor Michael J. Moriority of New York, the Premier of Canada, Governors Fanniman, Groves, McFeely, and Critchfield, and a brilliant array of European diplomats. Smurch did not in fact, come to in time to take part in the gigantic hullabaloo arranged at City Hall for the next day. He was rushed to a secluded nursing home and confined to bed. It was nine days before he was able to get up, or to be more exact, before he was permitted to get up. Meanwhile the greatest minds in the country, in solemn assembly, had arranged a secret conference of city, state, and government officials, which Smurch was to attend for the purpose of being instructed in the ethics and behavior of heroism.

On the day that the little mechanic was finally allowed to get up and dress and, for the first time in two weeks, took a great chew of tobacco, he was permitted to receive the newspapermen—this by way of testing him out. Smurch did not wait for questions. "Youse guys," he said—and the *Times* man winced—"youse guys can tell the cockeyed world dat I put it over on Lindbergh, see? Yeh—an' made an ass o' them two frogs." The "two frogs" was a reference to a pair of gallant French fliers who, in attempting a flight only halfway round the world, had, two weeks before, unhappily been lost at sea. The *Times* man was bold enough, at this point, to sketch out for Smurch the accepted formula for interviews in cases of this kind; he explained that there should be no arrogant statements belittling the achievements of other heroes, particularly heroes of foreign nations. "Ah, the hell with that," said Smurch. "I did it, see? I did it, an' I'm talkin' about it." And he did talk about it.

None of this extraordinary interview was, of course, printed. On the contrary, the newspapers, already under the disciplined direction of a secret directorate created for the occasion and composed of statesmen and editors, gave out to a panting and restless world that "Jacky," as he had been arbitrarily nicknamed, would consent to say only that he was very happy and that anyone could have done what he did. "My achievement has been, I fear, slightly exaggerated," the *Times* man's article had him protest, with a modest smile. These newspaper stories were kept from the hero, a restriction which did not serve to abate the rising malevolence of his temper. The situation was, indeed, extremely grave, for Pal Smurch was, as he kept insisting, "rarin' to go." He could not much longer be kept from a nation clamorous to lionize him. It was the most desperate crisis the United States of America had faced since the sinking of the *Lusitania*.

On the afternoon of the twenty-seventh of July, Smurch was spirited away to a conference room in which were gathered mayors, governors, government officials, behaviorist psychologists, and editors. He gave them each a limp, moist paw and a brief unlovely grin. "Hah ya?" he said. When Smurch was seated, the Mayor of New York arose and, with obvious pessimism, attempted to explain what he must say and how he must act when presented to the world, ending his talk with a high tribute to the hero's courage and integrity. The Mayor was followed by Governor Fanniman of New York, who, after a touching declaration of faith, introduced Cameron Spottiswood, Second Secretary of the American Embassy in Paris, the gentleman selected to coach Smurch in the amenities of public ceremonies. Sitting in a chair, with a soiled yellow tie in his hand and his shirt open at the throat, unshaved, smoking a rolled cigarette, Jack Smurch listened with a leer on his lips. "I get ya, I get ya," he cut in, nastily. "You want me to act like a softy, huh? Ya want me to act like that —— —— baby-faced Lindbergh, huh? Well, nuts to that, see?" Everyone took in his breath sharply; it was a sigh and a hiss. "Mr. Lindbergh," began a United States Senator, purple with rage, "and Mr. Byrd—" Smurch, who was paring his nails with a jackknife, cut in again. "Byrd!" he exclaimed. "Aw fa God's sake, dat big—" Somebody shut off his blasphemies with a sharp word. A newcomer had entered the room. Everyone stood up, except Smurch, who, still busy with his nails, did not even glance up. "Mr. Smurch," said someone sternly, "the President of the United States!" It had been thought that the presence of the Chief Executive might have a chastening effect upon the young hero, and the former had been, thanks to the remarkable cooperation of the press, secretly brought to the obscure conference room.

A great, painful silence fell. Smurch looked up, waved a hand at the President. "How ya comin'?" he asked, and began rolling a fresh cigarette. The silence deepened. Someone coughed in a strained way. "Geez, it's hot, ain't it?" said Smurch. He loosened two more shirt buttons, revealing a hairy chest and the tattooed word "Sadie" enclosed in a stencilled heart. The great and important men in the room, faced by the most serious crisis in recent American history, exchanged worried frowns. Nobody seemed to know how to proceed. "Come awn, come awn," said Smurch. "Let's get the hell out of here! When do I start cuttin' in on de parties, huh? And what's they goin' to be *in* it?" He rubbed a thumb and forefinger together meaningly. "Money!" exclaimed a state senator, shocked, pale. "Yeh, money," said Pal, flipping his cigarette out of a window. "An' big money." He began rolling a fresh cigarette. "Big money," he repeated, frowning over the rice paper. He tilted back in his chair, and leered at each gentleman, separately, the leer of an animal that knows its power, the leer of a leopard loose in a bird and dog shop. "Aw fa God's sake, let's get some place where it's cooler," he said. "I been cooped up plenty for three weeks!"

Smurch stood up and walked over to an open window, where he stood staring down into the street, nine floors below. The faint shouting of newsboys floated up to him. He made out his name. "Hot dog!" he cried, grinning, ecstatic. He leaned out over the sill. "You tell 'em, babies!" he shouted down. "Hot diggity dog!" In the tense little knot of men standing behind him, a quick, mad impulse flared up. An unspoken word of appeal, of command, seemed to ring through the room. Yet it was deadly silent. Charles K. L. Brand, secretary to the Mayor of New York City, happened to be standing nearest Smurch; he looked inquiringly at the President of the United States. The President, pale, grim, nodded shortly. Brand, a tall, powerfully built man, once a tackle at Rutgers, stepped forward, seized the greatest man in the world by his left shoulder and the seat of his pants, and pushed him out the window.

"My God, he's fallen out the window!" cried a quick-witted editor.

"Get me out of here!" cried the President. Several men sprang to his side and he was hurriedly escorted out of a door toward a side entrance of the building. The editor of the Associated Press took charge, being used to such things. Crisply he ordered certain men to leave, others to stay; quickly he outlined a story which all the papers were to agree on, sent two men to the street to handle that end of the tragedy, commanded a Senator to sob and two Congressmen to go to pieces nervously. In a word, he skillfully set the stage for the gigantic task that was to follow, the task of breaking to a grief-stricken world the sad story of the untimely, accidental death of its most illustrious and spectacular figure.

The funeral was, as you know, the most elaborate, the finest, the solemnist, and the saddest ever held in the United States of America. The monument in Arlington Cemetery, with its clean white shaft of marble and the simple device of a tiny plane carved on its base, is a place for pilgrims, in deep reverence, to visit. The nations of the world paid lofty tributes to little Jacky Smurch, America's greatest hero. At a given hour there were two minutes of silence throughout the nation. Even the inhabitants of the small, bewildered town of Westfield, Iowa, observed this touching ceremony; agents of the Department of Justice saw to that. One of them was especially assigned to stand grimly in the doorway of a little shack restaurant on the edge of the tourists' camping ground just outside the town. There, under his stern scrutiny, Mrs. Emma Smurch bowed her head above two hamburger steaks sizzling on her grill—

bowed her head and turned away, so that the Secret Service man could not see the twisted, strangely familiar, leer on her lips.

POETRY

Above All, Honor

One of the poet's traditional functions is to glorify and immortalize his nation's heroes. Ben Jonson, poet laureate of England during the reign of Elizabeth I, performs this function in his ode "To Sir Henry Cary." Cary had been captured—merely by chance, Jonson stresses—in a campaign in Germany, near Broick Castle and the Ruhr River. Nonetheless, Jonson portrays Cary as the traditional hero, who risks all for honor and whose only reward is glory.

The traditional hero's code of honor dominates all of his relationships. But sometimes conflicting claims upon his loyalty arise. The lover and would-be hero of Richard Lovelace's poem "To Lucasta, on Going to the Wars" puts his duty to his country before his loyalty to Lucasta. He justifies himself with the assertion that his honor is all-encompassing, for as it compels him to leave her for war, it ennobles his love for her through a sacrificial act.

To Sir Henry Cary

Ben Jonson

That neither fame nor love might wanting be
To greatness, Cary, I sing that and thee;
Whose house, if it no other honor had,
In only thee might be both great and glad;
Who, to upbraid the sloth of this our time, 5
Durst valor make almost, but not, a crime;
Which deed I know not, whether were more high,
Or thou more happy, it to justify
Against thy fortune: when no foe, that day,
Could conquer thee but chance, who did betray. 10
Love thy great loss, which a renown hath won,
To live when Broick not stands, nor Ruhr doth run.
Love honors, which of best example be

When they cost dearest and are done most free;
Though every fortitude deserves applause,   15
It may be much or little in the cause.
He's valiant'st that dares fight, and not for pay;
That virtuous is, when the reward's away.

To Lucasta, Going to the Wars

Richard Lovelace

Tell me not, sweet, I am unkind
That from the nunnery
Of thy chaste breast and quiet mind,
To war and arms I fly.

True, a new mistress now I chase,   5
The first foe in the field;
And with a stronger faith embrace
A sword, a horse, a shield.

Yet this inconstancy is such
As you too shall adore;   10
I could not love thee, dear, so much,
Loved I not honor more.

Ulysses: Hero, Villain, or Victim?

Glory can be a mixed blessing. A case in point is Ulysses (or Odysseus), the Greek hero whose cleverness, according to Homer's *Iliad,* was responsible for the stratagem of the Trojan horse and whose fortitude is demonstrated throughout Homer's *Odyssey.* His claims to the honor and glory traditionally accorded him have not, however, gone unchallenged, as some of the poems in the group that follows suggest. The more traditional view of Ulysses as hero *par excellence* is presented by two British poets laureate widely separated in time,

Samuel Daniel and Alfred, Lord Tennyson. In "Ulysses and the Siren" Daniel re-creates the incident in the *Odyssey* in which the seductive siren tries to lure Ulysses to his destruction. However, Daniel transforms this incident into a debate on a much-discussed issue in the Renaissance: The siren is the advocate of the quiet life of ease and pleasure, while Ulysses is the proponent of the active life of ceaseless striving.

Alfred, Lord Tennyson's "Ulysses" also involves a classic opposition—between the solitary man, the wanderer, and the more settled social man. Both can be committed to the active life and to honor and both can become heroes, but the commitment of an adventurer like Ulysses is intensely physical and essentially private; whereas that of a political figure like his son, Telemachus, is primarily intellectual and public. Ulysses' kind of commitment, of course, contains more possibilities for winning glory than does that of his son, and it is this difference between the romance of the adventurous life and the realism of the everyday life that is the central preoccupation of Tennyson's poem.

The heroic restlessness which both Daniel and Tennyson admire in Ulysses is perceived, not as an ennobling quality, but as a sign of the hero's guilt by W. S. Merwin in his poem "Odysseus." Like Tennyson, however, Merwin conveys a sense of the pathos in the wanderlust of a hero no longer young. The aging hero is also the subject of John Ciardi's "Ulysses." Nearing the end of his long quest, standing amidst the results of yet another of his butcheries, Ulysses asks the tragic hero's question, "Was this my life?"

Ulysses and the Siren

Samuel Daniel

SIREN. Come, worthy Greek, Ulysses, come,
Possess these shores with me;
The winds and seas are troublesome,
And here we may be free.
Here may we sit and view their toil   5
That travail in the deep,
And joy the day in mirth the while,
And spend the night in sleep.

ULYSSES. Fair nymph, if fame or honor were
To be attained with ease,   10
Then would I come and rest me there,
And leave such toils as these.
But here it dwells, and here must I
With danger seek it forth;
To spend the time luxuriously   15
Becomes not men of worth.

SIREN. Ulysses, Oh be not deceived
With that unreal name;
This honor is a thing conceived,
And rests on others' fame.   20
Begotten only to molest
Our peace, and to beguile
The best thing of our life, our rest,
And give us up to toil.

ULYSSES. Delicious nymph, suppose there were   25
Nor honor nor report,
Yet manliness would scorn to wear
The time in idle sport.
For toil doth give a better touch,
To make us feel our joy;   30
And ease finds tediousness, as much
As labor yields annoy.

SIREN. Then pleasure likewise seems the shore
Whereto tends all your toil,
Which you forgo to make it more,   35
And perish oft the while.
Who may disport them diversly,
Find never tedious day,
And ease may have variety
As well as action may.   40

ULYSSES. But natures of the noblest frame
These toils and dangers please,
And they take comfort in the same
As much as you in ease,
And with the thoughts of actions past   45
Are recreated still;
When pleasure leaves a touch at last
To show that it was ill.

SIREN. That doth opinion only cause
That's out of custom bred,   50
Which makes us many other laws
Than ever nature did.
No widows wail for our delights,
Our sports are without blood;
The world, we see, by warlike wights[1]   55
Receives more hurt than good.

ULYSSES. But yet the state of things require
These motions of unrest,
And these great spirits of high desire
Seem born to turn them best,   60
To purge the mischiefs that increase
And all good order mar;
For oft we see a wicked peace
To be well changed for war.

SIREN. Well, well, Ulysses, then I see   65
I shall not have thee here,
And therefore I will come to thee,
And take my fortunes there.
I must be won that cannot win,
Yet lost were I not won;   70
For beauty hath created been
T' undo, or be undone.

Ulysses

Alfred, Lord Tennyson

It little profits that an idle king,
By this still hearth, among these barren crags,
Match'd with an aged wife, I mete and dole
Unequal laws unto a savage race,
That hoard, and sleep, and feed, and know not me.   5
I cannot rest from travel; I will drink
Life to the lees.   All times I have enjoy'd

---

1. *wights* Persons.

Greatly, have suffer'd greatly, both with those
That loved me, and alone; on shore, and when
Thro' scudding drifts the rainy Hyades   10
Vext the dim sea.   I am become a name;
For always roaming with a hungry heart
Much have I seen and known,—cities of men
And manners, climates, councils, governments,
Myself not least, but honor'd of them all,—   15
And drunk delight of battle with my peers,
Far on the ringing plains of windy Troy.
I am a part of all that I have met;
Yet all experience is an arch wherethro'
Gleams that untravell'd world whose margin fades   20
For ever and for ever when I move.
How dull it is to pause, to make an end,
To rust unburnish'd, not to shine in use!
As tho' to breathe were life!   Life piled on life
Were all too little, and of one to me   25
Little remains; but every hour is saved
From that eternal silence, something more,
A bringer of new things; and vile it were
For some three suns to store and hoard myself,
And this gray spirit yearning in desire   30
To follow knowledge like a sinking star,
Beyond the utmost bound of human thought.
    This is my son, mine own Telemachus,
To whom I leave the scepter and the isle,—
Well-loved of me, discerning to fulfil   35
This labor, by slow prudence to make mild
A rugged people, and thro' soft degrees
Subdue them to the useful and the good.
Most blameless is he, centered in the sphere
Of common duties, decent not to fail   40
In offices of tenderness, and pay
Meet[1] adoration to my household gods,
When I am gone.   He works his work, I mine.
    There lies the port; the vessel puffs her sail;
There gloom the dark, broad seas.   My mariners,   45
Souls that have toil'd, and wrought, and thought with
    me,—
That ever with a frolic welcome took
The thunder and the sunshine, and opposed

---

1. *Meet* Fitting.

Free hearts, free foreheads,—you and I are old;
Old age hath yet his honor and his toil.   50
Death closes all; but something ere the end,
Some work of noble note, may yet be done,
Not unbecoming men that strove with Gods.
The lights begin to twinkle from the rocks;
The long day wanes; the slow moon climbs; the deep   55
Moans round with many voices.   Come, friends,
'T is not too late to seek a newer world.
Push off, and sitting well in order smite
The sounding furrows; for my purpose holds
To sail beyond the sunset, and the baths   60
Of all the western stars, until I die.
It may be that the gulfs will wash us down;
It may be we shall touch the Happy Isles,
And see the great Achilles, whom we knew.
Tho' much is taken, much abides; and tho'   65
We are not now that strength which in old days
Moved earth and heaven, that which we are, we are,—
One equal temper of heroic hearts,
Made weak by time and fate, but strong in will
To strive, to seek, to find, and not to yield.   70

Odysseus

for George Kirstein

W. S. Merwin

Always the setting forth was the same,
Same sea, same dangers waiting for him
As though he had got nowhere but older.
Behind him on the receding shore
The identical reproaches, and somewhere   5
Out before him, the unravelling patience
He was wedded to.   There were the islands
Each with its woman and twining welcome
To be navigated, and one to call "home."
The knowledge of all that he betrayed   10
Grew till it was the same whether he stayed
Or went.   Therefore he went.   And what wonder

If sometimes he could not remember
Which was the one who wished on his departure
Perils that he could never sail through,   15
And which, improbable, remote, and true,
Was the one he kept sailing home to?

Ulysses
John Ciardi

At the last mountain I stood to remember the sea
and it was not the sea of my remembering
but something from an augur's madness:
sheep guts, bird guts, ox guts, smoking
in a hot eye.   Was this my life?   Dull red,   5
dull green, blood black, the coils still writhing
the last of the living thing: a carnage
steaming into the smokes of a sick dawn.

I had planted the oar at the crossroads, there in the goat
    dust
where the oaf waited, chewing a stalk of garlic.   10
"Stranger," he said, "what have you on your shoulder?"
"A world," I said, and made a hole for it,
watched by the oaf and his goats.   I gave him money
for the fattest goat and asked to be alone,
and he would not leave me.   I gave him money again   15
for a peace-parting, and he would not go.
"Stranger," I said, "I have sailed to all lands,
killed in all lands, and come home poor.   I think
blood buys nothing, and I think it buys
all that's bought.   Leave me this goat and go."   20
Why should I want his blood on me?   The goat
stared at me like an old man, and the oaf
sat chewing garlic.   This much had been commanded.
Was the rest commanded, too?   Was it my life
or the god's laughter foresaw me?

                                        I prayed in anger: 25
"O coupling gods, if from your lecheries
among the bloods of man, a prayer may move you

to spare one life, call off this last sad dog
you have set on me.   Does Heaven need such meat?"
The heavens lurched on unheeding.   The fool stayed: 30
would not be scared off, and would not be whipped off.
Then he raised his staff against me.

                            Was it my life
or the gods' laughter answered?   I hacked him sidearm
across the middle: almost a stunt for practice—
dead level, no body weight to it, all in the shoulder   35
and wrist, and not three feet to the whole swing.
But it halved him like a melon!   A chop
the ships would have sung for a century!
. . . But there were no ships, and the oar was planted
    unknown
in a country of garlic and goat turds,   40
and what lay fallen was rags and bones.

                          "Take him, then!" I cried.
"Who else could stomach such a dusty tripe?"
I made the pyre with the planted oar at its center,
and as it flamed, I raised the libation cup,
but mouthed the wine and spat it at the blaze.   45
The fire roared up like Etna.   "At your pleasure!"
I shouted back, and threw the dead clown in,
first one piece, then the other.   The horns of the flame
raped him whole and blew for more.   The goats
stood watching, huddled like old crazy men   50
in a chorus round the fire, and one by one
I slit their throats and threw them to their master.
I say those goats were mad: they waited there
as if the fire were Medusa: the blood of the dead
ran down the legs of the living and they did not move,   55
not even to turn their heads.   And in the center
the flame went blood-mad in a shaft to Heaven.

It was dark when I turned away.   I lost my road
and slept the night in a grove.   When I awoke
I found a shrine to Apollo, a marble peace   60
leaned on by cypresses, but across his belly
a crack grinned hip to hip, and the right hand
lay palm-up in the dust.   On the road back
I came on many such, but that was the first
of the cracked gods and the dusty altars.   65

I returned to the sea, and at the last mountain
I stood to remember, and the memory
could not live in the fact.   I had grown old
in the wrong world.   Penelope wove for nothing
her fabric and delay.   I could not return.   70
I was woven to my dead men.   In the dust
of the dead shore by the dead sea I lay down
and named their names who had matched lives with me,
and won.   And they were all I loved.

Home and the Hero

To remain safely at home or to venture forth into danger is the classic dilemma faced by the hero of the old English ballad "Sir Patrick Spens."   The traditional hero, however, really has little choice—his honor is his fate.   This poem suggests that the ultimate irony of heroism, which makes it potentially tragic, is that all too often the best must sacrifice the most for lesser men.

This terrible waste of humanity's best leads the speaker of A. E. Housman's poem "Oh Stay at Home, My Lad" to discourage youthful aspirations toward honor and glory.   Not a siren's song urging mere pleasure and sloth, nor a cynical denial of the reality of heroic virtue, the poem is rather an affirmation of life and peace in the midst of death and war.

Sir Patrick Spens

Anonymous

The king sits in Dumferling town,
   Drinking the blude-reid[1] wine:
"O whar will I get guid sailor,
   To sail this ship of mine?"

Up and spak an eldern knicht,[2]   5
   Sat at the king's richt knee:

---

1. *blude-reid* Blood-red.   2. *eldern knicht* Old knight.

"Sir Patrick Spens is the best sailor
    That sails upon the sea."

The king has written a braid[3] letter
    And signed it wi' his hand,
And sent it to Sir Patrick Spens,
    Was walking on the sand.   10

The first line that Sir Patrick read,
    A loud lauch[4] lauched he;
The next line that Sir Patrick read,
    The tear blinded his ee.   15

"O wha is this has done this deed,
    This ill deed done to me,
To send me out this time o' the year,
    To sail upon the sea?   20

"Mak haste, mak haste, my mirry men all,
    Our guid ship sails the morn."
"O say na sae,[5] my master dear,
    For I fear a deadly storm.

"Late, late yestre'en I saw the new moon   25
    Wi' the auld moon in hir arm,
And I fear, I fear, my dear master,
    That we will come to harm."

O our Scots nobles were richt laith[6]
    To weet[7] their cork-heeled shoon,[8]   30
But lang or a' the play were played
    Their hats they swam aboon.[9]

O lang, lang may their ladies sit,
    Wi' their fans into their hand,
Or ere they see Sir Patrick Spens   35
    Come sailing to the land.

O lang, lang may the ladies stand
    Wi' their gold kems in their hair,

---

3. *braid* Broad.   4. *lauch* Laugh.   5. *sae* So.   6. *richt laith* Reluctant.
7. *weet* Wet.   8. *shoon* Shoes.   9. *aboon* Above.

Waiting for their ain dear lords,
For they'll see them na mair.

40

Half o'er, half o'er to Aberdour
It's fifty fadom deep,
And there lies guid Sir Patrick Spens
Wi' the Scots lords at his feet.

Oh stay at home, my lad, and plough

A. E. Housman

Oh stay at home, my lad, and plough
The land and not the sea,
And leave the soldiers at their drill,
And all about the idle hill
Shepherd your sheep with me.

5

Oh stay with company and mirth
And daylight and the air;
Too full already is the grave
Of fellows that were good and brave
And died because they were.

10

The Athlete as Hero

The traditional hero is seldom found at home, yet this locale does provide opportunities for one particular form of heroics: athletics. Sports are in a sense facsimiles of war and the athletes "combatants" in that "war." If the athlete is victorious, local or even national glory can be his. The athlete also has his code of honor. He is obliged to adhere to the rules of the game, to exert his maximum effort, and to obey all the unwritten rules of the game, such as exhibiting teamwork, discipline, and enthusiasm. Also like the warrior, the athlete lives on the razor's edge; defeat is an ever present threat, and the inevitable deterioration of even the best-conditioned body increases the odds against victory. Finally, in the controlled violence that is sport, as in the uncontrolled violence that is war, there always lurks the possibility of the athlete-hero's maiming or sudden death.

38

A. E. Housman does not tell us the cause of death of the title figure of his poem "To an Athlete Dying Young" but there is a special poignancy and a special irony in the death of any hero, and particularly a young hero. Such a death becomes symbolic of the transiency of youth, of life itself, and of fame.

John Updike's poem "Ex-Basketball Player" is also about transiency. Its subject is that pathetic figure, the high school hero who is reduced by time and circumstance to an ordinary human being. The ex-basketball player, Flick Webb, is one of Housman's "rout/Of lads that wore their honors out." The fading of Flick's glory becomes for him a kind of slow death.

Another kind of slow death—the life largely lacking in honor and glory—is portrayed in James Wright's "Autumn Begins in Martin's Ferry, Ohio." Like "Ex-Basketball Player," an intensely American poem, it sympathetically portrays the universal need for heroes and the universal compulsion of the young to become heroes. Like Housman's poem it suggests the transiency of the human condition and, in particular, the eventual displacement of fathers as heroes to their sons and the reversal of this process as the sons become heroes to their fathers.

To an Athlete Dying Young
A. E. Housman

The time you won your town the race
We chaired you through the market-place;
Man and boy stood cheering by,
And home we brought you shoulder-high.

Today, the road all runners come,   5
Shoulder-high we bring you home,
And set you at your threshold down,
Townsman of a stiller town.

Smart lad, to slip betimes away
From fields where glory does not stay   10
And early though the laurel grows
It withers quicker than the rose.

Eyes the shady night has shut
Cannot see the record cut,
And silence sounds no worse than cheers   15
After earth has stopped the ears:

Now you will not swell the rout
Of lads that wore their honors out,
Runners whom renown outran
And the name died before the man.   20

So set, before its echoes fade,
The fleet foot on the sill of shade,
And hold to the low lintel up
The still-defended challenge-cup.

And round that early-laureled head   25
Will flock to gaze the strengthless dead,
And find unwithered on its curls
The garland briefer than a girl's.

Ex-Basketball Player

John Updike

Pearl Avenue runs past the high-school lot,
Bends with the trolley tracks, and stops, cut off
Before it has a chance to go two blocks,
At Colonel McComsky Plaza.   Berth's Garage
Is on the corner facing west, and there,   5
Most days, you'll find Flick Webb, who helps Berth out.

Flick stands tall among the idiot pumps—
Five on a side, the old bubble-head style,
Their rubber elbows hanging loose and low.
One's nostrils are two S's, and his eyes   10
An E and O. And one is squat, without
A head at all—more of a football type.

Once Flick played for the high-school team, the Wizards.
He was good: in fact, the best.   In '46,

He bucketed three hundred ninety points,   15
A county record still.   The ball loved Flick.
I saw him rack up thirty-eight of forty
In one home game.   His hands were like wild birds.

He never learned a trade, he just sells gas,
Checks oil, and changes flats.   Once in a while,   20
As a gag, he dribbles an inner tube,
But most of us remember anyway.
His hands are fine and nervous on the lug wrench.
It makes no difference to the lug wrench, though.

Off work, he hangs around Mae's Luncheonette.   25
Grease-grey and kind of coiled, he plays pinball,
Sips lemon cokes, and smokes those thin cigars;
Flick seldom speaks to Mae, just sits and nods
Beyond her face towards bright applauding tiers
Of Necco Wafers, Nibs, and Juju Beads.   30

Autumn Begins in Martin's Ferry, Ohio

James Wright

In the Shreve High football stadium,
I think of Polacks nursing long beers in Tiltonsville,
And gray faces of Negroes in the blast furnace at
    Benwood,
And the ruptured night watchman of Wheeling Steel,
Dreaming of heroes.   5

All the proud fathers are ashamed to go home.
Their women cluck like starved pullets,
Dying for love.

Therefore,
Their sons grow suicidally beautiful   10
At the beginning of October,
And gallop terribly against each other's bodies.

Two American Heroes: Studies in Black and White

The heroes of the following poems both come out of the same era of American history—the building of the railroads in the nineteenth century. One, John Henry, is black; the other, Buffalo Bill, is white. John Henry lays track for the railroad while Buffalo Bill gets his start killing buffalo to supply meat for the railroad workers. The ballad "John Henry" reflects the contribution of blacks to the building of America in its portrayal of the strength, stamina, and simple dignity of its black hero. He pits his physical strength against the steam drill which threatens to replace him, and at stake is nothing less than his honor as a man. "Buffalo Bill" succinctly debunks a white hero, one whose honor and glory were more the result of showmanship and publicity than of genuinely heroic deeds.

John Henry

Anonymous

John Henry was a little baby,
Sittin' on his mammy's knee,
Said, "The Big Bend tunnel on the C. & O. road[1]
Gonna be the death of me,
Lawd, Lawd, gonna be the death of me."   5

John Henry was a little baby,
Sittin' on his daddy's knee,
Point his finger at a little piece of steel,
"That's gonna be the death of me,
Lawd, Lawd, that's gonna be the death of me."   10

John Henry had a little woman
And her name was Mary Magdelene,
She would go to the tunnel and sing for John
Jes' to hear John Henry's hammer ring,
Lawd, Lawd, jes' to hear John Henry's hammer ring.   15

---

1. *C. & O. road* Chesapeake and Ohio Railroad.

John Henry had a little woman
And her name was Polly Anne,
John Henry took sick and he had to go to bed,
Polly Anne drove steel like a man,
Lawd, Lawd, Polly Anne drove steel like a man.   20

Cap'n says to John Henry,
"Gonna bring me a steam drill 'round,
Gonna take that steam drill out on the job,
Gonna whop that steel on down,
Lawd, Lawd, gonna whop that steel on down."   25

John Henry told his cap'n,
Said, "A man ain't nothin' but a man,
And befo' I'd let that steam drill beat me down
I'd die with this hammer in my hand,
Lawd, Lawd, I'd die with the hammer in my hand."   30

Sun were hot and burnin',
Weren't no breeze atall,
Sweat ran down like water down a hill,
That day John let his hammer fall,
Lawd, Lawd, that day John let his hammer fall.   35

White man told John Henry,
"Nigger, damn yo' soul,
You may beat dis steam and drill of mine,—
When the rocks in the mountains turn to gold,
Lawd, Lawd, when the rocks in the mountains turn to
    gold."   40

John Henry said to his shaker,[2]
"Shaker, why don't you sing?
I'm throwin' twelve pounds from my hips on down,
Jes' lissen to the cold steel ring,
Lawd, Lawd, jes' lissen to the cold steel ring."   45

O the cap'n told John Henry,
"I b'lieve this mountain's sinkin' in,"
John Henry said to his cap'n, "O my,
It's my hammer just a-hossin' in the wind,
Lawd, Lawd, it's my hammer just a-hossin' in the wind."   50

2. *shaker* The man who holds the spike while it is being hammered.

John Henry told his shaker,
"Shaker, you better pray,
For, if I miss this six-foot steel
Tomorrow be yo' buryin' day,
Lawd, Lawd, tomorrow be yo' buryin' day."   55

John Henry told his captain,
"Looky yonder what I see—
Yo' drill's done broke an' yo' hole's done choke,
An' you can't drive steel like me,
Lawd, Lawd, an' you can't drive steel like me."   60

John Henry was hammerin' on the mountain,
An' his hammer was strikin' fire,
He drove so hard till he broke his pore heart
An' he lied down his hammer an' he died,
Lawd, Lawd, he lied down his hammer an' he died.   65

They took John Henry to the graveyard
An' they buried him in the sand
An' ev'ry locomotive come roarin' by,
Says, "There lays a steel drivin' man,"
Lawd, Lawd, "There lays a steel drivin' man."   70

Buffalo Bill's

e. e. cummings

Buffalo Bill's
defunct
         who used to
         ride a watersmooth-silver
                              stallion   5
and break onetwothreefourfive pigeonsjustlikethat
                                        Jesus
he was a handsome man
                    and what i want to know is
how do you like your blueeyed boy   10
Mister Death

The Hero as Memory

In spite of the ignorance or indifference of some and the cynicism or suspicion of others, in spite of defeat or death, the figure of the hero endures. He recurs throughout history, rising to meet challenges which make nonheroes quail. Those challenges met, he persists as historical figure and as legend, living in the memories of all who aspire to, or simply respect, greatness. That greatness, as the poem which follows suggests, is in a sense mainly spiritual. Although honor has different meanings to different people, it is usually summed up in the sense each of us has of the ideal human being within himself—that person we would like, but do not always try, to become. The hero has tried and succeeded. Thus he merits glory, which all of us can share to some degree, because with the hero we share a common humanity.

I Think Continually of Those Who Were Truly Great

Stephen Spender

I think continually of those who were truly great.
Who, from the womb, remembered the soul's history
Through corridors of light where the hours are suns,
Endless and singing.   Whose lovely ambition
Was that their lips, still touched with fire,   5
Should tell of the Spirit, clothed from head to foot in song.
And who hoarded from the Spring branches
The desires falling across their bodies like blossoms.

What is precious, is never to forget
The essential delight of the blood drawn from ageless
    springs   10
Breaking through rocks in worlds before our earth.
Never to deny its pleasure in the morning simple light
Nor its grave evening demand for love.
Never to allow gradually the traffic to smother
With noise and fog, the flowering of the Spirit.   15

Near the snow, near the sun, in the highest fields,
See how these names are fêted by the waving grass
And by the streamers of white cloud
And whispers of wind in the listening sky.
The names of those who in their lives fought for life,   20
Who wore at their hearts the fire's centre.
Born of the sun, they travelled a short while toward the
    sun,
And left the vivid air signed with their honour.

DRAMA

King Henry the Fourth, Part One

"Heroes and Anti-Heroes" would be an appropriate subtitle for *Henry IV, Part I,* for in his play Shakespeare explores and exploits both concepts to the fullest. By his father, King Henry IV, Prince Henry is regarded as being self-centered, self-indulgent, amoral, perhaps even seditious—what today we might well term an "anti-hero." But by the ne'er-do-wells, laggards, and roisterers with whom he consorts in the seedier sections of fifteenth-century London, this same young man is regarded as a hero. Here, amidst the taverns and the brothels, he is known, not as "Prince Henry," but as "Hal," or at best, "Prince Hal." It is frequently suggested that carousing, wenching, and playing dangerous games just within or without the law are his "princely" avocations, though—significantly—such behavior is more talked about than actually exhibited by Hal himself.

On the other hand, questionable activities seem to occupy most of the time of Hal's boon companion, Sir John Falstaff. This corpulent and aging knight is at once the complete hedonist—steadfastly devoted only to his own pleasure—and the complete amoralist—conspicuously lacking any sense of right and wrong. If the anti-hero is a character who not only is devoid of heroic virtue but also exhibits its very reverse, Sir John is a classic anti-hero. Cowardly, weak, self-centered, boastful, unserious, irreverent, given to wine, women, and song, Falstaff should be a contemptible character. But the reverse turns out to be the case: Falstaff manages to win not only the hearts of his companions but of generations of theatergoers. His comic nature only partially explains his enormous popularity. Part of that popularity must also be due to the fact that he is a life-affirming character. He has an indomitable sense of humor which he turns upon everything and everyone, including himself. He has extraordinary imaginative

46

powers which enable him to create fantasies of all kinds—and then enact them. But he is also a tough-minded realist who knows the world—and himself—only too well. Anti-hero though he may be, Sir John Falstaff is also an irresistible dramatic character.

The one significant delusion under which Falstaff labors is that he really knows Prince Hal. He imagines Hal to be mainly a younger version of himself, and thus, what in literature would be called a "rogue hero." The term refers to one whose status as a hero is to some extent compromised by the mischievous or even illegal nature of his adventures. Hal, however, knows—and will ultimately demonstrate—that he is more than a royal Robin Hood. Shakespeare's audience itself knew that the prince would eventually become one of England's hero-kings. That future is foreshadowed in Hal's soliloquy at the end of Act I, Scene 2, where he reveals that he is acting out a role, playing the part of a royal rogue so that his "reformation," when it comes, will be so dramatic as to receive everyone's attention. This hero then is in the process of creating his own myth.

But Hal is much more than an image. As the play progresses, it becomes clear that he has valor and strength, which will make him a good warrior, as well as political acumen and judiciousness, which will make him a good king. Tragic heroes aside, Hal is as complete and complex a hero figure as is to be found in literature.

Prince Hal is preeminent in a play which is almost overstocked with heroes. His foil or opposite number is "Hotspur," Henry Percy, who is—in King Henry's own words—"the theme of honour's tongue," and thus, in the monarch's view, everything that his own son is not. Hotspur's code of honor is so strict that he will become a rebel rather than compromise it, and to satisfy it he will fight at the drop of a gauntlet. Hotspur then is the concept of the chivalric hero carried to its logical extreme. Out of the contrast between Hotspur and Hal some provocative questions about the nature of true heroism emerge. For example, to what extent can the complete hero also be the complete man? Is there a point at which the hero's code of honor can become self-defeating or even nihilistic? Is it possible that the quest for glory can become obsessive and self-destructive?

Hotspur is also played off against Falstaff. To Hotspur honor and glory are everything; to that arch-realist or cynic, Falstaff, they are nothing—at least nothing worth risking life and limb for. To Hal, on the other hand, honor is neither a mere word nor the main goal of life. He balances considerations of honor against moral, political, and human considerations. The result is a happy compromise in which true honor and glory are attained, but not through the sacrifice of all else. Hal becomes the hero of the middle way.

King Henry the Fourth, Part One

William Shakespeare

CHARACTERS

KING HENRY THE FOURTH.
HENRY, *Prince of Wales,*
PRINCE JOHN *of Lancaster,* } *sons to the King.*
EARL OF WESTMORELAND.
SIR WALTER BLUNT.
THOMAS PERCY, *Earl of Worcester.*
HENRY PERCY, *Earl of Northumberland.*
HENRY PERCY, *surnamed* HOTSPUR, *his son.*
EDMUND MORTIMER, *Earl of March.*
RICHARD SCROOP, *Archbishop of York.*
ARCHIBALD, *Earl of Douglas.*
OWEN GLENDOWER.
SIR RICHARD VERNON.
SIR JOHN FALSTAFF.
SIR MICHAEL, *attending on the Archbishop of York.*
EDWARD POINS, *attending on Prince Henry.*
GADSHILL.
PETO.
BARDOLPH.
FRANCIS, *a drawer.*
LADY PERCY, *wife to Hotspur, and sister to Mortimer.*
LADY MORTIMER, *daughter to Glendower, and wife to Mortimer.*
MISTRESS QUICKLY, *hostess of a tavern in Eastcheap.*
LORDS, OFFICERS, SHERIFF, VINTNER, CHAMBERLAIN,
    DRAWERS, TWO CARRIERS, TRAVELLERS, OSTLER,
    and ATTENDANTS.

SCENE. England and Wales.

ACT I

SCENE 1

[*London.   The Palace.   Enter* KING HENRY, WESTMORELAND, SIR WALTER BLUNT, PRINCE JOHN *and others.*]

KING HENRY. So shaken as we are, so wan with care,

Find we a time for frighted peace to pant,
And breathe short-winded accents of new broils[1]
To be commenced in stronds[2] afar remote.
No more the thirsty entrance of this soil   5
Shall daub her lips with her own children's blood;
No more shall trenching war channel her fields,
Nor bruise her flowerets with the armed hoofs
Of hostile paces: those opposed eyes,
Which, like the meteors of a troubled heaven,   10
All of one nature, of one substance bred,
Did lately meet in the intestine shock
And furious close[3] of civil butchery,
Shall now, in mutual well-beseeming ranks,
March all one way, and be no more opposed   15
Against acquaintance, kindred, and allies.
The edge of war, like an ill-sheathed knife,
No more shall cut his master.   Therefore, friends
As far as to the sepulchre of Christ,
Whose soldier now, under whose blessed Cross   20
We are impressed and engaged to fight,
Forthwith a power[4] of English shall we levy,
Whose arms were moulded in their mothers' womb,
To chase these pagans in those holy fields,
Over whose acres walked those blessed feet   25
Which fourteen hundred years ago were nailed
For our advantage on the bitter Cross.
But this our purpose now is twelve month old,
And bootless[5] 'tis to tell you we will go:
Therefore we meet not now.[6]   Then let me hear   30
Of you, my gentle cousin Westmoreland,
What yesternight our council did decree
In forwarding this dear expedience.[7]
WESTMORELAND. My liege, this haste was hot in question,
And many limits of the charge[8] set down   35
But yesternight, when all athwart there came
A post from Wales loaden with heavy news,
Whose worst was that the noble Mortimer,
Leading the men of Herefordshire to fight
Against the irregular and wild Glendower,   40

1. *broils* Battles.   2. *stronds* Shores.   3. *close* Grappling or fighting.
4. *power* Army.   5. *bootless* Useless.
6. *Therefore . . . now.* This is not why we meet now.
7. *dear expedience* Important expedition.
8. *limits . . . charge* Assignments of responsibility.

Was by the rude hands of that Welshman taken,
A thousand of his people butchered;
Upon whose dead corpse there was such misuse,
Such beastly shameless transformation
By those Welshwomen done, as may not be   45
Without much shame retold or spoken of.
KING HENRY. It seems then that the tidings of this broil
Brake off our business for the Holy Land.
WESTMORELAND. This, matched with other did, my gracious lord,
For more uneven and unwelcome news   50
Came from the North, and thus it did import.
On Holy-rood day, the gallant Hotspur there,
Young Harry Percy, and brave Archibald,
That ever-valiant and approved Scot,
At Holmedon met,   55
Where they did spend a sad and bloody hour;
As by discharge of their artillery,
And shape of likelihood, the news was told;
For he that brought them, in the very heat
And pride of their contention[9] did take horse,   60
Uncertain of the issue[10] any way.
KING HENRY. Here is a dear, a true industrious friend,
Sir Walter Blunt, new lighted from his horse,
Stained with the variation of each soil
Betwixt that Holmedon and this seat of ours;   65
And he hath brought us smooth and welcome news.
The Earl of Douglas is discomfited,
Ten thousand bold Scots, two-and-twenty knights,
Balked[11] in their own blood, did Sir Walter see
On Holmedon's plains.   Of prisoners, Hotspur took   70
Mordake, Earl of Fife, and eldest son
To beaten Douglas, and the Earl of Athol,
Of Murray, Angus, and Menteith.
And is not this an honourable spoil?
A gallant prize? Ha, cousin, is it not?   75
WESTMORELAND. In faith,
It is a conquest for a prince to boast of.
KING HENRY. Yea, there thou makest me sad, and makest me sin
In envy that my Lord Northumberland
Should be the father to so blest a son.   80
A son who is the theme of honour's tongue,

9. *contention* Battle.   10. *issue* Outcome.   11. *Balked* Heaped up.

Amongst a grove, the very straightest plant,
Who is sweet Fortune's minion and her pride,
Whilst I, by looking on the praise of him,
See riot and dishonour stain the brow   85
Of my young Harry.   O, that it could be proved
That some night-tripping fairy had exchanged
In cradle clothes our children where they lay,
And called mine Percy, his Plantagenet!
Then would I have his Harry, and he mine.   90
But let him from my thoughts.   What think you, coz,
Of this young Percy's pride?   The prisoners,
Which he in this adventure hath surprised,
To his own use he keeps, and sends me word
I shall have none but Mordake, Earl of Fife.   95
WESTMORELAND. This is his uncle's teaching, this is Worcester,
Malevolent to you in all aspects,
Which makes him prune himself, and bristle up
The crest of youth against your dignity.
KING HENRY. But I have sent for him to answer this;   100
And for this cause awhile we must neglect
Our holy purpose to Jerusalem.
Cousin, on Wednesday next our council we
Will hold at Windsor, so inform the lords.
But come yourself with speed to us again,   105
For more is to be said and to be done
Than out of anger can be uttered.
WESTMORELAND. I will, my liege.   [*Exeunt.*]

SCENE 2

[*London.   The house of* PRINCE HENRY.   FALSTAFF *discovered asleep.
Enter* PRINCE HENRY *and wakes him.*]

FALSTAFF. Now, Hal, what time of day is it, lad?
PRINCE HENRY. Thou art so fat-witted with drinking of old sack,[1] and
unbuttoning thee after supper, and sleeping upon benches after noon,
that thou hast forgotten to demand that truly which thou wouldst
truly know.   What a devil hast thou to do with the time of the day?   5
Unless hours were cups of sack, and minutes capons, and clocks the
tongues of bawds, and dials the signs of leaping-houses,[2] and the
blessed sun himself a fair hot wench in flame-coloured taffeta, I see

1. *sack* Spanish white wine.   2. *leaping-houses* Brothels.

no reason why thou shouldst be so superfluous to demand the time of the day.

FALSTAFF. Indeed, you come near me now Hal, for we that take purses go by the moon and the seven stars, and not by Phœbus,[3] he, that wandering knight so fair. And, I prithee, sweet wag, when thou art King, as, God save thy Grace—Majesty I should say, for grace thou wilt have none—

PRINCE HENRY. What, none?

FALSTAFF. No, by my troth, not so much as will serve to be prologue to an egg and butter.

PRINCE HENRY. Well, how then? Come, roundly, roundly.

FALSTAFF. Marry, then, sweet wag, when thou art King, let not us that are squires of the night's body be called thieves of the day's beauty; let us be Diana's foresters,[4] gentlemen of the shade, minions of the moon, and let men say we be men of good government, being governed, as the sea is, by our noble and chaste mistress the moon, under whose countenance we steal.

PRINCE HENRY. Thou say'st well, and it holds well too, for the fortune of us that are the moon's men doth ebb and flow like the sea, being governed, as the sea is, by the moon. As, for proof, now: a purse of gold most resolutely snatched on Monday night, and most dissolutely spent on Tuesday morning; got with swearing "lay by,"[5] and spent with crying "bring in;"[6] now in as low an ebb as the foot of the ladder, and by and by in as high a flow as the ridge of the gallows.

FALSTAFF. By the Lord thou sayest true lad, and is not my hostess of the tavern a most sweet wench?

PRINCE HENRY. As the honey of Hybla, my old lad of the castle, and is not a buff jerkin a most sweet robe of durance?[7]

FALSTAFF. How now, how now, mad wag? What, in thy quips and thy quiddities? What a plague have I to do with a buff jerkin?

PRINCE HENRY. Why, what a pox have I to do with my hostess of the tavern?

FALSTAFF. Well, thou hast called her to a reckoning many a time and oft.

PRINCE HENRY. Did I ever call for thee to pay thy part?

FALSTAFF. No; I'll give thee thy due, thou hast paid all there.

PRINCE HENRY. Yea, and elsewhere, so far as my coin would stretch; and where it would not, I have used my credit.

3. *Phœbus* The sun. 4. *Diana's foresters* Thieves of the forest.
5. *"lay by"* Hand over your valuables. 6. *"bring in"* Bring in more wine.
7. *durance* Enduring or strong material, or imprisonment.

FALSTAFF. Yea, and so used it, that, were it not here apparent that thou art heir apparent—but, I prithee, sweet wag, shall there be gallows standing in England when thou art King? And resolution thus fobbed[8] as it is with the rusty curb of old father antic[9] the law? Do not thou, when thou art King, hang a thief. 50

PRINCE HENRY. No, thou shalt.

FALSTAFF. Shall I? O rare! By the Lord, I'll be a brave[10] judge.

PRINCE HENRY. Thou judgest false already: I mean thou shalt have the hanging of the thieves, and so become a rare hangman. 55

FALSTAFF. Well, Hal, well; and in some sort it jumps[11] with my humour as well as waiting[12] in the Court, I can tell you.

PRINCE HENRY. For obtaining of suits?

FALSTAFF. Yea, for obtaining of suits, whereof the hangman hath no lean wardrobe. 'Sblood, I am as melancholy as a gib-cat or a lugged 60 bear.

PRINCE HENRY. Or an old lion, or a lover's lute.

FALSTAFF. Yea, or the drone of a Lincolnshire bagpipe.

PRINCE HENRY. What sayest thou to a hare, or the melancholy of Moor-ditch?[13] 65

FALSTAFF. Thou hast the most unsavoury similes, and art, indeed, the most comparative, rascalliest, sweet young prince. But, Hal, I prithee, trouble me no more with vanity. I would to God thou and I knew where a commodity[14] of good names were to be bought. An old lord of the council rated me the other day in the street about you, 70 sir, but I marked him not; and yet he talked very wisely, but I regarded him not; and yet he talked wisely, and in the street too.

PRINCE HENRY. Thou didst well; for wisdom cries out in the streets, and no man regards it.

FALSTAFF. O, thou hast damnable iteration,[15] and art, indeed, able to 75 corrupt a saint. Thou hast done much harm upon me, Hal. God forgive thee for it! Before I knew thee, Hal, I knew nothing, and now am I, if a man should speak truly, little better than one of the wicked. I must give over this life, and I will give it over—by the Lord, an I do not, I am a villain! I'll be damned for never a king's 80 son in Christendom.

---

8. *resolution . . . fobbed* Courage thus thwarted (of its reward).
9. *antic* Buffoon.   10. *brave* Splendid.   11. *jumps* Suits.
12. *waiting* Being in attendance.
13. *Moor-ditch* An open sewer outside London's walls.
14. *commodity* Supply.
15. *O . . . iteration* O, you have the accursed trick of repeating what one says and twisting it to your own ends.

PRINCE HENRY. Where shall we take a purse to-morrow, Jack?

FALSTAFF. Zounds, where thou wilt, lad; I'll make one,[16] an I do not, call me villain, and baffle[17] me.

PRINCE HENRY. I see a good amendment of life in thee, from praying to purse-taking. 85

FALSTAFF. Why, Hal, 'tis my vocation, Hal; 'tis no sin for a man to labour in his vocation. [*Enter* POINS.] Poins! Now shall we know if Gadshill have set a match.[18] O, if men were to be saved by merit, what hole in hell were hot enough for him? This is the most omnip- 90 otent villain that ever cried "stand" to a true man.

PRINCE HENRY. Good morrow, Ned.

POINS. Good morrow, sweet Hal. What says Monsieur Remorse? What says Sir John Sack-and-sugar? Jack, how agrees the devil and thee about thy soul that thou soldest him on Good-Friday last for a 95 cup of Madeira and a cold capon's leg?

PRINCE HENRY. Sir John stands to his word, the devil shall have his bargain, for he was never yet a breaker of proverbs; he will give the devil his due.

POINS. Then art thou damned for keeping thy word with the devil. 100

PRINCE HENRY. Else he had been damned for cozening[19] the devil.

POINS. But, my lads, my lads, to-morrow morning, by four o'clock, early at Gadshill! There are pilgrims going to Canterbury with rich offer- ings, and traders riding to London with fat purses. I have vizards[20] for you all; you have horses for yourselves. Gadshill lies to-night in 105 Rochester. I have bespoke supper to-morrow night in Eastcheap. We may do it as secure as sleep. If you will go, I will stuff your purses full of crowns; if you will not, tarry at home and be hanged.

FALSTAFF. Hear ye, Yedward, if I tarry at home and go not, I'll hang you for going. 110

POINS. You will, chops?[21]

FALSTAFF. Hal, wilt thou make one?

PRINCE HENRY. Who, I rob? I a thief? Not I, by my faith.

FALSTAFF. There's neither honesty, manhood, nor good fellowship in thee, nor thou camest not of the blood royal, if thou darest not stand 115 for ten shillings.

PRINCE HENRY. Well, then, once in my days I'll be a madcap.

FALSTAFF. Why, that's well said.

PRINCE HENRY. Well, come what will, I'll tarry at home.

FALSTAFF. By the Lord, I'll be a traitor, then, when thou art King. 120

---

16. *make one* Be one of the party.   17. *baffle* Disgrace publicly.
18. *set a match* Arranged a robbery.   19. *cozening* Cheating.
20. *vizards* Masks.   21. *chops* Fat cheeks.

PRINCE HENRY. I care not.

POINS. Sir John, I prithee, leave the prince and me alone, I will lay him down such reasons for this adventure, that he shall go.

FALSTAFF. Well, God give thee the spirit of persuasion, and him the ears of profiting, that what thou speakest may move, and what he 125 hears may be believed, that the true prince may, for recreation sake, prove a false thief; for the poor abuses of the time want countenance.[22] Farewell, you shall find me in Eastcheap.

PRINCE HENRY. Farewell, thou latter spring! Farewell, All-hallown summer! [Exit FALSTAFF.] 130

POINS. Now, my good sweet honey lord, ride with us to-morrow. I have a jest to execute that I cannot manage alone. Falstaff, Bardolph, Peto, and Gadshill, shall rob those men that we have already waylaid; yourself and I will not be there; and when they have the booty, if you and I do not rob them, cut this head from my shoulders. 135

PRINCE HENRY. But how shall we part with them in setting forth?

POINS. Why, we will set forth before or after them, and appoint them a place of meeting, wherein it is at our pleasure to fail; and then will they adventure upon the exploit themselves, which they shall have no sooner achieved, but we'll set upon them. 140

PRINCE HENRY. Yea, but 'tis like that they will know us by our horses, by our habits, and by every other appointment, to be ourselves.

POINS. Tut! our horses they shall not see, I'll tie them in the wood; our vizards we will change after we leave them; and, sirrah, I have cases of buckram for the nonce, to immask our noted outward gar- 145 ments.

PRINCE HENRY. Yea, but I doubt they will be too hard for us.

POINS. Well, for two of them, I know them to be as true-bred cowards as ever turned back; and for the third, if he fight longer than he sees reason, I'll forswear arms. The virtue of this jest will be the incom- 150 prehensible lies that this same fat rogue will tell us when we meet at supper: how thirty, at least, he fought with; what wards, what blows, what extremities he endured; and in the reproof of this lies the jest.

PRINCE HENRY. Well, I'll go with thee. Provide us all things neces- 155 sary, and meet me to-night in Eastcheap; there I'll sup. Farewell.

POINS. Farewell, my lord. [Exit POINS.]

PRINCE HENRY. I know you all, and will awhile uphold
The unyoked humour of your idleness.
Yet herein will I imitate the sun, 160
Who doth permit the base contagious clouds

22. *want countenance* Lack encouragement.

To smother up his beauty from the world,
That, when he please again to be himself,
Being wanted, he may be more wonder'd at,
By breaking through the foul and ugly mists   165
Of vapours that did seem to strangle him.
If all the year were playing holidays,
To sport would be as tedious as to work;
But when they seldom come, they wished for come,
And nothing pleaseth but rare accidents.   170
So, when this loose behaviour I throw off,
And pay the debt I never promised,
By how much better than my word I am,
By so much shall I falsify men's hopes,
And, like bright metal on a sullen ground,   175
My reformation, glittering o'er my fault,
Shall show more goodly and attract more eyes,
Than that which hath no foil to set it off.
I'll so offend, to make offence a skill,
Redeeming time, when men think least I will.   *[Exit.]* 180

SCENE 3

[*Windsor.   The Castle.   Enter* KING HENRY, NORTHUMBERLAND, WOR-
CESTER, HOTSPUR, SIR WALTER BLUNT, *and others.*]

KING HENRY. My blood hath been too cold and temperate,
Unapt to stir at these indignities,
And you have found me; for accordingly
You tread upon my patience.   But be sure
I will from henceforth rather be myself,   5
Mighty, and to be feared, than my condition,
Which hath been smooth as oil, soft as young down,
And therefore lost that title of respect
Which the proud soul ne'er pays but to the proud.
WORCESTER. Our house, my sovereign liege, little deserves   10
The scourge of greatness to be used on it,
And that same greatness too, which our own hands
Have holp to make so portly.
NORTHUMBERLAND. My lord—
KING HENRY. Worcester, get thee gone, for I do see   15
Danger and disobedience in thine eye.
O, sir, your presence is too bold and peremptory,
And majesty might never yet endure
The moody frontier of a servant brow.

You have good leave to leave us.   When we need   20
Your use and counsel, we shall send for you.   [*Exit* WORCESTER.]
You were about to speak.
NORTHUMBERLAND.   Yea, my good lord.
Those prisoners in your Highness' name demanded,
Which Harry Percy here at Holmedon took,
Were, as he says, not with such strength denied   25
As is delivered[1] to your Majesty.
Either envy,[2] therefore, or misprision[3]
Is guilty of this fault, and not my son.
HOTSPUR. My liege, I did deny no prisoners,
But I remember when the fight was done,   30
When I was dry with rage and extreme toil,
Breathless and faint, leaning upon my sword,
Came there a certain lord, neat and trimly dressed,
Fresh as a bridegroom; and his chin new reaped
Showed like a stubble land at harvest home.   35
He was perfumed like a milliner,
And 'twixt his finger and his thumb he held
A pouncet-box,[4] which ever and anon
He gave his nose, and took't away again;
Who[5] therewith angry, when it next came there,   40
Took it in snuff,[6] and still he smiled and talked,
And as the soldiers bore dead bodies by,
He called them untaught knaves, unmannerly,
To bring a slovenly unhandsome corse
Betwixt the wind and his nobility.   45
With many holiday and lady terms
He questioned me, amongst the rest, demanded
My prisoners in your Majesty's behalf.
I then, all smarting with my wounds being cold,
To be so pestered with a popinjay,   50
Out of my grief and my impatience
Answered neglectingly, I know not what—
He should, or he should not; for he made me mad
To see him shine so brisk, and smell so sweet,
And talk so like a waiting-gentlewoman   55
Of guns and drums and wounds—God save the mark!

1. *delivered* Reported.   2. *envy* Malice.   3. *misprision* Misunderstanding
4. *pouncet-box* A small box containing spice to ward off unpleasant odors.
5. *Who* Refers to his nose.   6. *Took . . . snuff* Was offended.

And telling me the sovereignest thing on earth
Was parmaceti for an inward bruise,
And that it was great pity, so it was,
This villainous saltpetre should be digged   60
Out of the bowels of the harmless earth,
Which many a good tall fellow had destroyed
So cowardly, and but for these vile guns
He would himself have been a soldier.
This bald⁷ unjointed chat of his, my lord,   65
I answer'd indirectly, as I said,
And I beseech you, let not his report
Come current for an accusation
Betwixt my love and your high Majesty.
BLUNT. The circumstance considered, good my lord,   70
Whate'er Lord Harry Percy then had said
To such a person, and in such a place,
At such a time, with all the rest retold,
May reasonably die, and never rise
To do him wrong, or any way impeach   75
What then he said, so he unsay it now.
KING HENRY. Why, yet he doth deny his prisoners,
But with proviso and exception,
That we at our own charge shall ransom straight
His brother-in-law, the foolish Mortimer;   80
Who, on my soul, hath wilfully betrayed
The lives of those that he did lead to fight
Against the great magician, damned Glendower,
Whose daughter, as we hear, that Earl of March
Hath lately married.   Shall our coffers, then,   85
Be emptied to redeem a traitor home?
Shall we buy treason?   And indent⁸ with fears,⁹
When they have lost and forfeited themselves?
No, on the barren mountains let him starve;
For I shall never hold that man my friend   90
Whose tongue shall ask me for one penny cost
To ransom home revolted Mortimer.
HOTSPUR. Revolted Mortimer?
He never did fall off, my sovereign liege,
But by the chance of war—to prove that true   95
Needs no more but one tongue for all those wounds.
Those mouthed¹⁰ wounds, which valiantly he took,

---

7. *bald* Trivial.   8. *indent* Bargain.   9. *fears* Traitors.
10. *mouthed* Gaping.

When on the gentle Severn's sedgy bank,
In single opposition, hand to hand,
He did confound the best part of an hour   100
In changing hardiment with great Glendower.
Three times they breathed and three times did they drink,
Upon agreement, of swift Severn's flood,
Who then, affrighted with their bloody looks,
Ran fearfully among the trembling reeds   105
And hid his crisp head in the hollow bank,
Bloodstained with these valiant combatants.
Never did base and rotten policy
Colour her working with such deadly wounds,
Nor never could the noble Mortimer   110
Receive so many, and all willingly:
Then let him not be slandered with revolt.
KING HENRY. Thou dost belie him, Percy, thou dost belie him;
He never did encounter with Glendower.
I tell thee,   115
He durst as well have met the devil alone
As Owen Glendower for an enemy.
Art thou not ashamed?   But, sirrah, henceforth
Let me not hear you speak of Mortimer.
Send me your prisoners with the speediest means,   120
Or you shall hear in such a kind from me
As will displease you.   My Lord Northumberland,
We license your departure with your son.
Send us your prisoners, or you will hear of it.   [*Exeunt* KING HENRY,
    BLUNT, *and* ATTENDANTS.]
HOTSPUR. An if the devil come and roar for them,   125
I will not send them.   I will after straight
And tell him so, for I will ease my heart,
Albeit I make a hazard of my head.
NORTHUMBERLAND. What, drunk with choler?[11]   Stay, and pause
    awhile.
Here comes your uncle.

[*Enter* WORCESTER.]

HOTSPUR.   Speak of Mortimer!   130
Zounds, I will speak of him, and let my soul
Want mercy, if I do not join with him.
Yea, on his part I'll empty all these veins,

---

11. *choler* Anger.

And shed my dear blood drop by drop in the dust,
But I will lift the down-trod Mortimer   135
As high in the air as this unthankful King,
As this ingrate and cankered Bolingbroke.[12]
NORTHUMBERLAND. Brother, the King hath made your nephew mad.
WORCESTER. Who struck this heat up after I was gone?
HOTSPUR. He will, forsooth, have all my prisoners;   140
And when I urged the ransom once again
Of my wife's brother, then his cheek looked pale,
And on my face he turned an eye of death,
Trembling even at the name of Mortimer.
WORCESTER. I cannot blame him, was not he proclaimed   145
By Richard that dead is, the next of blood?
NORTHUMBERLAND. He was, I heard the proclamation.
And then it was when the unhappy King,
Whose wrongs in us God pardon, did set forth
Upon his Irish expedition;   150
From whence he intercepted did return
To be deposed, and shortly murdered.
WORCESTER. And for whose death we in the world's wide mouth
Live scandalized and foully spoken of.
HOTSPUR. But, soft, I pray you; did King Richard then   155
Proclaim my brother[13] Edmund Mortimer
Heir to the crown?
NORTHUMBERLAND.   He did, myself did hear it.
HOTSPUR. Nay, then I cannot blame his cousin King,
That wished him on the barren mountains starve.
But shall it be, that you, that set the crown   160
Upon the head of this forgetful man,
And for his sake wear the detested blot
Of murderous subornation,[14] shall it be
That you a world of curses undergo,
Being the agents, or base second means,   165
The cords, the ladder, or the hangman rather?
O, pardon me, that I descend so low
To show the line and the predicament
Wherein you range under this subtle King.
Shall it, for shame, be spoken in these days,   170
Or fill up chronicles in time to come,

12. *Bolingbroke* The family name of King Henry.   13. *brother* Brother-in-law.
14. *murderous subornation* Conspiracy to murder.

That men of your nobility and power
Did gage[15] them both in an unjust behalf,
As both of you, God pardon it, have done,
To put down Richard, that sweet lovely rose,   175
And plant this thorn, this canker, Bolingbroke?
And shall it, in more shame, be further spoken,
That you are fooled, discarded, and shook off
By him for whom these shames ye underwent?
No, yet time serves, wherein you may redeem   180
Your banished honours, and restore yourselves
Into the good thoughts of the world again,
Revenge the jeering and disdained contempt
Of this proud King, who studies day and night
To answer all the debt he owes to you,   185
Even with the bloody payment of your deaths.
Therefore, I say—
WORCESTER.   Peace, cousin, say no more.
And now I will unclasp a secret book,
And to your quick-conceiving discontents
I'll read you matter deep and dangerous,   190
As full of peril and adventurous spirit,
As to o'er-walk a current roaring loud
On the unsteadfast footing of a spear.
HOTSPUR. If he fall in, good night!—or sink or swim!
Send danger from the east unto the west,   195
So honour cross it from the north to south,
And let them grapple.   O, the blood more stirs
To rouse a lion than to start a hare!
NORTHUMBERLAND. Imagination of some great exploit
Drives him beyond the bounds of patience.   200
HOTSPUR. By heaven, methinks it were an easy leap,
To pluck bright honour from the pale-faced moon,
Or dive into the bottom of the deep,
Where fathom-line could never touch the ground,
And pluck up drowned honour by the locks,   205
So he that doth redeem her thence might wear
Without corrival all her dignities.
But out upon this half-faced fellowship!
WORCESTER. He apprehends a world of figures here,
But not the form of what he should attend.[16]   210

15. *gage* Pledge.
16. *He apprehends . . . attend.* He conceives a world out of mere figures of
speech, but does not pay attention to the true shape of things.

Good cousin, give me audience for a while.

HOTSPUR. I cry you mercy.

WORCESTER.   Those same noble Scots
That are your prisoners—

HOTSPUR.   I'll keep them all.
By God, he shall not have a Scot of them!
No, if a Scot would save his soul, he shall not: 215
I'll keep them, by this hand.

WORCESTER.   You start away,
And lend no ear unto my purposes.
Those prisoners you shall keep.

HOTSPUR.   Nay, I will; that's flat.
He said he would not ransom Mortimer;
Forbad my tongue to speak of Mortimer;   220
But will I find him when he lies asleep,
And in his ear I'll holla "Mortimer!"
Nay, I'll have a starling shall be taught to speak
Nothing but "Mortimer," and give it him,
To keep his anger still in motion.   225

WORCESTER. Hear you, cousin; a word.

HOTSPUR. All studies here I solemnly defy,
Save how to gall and pinch this Bolingbroke.
And that same sword-and-buckler Prince of Wales,
But that I think his father loves him not,   230
And would be glad he met with some mischance,
I would have him poisoned with a pot of ale.

WORCESTER. Farewell, kinsman, I'll talk to you
When you are better tempered to attend.

NORTHUMBERLAND. Why, what a wasp-stung and impatient fool   235
Art thou to break into this woman's mood,
Tying thine ear to no tongue but thine own!

HOTSPUR. Why, look you, I am whipped and scourged with rods,
Nettled, and stung with pismires,[17] when I hear
Of this vile politician, Bolingbroke.   240
In Richard's time—what do you call the place?
A plague upon it, it is in Gloucestershire;
'Twas where the madcap Duke his uncle kept
His uncle York, where I first bowed my knee
Unto this King of smiles, this Bolingbroke—   245
'Sblood!
When you and he came back from Ravenspurgh.

17. *pismires* Ants.

62

NORTHUMBERLAND. At Berkeley Castle.

HOTSPUR. You say true.

Why, what a candy deal of courtesy   250
This fawning greyhound then did proffer me!
Look, "when his infant fortune came to age,"
And, "gentle Harry Percy," and, "kind cousin"—
O, the devil take such cozeners!   —God forgive me!—
Good uncle, tell your tale, I have done.   255

WORCESTER. Nay, if you have not, to it again;
We will stay your leisure.

HOTSPUR.   I have done, i' faith.

WORCESTER. Then once more to your Scottish prisoners.
Deliver them up without their ransom straight,
And make the Douglas' son your only mean   260
For powers in Scotland; which, for divers reasons
Which I shall send you written, be assured,
Will easily be granted.   [*To* NORTHUMBERLAND] You, my lord,
Your son in Scotland being thus employed,
Shall secretly into the bosom creep   265
Of that same noble prelate, well beloved,
The archbishop.

HOTSPUR. Of York, is it not?

WORCESTER. True; who bears hard
His brother's death at Bristol, the Lord Scroop.   270
I speak not this in estimation,
As what I think might be, but what I know
Is ruminated, plotted, and set down,
And only stays but to behold the face
Of that occasion that shall bring it on.   275

HOTSPUR. I smell it: upon my life, it will do well.

NORTHUMBERLAND. Before the game is afoot, thou still lett'st slip.

HOTSPUR. Why, it cannot choose but be a noble plot.
And then the power of Scotland and of York,
To join with Mortimer, ha?

WORCESTER.   And so they shall.   280

HOTSPUR. In faith, it is exceedingly well aimed.

WORCESTER. And 'tis no little reason bids us speed,
To save our heads by raising of a head;[18]
For, bear ourselves as even as we can,
The King will always think him in our debt,   285
And think we think ourselves unsatisfied,

18. *head* Army.

Till he hath found a time to pay us home.[19]
And see already how he doth begin
To make us strangers to his looks of love.
HOTSPUR. He does, he does; we'll be revenged on him. 290
WORCESTER. Cousin, farewell. No further go in this
Than I by letters shall direct your course.
When time is ripe, which will be suddenly,
I'll steal to Glendower and Lord Mortimer,
Where you and Douglas and our powers at once, 295
As I will fashion it, shall happily meet,
To bear our fortunes in our own strong arms,
Which now we hold at much uncertainty.
NORTHUMBERLAND. Farewell, good brother. We shall thrive, I trust.
HOTSPUR. Uncle, adieu. O, let the hours be short, 300
Till fields and blows and groans applaud our sport! [*Exeunt.*]

ACT II

SCENE 1

[*Rochester. An innyard. Enter* FIRST CARRIER *with a lantern in his hand.*]

FIRST CARRIER. Heigh-ho! An't be not four by the day,[1] I'll be hanged.
Charles' wain[2] is over the new chimney, and yet our horse not packed.
What, ostler!
OSTLER [*within*]. Anon, anon.
FIRST CARRIER. I prithee, Tom, beat Cut's saddle, put a few flocks in 5
the point; poor jade is wrung in the withers out of all cess.[3]

[*Enter* SECOND CARRIER.]

SECOND CARRIER. Peas and beans are as dank here as a dog, and that is
the next way to give poor jades the bots.[4] This house is turn'd upside
down since Robin ostler died.
FIRST CARRIER. Poor fellow never joyed since the price of oats rose; it 10
was the death of him.

19. *pay . . . home* Put us out of his way.
1. *by the day* In the morning. 2. *Charles' wain* The Big Dipper.
3. *I . . . cess*. I pray thee, soften Cut's pack saddle, put some wool in the pommel;
the poor nag is terribly sore in the shoulders.
4. *Peas . . . bots*. The horse feed is as damp as a dog, and that's the quickest way
to give nags worms.

SECOND CARRIER. I think this be the most villainous house in all London road for fleas: I am stung like a tench.[5]
FIRST CARRIER. Like a tench! By the mass, there is ne'er a king christen could be better bit than I have been since the first cock. 15
SECOND CARRIER. Why, they will allow us ne'er a jordan,[6] and then we leak in the chimney, and your chamber-lye breeds fleas like a loach.[7]
FIRST CARRIER. What, ostler! Come away, and be hanged! Come away.
SECOND CARRIER. I have a gammon[8] of bacon and two razes[9] of ginger 20 to be delivered as far as Charing Cross.
FIRST CARRIER. God's body, the turkeys in my pannier[10] are quite starved. What, ostler! A plague on thee! Hast thou never an eye in thy head? Canst not hear? An 'twere not as good a deed as drink to break the pate on thee, I am a very villain. Come, and be hanged! 25
Hast no faith in thee?

[*Enter* GADSHILL.]

GADSHILL. Good morrow, carriers. What's o'clock?
FIRST CARRIER. I think it be two o'clock.
GADSHILL. I prithee, lend me thy lantern, to see my gelding in the stable. 30
FIRST CARRIER. Nay, by God, soft; I know a trick worth two of that, i' faith.
GADSHILL. I pray thee, lend me thine.
SECOND CARRIER. Ay, when? Canst tell? Lend me thy lantern, quoth'a? Marry, I'll see thee hanged first. 35
GADSHILL. Sirrah carrier, what time do you mean to come to London?
SECOND CARRIER. Time enough to go to bed with a candle, I warrant thee. Come, neighbour Mugs, we'll call up the gentlemen: they will along with company, for they have great charge.[11] [*Exeunt* CARRIERS.]
GADSHILL. What, ho! chamberlain! 40
CHAMBERLAIN [*within*]. At hand, quoth pick-purse.
GADSHILL. That's even as fair as—at hand, quoth the chamberlain; for thou variest no more from picking of purses than giving direction doth from labouring; thou layest the plot how.

[*Enter* CHAMBERLAIN.]

5. *tench* A spotted fish.   6. *jordan* Chamberpot.
7. *loach* A fish that breeds often.   8. *gammon* A haunch.   9. *razes* Roots.
10. *pannier* Basket.   11. *great charge* Considerable wealth.

CHAMBERLAIN. Good morrow, Master Gadshill. It holds current that 45
I told you yesternight: there's a franklin[12] in the wild of Kent hath
brought three hundred marks with him in gold. I heard him tell it to
one of his company last night at supper, a kind of auditor, one that
hath abundance of charge too, God knows what. They are up already, and call for eggs and butter; they will away presently. 50
GADSHILL. Sirrah, if they meet not with Saint Nicholas' clerks,[13] I'll
give thee this neck.
CHAMBERLAIN. No, I'll none of it. I prithee, keep that for the hangman; for I know thou worshipest Saint Nicholas as truly as a man of
falsehood may. 55
GADSHILL. What talkest thou to me of the hangman? If I hang, I'll
make a fat pair of gallows; for if I hang, old Sir John hangs with me,
and thou knowest he's no starveling! Tut! there are other Trojans
that thou dreamest not of, the which, for sport sake, are content to do
the profession some grace; that would, if matters should be looked 60
into, for their own credit sake, make all whole. I am joined with no
foot land-rakers,[14] no long-staff sixpenny strikers,[15] none of these mad
mustachio purple-hued malt-worms;[16] but with nobility and tranquil-
lity, burgomasters and great oneyers,[17] such as can hold in, such as
will strike sooner than speak, and speak sooner than drink, and drink 65
sooner than pray. And yet, zounds, I lie, for they pray continually to
their saint, the commonwealth; or, rather, not pray to her, but prey
on her, for they ride up and down on her, and make her their boots.[18]
CHAMBERLAIN. What, the commonwealth their boots? Will she hold
out water in foul way?[19] 70
GADSHILL. She will, she will; justice hath liquored[20] her. We steal as
in a castle, cock-sure; we have the receipt of fern-seed,[21] we walk
invisible.
CHAMBERLAIN. Nay, by my faith, I think you are more beholding to
the night than to fern-seed for your walking invisible. 75
GADSHILL. Give me thy hand, thou shalt have a share in our purchase,
as I am a true man.
CHAMBERLAIN. Nay, rather let me have it, as you are a false thief.
GADSHILL. Go to, homo is a common name to all men. Bid the ostler
bring my gelding out of the stable. Farewell, you muddy knave. 80
[Exeunt.]

12. *franklin* A rich farmer or small landowner.
13. *Saint Nicholas' clerks* Highwaymen.
14. *foot land-rakers* Vagabond robbers.   15. *strikers* Hold-up men.
16. *malt-worms* Drunkards.   17. *oneyers* Ones.   18. *boots* Booty.
19. *foul way* Muddy road.   20. *liquored* Waterproofed.
21. *fern-seed* A herb reputed to make one invisible.

[The road by Gadshill. Enter PRINCE HENRY, POINS, and PETO.]

POINS. Come, shelter, shelter. I have removed Falstaff's horse, and he frets like a gummed velvet.

PRINCE HENRY. Stand close. *[They retire. Enter FALSTAFF.]*

FALSTAFF. Poins! Poins, and be hanged! Poins!

PRINCE HENRY *[coming forward]*. Peace, ye fat-kidney'd rascal! What 5 a brawling dost thou keep!

FALSTAFF. Where's Poins, Hal?

PRINCE HENRY. He is walked up to the top of the hill. I'll go seek him. *[Retires.]*

FALSTAFF. I am accurst to rob in that thief's company. The rascal 10 hath removed my horse and tied him, I know not where. If I travel but four foot by the squier[1] further a-foot, I shall break my wind. Well, I doubt not but to die a fair death for all this, if I scape hanging for killing that rogue. I have forsworn his company hourly any time this two-and-twenty year, and yet I am bewitched with the rogue's 15 company. If the rascal have not given me medicines to make me love him, I'll be hanged. It could not be else; I have drunk medicines. Poins, Hal, a plague upon you both! Bardolph! Peto! I'll starve, ere I'll rob a foot further. An 'twere not as good a deed as drink to turn true man and to leave these rogues, I am the veriest 20 varlet that ever chewed with a tooth. Eight yards of uneven ground is threescore and ten miles a-foot with me; and the stony-hearted villains know it well enough. A plague upon't, when thieves cannot be true one to another! *[They whistle.]* Whew! A plague upon you all! Give me my horse, you rogues; give me my horse, and be 25 hanged!

PRINCE HENRY *[coming forward]*. Peace, ye fat-guts! Lie down; lay thine ear close to the ground, and list if thou canst hear the tread of travellers.

FALSTAFF. Have you any levers to lift me up again, being down? 30 'Sblood, I'll not bear mine own flesh so far a-foot again for all the coin in thy father's exchequer. What a plague mean ye to colt[2] me thus?

PRINCE HENRY. Thou liest, thou art not colted, thou art uncolted.[3]

FALSTAFF. I prithee, good Prince Hal, help me to my horse, good King's son. 35

PRINCE HENRY. Out, ye rogue! Shall I be your ostler?

FALSTAFF. Go, hang thyself in thine own heir-apparent garters! If I

---

1. *squier* Foot-rule.   2. *colt* Trick.   3. *uncolted* Unhorsed.

be ta'en, I'll peach⁴ for this. An I have not ballads made on you all, and sung to filthy tunes, let a cup of sack be my poison. When a jest is so forward, and a-foot too, I hate it. 40

[*Enter* GADSHILL *and* BARDOLPH.]

GADSHILL. Stand!

FALSTAFF. So I do, against my will.

POINS. O, 'tis our setter, I know his voice. [*Comes forward with* PETO.] Bardolph, what news?

BARDOLPH. Case ye, case ye, on with your vizards; there's money of 45 the King's coming down the hill, 'tis going to the King's exchequer.

FALSTAFF. You lie, ye rogue, 'tis going to the King's tavern.

GADSHILL. There's enough to make us all.

FALSTAFF. To be hanged.

PRINCE HENRY. Sirs, you four shall front them in the narrow lane; Ned 50 Poins and I will walk lower. If they scape from your encounter, then they light on us.

PETO. How many be there of them?

GADSHILL. Some eight or ten.

FALSTAFF. Zounds, will they not rob us? 55

PRINCE HENRY. What, a coward, Sir John Paunch?

FALSTAFF. Indeed, I am not John of Gaunt, your grandfather; but yet no coward, Hal.

PRINCE HENRY. Well, we leave that to the proof.

POINS. Sirrah Jack, thy horse stands behind the hedge; when thou 60 need'st him, there thou shalt find him. Farewell, and stand fast.

FALSTAFF. Now cannot I strike him, if I should be hanged.

PRINCE HENRY [*aside to* POINS]. Ned, where are our disguises?

POINS [*aside to* PRINCE HENRY]. Here, hard by, stand close.

[*Exeunt* PRINCE HENRY *and* POINS.]

FALSTAFF. Now, my masters, happy man be his dole,⁵ say I. Every 65 man to his business.

[*Enter* TRAVELLERS.]

FIRST TRAVELLER. Come, neighbour, the boy shall lead our horses down the hill; we'll walk a-foot awhile, and ease our legs.

THIEVES. Stand!

TRAVELLERS. Jesus bless us! 70

FALSTAFF. Strike, down with them, cut the villains' throats. Ah, whoreson caterpillars, bacon-fed knaves, they hate us youth; down with them, fleece them.

---

4. *peach* Inform on you.   5. *dole* Lot.

68

TRAVELLERS. O, we are undone, both we and ours for ever!

FALSTAFF. Hang ye, gorbellied knaves, are ye undone? No, ye fat   75
chuffs;[6] I would your store were here! On, bacons, on! What, ye
knaves! Young men must live. You are grand-jurors, are ye? We'll
jure ye, i' faith.

[*They rob and bind them, and exeunt with them. Enter* PRINCE
HENRY *and* POINS *disguised.*]

PRINCE HENRY. The thieves have bound the true men. Now could
thou and I rob the thieves, and go merrily to London, it would be   80
argument for a week, laughter for a month, and a good jest for ever.

POINS. Stand close, I hear them coming.

[*They retire. Reenter* THIEVES.]

FALSTAFF. Come, my masters, let us share, and then to horse before
day. An the Prince and Poins be not two arrant cowards, there's no
equity stirring. There's no more valour in that Poins than in a wild   85
duck.

PRINCE HENRY. Your money!

POINS. Villains!

[*As they are sharing, the* PRINCE *and* POINS *set upon them. They all
run away, and* FALSTAFF *after a blow or two runs away too, leaving
the booty behind them.*]

PRINCE HENRY. Got with much ease. Now merrily to horse.
The thieves are scattered, and possessed with fear   90
So strongly that they dare not meet each other.
Each takes his fellow for an officer.
Away, good Ned. Falstaff sweats to death,
And lards the lean earth as he walks along.
Were't not for laughing, I should pity him.   95

POINS. How the fat rogue roared!   [*Exeunt.*]

SCENE 3

[*Warkworth Castle. Enter* HOTSPUR *reading a letter.*]

HOTSPUR. "But, for mine own part, my lord, I could be well contented
to be there, in respect of the love I bear your house." He could be
contented. Why is he not, then? In respect of the love he bears our
house; he shows in this, he loves his own barn better than he loves
our house. Let me see some more. "The purpose you undertake is   5

6. *chuffs* Misers.

The Quest for Honor and Glory   69

dangerous"—why, that's certain, 'tis dangerous to take a cold, to
sleep, to drink, but I tell you, my lord fool, out of this nettle, danger,
we pluck this flower, safety. "The purpose you undertake is dangerous; the friends you have named uncertain; the time itself unsorted;
and your whole plot too light for the counterpoise of so great an op-   10
position." Say you so, say you so? I say unto you again, you are a
shallow, cowardly hind, and you lie. What a lack-brain is this! By
the Lord, our plot is a good plot as ever was laid; our friends true and
constant: a good plot, good friends, and full of expectation; an excellent plot, very good friends. What a frosty-spirited rogue is this!   15
Why, my Lord of York commends the plot and the general course of
the action. Zounds, an I were now by this rascal, I could brain him
with his lady's fan. Is there not my father, my uncle, and myself?
Lord Edmund Mortimer, my Lord of York, and Owen Glendower?
Is there not, besides, the Douglas? Have I not all their letters to   20
meet me in arms by the ninth of the next month, and are they not
some of them set forward already? What a pagan rascal is this, an
infidel! Ha, you shall see now, in very sincerity of fear and cold
heart, will he to the King, and lay open all our proceedings. O, I
could divide myself, and go to buffets, for moving such a dish of skim   25
milk with so honourable an action! Hang him! Let him tell the
King: we are prepared. I will set forward tonight. [*Enter* LADY
PERCY.] How now, Kate! I must leave you within these two hours.
LADY PERCY. O, my good lord, why are you thus alone?
For what offence have I this fortnight been   30
A banished woman from my Harry's bed?
Tell me, sweet lord, what is't that takes from thee
Thy stomach, pleasure, and thy golden sleep?
Why dost thou bend thine eyes upon the earth,
And start so often when thou sit'st alone?   35
Why hast thou lost the fresh blood in thy cheeks,
And given my treasures and my rights of thee
To thick-eyed musing and curst melancholy?
In thy faint slumbers I by thee have watched,
And heard thee murmur tales of iron wars;   40
Speak terms of manage to thy bounding steed;
Cry, "Courage! to the field!" and thou hast talked
Of sallies and retires, of trenches, tents,
Of palisadoes,[1] frontiers,[2] parapets,
Of basilisks, of cannon, culverin,[3]   45

1. *palisadoes* Stakes set in the ground to stop a charge.
2. *frontiers* Fortifications.   3. *basilisks . . . culverin* Cannon of various sizes.

Of prisoners' ransom, and of soldiers slain,
And all the currents of a heady fight.
Thy spirit within thee hath been so at war,
And thus hath so bestirred thee in thy sleep,
That beads of sweat have stood upon thy brow,   50
Like bubbles in a late-disturbed stream,
And in thy face strange motions have appeared,
Such as we see when men restrain their breath
On some great sudden hest.[4] O, what portents are these?
Some heavy business hath my lord in hand,   55
And I must know it, else he loves me not.
HOTSPUR. What, ho! [*Enter a* SERVANT.]
                Is Gilliams with the packet gone?
SERVANT. He is, my lord, an hour ago.
HOTSPUR. Hath Butler brought those horses from the sheriff?
SERVANT. One horse, my lord, he brought even now.   60
HOTSPUR. What horse? A roan, a crop-ear, is it not?
SERVANT. It is, my lord.
HOTSPUR.   That roan shall be my throne.
Well, I will back him straight: O esperance![5]
Bid Butler lead him forth into the park.   [*Exit* SERVANT.]
LADY PERCY. But hear you, my lord.   65
HOTSPUR. What sayest thou, my lady?
LADY PERCY. What is it carries you away?
HOTSPUR. Why, my horse, my love, my horse.
LADY PERCY. Out, you mad-headed ape!
A weasel hath not such a deal of spleen   70
As you are tossed with. In faith,
I'll know your business, Harry, that I will.
I fear my brother Mortimer doth stir
About his title, and hath sent for you
To line[6] his enterprise, but if you go—   75
HOTSPUR. So far a-foot, I shall be weary, love.
LADY PERCY. Come, come, you paraquito,[7] answer me
Directly unto this question that I ask.
In faith, I'll break thy little finger, Harry,
An if thou wilt not tell me all things true.   80
HOTSPUR. Away, away, you trifler! Love, I love thee not,
I care not for thee, Kate. This is no world
To play with mammets[8] and to tilt with lips.

---

4. *hest* Command.   5. *esperance* Hope.   6. *line* Strengthen.
7. *paraquito* Parrot.   8. *mammets* Dolls.

We must have bloody noses and cracked crowns,
And pass them current too.   God's me, my horse!   85
What sayest thou, Kate?   What wouldst thou have with me?
LADY PERCY. Do you not love me?   Do you not, indeed?
Well, do not, then, for since you love me not,
I will not love myself.   Do you not love me?
Nay, tell me if you speak in jest or no.   90
HOTSPUR. Come, wilt thou see me ride?
And when I am o'horseback, I will swear
I love thee infinitely.   But hark you, Kate,
I must not have you henceforth question me
Whither I go, nor reason whereabout.   95
Whither I must, I must, and to conclude,
This evening must I leave you, gentle Kate.
I know you wise, but yet no further wise
Than Harry Percy's wife.   Constant you are,
But yet a woman, and for secrecy,   100
No lady closer, for I well believe
Thou wilt not utter what thou dost not know,
And so far will I trust thee, gentle Kate.
LADY PERCY. How!   so far?
HOTSPUR. Not an inch further.   But hark you, Kate,   105
Whither I go, thither shall you go too.
To-day will I set forth, to-morrow you.
Will this content you, Kate?
LADY PERCY.   It must of force.   [*Exeunt.*]

SCENE 4

[*Eastcheap.   The Boar's Head Tavern.   Enter* PRINCE HENRY.]

PRINCE HENRY. Ned, prithee, come out of that fat¹ room, and lend me
thy hand to laugh a little.

[*Enter* POINS.]

POINS. Where hast been, Hal?
PRINCE HENRY. With three or four loggerheads² amongst three or
fourscore hogsheads.   I have sounded the very base-string of humil-   5
ity.   Sirrah, I am sworn brother to a leash of drawers,³ and can tell
them all by their christen names, as—Tom, Dick, and Francis.   They
take it already upon their salvation, that though I be but Prince of

1. *fat* Hot.   2. *loggerheads* Blockheads.
3. *leash of drawers* A trio of waiters.

72

Wales, yet I am the king of courtesy; and tell me flatly I am no proud
Jack, like Falstaff, but a Corinthian,[4] a lad of mettle, a good boy, by   10
the Lord, so they call me, and when I am King of England, I shall
command all the good lads in Eastcheap. They call drinking deep,
dyeing scarlet; and when you breathe in your watering, they cry
"hem!" and bid you play it off. To conclude, I am so good a proficient in one quarter of an hour, that I can drink with any tinker in   15
his own language during my life. I tell thee, Ned, thou hast lost
much honour, that thou wert not with me in this action. But, sweet
Ned, to sweeten which name of Ned, I give thee this pennyworth of
sugar, clapped even now into my hand by an underskinker,[5] one that
never spake other English in his life than "Eight shillings and six-   20
pence," and "You are welcome," with this shrill addition, "Anon,
anon, sir! Score a pint of bastard[6] in the Half-moon," or so. But,
Ned, to drive away the time till Falstaff come, I prithee, do thou
stand in some by-room, while I question my puny drawer to what end
he gave me the sugar; and do thou never leave calling "Francis," that   25
his tale to me may be nothing but "anon." Step aside, and I'll show
thee a precedent.   [Exit POINS.]
POINS [within]. Francis!
PRINCE HENRY. Thou art perfect.
POINS [within]. Francis!   30

[Enter FRANCIS.]

FRANCIS. Anon, anon, sir. Look down into the Pomgarnet, Ralph.
PRINCE HENRY. Come hither, Francis.
FRANCIS. My lord?
PRINCE HENRY. How long hast thou to serve, Francis?
FRANCIS. Forsooth, five years, and as much as to—   35
POINS [within]. Francis!
FRANCIS. Anon, anon, sir.
PRINCE HENRY. Five years! By'r lady, a long lease for the clinking of
pewter. But, Francis, darest thou be so valiant as to play the coward
with thy indenture and show it a fair pair of heels and run from it?   40
FRANCIS. O Lord, sir, I'll be sworn upon all the books in England, I
could find in my heart—
POINS [within]. Francis!
FRANCIS. Anon, anon, sir.
PRINCE HENRY. How old art thou, Francis?   45
FRANCIS. Let me see—about Michaelmas next I shall be—

4. *Corinthian* A good sport.   5. *underskinker* A bartender's assistant.
6. *bastard* Spanish wine.

POINS [*within*]. Francis!

FRANCIS. Anon, sir. Pray you, stay a little, my lord.

PRINCE HENRY. Nay, but hark you, Francis, for the sugar thou gavest
me—'twas a pennyworth, was't not?   50

FRANCIS. O Lord, sir, I would it had been two!

PRINCE HENRY. I will give thee for it a thousand pound: ask me
when thou wilt, and thou shalt have it.

POINS [*within*]. Francis!

FRANCIS. Anon, anon.   55

PRINCE HENRY. Anon, Francis? No, Francis; but to-morrow, Francis;
or, Francis, o' Thursday; or, indeed, Francis, when thou wilt.   But,
Francis—

FRANCIS. My lord?

PRINCE HENRY. Wilt thou rob this leathern-jerkin, crystal-button, nott-   60
pated,   agate-ring,   puke-stocking,   caddis-garter,   smooth-tongue,
Spanish-pouch—

FRANCIS. O Lord, sir, what do you mean?

PRINCE HENRY. Why, then, your brown bastard is your only drink; for,
look you, Francis, your white canvas doublet will sully: in Barbary,   65
sir, it cannot come to so much.[7]

FRANCIS. What, sir?

POINS [*within*]. Francis!

PRINCE HENRY. Away, you rogue! dost thou not hear them call?

[*Here they both call him;* FRANCIS *stands amazed, not knowing which
way to go.   Enter* VINTNER.]

VINTNER. What, stand'st thou still, and hear'st such a calling?   Look   70
to the guests within.   [*Exit* FRANCIS.]   My lord, old Sir John, with
half-a-dozen more, are at the door, shall I let them in?

PRINCE HENRY. Let them alone awhile, and then open the door.
[*Exit* VINTNER.] Poins!

[*Enter* POINS.]

POINS. Anon, anon, sir.   75

PRINCE HENRY. Sirrah, Falstaff and the rest of the thieves are at the
door, shall we be merry?

POINS. As merry as crickets, my lad.   But hark ye; what cunning
match have you made with this jest of the drawer?   Come, what's the
issue?   80

PRINCE HENRY. I am now of all humours that have showed themselves

---

7. *Why, then ... so much.* This is largely a nonsense speech to confuse Francis.

humours since the old days of goodman Adam to the pupil age of this present twelve o'clock at midnight. [*Enter* FRANCIS, *passing over.*] What's o'clock, Francis?

FRANCIS. Anon, anon, sir.   85

PRINCE HENRY. That ever this fellow should have fewer words than a parrot, and yet the son of a woman! His industry is upstairs and downstairs; his eloquence the parcel of a reckoning.[8] I am not yet of Percy's mind, the Hotspur of the north, he that kills me some six or seven dozen of Scots at a breakfast, washes his hands, and says to his   90 wife, "Fie upon this quiet life! I want work." "O my sweet Harry," says she, "how many hast thou killed to-day?" "Give my roan horse a drench," says he, and answers, "Some fourteen," an hour after—"a trifle, a trifle." I prithee, call in Falstaff: I'll play Percy, and that damned brawn shall play Dame Mortimer his wife. "Rivo," says   95 the drunkard. Call in ribs, call in tallow.

[*Enter* FALSTAFF, GADSHILL, BARDOLPH, *and* PETO; *followed by* FRANCIS *with wine.*]

POINS. Welcome, Jack, where hast thou been?

FALSTAFF. A plague of all cowards, I say, and a vengeance too! Marry, and amen! Give me a cup of sack, boy. Ere I lead this life long, I'll sew netherstocks and mend them and foot them too. A   100 plague of all cowards! Give me a cup of sack, rogue. Is there no virtue extant? [*Drinks.*]

PRINCE HENRY. Didst thou never see Titan[9] kiss a dish of butter— pitiful-hearted Titan—that melted at the sweet tale of the sun! If thou didst, then behold that compound.   105

FALSTAFF. You rogue, here's lime[10] in this sack too; there is nothing but roguery to be found in villainous man, yet a coward is worse than a cup of sack with lime in it—a villainous coward. Go thy ways, old Jack, die when thou wilt, if manhood, good manhood, be not forgot upon the face of the earth, then am I a shotten herring.[11] There lives   110 not three good men unhanged in England, and one of them is fat and grows old. God help the while! A bad world, I say. I would I were a weaver; I could sing psalms or any thing. A plague of all cowards! I say still.

PRINCE HENRY. How now, wool-sack! What mutter you?   115

FALSTAFF. A king's son! If I do not beat thee out of thy kingdom with a dagger of lath,[12] and drive all thy subjects afore thee like a

8. *his . . . reckoning.* His only eloquence is in the itemization of a bill.
9. *Titan* The sun.   10. *lime* A substance used to mask the taste of cheap wine.
11. *shotten herring* A herring that has deposited its roe and is therefore long and lean.   12. *lath* Wood.

flock of wild geese, I'll never wear hair on my face more. You Prince of Wales!

PRINCE HENRY. Why, you whoreson round man, what's the matter? 120

FALSTAFF. Are not you a coward? Answer me to that—and Poins there?

POINS. Zounds, ye fat paunch, an ye call me coward, by the Lord, I'll stab thee.

FALSTAFF. I call thee coward? I'll see thee damned ere I call thee 125 coward: but I would give a thousand pound, I could run as fast as thou canst. You are straight enough in the shoulders—you care not who sees your back. Call you that backing of your friends? A plague upon such backing, give me them that will face me. Give me a cup of sack—I am a rogue, if I drunk to-day. 130

PRINCE HENRY. O villain! thy lips are scarce wiped since thou drunk'st last.

FALSTAFF. All's one for that. [*Drinks.*] A plague of all cowards still say I.

PRINCE HENRY. What's the matter? 135

FALSTAFF. What's the matter? There be four of us here have ta'en a thousand pound this day morning.

PRINCE HENRY. Where is it, Jack? Where is it?

FALSTAFF. Where is it? Taken from us it is: a hundred upon poor four of us. 140

PRINCE HENRY. What, a hundred, man?

FALSTAFF. I am a rogue, if I were not at half-sword[13] with a dozen of them two hours together. I have scaped by miracle. I am eight times thrust through the doublet, four through the hose, my buckler cut through and through; my sword hacked like a handsaw—*ecce* 145 *signum!*[14] I never dealt better since I was a man: all would not do. A plague of all cowards! Let them speak: if they speak more or less than truth, they are villains and the sons of darkness.

PRINCE HENRY. Speak, sirs; how was it?

GADSHILL. We four set upon some dozen— 150

FALSTAFF. Sixteen at least, my lord.

GADSHILL. And bound them.

PETO. No, no, they were not bound.

FALSTAFF. You rogue, they were bound, every man of them, or I am a Jew else, an Ebrew Jew. 155

GADSHILL. As we were sharing, some six or seven fresh men set upon us—

---

13. *at half-sword* Fighting at close quarters.
14. *ecce signum* Behold the evidence.

FALSTAFF. And unbound the rest, and then come in the other.

PRINCE HENRY. What, fought you with them all?

FALSTAFF. All! I know not what you call all; but if I fought not with fifty of them, I am a bunch of radish. If there were not two or three and fifty upon poor old Jack, then am I no two-legged creature. 160

PRINCE HENRY. Pray God you have not murdered some of them.

FALSTAFF. Nay, that's past praying for: I have peppered two of them. Two I am sure I have paid, two rogues in buckram suits. I 165 tell thee what, Hal, if I tell thee a lie, spit in my face, call me horse. Thou knowest my old ward—here I lay, and thus I bore my point. Four rogues in buckram let drive at me—

PRINCE HENRY. What, four? Thou saidst but two even now.

FALSTAFF. Four, Hal; I told thee four. 170

POINS. Ay, ay, he said four.

FALSTAFF. These four came all a-front, and mainly thrust at me. I made me no more ado but took all their seven points in my target, thus.

PRINCE HENRY. Seven? Why, there were but four even now. 175

FALSTAFF. In buckram?

POINS. Ay, four, in buckram suits.

FALSTAFF. Seven, by these hilts, or I am a villain else.

PRINCE HENRY. Prithee, let him alone; we shall have more anon.

FALSTAFF. Dost thou hear me, Hal? 180

PRINCE HENRY. Ay, and mark thee too, Jack.

FALSTAFF. Do so, for it is worth the listening to. These nine in buckram that I told thee of—

PRINCE HENRY. So, two more already.

FALSTAFF. Their points[15] being broken— 185

POINS. Down fell their hose.

FALSTAFF. Began to give me ground; but I followed me close, came in foot and hand, and with a thought seven of the eleven I paid.

PRINCE HENRY. O monstrous! Eleven buckram men grown out of two! 190

FALSTAFF. But, as the devil would have it, three misbegotten knaves in Kendal green came at my back and let drive at me—for it was so dark, Hal, that thou couldst not see thy hand.

PRINCE HENRY. These lies are like their father that begets them, gross as a mountain, open, palpable. Why, thou clay-brained guts, thou 195 nott-pated fool, thou whoreson, obscene, greasy tallow-keech—

FALSTAFF. What, art thou mad? Art thou mad? Is not the truth the truth?

15. *points* Sword points, but also lacings that hold breeches and stockings together.

PRINCE HENRY. Why, how couldst thou know these men in Kendal green, when it was so dark thou couldst not see thy hand? Come, tell us your reason. What sayest thou to this? 200

POINS. Come, your reason, Jack, your reason.

FALSTAFF. What, upon compulsion? Zounds, an I were at the strappado,[16] or all the racks in the world, I would not tell you on compulsion. Give you a reason on compulsion! If reasons were as plentiful 205 as blackberries, I would give no man a reason upon compulsion, I.

PRINCE HENRY. I'll be no longer guilty of this sin. This sanguine coward, this bed-presser, this horse-back-breaker, this huge hill of flesh—

FALSTAFF. Away, you starveling, you eel-skin, you dried neat's- 210 tongue, you bull's-pizzle, you stock-fish—O, for breath to utter what is like thee—you tailor's-yard, you sheath, you bow-case, you vile standing-tuck—

PRINCE HENRY. Well, breathe awhile, and then to it again, and when thou hast tired thyself in base comparisons, hear me speak but this. 215

POINS. Mark, Jack.

PRINCE HENRY. We two saw you four set on four and bound them, and were masters of their wealth. Mark now, how a plain tale shall put you down. Then did we two set on you four; and, with a word, out-faced you from your prize, and have it; yea, and can show it you 220 here in the house. And, Falstaff, you carried your guts away as nimbly, with as quick dexterity, and roared for mercy, and still ran and roared, as ever I heard bull-calf. What a slave art thou, to hack thy sword as thou hast done, and then say it was in fight! What trick, what device, what starting-hole, canst thou now find out to 225 hide thee from this open and apparent shame?

POINS. Come, let's hear, Jack; what trick hast thou now?

FALSTAFF. By the Lord, I knew ye as well as he that made ye. Why, hear you, my masters, was it for me to kill the heir-apparent? Should I turn upon the true Prince? Why, thou knowest I am as valiant as 230 Hercules; but beware instinct, the lion will not touch the true Prince. Instinct is a great matter; I was a coward on instinct. I shall think the better of myself and thee during my life; I for a valiant lion, and thou for a true Prince. But, by the Lord, lads, I am glad you have the money. Hostess, clap-to the doors. Watch to-night, pray to- 235 morrow. Gallants, lads, boys, hearts of gold, all the titles of good fellowship come to you! What, shall we be merry? Shall we have a play extempore?

16. *strappado* A kind of torture.

PRINCE HENRY. Content—and the argument shall be thy running away. 240
FALSTAFF. Ah, no more of that, Hal, an thou lovest me!

[*Enter* HOSTESS.]

HOSTESS. O Jesu, my lord the prince—
PRINCE HENRY. How now, my lady the hostess! What say'st thou to me?
HOSTESS. Marry, my lord, there is a nobleman of the court at door 245
would speak with you. He says he comes from your father.
PRINCE HENRY. Give him as much as will make him a royal man, and send him back again to my mother.
FALSTAFF. What manner of man is he?
HOSTESS. An old man. 250
FALSTAFF. What doth gravity out of his bed at midnight? Shall I give him his answer?
PRINCE HENRY. Prithee, do, Jack.
FALSTAFF. Faith, and I'll send him packing. [*Exit.*]
PRINCE HENRY. Now, sirs, by'r lady you fought fair, so did you, Peto, 255
so did you, Bardolph. You are lions too, you ran away upon instinct; you will not touch the true Prince, no—fie!
BARDOLPH. Faith, I ran when I saw others run.
PRINCE HENRY. Faith, tell me now in earnest, how came Falstaff's sword so hacked? 260
PETO. Why, he hacked it with his dagger, and said he would swear truth out of England, but he would make you believe it was done in fight, and persuaded us to do the like.
BARDOLPH. Yea, and to tickle our noses with spear-grass to make them bleed; and then to beslubber our garments with it, and swear it was 265
the blood of true men. I did that I did not this seven year before—I blushed to hear his monstrous devices.
PRINCE HENRY. O villain, thou stolest a cup of sack eighteen years ago, and wert taken with the manner, and ever since thou hast blushed extempore. Thou hadst fire and sword on thy side, and yet thou 270
ran'st away. What instinct hadst thou for it?
BARDOLPH. My lord, do you see these meteors? Do you behold these exhalations?[17]
PRINCE HENRY. I do.
BARDOLPH. What think you they portend? 275

17. *meteors . . . exhalations* Bardolph is pointing to his red nose and blotched complexion.

PRINCE HENRY. Hot livers and cold purses.[18]

BARDOLPH. Choler,[19] my lord, if rightly taken.

PRINCE HENRY. No, if rightly taken, halter.[20] Here comes lean Jack, here comes bare-bone. [*Enter* FALSTAFF.] How now, my sweet creature of bombast! How long is't ago, Jack, since thou sawest 280 thine own knee?

FALSTAFF. My own knee! When I was about thy years, Hal, I was not an eagle's talon in the waist; I could have crept into any alderman's thumb-ring; a plague of sighing and grief! It blows a man up like a bladder. There's villainous news abroad: here was Sir John 285 Bracy from your father; you must to the court in the morning. That same mad fellow of the north, Percy, and he of Wales, that gave Amamon[21] the bastinado,[22] and made Lucifer cuckold, and swore the devil his true liegeman upon the cross of a Welsh hook—what, a plague, call you him? 290

POINS. Owen Glendower.

FALSTAFF. Owen, Owen—the same; and his son-in-law, Mortimer; and old Northumberland; and that sprightly Scot of Scots, Douglas, that runs o' horseback up a hill perpendicular—

PRINCE HENRY. He that rides at high speed and with his pistol kills a 295 sparrow flying.

FALSTAFF. You have hit it.

PRINCE HENRY. So did he never the sparrow.

FALSTAFF. Well, that rascal hath good mettle in him, he will not run.

PRINCE HENRY. Why, what a rascal art thou, then, to praise him so for 300 running!

FALSTAFF. O' horseback, ye cuckoo; but a-foot he will not budge a foot.

PRINCE HENRY. Yes, Jack, upon instinct.

FALSTAFF. I grant ye, upon instinct. Well, he is there too, and one 305 Mordake, and a thousand blue-caps[23] more. Worcester is stolen away to-night; thy father's beard is turned white with the news. You may buy land now as cheap as stinking mackerel.

PRINCE HENRY. Why, then, it is like if there come a hot June, and this civil buffeting hold, we shall buy maidenheads as they buy hobnails, 310 by the hundreds.

FALSTAFF. By the mass, lad, thou sayest true; it is like we shall have good trading that way. But tell me, Hal, art thou not horrible afeard? Thou being heir-apparent, could the world pick thee out

---

18. *Hot . . . purses.* The results of excessive drinking. 19. *Choler* Anger.
20. *halter* Collar, the hangman's noose. 21. *Amamon* A devil.
22. *bastinado* A beating on the soles of the feet. 23. *blue-caps* Scots.

three such enemies again as that fiend Douglas, that spirit Percy, and 315
that devil Glendower? Art thou not horribly afraid? Doth not thy
blood thrill at it?

PRINCE HENRY. Not a whit, i'faith; I lack some of thy instinct.

FALSTAFF. Well, thou wilt be horribly chid to-morrow when thou
comest to thy father. If thou love me, practise an answer.   320

PRINCE HENRY. Do thou stand for my father, and examine me upon
the particulars of my life.

FALSTAFF. Shall I? Content. This chair shall be my state, this dagger my sceptre, and this cushion my crown.

PRINCE HENRY. Thy state is taken for a joint-stool, thy golden sceptre 325
for a leaden dagger, and thy precious rich crown for a pitiful bald
crown!

FALSTAFF. Well, an the fire of grace be not quite out of thee, now
shalt thou be moved. Give me a cup of sack to make my eyes look
red, that it may be thought I have wept; for I must speak in passion, 330
and I will do it in King Cambyses'[24] vein. [Drinks.]

PRINCE HENRY. Well, here is my leg.[25]

FALSTAFF. And here is my speech. Stand aside, nobility.

HOSTESS. O Jesu, this is excellent sport, i' faith!

FALSTAFF. Weep not, sweet queen; for trickling tears are vain.   335

HOSTESS. O, the father, how he holds his countenance!

FALSTAFF. For God's sake, lords, convey my tristful queen; for tears
do stop the flood-gates of her eyes.

HOSTESS. O Jesu, he doth it as like one of these harlotry players[26] as
ever I see!   340

FALSTAFF. Peace, good pint-pot; peace, good tickle-brain. [Exeunt
BARDOLPH, FRANCIS, and HOSTESS.]   Harry, I do not only marvel where
thou spendest thy time, but also how thou art accompanied: for
though the camomile, the more it is trodden on, the faster it grows,
yet youth, the more it is wasted, the sooner it wears. That thou art 345
my son, I have partly thy mother's word, partly my own opinion; but
chiefly a villainous trick of thine eye, and a foolish hanging of thy
nether lip, that doth warrant me. If, then, thou be son to me, here
lies the point—why, being son to me, art thou so pointed at? Shall
the blessed sun of heaven prove a micher,[27] and eat blackberries? A 350
question not to be asked. Shall the son of England prove a thief, and
take purses? A question to be asked. There is a thing, Harry,
which thou hast often heard of, and it is known to many in our land

24. *King Cambyses* The hero of a gaudy play of the period.
25. *Well . . . leg.* Hal kneels.   26. *harlotry players* Rascally actors.
27. *micher* Truant.

by the name of pitch. This pitch, as ancient writers do report, doth defile; so doth the company thou keepest. For, Harry, now I do not speak to thee in drink, but in tears; not in pleasure, but in passion; not in words only, but in woes also. And yet there is a virtuous man whom I have often noted in thy company, but I know not his name. 355

PRINCE HENRY. What manner of man, an it like your Majesty?

FALSTAFF. A goodly portly man, i' faith, and a corpulent, of a cheerful look, a pleasing eye, and a most noble carriage; and, as I think, his age some fifty, or, by'r lady, inclining to three-score; and now I remember me, his name is Falstaff. If that man should be lewdly given, he deceiveth me; for, Harry, I see virtue in his looks. If, then, the tree may be known by the fruit, as the fruit by the tree, then, peremptorily I speak it, there is virtue in that Falstaff; him keep with, the rest banish. And tell me now, thou naughty varlet, tell me where hast thou been this month? 360 365

PRINCE HENRY. Dost thou speak like a king? Do thou stand for me, and I'll play my father. 370

FALSTAFF. Depose me? If thou dost it half so gravely, so majestically, both in word and matter, hang me up by the heels for a rabbit-sucker or a poulter's hare.

PRINCE HENRY. Well, here I am set.

FALSTAFF. And here I stand—judge, my masters. 375

PRINCE HENRY. Now, Harry, whence come you?

FALSTAFF. My noble lord, from Eastcheap.

PRINCE HENRY. The complaints I hear of thee are grievous.

FALSTAFF. 'Sblood, my lord, they are false—nay, I'll tickle ye for a young prince, i' faith. 380

PRINCE HENRY. Swearest thou, ungracious boy? Henceforth ne'er look on me. Thou art violently carried away from grace; there is a devil haunts thee, in the likeness of an old fat man, a tun of man is thy companion. Why dost thou converse with that trunk of humours, that bolting-hutch of beastliness, that swollen parcel of dropsies, that huge bombard of sack, that stuffed cloakbag of guts, that roasted Manningtree ox with the pudding in his belly, that reverend vice, that gray iniquity, that father ruffian, that vanity in years? Wherein is he good, but to taste sack and drink it? Wherein neat and cleanly, but to carve a capon and eat it? Wherein cunning, but in craft? Wherein crafty, but in villainy? Wherein villainous, but in all things? Wherein worthy, but in nothing? 385 390

FALSTAFF. I would your Grace would take me with you: whom means your Grace?

PRINCE HENRY. That villainous abominable misleader of youth, Falstaff, that old white-bearded Satan. 395

FALSTAFF. My lord, the man I know.

PRINCE HENRY. I know thou dost.

FALSTAFF. But to say I know more harm in him than in myself, were to say more than I know. That he is old, the more the pity, his white hairs do witness it, but that he is, saving your reverence, a whoremaster, that I utterly deny. If sack and sugar be a fault, God help the wicked! If to be old and merry be a sin, then many an old host that I know is damned. If to be fat be to be hated, then Pharaoh's lean kine are to be loved. No, my good lord, banish Peto, banish Bardolph, banish Poins, but, for sweet Jack Falstaff, kind Jack Falstaff, true Jack Falstaff, valiant Jack Falstaff, and therefore more valiant, being, as he is, old Jack Falstaff, banish not him thy Harry's company, banish not him thy Harry's company—banish plump Jack, and banish all the world.

PRINCE HENRY. I do, I will.

[Enter BARDOLPH, *running.]*

BARDOLPH. O, my lord, my lord! The sheriff with a most monstrous watch[28] is at the door.

FALSTAFF. Out, ye rogue! Play out the play: I have much to say in the behalf of that Falstaff.

[Enter HOSTESS, *hastily.]*

HOSTESS. O Jesu, my lord, my lord—

PRINCE HENRY. Heigh, heigh! the devil rides upon a fiddlestick: what's the matter?

HOSTESS. The sheriff and all the watch are at the door: they are come to search the house. Shall I let them in?

FALSTAFF. Dost thou hear, Hal? Never call a true piece of gold a counterfeit. Thou art essentially mad, without seeming so.

PRINCE HENRY. And thou a natural coward, without instinct.

FALSTAFF. I deny your major;[29] if you will deny the sheriff, so; if not, let him enter. If I become not a cart as well as another man, a plague on my bringing up! I hope I shall as soon be strangled with a halter as another.

PRINCE HENRY. Go, hide thee behind the arras, the rest walk up above. Now, my masters, for a true face and good conscience.

FALSTAFF. Both which I have had, but their date is out, and therefore I'll hide me.

PRINCE HENRY. Call in the sheriff.

400

405

410

415

420

425

430

---

28. *watch* A band of watchmen.   29. *major* Premise.

[*Exeunt all except the* PRINCE *and* POINS. *Enter* SHERIFF *and* CARRIER.]

Now, master sheriff, what's your will with me?

SHERIFF. First, pardon me, my lord. A hue and cry
Hath followed certain men unto this house.   435

PRINCE HENRY. What men?

SHERIFF. One of them is well known, my gracious lord,
A gross fat man.

CARRIER.   As fat as butter.

PRINCE HENRY. The man, I do assure you, is not here;
For I myself at this time have employed him.   440
And, sheriff, I will engage my word to thee,
That I will, by to-morrow dinner-time,
Send him to answer thee, or any man,
For any thing he shall be charged withal:
And so, let me entreat you leave the house.   445

SHERIFF. I will, my lord. There are two gentlemen
Have in this robbery lost three hundred marks.

PRINCE HENRY. It may be so: if he have robbed these men,
He shall be answerable; and so, farewell.

SHERIFF. Good night, my noble lord.   450

PRINCE HENRY. I think it is good morrow, is it not?

SHERIFF. Indeed, my lord, I think it be two o'clock. [*Exeunt* SHERIFF
     and CARRIER.]

PRINCE HENRY. This oily rascal is known as well as Paul's.[30]
Go, call him forth.

POINS. Falstaff!—fast asleep behind the arras, and snorting like a   455
horse.

PRINCE HENRY. Hark, how hard he fetches breath. Search his
pockets. [POINS *searches.*] What hast thou found?

POINS. Nothing but papers, my lord.

PRINCE HENRY. Let's see what they be: read them.   460

POINS [*reads*]. Item, A capon, . 2*s.* 2*d.* Item, Sauce, . . 4*d.* Item,
Sack, two gallons, . . . 5*s.* 8*d.* Item, Anchovies and sack after supper,
2*s.* 6*d.* Item, Bread, . . *ob.*

PRINCE HENRY. O monstrous! But one half-pennyworth of bread to
this intolerable deal of sack? What there is else, keep close, we'll   465
read it at more advantage; there let him sleep till day. I'll to the
Court in the morning. We must all to the wars, and thy place shall
be honourable. I'll procure this fat rogue a charge of foot;[31.] and I

30. *Paul's* St. Paul's Cathedral.
31. *charge of foot* The command of an infantry company.

84

know his death will be a march of twelve-score.   The money shall be paid back again with advantage.[32]   Be with me betimes in the morn- 470 ing; and so, good morrow, Poins.

POINS. Good morrow, good my lord.   [*Exeunt.*]

Act III

Scene 1

[*Wales.   Glendower's castle.   Enter* HOTSPUR, WORCESTER, MORTIMER, *and* GLENDOWER.]

MORTIMER. These promises are fair, the parties sure,
And our induction[1] full of prosperous hope.
HOTSPUR. Lord Mortimer, and cousin Glendower, will you sit down?
And Uncle Worcester—a plague upon it, I have forgot the map.
GLENDOWER. No, here it is.   Sit cousin Percy,   5
Sit good cousin Hotspur, for by that name,
As oft as Lancaster[2] doth speak of you,
His cheek looks pale, and with a rising sigh
He wisheth you in heaven.
HOTSPUR. And you in hell, as oft as he hears Owen Glendower spoke   10
of.
GLENDOWER. I cannot blame him.   At my nativity
The front of heaven was full of fiery shapes
Of burning cressets,[3] and at my birth
The frame and huge foundation of the earth   15
Shaked like a coward.
HOTSPUR. Why so it would have done at the same season if your mother's cat had but kittened, though yourself had never been born.
GLENDOWER. I say the earth did shake when I was born.
HOTSPUR. And I say the earth was not of my mind,   20
If you suppose as fearing you it shook.
GLENDOWER. The heavens were all on fire, the earth did tremble.
HOTSPUR. O, then the earth shook to see the heavens on fire,
And not in fear of your nativity.
Diseased nature oftentimes breaks forth   25
In strange eruptions; oft the teeming earth
Is with a kind of colic pinched and vexed,

---

32. *advantage* Interest.

1. *induction* First step.   2. *Lancaster* King Henry.   3. *cressets* Lamps.

By the imprisoning of unruly wind
Within her womb, which for enlargement striving
Shakes the old beldam earth, and topples down   30
Steeples and moss-grown towers.   At your birth
Our grandam earth, having this distemperature,[4]
In passion[5] shook.
GLENDOWER.   Cousin, of many men
I do not bear these crossings.   Give me leave
To tell you once again that at my birth   35
The front of heaven was full of fiery shapes,
The goats ran from the mountains, and the herds
Were strangely clamorous to the frighted fields.
These signs have marked me extraordinary,
And all the courses of my life do show   40
I am not in the roll of common men.
Where is he living, clipped in with the sea
That chides the banks of England, Scotland, Wales,
Which calls me pupil or hath read to me?
And bring him out that is but woman's son   45
Can trace me in the tedious ways of art,
And hold me pace in deep experiments.
HOTSPUR. I think there's no man speaks better Welsh.   I'll to dinner.
MORTIMER. Peace, cousin Percy, you will make him mad.
GLENDOWER. I can call spirits from the vasty deep.   50
HOTSPUR. Why so can I, or so can any man,
But will they come when you do call for them?
GLENDOWER. Why I can teach you, cousin, to command the devil.
HOTSPUR. And I can teach thee, coz, to shame the devil
By telling truth.   Tell truth and shame the devil.   55
If thou have power to raise him, bring him hither,
And I'll be sworn I have power to shame him hence.
O, while you live, tell truth, and shame the devil!
MORTIMER. Come, come, no more of this unprofitable chat.
GLENDOWER. Three times hath Henry Bolingbroke made head   60
Against my power; thrice from the banks of Wye
And sandy-bottomed Severn have I sent him
Bootless home and weather-beaten back.
HOTSPUR. Home without boots, and in foul weather too!
How scapes he agues, in the devil's name?   65
GLENDOWER. Come, here's the map, shall we divide our right
According to our threefold order ta'en?

4. *distemperature* Physical disorder.   5. *passion* Pain.

MORTIMER. The archdeacon hath divided it
Into three limits very equally.
England, from Trent and Severn hitherto,   70
By south and east is to my part assigned.
All westward, Wales beyond the Severn shore,
And all the fertile land within that bound,
To Owen Glendower.   And, dear coz, to you
The remnant northward, lying off from Trent.   75
And our indentures tripartite are drawn,
Which being sealed interchangeably,
A business that this night may execute,
To-morrow, cousin Percy, you, and I,
And my good Lord of Worcester, will set forth   80
To meet your father[6] and the Scottish power,
As is appointed us at Shrewsbury.
My father Glendower is not ready yet,
Nor shall we need his help these fourteen days.
[*to* GLENDOWER] Within that space you may have drawn together   85
Your tenants, friends, and neighbouring gentlemen.
GLENDOWER. A shorter time shall send me to you, lords,
And in my conduct shall your ladies come,
From whom you now must steal, and take no leave,
For there will be a world of water shed   90
Upon the parting of your wives and you.
HOTSPUR. Methinks my moiety,[7] north from Burton here,
In quantity equals not one of yours.
See how this river comes me cranking in,
And cuts me from the best of all my land   95
A huge half-moon, a monstrous cantle out.
I'll have the current in this place dammed up,
And here the smug and silver Trent shall run
In a new channel, fair and evenly.
It shall not wind with such a deep indent,   100
To rob me of so rich a bottom here.
GLENDOWER. Not wind?   It shall, it must; you see it doth.
MORTIMER. Yea, but
Mark how he bears his course, and runs me up
With like advantage on the other side,   105
Gelding the opposed continent as much
As on the other side it takes from you.
WORCESTER. Yea, but a little charge will trench him here,

6. *father* Father-in-law.   7. *moiety* Share.

And on this north side win this cape of land;
And then he runs straight and even. 110
HOTSPUR. I'll have it so, a little charge will do it.
GLENDOWER. I'll not have it altered.
HOTSPUR.   Will not you?
GLENDOWER. No, nor you shall not.
HOTSPUR.   Who shall say me nay?
GLENDOWER. Why, that will I.
HOTSPUR.   Let me not understand you, then;
Speak it in Welsh. 115
GLENDOWER. I can speak English, lord, as well as you,
For I was trained up in the English Court,
Where, being but young, I framed to the harp
Many an English ditty lovely well,
And gave the tongue a helpful ornament, 120
A virtue that was never seen in you.
HOTSPUR. Marry, and I am glad of it with all my heart.
I had rather be a kitten and cry mew,
Than one of these same metre ballet-mongers.
I had rather hear a brazen canstick turned,[8] 125
Or a dry wheel grate on the axletree,
And that would set my teeth nothing on edge,
Nothing so much as mincing poetry;
'Tis like the forced gait of a shuffling nag.
GLENDOWER. Come, you shall have Trent turned. 130
HOTSPUR. I do not care, I'll give thrice so much land
To any well-deserving friend;
But in the way of bargain, mark ye me,
I'll cavil on the ninth part of a hair.
Are the indentures drawn? Shall we be gone? 135
GLENDOWER. The moon shines fair, you may away by night.
I'll in and haste the writer, and withal
Break with your wives of your departure hence.
I am afraid my daughter will run mad,
So much she doteth on her Mortimer. [*Exit.*] 140
MORTIMER. Fie, cousin Percy! How you cross my father!
HOTSPUR. I cannot choose, sometime he angers me
With telling me of the moldwarp[9] and the ant,
Of the dreamer Merlin and his prophecies,
And of a dragon and a finless fish, 145
A clip-winged griffin and a moulten raven,

8. *canstick turned* A candlestick being burnished.   9. *moldwarp* Mole.

88

A couching lion and a ramping cat,
And such a deal of skimble-skamble stuff
As puts me from my faith.   I tell you what,
He held me last night at least nine hours   150
In reckoning up the several devils' names
That were his lackeys.   I cried "hum," and "well, go to,"
But marked him not a word.   O, he is as tedious
As a tired horse, a railing wife,
Worse than a smoky house.   I had rather live   155
With cheese and garlic in a windmill, far,
Than feed on cates[10] and have him talk to me
In any summer-house in Christendom.
MORTIMER.   In faith, he is a worthy gentleman,
Exceedingly well-read, and profited   160
In strange concealments,[11] valiant as a lion,
And wondrous affable, and as bountiful
As mines of India.   Shall I tell you, cousin?
He holds your temper in a high respect,
And curbs himself even of his natural scope   165
When you come 'cross his humour, faith, he does.
I warrant you, that man is not alive
Might so have tempted him as you have done,
Without the taste of danger and reproof.
But do not use it oft, let me entreat you.   170
WORCESTER.   In faith, my lord, you are too wilful-blame,[12]
And since your coming hither have done enough
To put him quite beside his patience.
You must needs learn, lord, to amend this fault,
Though sometimes it show greatness, courage, blood,   175
And that's the dearest grace it renders you.
Yet oftentimes it doth present harsh rage,
Defect of manners, want of government,[13]
Pride, haughtiness, opinion,[14] and disdain,
The least of which haunting a nobleman   180
Loseth men's hearts and leaves behind a stain
Upon the beauty of all parts besides,
Beguiling them of commendation.
HOTSPUR.   Well, I am schooled, good manners be your speed!
Here come our wives, and let us take our leave.   185

10. *cates* Delicacies.   11. *profited . . . concealments* Proficient in secret arts.
12. *wilful-blame* Headstrong.
13. *want of government* Insufficient self-control.   14. *opinion* Conceitedness.

[*Enter* GLENDOWER, *with* LADY MORTIMER *and* LADY PERCY.]

MORTIMER. This is the deadly spite[15] that angers me,
My wife can speak no English, I no Welsh.
GLENDOWER. My daughter weeps, she will not part with you;
She'll be a soldier too, she'll to the wars.
MORTIMER. Good father, tell her that she and my aunt Percy   190
Shall follow in your conduct speedily.

[GLENDOWER *speaks to her in Welsh, and she answers him in the
same.*]

GLENDOWER. She is desperate here, a peevish self-willed harlotry, one
that no persuasion can do good upon.

[*The* LADY *speaks in Welsh.*]

MORTIMER. I understand thy looks. That pretty Welsh
Which thou pourest down from these swelling heavens   195
I am too perfect in, and, but for shame,
In such a parley should I answer thee.   [*The* LADY *speaks again in
Welsh.*]
I understand thy kisses, and thou mine,
And that's a feeling disputation.
But I will never be a truant, love,   200
Till I have learned thy language, for thy tongue
Makes Welsh as sweet as ditties highly penned,
Sung by a fair queen in a summer's bower,
With ravishing division, to her lute.
GLENDOWER. Nay, if you melt, then will she run mad.   205

[*The* LADY *speaks again in Welsh.*]

MORTIMER. O, I am ignorance itself in this!
GLENDOWER. She bids you on the wanton rushes lay you down,
And rest your gentle head upon her lap,
And she will sing the song that pleaseth you,
And on your eyelids crown the god of sleep,   210
Charming your blood with pleasing heaviness,
Making such difference 'twixt wake and sleep,
As is the difference betwixt day and night,
The hour before the heavenly-harnessed team
Begins his golden progress in the east.   215
MORTIMER. With all my heart I'll sit and hear her sing;
By that time will our book, I think, be drawn.

15. *spite* Misfortune.

GLENDOWER. Do so;
And those musicians that shall play to you
Hang in the air a thousand leagues from hence, 220
And straight they shall be here: sit, and attend.
HOTSPUR. Come, Kate, thou art perfect in lying down. Come, quick,
quick, that I may lay my head in thy lap.
LADY PERCY. Go, ye giddy goose.

[*The music plays.*]

HOTSPUR. Now I perceive the devil understands Welsh, 225
And 'tis no marvel he is so humorous.
By'r lady, he is a good musician.
LADY PERCY. Then should you be nothing but musical, for you are
altogether governed by humours. Lie still, ye thief, and hear the
lady sing in Welsh. 230
HOTSPUR. I had rather hear Lady, my brach,[16] howl in Irish.
LADY PERCY. Wouldst thou have thy head broken?
HOTSPUR. No.
LADY PERCY. Then be still.
HOTSPUR. Neither; 'tis a woman's fault. 235
LADY PERCY. Now God help thee!
HOTSPUR. To the Welsh lady's bed.
LADY PERCY. What's that?
HOTSPUR. Peace! She sings. [*Here the* LADY *sings a Welsh song.*]
Come, Kate, I'll have your song too. 240
LADY PERCY. Not mine, in good sooth.
HOTSPUR. Not yours, in good sooth! Heart! You swear like a comfit-
maker's[17] wife. "Not you, in good sooth"; and "as true as I live"; and
"as God shall mend me"; and "as sure as day"; and givest such sar-
cenet surety[18] for thy oaths, as if thou never walkst further than 245
Finsbury.[19] Swear me, Kate, like a lady as thou art, a good mouth-
filling oath, and leave "in sooth," and such protest of pepper-
gingerbread,[20] to velvet-guards[21] and Sunday-citizens. Come, sing.
LADY PERCY. I will not sing.
HOTSPUR. 'Tis the next way to turn tailor, or be redbreast teacher.[22] 250

16. *brach* Female hound.   17. *comfit-maker's* Confectioner's.
18. *sarcenet surety* Flimsy confirmation.
19. *Finsbury* A field near London frequented on Sundays by citizens.
20. *pepper-gingerbread* Insubstantial, mealy-mouthed.
21. *velvet-guards* Women who favored velvet trim (usually women of the lower
classes).
22. *'Tis . . . teacher.* It's the quickest way to become like the tailor (who always
sings at his work), or like one who teaches robins to sing.

An the indentures be drawn, I'll away within these two hours; and
so, come in when ye will.   [*Exit*]
GLENDOWER. Come, come, Lord Mortimer; you are as slow
As hot Lord Percy is on fire to go.
By this our book is drawn; we'll but seal   255
And then to horse immediately.
MORTIMER.   With all my heart.   [*Exeunt.*]

SCENE 2

[*London.   The palace.   Enter* KING HENRY, PRINCE HENRY, *and*
LORDS.]

KING HENRY. Lords, give us leave; the Prince of Wales and I
Must have some private conference; but be near at hand,
For we shall presently have need of you.   [*Exeunt*]
I know not whether God will have it so,
For some displeasing service I have done,   5
That, in his secret doom, out of my blood
He'll breed revengement and a scourge for me;
But thou dost, in thy passages of life,
Make me believe that thou art only marked
For the hot vengeance and the rod of heaven   10
To punish my mistreadings.   Tell me else,
Could such inordinate and low desires,
Such poor, such base, such lewd, such mean attempts,
Such barren pleasures, rude society,
As thou art matched withal and grafted to,   15
Accompany the greatness of thy blood,
And hold their level with thy princely heart?
PRINCE HENRY. So please your Majesty, I would I could
Quit all offences with as clear excuse
As well as I am doubtless I can purge   20
Myself of many I am charged withal.
Yet such extenuation let me beg,
As, in reproof of many tales devised,
Which oft the ear of greatness needs must hear,
By smiling pick-thanks and base news-mongers,   25
I may, for some things true, wherein my youth
Hath faulty wandered and irregular,
Find pardon on my true submission.
KING HENRY. God pardon thee!   Yet let me wonder, Harry,
At thy affections, which do hold a wing   30

Quite from the flight of all thy ancestors.
Thy place in council thou hast rudely lost,
Which by thy younger brother is supplied,
And art almost an alien to the hearts
Of all the Court and princes of my blood.   35
The hope and expectation of thy time
Is ruined, and the soul of every man
Prophetically do forethink thy fall.
Had I so lavish of my presence been,
So common-hackneyed in the eyes of men,   40
So stale and cheap to vulgar company,
Opinion, that did help me to the crown,
Had still kept loyal to possession,
And left me in reputeless banishment,
A fellow of no mark nor likelihood.   45
By being seldom seen, I could not stir
But, like a comet, I was wondered at;
That men would tell their children, "This is he;"
Others would say, "Where, which is Bolingbroke?"
And then I stole all courtesy from heaven,   50
And drest myself in such humility
That I did pluck allegiance from men's hearts,
Loud shouts and salutations from their mouths,
Even in the presence of the crowned King.
Thus did I keep my person fresh and new;   55
My presence, like a robe pontifical,
Ne'er seen but wondered at; and so my state,
Seldom but sumptuous, showed like a feast,
And won by rareness such solemnity.
The skipping King, he ambled up and down   60
With shallow jesters and rash bavin wits,
Soon kindled and soon burnt; carded[1] his state;
Mingled his royalty with capering fools;
Had his great name profaned with their scorns;
And gave his countenance, against his name,   65
To laugh at gibing boys, and stand the push[2]
Of every beardless vain comparative;[3]
Grew a companion to the common streets,
Enfeoft himself to popularity,
That, being daily swallowed by men's eyes,   70

1. *carded* Debased.   2. *stand the push* Serve as the butt.
3. *comparative* Amateur satirist.

They surfeited with honey, and began
To loathe the taste of sweetness, whereof a little
More than a little is by much too much.
So, when he had occasion to be seen,
He was but as the cuckoo is in June,   75
Heard, not regarded—seen, but with such eyes
As, sick and blunted with community,[4]
Afford no extraordinary gaze,
Such as is bent on sun-like majesty
When it shines seldom in admiring eyes;   80
But rather drowzed, and hung their eyelids down,
Slept in his face and rendered such aspect
As cloudy men use to their adversaries,
Being with his presence glutted, gorged, and full.
And in that very line, Harry, standest thou;   85
For thou hast lost thy princely privilege
With vile participation.   Not an eye
But is a-weary of thy common sight,
Save mine, which hath desired to see thee more,
Which now doth that I would not have it do—   90
Make blind itself with foolish tenderness.
PRINCE HENRY. I shall hereafter, my thrice-gracious lord,
Be more myself.
KING HENRY.   For all the world,
As thou art to this hour, was Richard then
When I from France set foot at Ravenspurgh;
And even as I was then is Percy now.   95
Now, by my sceptre, and my soul to boot,
He hath more worthy interest to the state
Than thou, the shadow of succession.
For, of no right, nor colour[5] like to right,
He doth fill fields with harness in the realm;   100
Turns head against the lion's armed jaws;
And, being no more in debt to years than thou,
Leads ancient lords and reverend bishops on
To bloody battles and to bruising arms.
What never-dying honour hath he got   105
Against renowned Douglas, whose high deeds,
Whose hot incursions, and great name in arms,
Holds from all soldiers chief majority
And military title capital

4. *community* Familiarity.   5. *colour* Pretense.

Through all the kingdoms that acknowledge Christ. 110
Thrice hath this Hotspur, Mars in swathling clothes,
This infant warrior, in his enterprises
Discomfited great Douglas, ta'en him once,
Enlarged[6] him, and made a friend of him,
To fill the mouth of deep defiance up,[7] 115
And shake the peace and safety of our throne.
And what say you to this? Percy, Northumberland,
The Archbishop's Grace of York, Douglas, Mortimer,
Capitulate against us, and are up.
But wherefore do I tell these news to thee? 120
Why, Harry, do I tell thee of my foes,
Which art my nearest and dearest enemy?
Thou that art like enough—through vassal[8] fear,
Base inclination, and the start of spleen[9]
To fight against me under Percy's pay, 125
To dog his heels, and curtsy at his frowns,
To show how much thou art degenerate.
PRINCE HENRY. Do not think so; you shall not find it so:
And God forgive them that so much have swayed
Your Majesty's good thoughts away from me! 130
I will redeem all this on Percy's head,
And, in the closing of some glorious day,
Be bold to tell you that I am your son;
When I will wear a garment all of blood,
And stain my favours in a bloody mask, 135
Which, washed away, shall scour my shame with it.
And that shall be the day, whene'er it lights,
That this same child of honour and renown,
This gallant Hotspur, this all-praised knight,
And your unthought-of Harry chance to meet. 140
For every honour sitting on his helm,
Would they were multitudes, and on my head
My shames redoubled! For the time will come
That I shall make this northern youth exchange
His glorious deeds for my indignities. 145
Percy is but my factor, good my lord,
To engross up glorious deeds on my behalf;
And I will call him to so strict account

6. *Enlarged* Released.
7. *To . . . up* In order to increase his ability to defy us.   8. *vassal* Lowly.
9. *spleen* Irrationality.

That he shall render every glory up,
Yea, even the slightest worship[10] of his time,   150
Or I will tear the reckoning from his heart.
This, in the name of God, I promise here:
The which if He be pleased I shall perform,
I do beseech your Majesty, may salve
The long-grown wounds of my intemperance.   155
If not, the end of life cancels all bands;
And I will die a hundred thousand deaths
Ere break the smallest parcel of this vow.
KING HENRY. A hundred thousand rebels die in this—
Thou shalt have charge and sovereign trust herein.   160

[*Enter* SIR WALTER BLUNT.]

How now, good Blunt! Thy looks are full of speed.
BLUNT. So hath the business that I come to speak of.
Lord Mortimer of Scotland hath sent word
That Douglas and the English rebels met
The eleventh of this month at Shrewsbury.   165
A mighty and a fearful head they are,
If promises be kept on every hand,
As ever offered foul play in a state.
KING HENRY. The Earl of Westmoreland set forth to-day,
With him my son, Lord John of Lancaster,   170
For this advertisement is five days old.
On Wednesday next, Harry, you shall set forward;
On Thursday we ourselves will march. Our meeting
Is Bridgenorth; And, Harry, you shall march
Through Gloucestershire, by which account,   175
Our business valued,[11] some twelve days hence
Our general forces at Bridgenorth shall meet.
Our hands are full of business, let's away;
Advantage feeds him fat, while men delay.   [*Exeunt.*]

SCENE 3

[*Eastcheap. The Boar's Head Tavern. Enter* FALSTAFF *and* BAR-DOLPH.]

FALSTAFF. Bardolph, am I not fallen away vilely since this last action?
Do I not bate? Do I not dwindle? Why, my skin hangs about me

10. *worship* Honor.
11. *Our . . . valued* Our undertaking being well thought out.

96

like an old lady's loose gown; I am withered like an old apple-john.[1]
Well, I'll repent, and that suddenly, while I am in some liking; I shall
be out of heart shortly, and then I shall have no strength to repent. 5
An I have not forgotten what the inside of a church is made of, I am
a peppercorn, a brewer's horse.[2] The inside of a church! Company,
villainous company, hath been the spoil of me.

BARDOLPH. Sir John, you are so fretful, you cannot live long.

FALSTAFF. Why, there is it. Come, sing me a bawdy song, make me 10
merry. I was as virtuously given as a gentleman need to be; virtuous
enough; swore little; diced not above seven times a week; went to
a bawdy-house not above once in a quarter—of an hour; paid money
that I borrowed—three or four times; lived well, and in good compass. And now I live out of all order, out of all compass. 15

BARDOLPH. Why, you are so fat, Sir John, that you must needs be
out of all compass—out of all reasonable compass; Sir John.

FALSTAFF. Do thou amend thy face, and I'll amend my life. Thou
art our admiral, thou bearest the lantern in the poop—but 'tis in the
nose of thee; thou art the Knight of the Burning Lamp. 20

BARDOLPH. Why, Sir John, my face does you no harm.

FALSTAFF. No, I'll be sworn; I make as good use of it as many a man
doth of a death's-head or a memento mori.[3] I never see thy face but
I think upon hell-fire, and Dives[4] that lived in purple; for there he
is in his robes, burning, burning. If thou wert any way given to 25
virtue, I would swear by thy face; my oath should be, "By this fire,
that's God's angel." But thou art altogether given over; and wert
indeed, but for the light in thy face, the son of utter darkness. When
thou ran'st up Gadshill in the night to catch my horse, if I did not
think thou hadst been an ignis fatuus[5] or a ball of wildfire,[6] there's 30
no purchase in money. O, thou art a perpetual triumph,[7] an everlasting bonfire-light! Thou hast saved me a thousand marks in links[8]
and torches, walking with thee in the night betwixt tavern and tavern;
but the sack that thou hast drunk me would have bought me lights
as good cheap at the dearest chandler's in Europe. I have main- 35
tained that salamander[9] of yours with fire any time this two-and-
thirty years; God reward me for it!

BARDOLPH. 'Sblood, I would my face were in your belly!

---

1. *apple-john* Dried apple.
2. *brewer's horse* A horse that is lean and worn out.
3. *memento mori* A reminder of death.
4. *Dives* In Luke, Chapter 16, he is the uncharitable rich man who burns in
Hell. 5. *ignis fatuus* Will-o'-the-wisp. 6. *wildfire* Fireworks.
7. *triumph* A parade with torches such as the Romans held for victorious generals.
8. *links* Torches. 9. *salamander* A fabled lizard that lived in fire.

FALSTAFF. God-a-mercy!   So should I be sure to be heart-burned. [*Enter* HOSTESS.]   How now, Dame Partlet the hen!   Have you in- 40 quired yet who picked my pocket?

HOSTESS. Why, Sir John, what do you think, Sir John?   Do you think I keep thieves in my house?   I have searched, I have inquired, so has my husband, man by man, boy by boy, servant by servant.   The tithe of a hair was never lost in my house before. 45

FALSTAFF. Ye lie, hostess: Bardolph was shaved, and lost many a hair; and I'll be sworn my pocket was picked.   Go to, you are a woman, go.

HOSTESS. Who, I?   No, I defy thee!   God's light, I was never called so in mine own house before. 50

FALSTAFF. Go to, I know you well enough.

HOSTESS. No, Sir John; you do not know me, Sir John.   I know you, Sir John: you owe me money, Sir John; and now you pick a quarrel to beguile me of it.   I bought you a dozen of shirts to your back.

FALSTAFF. Dowlas,[10] filthy dowlas: I have given them away to 55 bakers' wives, and they have made bolters[11] of them.

HOSTESS. Now, as I am a true woman, holland[12] of eight shillings an ell.   You owe money here besides, Sir John, for your diet and by-drinkings, and money lent you, four-and-twenty pound.

FALSTAFF. He had his part of it; let him pay. 60

HOSTESS. He?   Alas, he is poor; he hath nothing.

FALSTAFF. How!   poor?   Look upon his face.   What call you rich? Let them coin his nose, let them coin his cheeks, I'll not pay a denier. What, will you make a younker[13] of me?   Shall I not take mine ease in mine inn, but I shall have my pocket picked?   I have lost a seal- 65 ring of my grandfather's worth forty mark.

HOSTESS. O Jesu, I have heard the Prince tell him, I know not how oft, that that ring was copper!

FALSTAFF. How!   The Prince is a Jack,[14] a sneakup.   'Sblood, an he were here, I would cudgel him like a dog, if he would say so.   [*Enter* 70 *the* PRINCE *and* POINS, *marching, and* FALSTAFF *meets them, playing on his truncheon like a fife.*]   How now, lad, is the wind in that door, i' faith?   Must we all march?

BARDOLPH. Yea, two and two, Newgate fashion.[15]

HOSTESS. My lord, I pray you, hear me.

PRINCE HENRY. What sayest thou, Mistress Quickly!   How doth thy 75 husband?   I love him well; he is an honest man.

---

10. *Dowlas* Coarse, cheap linen.   11. *bolters* Flour-sifters.
12. *holland* Fine linen.   13. *younker* Greenhorn.   14. *Jack* Rascal.
15. *Newgate fashion* Chained together as in Newgate prison.

HOSTESS. Good my lord, hear me.

FALSTAFF. Prithee, let her alone, and list to me.

PRINCE HENRY. What sayest thou, Jack?

FALSTAFF. The other night I fell asleep here behind the arras, and 80
had my pocket picked. This house is turned bawdy-house; they pick
pockets.

PRINCE HENRY. What didst thou lose, Jack?

FALSTAFF. Wilt thou believe me, Hal? Three or four bonds of forty
pound a-piece, and a seal-ring of my grandfather's. 85

PRINCE HENRY. A trifle, some eight-penny matter.

HOSTESS. So I told him, my lord; and I said I heard your Grace say
so; and, my lord, he speaks most vilely of you, like a foul-mouthed
man as he is; and said he would cudgel you.

PRINCE HENRY. What! He did not? 90

HOSTESS. There's neither faith, truth, nor womanhood in me else.

FALSTAFF. There's no more faith in thee than in a stewed prune; nor
no more truth in thee than in a drawn fox; and for womanhood, Maid
Marian[16] may be the deputy's wife[17] of the ward to thee. Go, you
thing, go. 95

HOSTESS. Say, what thing? What thing?

FALSTAFF. What thing! Why, a thing to thank God on.

HOSTESS. I am no thing to thank God on, I would thou shouldst know
it; I am an honest man's wife; and, setting thy knighthood aside, thou
art a knave to call me so. 100

FALSTAFF. Setting thy womanhood aside, thou art a beast to say otherwise.

HOSTESS. Say, what beast, thou knave, thou?

FALSTAFF. What beast? Why, an otter.

PRINCE HENRY. An otter, Sir John, why an otter? 105

FALSTAFF. Why, she's neither fish nor flesh; a man knows not where
to have her.

HOSTESS. Thou art an unjust man in saying so: thou or any man
knows where to have me, thou knave, thou!

PRINCE HENRY. Thou sayest true, hostess; and he slanders thee most 110
grossly.

HOSTESS. So he doth you, my lord, and said this other day you ought
him a thousand pound.

PRINCE HENRY. Sirrah, do I owe you a thousand pound?

FALSTAFF. A thousand pound, Hal? A million, thy love is worth a 115
million, thou owest me thy love.

16. *Maid Marian* A disreputable woman in country May dances.
17. *deputy's wife* A very respectable woman.

HOSTESS. Nay, my lord, he called you Jack, and said he would cudgel you.

FALSTAFF. Did I, Bardolph?

BARDOLPH. Indeed, Sir John, you said so.   120

FALSTAFF. Yea—if he said my ring was copper.

PRINCE HENRY. I say 'tis copper; darest thou be as good as thy word now?

FALSTAFF. Why, Hal, thou knowest, as thou art but man, I dare; but as thou art Prince, I fear thee as I fear the roaring of the lion's whelp.   125

PRINCE HENRY. And why not as the lion?

FALSTAFF. The King himself is to be feared as the lion: dost thou think I'll fear thee as I fear thy father? Nay, an I do, I pray God my girdle break.

PRINCE HENRY. O, if it should, how would thy guts fall about thy   130
knees! But, sirrah, there's no room for faith, truth, nor honesty in this bosom of thine—it is all filled up with guts and midriff. Charge an honest woman with picking thy pocket! Why, thou whoreson, impudent, embost rascal, if there were anything in thy pocket but tavern-reckonings, memorandums of bawdy-houses, and one poor   135
pennyworth of sugar-candy to make thee long-winded—if thy pocket were enriched with any other injuries but these, I am a villain. And yet you will stand to it; you will not pocket-up wrong. Art thou not ashamed?

FALSTAFF. Dost thou hear, Hal? Thou knowest in the state of inno-   140
cency Adam fell; and what should poor Jack Falstaff do in the days of villainy? Thou seest I have more flesh than another man, and therefore more frailty. You confess, then, you picked my pocket?

PRINCE HENRY. It appears so by the story.

FALSTAFF. Hostess, I forgive thee: go, make ready breakfast; love   145
thy husband, look to thy servants, cherish thy guests. Thou shalt find me tractable to any honest reason; thou seest I am pacified still. Nay, prithee, be gone. [*Exit* Hostess.] Now, Hal, to the news at Court; for the robbery, lad—how is that answered?

PRINCE HENRY. O, my sweet beef, I must still be good angel to thee;   150
the money is paid back again.

FALSTAFF. O, I do not like that paying back; 'tis a double labour.

PRINCE HENRY. I am good friends with my father, and may do any thing.

FALSTAFF. Rob me the exchequer the first thing thou dost, and do it   155
with unwashed hands too.

BARDOLPH. Do, my lord.

PRINCE HENRY. I have procured thee, Jack, a charge of foot.

FALSTAFF. I would it had been of horse. Where shall I find one that

can steal well? O, for a fine thief, of the age of two-and-twenty or 160
thereabouts! I am heinously unprovided. Well, God be thanked for
these rebels—they offend none but the virtuous. I laud them, I praise
them.

PRINCE HENRY. Bardolph—

BARDOLPH. My lord? 165

PRINCE HENRY. Go bear this letter to Lord John of Lancaster, to my
brother John; this to my Lord of Westmoreland. [*Exit* BARDOLPH.]
Go, Poins, to horse, to horse, for thou and I have thirty miles to ride
yet ere dinner-time. [*Exit* POINS.] Jack, meet me to-morrow in the
Temple-hall at two o'clock in the afternoon: 170
There shalt thou know thy charge; and there receive
Money and order for their furniture.[18]
The land is burning; Percy stands on high;
And either we or they must lower lie.   [*Exit.*]

FALSTAFF. Rare words! brave world! Hostess, my breakfast, come. 175
O, I could wish this tavern were my drum![19]   [*Exit.*]

ACT IV

SCENE 1

[*The rebel camp near Shrewsbury. Enter* HOTSPUR, WORCESTER, *and*
DOUGLAS.]

HOTSPUR. Well said, my noble Scot: if speaking truth
In this fine age were not thought flattery,
Such attribution[1] should the Douglas have,
As not a soldier of this season's stamp
Should go so general current[2] through the world. 5
By God, I cannot flatter; I defy[3]
The tongues of soothers; but a braver place
In my heart's love hath no man than yourself.
Nay, task to my word; approve me, lord.

DOUGLAS. Thou art the king of honour. 10
No man so potent breathes upon the ground
But I will beard[4] him.

HOTSPUR.   Do so, and 'tis well.

[*Enter a* MESSENGER *with letters.*]

18. *furniture* Equipment.   19. *drum* Recruiting center.
1. *attribution* Recognition.   2. *go . . . current* Be accepted.
3. *defy* Despise.   4. *beard* Challenge.

What letters hast thou there?   I can but thank you.
MESSENGER. These letters come from your father.
HOTSPUR. Letters from him!   Why comes he not himself?   15
MESSENGER. He cannot come, my lord; he is grievous sick.
HOTSPUR. Zounds!   How has he the leisure to be sick
In such a justling time?   Who leads his power?
Under whose government come they along?
MESSENGER. His letters bear his mind, not I, my lord.   20
WORCESTER. I prithee, tell me, doth he keep his bed?
MESSENGER. He did, my lord, four days ere I set forth;
And at the time of my departure thence
He was much feared by his physicians.
WORCESTER. I would the state of time had first been whole   25
Ere he by sickness had been visited:
His health was never better worth than now.
HOTSPUR. Sick now!   Droop now!   This sickness doth infect
The very life-blood of our enterprise;
'Tis catching hither, even to our camp.   30
He writes me here, that inward sickness—
And that his friends by deputation could not
So soon be drawn; nor did he think it meet
To lay so dangerous and dear a trust
On any soul removed, but on his own.   35
Yet doth he give us bold advertisement,
That with our small conjunction we should on,
To see how fortune is disposed to us;
For, as he writes, there is no quailing now,
Because the King is certainly possessed   40
Of all our purposes.   What say you to it?
WORCESTER. Your father's sickness is a maim to us.
HOTSPUR. A perilous gash, a very limb lopped off;
And yet, in faith, it is not; his present want⁵
Seems more than we shall find it.   Were it good   45
To set the exact wealth of all our states
All at one cast?   To set so rich a main
On the nice hazard of one doubtful hour?
It were not good, for therein should we read
The very bottom and the soul of hope,   50
The very list, the very utmost bound
Of all our fortunes.
DOUGLAS.   Faith, and so we should;

5. *want* Absence.

Where now remains a sweet reversion;[6]
We may boldly spend upon the hope of what
Is to come in.   55
A comfort of retirement[7] lives in this.
HOTSPUR. A rendezvous, a home to fly unto,
If that the devil and mischance look big
Upon the maidenhead of our affairs.
WORCESTER. But yet I would your father had been here.   60
The quality and hair of our attempt
Brooks no division: it will be thought
By some, that know not why he is away,
That wisdom, loyalty, and mere dislike
Of our proceedings, kept the earl from hence.   65
And think how such an apprehension
May turn the tide of fearful faction,
And breed a kind of question in our cause;
For well you know we of the offering[8] side
Must keep aloof from strict arbitrement,[9]   70
And stop all sight-holes, every loop from whence
The eye of reason may pry in upon us.
This absence of your father's draws a curtain
That shows the ignorant a kind of fear
Before not dreamt of.
HOTSPUR.   You strain too far.   75
I, rather, of his absence make this use:
It lends a lustre and more great opinion,
A larger dare to our great enterprise,
Than if the earl were here; for men must think,
If we, without his help, can make a head   80
To push against a kingdom, with his help
We shall o'erturn it topsy-turvy down.
Yet all goes well, yet all our joints are whole.
DOUGLAS. As heart can think. There is not such a word
Spoke of in Scotland as this term of fear.   85

[*Enter* SIR RICHARD VERNON.]

HOTSPUR. My cousin Vernon!   Welcome, by my soul.
VERNON. Pray God my news be worth a welcome, lord.
The Earl of Westmoreland, seven thousand strong,
Is marching hitherwards; with him, Prince John.

6. *sweet reversion* Expectation of gain.   7. *retirement* Refuge.
8. *offering* Attacking.   9. *arbitrement* Evaluation or scrutiny.

HOTSPUR. No harm—what more?

VERNON.   And further, I have learned,   90
The King himself in person is set forth,
Or hitherwards intended speedily,
With strong and mighty preparation.

HOTSPUR. He shall be welcome too.   Where is his son,
The nimble-footed madcap Prince of Wales,   95
And his comrades, that daft the world aside,
And bid it pass?

VERNON.   All furnished, all in arms;
All plumed like estridges that wing the wind;
Bated like eagles having lately bathed;
Glittering in golden coats, like images;   100
As full of spirit as the month of May,
And gorgeous as the sun at midsummer;
Wanton as youthful goats, wild as young bulls.
I saw young Harry with his beaver[10] on,
His cuisses[11] on his thighs, gallantly armed—   105
Rise from the ground like feathered Mercury,
And vaulted with such ease into his seat,
As if an angel dropped down from the clouds,
To turn and wind a fiery Pegasus,
And witch the world with noble horsemanship.   110

HOTSPUR. No more, no more: worse than the sun in March,
This praise doth nourish agues.   Let them come;
They come like sacrifices in their trim,
And to the fire-eyed maid of smoky war,
All hot and bleeding, will we offer them.   115
The mailed Mars shall on his altar sit
Up to the ears in blood.   I am on fire
To hear this rich reprisal[12] is so nigh,
And yet not ours.   Come, let me taste my horse,
Who is to bear me, like a thunderbolt,   120
Against the bosom of the Prince of Wales:
Harry to Harry shall, hot horse to horse,
Meet, and ne'er part till one drop down a corse.
O, that Glendower were come!

VERNON.   There is more news:
I learned in Worcester, as I rode along,   125
He cannot draw his power this fourteen days.

DOUGLAS. That's the worst tidings that I hear of yet.

---

10. *beaver* Helmet.   11. *cuisses* Leg armor.   12. *reprisal* Prize.

WORCESTER. Ay, by my faith, that bears a frosty sound.
HOTSPUR. What may the King's whole battle reach unto?
VERNON. To thirty thousand.
HOTSPUR.   Forty let it be: 130
My father and Glendower being both away,
The powers of us may serve so great a day.
Come, let us take a muster speedily:
Doomsday is near; die all, die merrily.
DOUGLAS. Talk not of dying: I am out of fear   135
Of death or death's hand for this one half-year.   [*Exeunt.*]

SCENE 2

[*A public road near Coventry.   Enter* FALSTAFF *and* BARDOLPH.]

FALSTAFF. Bardolph, get thee before to Coventry; fill me a bottle of
sack.   Our soldiers shall march through; we'll to Sutton-Co'fil' to-night.
BARDOLPH. Will you give me money, captain?
FALSTAFF. Lay out,[1] lay out.
BARDOLPH. This bottle makes an angel.[2]   5
FALSTAFF. And if it do, take it for thy labour; and if it make twenty,
take them all; I'll answer the coinage.   Bid my lieutenant Peto meet
me at town's end.
BARDOLPH. I will, captain: farewell.   [*Exit.*]
FALSTAFF. If I be not ashamed of my soldiers, I am a soused gurnet.[3]   10
I have misused the King's press[4] damnably.   I have got, in exchange
of a hundred and fifty soldiers, three hundred and odd pounds.   I
press me none but good householders, yeomen's sons; inquire me out
contracted bachelors, such as had been asked twice on the banns;[5]
such a commodity of warm slaves as had as lieve hear the devil as a   15
drum; such as fear the report of a caliver[6] worse than a struck fowl
or a hurt wild duck.   I prest me none but such toasts-and-butter,
with hearts in their bellies no bigger than pins'-heads, and they have
bought out their services; and now my whole charge consists of
ancients, corporals, lieutenants, gentlemen of companies, slaves as   20
ragged as Lazarus in the painted cloth, where the glutton's dogs
licked his sores; and such as, indeed, were never soldiers, but discarded unjust serving-men, younger sons to younger brothers, revolted
tapsters, and ostlers trade-fallen; the cankers of a calm world and a
long peace; ten times more dishonourable ragged than an old fazed   25

1. *Lay out* Pay for it yourself.
2. *This . . . angel* Including this bottle you owe me ten shillings.
3. *soused gurnet* Pickled fish.   4. *press* Conscription.
5. *asked . . . banns* Men just about to be married.   6. *caliver* Musket.

ancient: and such have I, to fill up the rooms of them that have bought out their services, that you would think that I had a hundred and fifty tattered prodigals lately come from swine-keeping, from eating draff and husks. A mad fellow met me on the way, and told me I had unloaded all the gibbets, and prest the dead bodies. No eye 30 hath seen such scarecrows. I'll not march through Coventry with them, that's flat—nay, and the villains march wide betwixt the legs, as if they had gyves on; for, indeed, I had the most of them out of prison. There's but a shirt and a half in all my company; and the half-shirt is two napkins tacked together and thrown over the shoul- 35 ders like a herald's coat without sleeves; and the shirt, to say the truth, stolen from my host at Saint Albans, or the red-nose innkeeper of Daventry. But that's all one; they'll find linen enough on every hedge.[7]

[*Enter the* PRINCE *and* WESTMORELAND.]

PRINCE HENRY. How now, blown Jack! How now, quilt! 40
FALSTAFF. What, Hal! How now, mad wag! What a devil dost thou in Warwickshire? My good Lord of Westmoreland, I cry you mercy. I thought your honour had already been at Shrewsbury.
WESTMORELAND. Faith, Sir John, 'tis more than time that I were there, and you too; but my powers are there already. The King, I can tell 45 you, looks for us all, we must away all night.
FALSTAFF. Tut, never fear me: I am as vigilant as a cat to steal cream.
PRINCE HENRY. I think, to steal cream, indeed; for thy theft hath already made thee butter. But tell me, Jack, whose fellows are these 50 that come after?
FALSTAFF. Mine, Hal, mine.
PRINCE HENRY. I did never see such pitiful rascals.
FALSTAFF. Tut, tut; good enough to toss; food for powder, food for powder; they'll fill a pit as well as better. Tush, man, mortal men, 55 mortal men.
WESTMORELAND. Ay, but, Sir John, methinks they are exceeding poor and bare—too beggarly.
FALSTAFF. Faith, for their poverty, I know not where they had that; and for their bareness, I am sure they never learned that of me. 60
PRINCE HENRY. No, I'll be sworn, unless you call three fingers on the ribs bare. But, sirrah, make haste, Percy is already in the field.

[*Exit.*]

7. *they'll . . . hedge* They will be able to steal clothes that have been spread out on hedges to dry.

FALSTAFF. What, is the King encamped?

WESTMORELAND. He is, Sir John. I fear we shall stay too long.

[*Exit.*]

FALSTAFF. Well,   65
To the latter end of a fray and the beginning of a feast
Fits a dull fighter and a keen guest.   [*Exit.*]

Scene 3

[*The rebel camp near Shrewsbury.   Enter* HOTSPUR, WORCESTER,
DOUGLAS, *and* VERNON.]

HOTSPUR. We'll fight with him to-night.

WORCESTER.   It may not be.

DOUGLAS. You give him, then, advantage.

VERNON.   Not a whit.

HOTSPUR. Why say you so? Looks he not for supply?

VERNON. So do we.

HOTSPUR.   His is certain, ours is doubtful.

WORCESTER. Good cousin, be advised; stir not to-night.   5

VERNON. Do not, my lord.

DOUGLAS.   You do not counsel well:
You speak it out of fear and cold heart.

VERNON. Do me no slander, Douglas, by my life—
And I dare well maintain it with my life—
If well-respected honour bid me on,   10
I hold as little counsel with weak fear
As you, my lord, or any Scot that this day lives.
Let it be seen to-morrow in the battle,
Which of us fears.

DOUGLAS.   Yea, or to-night.

VERNON.   Content.

HOTSPUR. To-night, say I.   15

VERNON. Come, come, it may not be. I wonder much,
Being men of such great leading as you are,
That you foresee not what impediments
Drag back our expedition: certain horse
Of my cousin Vernon's are not yet come up;   20
Your uncle Worcester's horse came but to-day;
And now their pride and mettle is asleep,
Their courage with hard labour tame and dull,
That not a horse is half the half of himself.

HOTSPUR. So are the horses of the enemy   25

In general, journey-bated and brought low:
The better part of ours are full of rest.
WORCESTER. The number of the King exceedeth ours.
Fod God's sake, cousin, stay till all come in.

[*The trumpet sounds a parley. Enter* SIR WALTER BLUNT.]

BLUNT. I come with gracious offers from the King,   30
If you vouchsafe me hearing and respect.
HOTSPUR. Welcome, Sir Walter Blunt; and would to God
You were of our determination!
Some of us love you well; and even those some
Envy your great deservings and good name,   35
Because you are not of our quality,[1]
But stand against us like an enemy.
BLUNT. And God defend but still I should stand so,
So long as out of limit and true rule
You stand against anointed Majesty!   40
But, to my charge.   The King hath sent to know
The nature of your griefs, and whereupon
You conjure from the breast of civil peace
Such bold hostility, teaching his duteous land
Audacious cruelty.   If that the King   45
Have any way your good deserts forgot,
Which he confesseth to be manifold,
He bids you name your griefs, and with all speed
You shall have your desires with interest,
And pardon absolute for yourself and these   50
Herein misled by your suggestion.
HOTSPUR. The King is kind; and well we know the King
Knows at what time to promise, when to pay.
My father and my uncle and myself
Did give him that same royalty he wears;   55
And when he was not six-and-twenty strong,
Sick in the world's regard, wretched and low,
A poor unminded outlaw sneaking home,
My father gave him welcome to the shore;
And when he heard him swear and vow to God,   60
He came but to be Duke of Lancaster,
To sue his livery[2] and beg his peace,
With tears of innocency and terms of zeal,

---

1. *quality* Party.   2. *To . . . livery* To claim his inheritance.

My father, in kind heart and pity moved,
Swore him assistance, and performed it too.   65
Now, when the lords and barons of the realm
Perceived Northumberland did lean to him,
The more and less came in with cap and knee;
Met him in boroughs, cities, villages,
Attended him on bridges, stood in lanes,   70
Laid gifts before him, proffered him their oaths,
Gave him their heirs as pages, followed him
Even at the heels in golden multitudes.
He presently—as greatness knows itself—
Steps me a little higher than his vow   75
Made to my father, while his blood was poor,
Upon the naked shore at Ravenspurgh;
And now, forsooth, takes on him to reform
Some certain edicts and some strait decrees
That lie too heavy on the commonwealth;   80
Cries out upon abuses, seems to weep
Over his country's wrongs; and, by this face,
This seeming brow of justice, did he win
The hearts of all that he did angle for;
Proceeded further; cut me off the heads   85
Of all the favourites, that the absent King[3]
In deputation left behind him here
When he was personal in the Irish war.
BLUNT. Tut, I came not to hear this.
HOTSPUR.   Then to the point.
In short time after, he deposed the King;   90
Soon after that, deprived him of his life;
And, in the neck of that, tasked the whole state;
To make that worse, suffered his kinsman March—
Who is, if every owner were well placed,
Indeed his King—to be engaged in Wales,   95
There without ransom to lie forfeited;
Disgraced me in my happy victories,
Sought to entrap me by intelligence;[4]
Rated my uncle from the council-board;
In rage dismissed my father from the Court;   100
Broke oath on oath, committed wrong on wrong;
And, in conclusion, drove us to seek out

3. *absent King* Refers to Richard II.   4. *intelligence* Spies.

This head of safety, and withal to pry
Into his title, the which we find
Too indirect⁵ for long continuance.   105
BLUNT. Shall I return this answer to the King?
HOTSPUR. Not so, Sir Walter: we'll withdraw awhile.
Go to the King, and let there be impawned
Some surety for a safe return again,
And in the morning early shall mine uncle   110
Bring him our purposes; and so, farewell.
BLUNT. I would you would accept of grace and love.
HOTSPUR. And may be so we shall.
BLUNT.   Pray God you do.   [*Exeunt.*]

SCENE 4

[*York.   The* ARCHBISHOP's *palace.   Enter the* ARCHBISHOP OF YORK *and*
SIR MICHAEL.]

ARCHBISHOP OF YORK. Hie, good Sir Michael; bear this sealed brief
With winged haste to the lord marshal;
This to my cousin Scroop; and all the rest
To whom they are directed.   If you knew
How much they do import, you would make haste.   5
SIR MICHAEL. My good lord,
I guess their tenour.
ARCHBISHOP OF YORK.   Like enough you do.
To-morrow, good Sir Michael, is a day
Wherein the fortune of ten thousand men
Must bide the touch; for, sir, at Shrewsbury,   10
As I am truly given to understand,
The King, with mighty and quick-raised power,
Meets with Lord Harry.   And, I fear, Sir Michael,
What with the sickness of Northumberland,
Whose power was in the first proportion,   15
And what with Owen Glendower's absence thence,
Who with them was a rated sinew too,
And comes not in, o'er-ruled by prophecies,
I fear the power of Percy is too weak
To wage an instant trial with the king.   20
SIR MICHAEL. Why, my good lord, you need not fear;
There is Douglas and Lord Mortimer.

5. *indirect* Irregular.

ARCHBISHOP OF YORK. No, Mortimer is not there.

SIR MICHAEL. But there is Mordake, Vernon, Lord Harry Percy.
And there is my Lord of Worcester, and a head   25
Of gallant warriors, noble gentlemen.

ARCHBISHOP OF YORK. And so there is; but yet the King hath drawn
The special head of all the land together:
The Prince of Wales, Lord John of Lancaster,
The noble Westmoreland, and warlike Blunt,   30
And many moe corrivals and dear men
Of estimation and command in arms.

SIR MICHAEL. Doubt not, my lord, they shall be well opposed.

ARCHBISHOP OF YORK. I hope no less, yet needful 'tis to fear;
And, to prevent the worst, Sir Michael, speed: 35
For if Lord Percy thrive not, ere the King
Dismiss his power, he means to visit us,
For he hath heard of our confederacy—
And 'tis but wisdom to make strong against him.
Therefore make haste.   I must go write again   40
To other friends; and so, farewell, Sir Michael.   [*Exeunt.*]

ACT V

SCENE 1

[*The* KING'S *camp near Shrewsbury.   Enter the* KING, PRINCE HENRY,
PRINCE JOHN, SIR WALTER BLUNT, *and* FALSTAFF.]

KING HENRY. How bloodily the sun begins to peer
Above yon busky hill!   The day looks pale
At his distemperature.

PRINCE HENRY.   The southern wind
Doth play the trumpet to his purposes,
And by his hollow whistling in the leaves   5
Foretells a tempest and a blustering day.

KING HENRY. Then with the losers let it sympathise,
For nothing can seem foul to those that win.

[*The trumpet sounds.   Enter* WORCESTER *and* VERNON.]

How now, my Lord of Worcester! 'Tis not well
That you and I should meet upon such terms   10
As now we meet.   You have deceived our trust,
And made us doff our easy robes of peace,
To crush our old limbs in ungentle steel.
This is not well, my lord, this is not well.

What say you to it?   Will you again unknit   15
This churlish knot of all-abhorred war
And move in that obedient orb again
Where you did give a fair and natural light,
And be no more an exhaled meteor,
A prodigy of fear, and a portent   20
Of broached mischief to the unborn times?
WORCESTER. Hear me, my liege:
For mine own part, I could be well content
To entertain the lag-end of my life
With quiet hours; for, I do protest,   25
I have not sought the day of this dislike.
KING HENRY. You have not sought it!   How comes it, then?
FALSTAFF. Rebellion lay in his way, and he found it.
PRINCE HENRY. Peace, chewet, peace!
WORCESTER. It pleased your Majesty to turn your looks   30
Of favour from myself and all our house;
And yet I must remember you, my lord,
We were the first and dearest of your friends.
For you my staff of office did I break
In Richard's time; and posted day and night   35
To meet you on the way, and kiss your hand,
When yet you were in place and in account
Nothing so strong and fortunate as I.
It was myself, my brother, and his son,
That brought you home, and boldly did outdare   40
The dangers of the time. You swore to us,
And you did swear that oath at Doncaster,
That you did nothing purpose 'gainst the state,
Nor claim no further than your new-fallen right,
The seat of Gaunt, dukedom of Lancaster.   45
To this we swore our aid.   But in short space,
It rained down fortune showering on your head,
And such a flood of greatness fell on you—
What with our help, what with the absent King,
What with the injuries of a wanton time,   50
The seeming sufferances that you had borne,
And the contrarious winds that held the King
So long in his unlucky Irish wars
That all in England did repute him dead—
And from this swarm of fair advantages   55
You took occasion to be quickly woo'd
To gripe the general sway into your hand;
Forgot your oath to us at Doncaster;

And, being fed by us, you used us so
As that ungentle gull, the cuckoo's bird,   60
Useth the sparrow, did oppress our nest;
Grew by our feeding to so great a bulk,
That even our love durst not come near your sight
For fear of swallowing, but with nimble wing
We were enforced, for safety sake, to fly   65
Out of your sight, and raise this present head:
Whereby we stand opposed by such means
As you yourself have forged against yourself,
By unkind usage, dangerous countenance,
And violation of all faith and troth   70
Sworn to us in your younger enterprise.
KING HENRY. These things, indeed, you have articulate,
Proclaimed at market-crosses, read in churches,
To face¹ the garment of rebellion
With some fine colour that may please the eye   75
Of fickle changelings and poor discontents,
Which gape and rub the elbow at the news
Of hurlyburly innovation:²
And never yet did insurrection want
Such water-colours to impaint his cause,   80
Nor moody beggars, starving for a time
Of pellmell havoc and confusion.
PRINCE HENRY. In both our armies there is many a soul
Shall pay full dearly for this encounter,
If once they join in trial. Tell your nephew   85
The Prince of Wales doth join with all the world
In praise of Henry Percy. By my hopes,
This present enterprise set off his head,³
I do not think a braver gentleman,
More active-valiant or more valiant-young,   90
More daring or more bold, is now alive
To grace this latter age with noble deeds.
For my part, I may speak it to my shame,
I have a truant been to chivalry;
And so I hear he doth account me too: 95
Yet this before my father's Majesty—
I am content that he shall take the odds
Of his great name and estimation,
And will, to save the blood on either side,
Try fortune with him in a single fight.   100

1. *face* Adorn.   2. *innovation* Rebellion.   3. *set . . . head* Disregarded.

KING HENRY. And, Prince of Wales, so dare we venture thee,
Albeit considerations infinite
Do make against it.—No, good Worcester, no,
We love our people well; even those we love
That are misled upon your cousin's part;   105
And, will they take the offer of our grace,
Both he and they, and you, yea, every man
Shall be my friend again, and I'll be his:
So tell your cousin, and bring me word
What he will do.   But if he will not yield,   110
Rebuke and dread correction wait on us,
And they shall do their office.   So, be gone;
We will not now be troubled with reply:
We offer fair; take it advisedly.   [*Exeunt* WORCESTER *and* VERNON.]
PRINCE HENRY. It will not be accepted, on my life.   115
The Douglas and the Hotspur both together
Are confident against the world in arms.
KING HENRY. Hence, therefore, every leader to his charge,
For, on their answer, will we set on them,
And God befriend us, as our cause is just!   120
                    [*Exeunt* KING, BLUNT, *and* PRINCE JOHN.]
FALSTAFF. Hal, if thou see me down in the battle, and bestride me,[4]
so; 'tis a point of friendship.
PRINCE HENRY. Nothing but a colossus can do thee that friendship.
Say thy prayers, and farewell.
FALSTAFF. I would 'twere bedtime, Hal, and all well.   125
PRINCE HENRY. Why, thou owest God a death.   [*Exit.*]
FALSTAFF. 'Tis not due yet; I would be loth to pay him before his day.
What need I be so forward with him that calls not on me?   Well, 'tis
no matter; honour pricks me on.   Yea, but how if honour prick me
off when I come on?   How then?   Can honour set to a leg?   No.   Or 130
an arm?   No.   Or take away the grief of a wound?   No. Honour hath
no skill in surgery, then?   No.   What is honour?   A word.   What is
that word honour?   Air.   A trim reckoning!   Who hath it?   He that
died o' Wednesday.   Doth he feel it?   No.   Doth he hear it?   No.
'Tis insensible, then?   Yea, to the dead.   But will it not live with the 135
living?   No.   Why?   Detraction will not suffer it.   Therefore I'll
none of it: honour is a mere scutcheon[5]—and so ends my catechism.
                                                          [*Exit.*]

4. *bestride me* Stand over, straddle, so as to defend.
5. *scutcheon* The deceased's coat of arms borne at his funeral.

114

Scene 2

[*The rebel camp. Enter* WORCESTER *and* VERNON.]

WORCESTER. O, no, my nephew must not know Sir Richard,
The liberal and kind offer of the King.
VERNON. 'Twere best he did.
WORCESTER.   Then are we all undone.
It is not possible, it cannot be,
The King should keep his word in loving us.   5
He will suspect us still, and find a time
To punish this offence in other faults.
Suspicion all our lives shall be stuck full of eyes,
For treason is but trusted like the fox,
Who, ne'er so tame, so cherished, and locked up,   10
Will have a wild trick of his ancestors.
Look how we can, or sad or merrily,
Interpretation will misquote our looks;
And we shall feed like oxen at a stall,
The better cherished, still the nearer death.   15
My nephew's trespass may be well forgot.
It hath the excuse of youth and heat of blood,
And an adopted name of privilege—
A hare-brained Hotspur, governed by a spleen.
All his offences live upon my head   20
And on his father's: we did train¹ him on,
And, his corruption being ta'en from us,
We, as the spring of all, shall pay for all.
Therefore, good cousin, let not Harry know,
In any case, the offer of the King.   25
VERNON. Deliver what you will, I'll say 'tis so.
Here comes your cousin.

[*Enter* HOTSPUR *and* DOUGLAS *with* OFFICERS *and* SOLDIERS *behind.*]

HOTSPUR.   My uncle is returned:
Deliver up my Lord of Westmoreland.
Uncle, what news?
WORCESTER. The King will bid you battle presently.   30
DOUGLAS. Defy him by the Lord of Westmoreland.
HOTSPUR. Lord Douglas, go you and tell him so.
DOUGLAS. Marry, and shall, and very willingly.   [*Exit.*]

---

1. *train* Draw.

WORCESTER. There is no seeming mercy in the King.
HOTSPUR. Did you beg any?   God forbid!   35
WORCESTER. I told him gently of our grievances,
Of his oath-breaking, which he mended thus:
By now forswearing that he is forsworn.
He calls us rebels, traitors, and will scourge
With haughty arms this hateful name in us.   40

[*Enter* DOUGLAS.]

DOUGLAS. Arm, gentlemen, to arms!   For I have thrown
A brave defiance in King Henry's teeth,
And Westmoreland, that was engaged, did bear it,
Which cannot choose but bring him quickly on.
WORCESTER. The Prince of Wales stept forth before the King   45
And, nephew, challenged you to single fight.
HOTSPUR. O, would the quarrel lay upon our heads,
And that no man might draw short breath to-day
But I and Harry Monmouth!   Tell me, tell me,
How showed his tasking?   Seemed it in contempt?   50
VERNON. No, by my soul; I never in my life
Did hear a challenge urged more modestly,
Unless a brother should a brother dare
To gentle exercise and proof of arms.
He gave you all the duties of a man;   55
Trimmed up your praises with a princely tongue;
Spoke your deservings like a chronicle;
Making you ever better than his praise,
By still dispraising praise valued with you;[2]
And, which became him like a prince indeed,   60
He made a blushing cital of[3] himself;
And chid his truant youth with such a grace,
As if he mastered there a double spirit,
Of teaching and of learning instantly.
There did he pause: but let me tell the world—   65
If he outlive the envy[4] of this day,
England did never owe[5] so sweet a hope,
So much misconstrued in his wantonness.
HOTSPUR. Cousin, I think thou art enamoured
On his follies; never did I hear   70
Of any prince so wild a liberty.
But be he as he will, yet once ere night

2. *By . . . you* By continuing to insist that mere praise could not do you justice.
3. *cital of* Reference to.   4. *envy* Malice.   5. *owe* Own.

116

I will embrace him with a soldier's arm,
That he shall shrink under my courtesy.
Arm, arm with speed—and fellows, soldiers, friends—   75
Better consider what you have to do
Than I, that have not well the gift of tongue,
Can lift your blood up with persuasion.

[*Enter a* MESSENGER.]

MESSENGER. My lord, here are letters for you.
HOTSPUR. I cannot read them now.   80
O gentlemen, the time of life is short!
To spend that shortness basely were too long,
If life did ride upon a dial's point,
Still ending at the arrival of an hour.
An if we live, we live to tread on Kings;   85
If die, brave death, when princes die with us!
Now, for our consciences, the arms are fair,
When the intent of bearing them is just.

[*Enter another* MESSENGER.]

MESSENGER. My lord, prepare; the King comes on apace.
HOTSPUR. I thank him, that he cuts me from my tale,   90
For I profess not talking; only this—
Let each man do his best; and here draw I
A sword, whose temper I intend to stain
With the best blood that I can meet withal
In the adventure of this perilous day.   95
Now.—Esperance!—Percy!—and set on!
Sound all the lofty instruments of war,
And by that music let us all embrace;
For, heaven to earth, some of us never shall
A second time do such a courtesy.   100
          [*The trumpets sound. They embrace, and exeunt.*]

SCENE 3

[*Plain between the camps. Enter* KING HENRY *and his army, pass
over the stage and exeunt. Then enter* DOUGLAS, *and* BLUNT *disguised
as the* KING.]

BLUNT. What is thy name, that in the battle thus
Thou crossest me? What honour dost thou seek
Upon my head?
DOUGLAS.   Know, then, my name is Douglas;

And I do haunt thee in the battle thus
Because some tell me that thou art a King.   5
BLUNT. They tell thee true.
DOUGLAS. The Lord of Stafford dear to-day hath bought
Thy likeness; for, instead of thee, King Harry,
This sword hath ended him.   So shall it thee,
Unless thou yield thee as my prisoner.   10
BLUNT. I was not born a yielder, thou proud Scot;
And thou shalt find a King that will revenge
Lord Stafford's death.

[*They fight,* DOUGLAS *kills* BLUNT.   *Enter* HOTSPUR.]

HOTSPUR. O Douglas, hadst thou fought at Holmedon thus,
I never had triumphed upon a Scot.   15
DOUGLAS. All's done, all's won; here breathless lies the King.
HOTSPUR. Where?
DOUGLAS. Here.
HOTSPUR. This, Douglas?   No; I know this face full well.
A gallant knight he was, his name was Blunt,   20
Semblably furnished like the King himself.
DOUGLAS. Ah fool go with thy soul, whither it goes!
A borrowed title hast thou bought too dear.
Why didst thou tell me that thou wert a King?
HOTSPUR. The King hath many masking in his coats.¹   25
DOUGLAS. Now, by my sword, I will kill all his coats;
I'll murder all his wardrobe piece by piece,
Until I meet the King.
HOTSPUR.   Up, and away!
Our soldiers stand full fairly for the day.
                              [*Exeunt.   Alarum.   Enter* FALSTAFF.]
FALSTAFF. Though I could scape shot-free² at London, I fear the shot   30
here; here's no scoring³ but upon the pate.   Soft!   Who are you?   Sir
Walter Blunt—there's honour for you!   Here's no vanity!   I am as
hot as molten lead, and as heavy too: God keep lead out of me!   I
need no more weight than mine own bowels.   I have led my raga-
muffins where they are peppered: there's but three of my hundred   35
and fifty left alive; and they are for the town's end—to beg during life.
But who comes here?

[*Enter* PRINCE HENRY.]

1. *coats* Coats of arms.   2. *shot-free* Without paying bills.
3. *scoring* Billing.

118

PRINCE HENRY. What, stand'st thou idle here?   Lend me thy sword.
Many a nobleman lies stark and stiff
Under the hoofs of vaunting enemies,   40
Whose deaths are yet unrevenged.
I prithee, lend me thy sword.
FALSTAFF. O Hal, I prithee, give me leave to breathe awhile.   Turk
Gregory never did such deeds in arms as I have done this day.   I
have paid Percy, I have made him sure.   45
PRINCE HENRY. He is, indeed, and living to kill thee.   I prithee, lend
me thy sword.
FALSTAFF. Nay, before God, Hal, if Percy be alive, thou gets not my
sword; but take my pistol, if thou wilt.
PRINCE HENRY. Give it me.   What, is it in the case?   50
FALSTAFF. Ay, Hal.   'Tis hot, 'tis hot: there's that will sack a city.

[*The* PRINCE *draws it out, and finds it to be a bottle of sack.*]

PRINCE HENRY. What, is it a time to jest and dally now?
                         [*He throws the bottle at him.   Exit.*]
FALSTAFF. Well, if Percy be alive, I'll pierce him. If he do come in
my way, so; if he do not, if I come in his willingly, let him make a
carbonado[4] of me.   I like not such grinning honour as Sir Walter   55
hath: give me life, which if I can save, so; if not, honour comes
unlooked for, and there's an end.   [*Exit.*]

SCENE 4

[*Another part of the field.   Alarum.   Excursions.   Enter* KING HENRY,
PRINCE HENRY, PRINCE JOHN, *and* WESTMORELAND.]

KING HENRY. I prithee, Harry, withdraw thyself, thou bleed'st too
        much.
Lord John of Lancaster, go you with him.
PRINCE JOHN. Not I, my lord, unless I did bleed too.
PRINCE HENRY. I beseech your majesty, make up,[1]
Lest your retirement do amaze[2] your friends.   5
KING HENRY. I will do so.
My Lord of Westmoreland, lead him to his tent.
WESTMORELAND. Come, my lord, I will lead you to your tent.
PRINCE HENRY. Lead me, my lord?   I do not need your help:

---

4. *carbonado* Slashed meat.

1. *make up* Advance.   2. *amaze* Dismay.

And God forbid, a shallow scratch should drive 10
The Prince of Wales from such a field as this,
Where stained nobility lies trodden on,
And rebels' arms triumph in massacres!
PRINCE JOHN. We breathe too long: come, cousin Westmoreland,
Our duty this way lies; for God's sake, come. 15
                       [*Exeunt* PRINCE JOHN *and* WESTMORELAND.]
PRINCE HENRY. By God, thou hast deceived me, Lancaster;
I did not think thee lord of such a spirit:
Before, I loved thee as a brother, John;
But now, I do respect thee as my soul.
KING HENRY. I saw him hold Lord Percy at the point 20
With lustier maintenance than I did look for
Of such an ungrown warrior.
PRINCE HENRY.   O, this boy
Lends mettle to us all!   [*Exit. Enter* DOUGLAS.]
DOUGLAS. Another King! They grow like Hydra's heads:
I am the Douglas, fatal to all those 25
That wear those colours on them. What art thou,
That counterfeit'st the person of a King?
KING HENRY. The King himself, who, Douglas, grieves at heart,
So many of his shadows thou hast met,
And not the very King. I have two boys 30
Seek Percy and thyself about the field:
But, seeing thou fallest on me so luckily,
I will assay thee: so, defend thyself.
DOUGLAS. I fear thou art another counterfeit;
And yet, in faith, thou bearest thee like a King: 35
But mine I am sure thou art, whoe'er thou be,
And thus I win thee.

[*They fight; the* KING *being in danger, enter* PRINCE HENRY.]

PRINCE HENRY. Hold up thy head, vile Scot, or thou art like
Never to hold it up again! The spirits
Of valiant Shirley, Stafford, Blunt, are in my arms. 40
It is the Prince of Wales that threatens thee,
Who never promiseth but he means to pay. [*They fight;* DOUGLAS
flies.]
Cheerly, my lord, how fares your Grace?
Sir Nicholas Gawsey hath for succour sent,
And so hath Clifton. I'll to Clifton straight. 45
KING HENRY. Stay, and breathe awhile.

Thou hast redeemed thy lost opinion,
And showed thou makest some tender³ of my life,
In this fair rescue thou hast brought to me.
PRINCE HENRY. O God, they did me too much injury   50
That ever said I hearkened for your death!
If it were so, I might have let alone
The insulting hand of Douglas over you,
Which would have been as speedy in your end
As all the poisonous potions in the world,   55
And saved the treacherous labour of your son.
KING HENRY. Make up to Clifton; I'll to Sir Nicholas Gawsey.
                              [*Exit.   Enter* HOTSPUR.]
HOTSPUR. If I mistake not, thou art Harry Monmouth.
PRINCE HENRY. Thou speakest as if I would deny my name.
HOTSPUR. My name is Harry Percy.
PRINCE HENRY.   Why, then I see   60
A very valiant rebel of the name.
I am the Prince of Wales, and think not, Percy,
To share with me in glory any more.
Two stars keep not their motion in one sphere,
Nor can one England brook a double reign,   65
Of Harry Percy and the Prince of Wales.
HOTSPUR. Nor shall it, Harry, for the hour is come
To end the one of us; and would to God
Thy name in arms were now as great as mine!
PRINCE HENRY. I'll make it greater ere I part from thee; 70
And all the budding honours on thy crest
I'll crop, to make a garland for my head.
HOTSPUR. I can no longer brook thy vanities.

[*They fight.   Enter* FALSTAFF.]

FALSTAFF. Well said, Hal! To it, Hal! Nay, you shall find no boy's
play here, I can tell you.   75

[*Enter* DOUGLAS; *he fights with* FALSTAFF, *who falls down as if he
were dead.   Exit* DOUGLAS.   PRINCE HENRY *wounds* HOTSPUR, *who
falls.*]

HOTSPUR. O Harry, thou hast robbed me of my youth!
I better brook the loss of brittle life
Than those proud titles thou hast won of me;
They wound my thoughts worse than thy sword my flesh.

3. *tender* Value.

But thought's the slave of life, and life time's fool;   80
And time, that takes survey of all the world,
Must have a stop.   O, I could prophesy,
But that the earthy and cold hand of death
Lies on my tongue.   No, Percy, thou art dust,
And food for—   [*Dies.*] 85
PRINCE HENRY. For worms, brave Percy: fare thee well, great heart!
Ill-weaved ambition, how much art thou shrunk!
When that this body did contain a spirit,
A kingdom for it was too small a bound;
But now two paces of the vilest earth   90
Is room enough.   This earth that bears thee dead
Bears not alive so stout a gentleman.
If thou wert sensible of courtesy,
I should not make so dear a show of zeal;
But let my favours hide thy mangled face,   95
And even in thy behalf, I'll thank myself
For doing these fair rites of tenderness.
Adieu, and take thy praise with thee to heaven!
Thy ignomy sleep with thee in the grave,
But not remembered in thy epitaph!   [*He spieth* FALSTAFF *on the* 100
ground.]
What, old acquaintance!   Could not all this flesh
Keep in a little life?   Poor Jack, farewell!
I could have better spared a better man.
O, I should have a heavy miss of thee,
If I were much in love with vanity![4]   105
Death hath not struck so fat a deer to-day,
Though many dearer, in this bloody fray.
Embowelled will I see thee by and by;
Till then in blood by noble Percy lie.   [*Exit.*   FALSTAFF *riseth up.*]
FALSTAFF. Embowelled!   If thou embowel me to-day, I'll give you 110
leave to powder me and eat me too to-morrow. 'Sblood, 'twas time
to counterfeit, or that hot termagant Scot had paid me scot and lot
too.   Counterfeit?   I lie, I am no counterfeit: to die, is to be a
counterfeit; for he is but the counterfeit of a man who hath not the
life of a man.   But to counterfeit dying, when a man thereby liveth, 115
is to be no counterfeit, but the true and perfect image of life indeed.
The better part of valour is discretion, in the which better part I have
saved my life.   Zounds, I am afraid of this gunpowder Percy, though

4. *vanity* Frivolity.

he be dead. How, if he should counterfeit too, and rise? By my
faith, I am afraid he would prove the better counterfeit. Therefore 120
I'll make him sure; yea, and I'll swear I killed him. Why may not
he rise as well as I? Nothing confutes me but eyes, and nobody sees
me. Therefore, sirrah [*stabbing him*], with a new wound in your
thigh, come you along with me.

[*He takes up* HOTSPUR *on his back. Enter* PRINCE HENRY *and* PRINCE
JOHN.]

PRICE HENRY. Come, brother John; full bravely hast thou fleshed   125
Thy maiden sword.
PRINCE JOHN.   But, soft!   Whom have we here?
Did you not tell me this fat man was dead?
PRINCE HENRY. I did; I saw him dead,
Breathless and bleeding on the ground.
Art thou alive?   Or is it fantasy   130
That plays upon our eyesight?   I prithee, speak;
We will not trust our eyes without our ears;
Thou art not what thou seemest.
FALSTAFF. No, that's certain; I am not a double man: but if I be not
Jack Falstaff, then am I a Jack.   There is Percy [*throwing the body* 135
down], if your father will do me any honour, so; if not, let him kill
the next Percy himself.   I look to be either earl or duke, I can assure
you.
PRINCE HENRY. Why, Percy I killed myself, and saw thee dead.
FALSTAFF. Didst thou?—Lord, Lord how this world is given to lying! 140
—I grant you I was down and out of breath, and so was he, but we
rose both at an instant, and fought a long hour by Shrewsbury clock.
If I may be believed, so; if not, let them that should reward valour
bear the sin upon their own heads.   I'll take it upon my death, I gave
him this wound in the thigh: if the man were alive, and would deny 145
it, zounds, I would make him eat a piece of my sword.
PRINCE JOHN. This is the strangest tale that e'er I heard.
PRINCE HENRY. This is the strangest fellow, brother John.
Come, bring your luggage nobly on your back:
For my part, if a lie may do thee grace,   150
I'll gild it with the happiest terms I have.

[*A retreat is sounded.*]

The trumpet sounds retreat; the day is ours.
Come, brother, let's to the highest of the field,
To see what friends are living, who are dead.   [*Exeunt* PRINCES.]

FALSTAFF. I'll follow, as they say, for reward.   He that rewards me, 155
God reward him!   If I do grow great, I'll grow less; for I'll purge,
and leave sack, and live cleanly as a nobleman should do.

[*Exit, bearing off the body.*]

SCENE 5

[*Another part of the field.   The trumpets sound.   Enter* KING HENRY,
PRINCE HENRY, PRINCE JOHN, WESTMORELAND, *and others, with* WOR-
CESTER *and* VERNON *prisoners.*]

KING HENRY.   Thus ever did rebellion find rebuke.
Ill-spirited Worcester!   Did we not send grace,
Pardon, and terms of love to all of you?
And wouldst thou turn our offers contrary?
Misuse the tenour of thy kinsman's trust?   5
Three knights upon our party slain to-day,
A noble earl, and many a creature else,
Had been alive this hour,
If, like a Christian, thou hadst truly borne
Betwixt our armies true intelligence.   10
WORCESTER.   What I have done my safety urged me to;
And I embrace this fortune patiently,
Since not to be avoided it falls on me.
KING HENRY.   Bear Worcester to the death, and Vernon too.
Other offenders we will pause upon.   15

[*Exeunt* WORCESTER *and* VERNON, *guarded.*]

How goes the field?
PRINCE HENRY.   The noble Scot, Lord Douglas, when he saw
The fortune of the day quite turned from him,
The noble Percy slain, and all his men
Upon the foot of fear, fled with the rest;   20
And falling from a hill, he was so bruised
That the pursuers took him.   At my tent
The Douglas is; and I beseech your Grace
I may dispose of him.
KING HENRY.   With all my heart.
PRINCE HENRY.   Then, brother John of Lancaster, to you   25
This honourable bounty shall belong:
Go to the Douglas, and deliver him
Up to his pleasure, ransomless and free;
His valour, shown upon our crests to-day,
Hath taught us how to cherish such high deeds   30
Even in the bosom of our adversaries.

124

PRINCE JOHN. I thank your Grace for this high courtesy
Which I shall give away immediately.
KING HENRY. Then this remains, that we divide our power.
You, son John, and my cousin Westmoreland,   35
Towards York shall bend you with your dearest speed,
To meet Northumberland and the prelate Scroop,
Who, as we hear, are busily in arms.
Myself, and you, son Harry, will towards Wales,
To fight with Glendower and the Earl of March.   40
Rebellion in this land shall lose his sway,
Meeting the check of such another day.
And since this business so fair is done,
Let us not leave till all our own be won.   *[Exeunt.]*

The Quest for Victory

CHAPTER TWO

Every hero seeks victory in some form, though not every hero, of course, finds it. In literature the most successful hero is found in the story of high adventure, the literary term for which is "romance." The romance hero's role is more often than not that of warrior—a knight or soldier in traditional romance, a cowboy, policeman, or spy in modern romance. Because he most closely approximates the ideal hero, the romance hero—whether his battle is with dragons, enemy armies, cattle rustlers, criminals, or foreign agents—usually triumphs. Because he represents Good, that triumph is not only physical but moral. And since that good tends to be identified with the value system of a particular community or state, the hero's victory is social and political as well as personal.

On the psychological level the hero of romance functions as a potent wish-fulfillment figure. He is the extraordinarily strong, brave, successful figure we sometimes fantasize ourselves as being. The evil forces arrayed against the hero represent our conscious and unconscious anxieties about whatever it is that seems to threaten our lives, liberty, or happiness. Those anxieties are laid to rest and our wishes fulfilled by the hero's victory, which produces pleasure. The considerable popularity of romance in the form of novels, movies, and television programs suggest that we very much want, and perhaps even need, the kind of "therapy" it provides.

Comedy likewise is an extremely popular literary mode, and it too invariably involves a hero, a conflict, and a victory—often in the form of the hero winning the girl from an older and/or more powerful rival. In a sense, then, comedy represents the victory of the individual over society, of man's instinctual biological drives over those societal structures designed to control or suppress them.

Because the premises upon which they are based are relatively simple and fundamental, comedy and romance do not usually find favor as literary forms with writers who feel that life is complex and ambiguous and who reflect that feeling in the types of heroes and stories they create. The tragic dramatist, for example, shows his hero going down to defeat, yet achieving at the same time a kind of victory. That victory may be in part physical, but it is also moral and spiritual. Nonetheless, the tragic hero's victory is never complete and never clear-cut. This is also the case with heroes in satiric and realistic fiction. Such heroes are seldom godlike. They are, rather, recognizably human and imperfect. Frequently they are ordinary persons caught up in quests against their wills or faced with opportunities for heroism which they have not sought. Since they are very much like us, it is easy to identify with them, to feel their dilemmas intensely, and to rejoice when they rise to meet the demands of the crucial occasion or regret it when they fall short. Most of the main characters found in the works contained in this section are such figures.

Victory for the typical hero of satiric or realistic fiction is often elusive and sometimes illusory. It seldom involves anything so obvious as slaying a dragon or so monumental as defeating an opposing army. While the ultimate victory such heroes seek can be the preservation of their comrades ·or their nation, the victory most often achieved is a minor or private one like gaining an insight into the true nature of reality or of oneself, or simply managing to survive. Whether such victories be large or small, they always cost something. This is a fact of heroic life. Any hero, whether he wins his victory or suffers his defeat, must pay for it—sometimes with his energy, his happiness, or his well-being, sometimes with this life.

SHORT STORIES

The Ironies of Victory

The victory of good over evil is the basic theme of romance and that which gives romance its moral implications. A common variation on that theme is that the victory of good over evil also becomes the victory of youth over age, innocence over experience, and weakness over strength. Such a pattern, seen in primitive romances like the fairy tale of Jack the giant-killer and in more sophisticated ones like the story of David and Goliath, has psychological as well as moral implications. It suggests that recurrent rebellion of the young against those forces and factors which keep them subservient, and its outcome in favor of the young, suggests a wish-fulfillment dream. In this case the victory of the hero would represent youth's coming-of-age and forcibly taking his rightful place in society. The irony of this process is that youth inevitably ages and then finds itself challenged by the next generation.

Such is the pattern of the life of David as recounted in First and Second Samuel and First Kings of the Old Testament. This pattern also conforms in a number of respects to the one anthropologists have described as the typical life story of the hero. In brief, David, the youngest son, is singled out early as an exceptional person. He achieves a great victory over a powerful adversary and marries a woman of stature. He is proclaimed King and reigns successfully. But after a time he falls out of favor with God and must endure troubles of various kinds. Finally he regains God's favor and when he dies is revered as a hero.

The selection from First Samuel in this unit contains only the story of David's encounter with Goliath. It is, of course, a short story by editorial license only. Yet, like the conventional short story, it treats one main character, involves a single action, and entails both a conflict and its resolution. Viewed in isolation, the story of David's victory conforms to the definition of a romance. This view finds its parallel in the poem "David" by Josephine Miles. Viewed in the context of the hero's whole life story, however, this romance has ironic overtones, as Don Geiger's poem "David and Goliath" suggests.

Unlike David, the main character of Stephen Crane's story "A Mystery of Heorism" does not fit the pattern of the traditional hero. Fred Collins, an ordinary soldier in the Civil War, is far from exceptional, though he is singled out by circumstances. Taunted by his comrades into risking his life to obtain water that is not really needed, he suddenly finds that a simple, even foolish, action can become a kind of quest, with all of the quest's potentialities for heroism. Yet he cannot rid himself of the feeling that real heroes are quite different from ordinary men like himself. Through the character of Fred Collins, Crane explores the relationship between facts and myths, the psychological puzzle that is heroism, and the effects of heroism upon those who come in contact with it.

The last two stories in this section both happen to be by Italian writers. Giovanni Verga's "Buddies" takes place during one of Italy's several wars with Austria during the latter part of the nineteenth century. Victory in this war would mean Italy's freedom from Austria. Large political issues such as this, however, are only vaguely perceived by common soldiers like Malerba. A stolid peasant, the butt of numerous jokes by his buddies, Malerba is something of an anti-hero until he finds himself in actual combat. The muddled conclusion of the battle and the ironic conclusion of the story pose the problem of whether victory or defeat has any real meaning for ordinary human beings.

The war referred to in the title of Luigi Pirandello's short story is World War I, but it could be any war. For in all wars parents confront the possibility that victory will be purchased by the lives of their sons. Whether the glorification of these young men as heroes is worth the frightful cost is the grim question such parents must face—if they can. To do so requires of them, too, a kind of heroism.

David and Goliath
Old Testament
I Samuel 17:1-54

Now the Philistines gathered together their armies to battle, and were gathered together at Shochoh, which belongeth to Judah, and pitched between Shochoh and Azekah, in Ephesdammim. And Saul[1] and the men of Israel were gathered together, and pitched by the valley of Elah, and set the battle in array against the Philistines. And the Philistines stood on a mountain on the one side, and Israel stood on a mountain on the other side: and there was a valley between them. And there went out a champion out of the camp of the Philistines, named Goliath, of Gath, whose height was six cubits and a span. And he had a helmet of brass upon his head, and he was armed with a coat of mail; and the weight of the coat was five thousand shekels of brass. And he had greaves of brass upon his legs, and a target of brass between his shoulders. And the staff of his spear was like a weaver's beam; and his spear's head weighed six hundred shekels of iron: and one bearing a shield went before him. And he stood and cried unto the armies of Israel, and said unto them, "Why are ye come out to set your battle in array? am not I a Philistine, and ye servants to Saul? choose you a man for you, and let him come down to me. If he be able to fight with me, and to kill me, then will we be your servants: but if I prevail against him, and kill him, then shall ye be our servants, and serve us." And the Philistine said, "I defy the armies of Israel this day; give me a man, that

1. *Saul* Israel's reigning king.

we may fight together." When Saul, and all Israel heard those words of the Philistine, they were dismayed, and greatly afraid.

Now David was the son of that Ephrathite of Bethlehem-judah, whose name was Jesse; and he had eight sons: and the man went among men for an old man in the days of Saul. And the three eldest sons of Jesse went and followed Saul to the battle: and the names of his three sons that went to the battle were Eliab the firstborn, and next unto him Abinadab, and the third Shammah. And David was the youngest: and the three eldest followed Saul. But David went and returned from Saul to feed his father's sheep at Bethlehem. And the Philistine drew near morning and evening, and presented himself forty days.

And Jesse said unto David his son, "Take now for thy brethren an ephah of this parched corn, and these ten loaves, and run to the camp to thy brethren; and carry these ten cheeses unto the captain of their thousand, and look how thy brethren fare, and take their pledge."

Now Saul, and they, and all the men of Israel, were in the valley of Elah, fighting with the Philistines. And David rose up early in the morning, and left the sheep with a keeper, and took, and went, as Jesse had commanded him; and he came to the trench, as the host was going forth to the fight, and shouted for the battle. For Israel and the Philistines had put the battle in array, army against army. And David left his carriage, and ran into the army, and came and saluted his brethren. And as he talked with them, behold, there came up the champion, the Philistine of Gath, Goliath by name, out of the armies of the Philistines, and spake according to the same words: and David heard them.

And all the men of Israel, when they saw the man, fled from him, and were sore afraid. And the men of Israel said, 'Have ye seen this man that is come up? surely to defy Israel is he come up: and it shall be, that the man who killeth him, the king will enrich him with great riches, and will give him his daughter, and make his father's house free in Israel." And David spake to the men that stood by him, saying, "What shall be done to the man that killeth this Philistine, and taketh away the reproach from Israel? for who is this uncircumcised Philistine, that he should defy the armies of the living God?" And the people answered him after this manner, saying, "So shall it be done to the man that killeth him."

And Eliab his eldest brother heard when he spake unto the men; and Eliab's anger was kindled against David, and he said, "Why camest thou down hither? and with whom has thou left those few sheep in the wilderness? I know thy pride, and the naughtiness of thine heart; for thou art come down that thou mightest see the battle." And David said, "What have I now done? Is there not a cause?" And he turned from him toward another, and spake after the same manner: and the people answered him again after the former manner.

And when the words were heard which David spake, they rehearsed them before Saul: and he sent for him. And David said to Saul, "Let no man's heart fail because of him; thy servant will go and fight with this Philistine." And Saul said to David, "Thou art not able to go against this Philistine to fight with him: for thou art but a youth, and he a man of war from his youth." And David said unto Saul, "Thy servant kept his father's sheep, and there came a lion, and a bear, and took a lamb out of the flock: and I went out after him, and smote him, and delivered it out of his mouth: and when he arose against me, I caught him by his beard, and smote him, and slew him. Thy servant slew both the lion and the bear: and this uncircumcised Philistine shall be as one of them, seeing he hath defied the armies of the living God." David said moreover, "The Lord that delivered me out of the paw of the lion, and out of the paw of the bear, he will deliver me out of the hand of this Philistine." And Saul said unto David, "Go, and the Lord be with thee." And Saul armed David with his armor, and he put a helmet of brass upon his head; also he armed him with a coat of mail. And David girded his sword upon his armor, and he assayed to go; for he had not proved it. And David said unto Saul, "I cannot go with these; for I have not proved them." And David put them off him. And he took his staff in his hand, and chose him five smooth stones out of the brook, and put them in a shepherd's bag which he had, even in a scrip; and his sling was in his hand: and he drew near to the Philistine.

And the Philistine came on and drew near unto David; and the man that bare the shield went before him. And when the Philistine looked about, and saw David, he disdained him: for he was but a youth, and ruddy, and of a fair countenance. And the Philistine said unto David, "Am I a dog, that thou comest to me with staves?" And the Philistine cursed David by his gods. And the Philistine said to David, "Come to me, and I will give thy flesh unto the fowls of the air, and to the beasts of the field." Then said David to the Philistine, "Thou comest to me with a sword, and with a spear, and with a shield: but I come to thee in the name of the Lord of hosts, the God of the armies of Israel, who thou hast defied. This day will the Lord deliver thee into mine hand; and I will smite thee, and take thine head from thee; and I will give the carcasses of the host of the Philistines this day unto the fowls of the air, and to the wild beasts of the earth; that all the earth may know that there is a God in Israel. And all this assembly shall know that the Lord saveth not with sword and spear: for the battle is the Lord's and he will give you into our hands."

And it came to pass, when the Philistine arose, and came and drew nigh to meet David, that David hasted, and ran toward the army to meet the Philistine. And David put his hand in his bag, and took thence a stone, and slang it, and smote the Philistine in his forehead, that the stone sunk into his forehead; and he fell upon his face to the earth.

So David prevailed over the Philistine with a sling and with a stone, and smote the Philistine, and slew him; but there was no sword in the hand of David. Therefore David ran, and stood upon the Philistine, and took his sword, and drew it out of the sheath thereof, and slew him, and cut off his head therewith. And when the Philistines saw their champion was dead, they fled. And the men of Israel and of Judah arose, and shouted, and pursued the Philistines, until thou come to the valley, and to the gates of Ekron. And the wounded of the Philistines fell down by the way to Sha-araim, even unto Gath, and unto Ekron. And the children of Israel returned from chasing after the Philistines, and they spoiled their tents. And David took the head of the Philistine, and brought it to Jerusalem; but he put his armor in his tent.

David

Josephine Miles

Goliath stood up clear in the assumption of status,
Strong and unquestioning of himself and others,
Fully determined by the limits of his experience.
I have seen such a one among surgeons, sergeants,
Deans, and giants, the power implicit.   5

Then there was David, who made few assumptions,
Had little experience, but for more was ready,
Testing and trying this pebble or that pebble,
This giant or that giant.
He is not infrequent.   10

How could Goliath guess, with his many assumptions,
The force of the sling shot of the pure-hearted?
How could David fear, with his few hypotheses,
The power of status which is but two-footed?
So he shot, and shouted!   15

David and Goliath

Don Geiger

Down went Goliath,
to send the evil pennons flying,
and how was that God-sent boy
(ruddy, handsome, and with beautiful eyes),
flushed with his inevitable triumph   5
in the impossible struggle,
to know what he would yet become?
How could bold David,
putting off the gift of armor
in which he felt so unlike himself,   10
and with only his spirited sling
to face that loathsome power
of self-sufficient pride,
know what a blow it would be
to learn that good men may be dangerous,   15
that lieutenants are not to be trusted,
that a beloved son can plot
to steal his father's place,
or how it would stun him to learn
that he himself could conspire   20
to kill, from lust for a woman,
a harmless and loyal man?
Nor could he, apple of his Lord's eye,
foretell the bitterness
of isolation in the sense of sin,   25
with nowhere to turn for support,
a nation's fate in the balance,
unless he fell to his knees like a beggar
to whimper for charity.
For whatever assurances were David's,   30
cheerfully sorting the stones for his sling,
his was not yet the acknowledged power,
nor he the king—
vengeful and lickerish,
crafty, afraid, and indispensable.   35

A Mystery of Heroism

Stephen Crane

The dark uniforms of the men were so coated with dust from the incessant wrestling of the two armies that the regiment almost seemed a part of the clay bank which shielded them from the shells. On the top of the hill a battery was arguing in tremendous roars with some other guns, and to the eye of the infantry the artillerymen, the guns, the caissons, the horses, were distinctly outlined upon the blue sky. When a piece was fired, a red streak as round as a log flashed low in the heavens, like a monstrous bolt of lightning. The men of the battery wore white duck trousers, which somehow emphasized their legs; and when they ran and crowded in little groups at the bidding of the shouting officers, it was more impressive than usual to the infantry.

Fred Collins, of A Company, was saying: "Thunder! I wisht I had a drink. Ain't there any water round here?" Then somebody yelled: "There goes th' bugler!"

As the eyes of half the regiment swept in one machine-like movement, there was an instant's picture of a horse in a great convulsive leap of a death-wound and a rider leaning back with a crooked arm and spread fingers before his face. On the ground was the crimson terror of an exploding shell, with fibres of flame that seemed like lances. A glittering bugle swung clear of the rider's back as fell headlong the horse and the man. In the air was an odour as from a conflagration.

Sometimes they of the infantry looked down at a fair little meadow which spread at their feet. Its long green grass was rippling gently in a breeze. Beyond it was the grey form of a house half torn to pieces by shells and by the busy axes of soldiers who had pursued firewood. The line of an old fence was now dimly marked by long weeds and by an occasional post. A shell had blown the well-house to fragments. Little lines of grey smoke ribboning upward from some embers indicated the place where had stood the barn.

From beyond a curtain of green woods there came the sound of some stupendous scuffle, as if two animals of the size of islands were fighting. At a distance there were occasional appearances of swift-moving men, horses, batteries, flags, and with the crashing of infantry volleys were heard, often, wild and frenzied cheers. In the midst of it all Smith and Ferguson, two privates of A Company, were engaged in a heated discussion which involved the greatest questions of the national existence.

The battery on the hill presently engaged in a frightful duel. The white legs of the gunners scampered this way and that way, and the officers redoubled their shouts. The guns, with their demeanors of stolidity and courage, were typical of something infinitely self-possessed in this clamor of death that swirled around the hill.

One of a "swing" team was suddenly smitten quivering to the ground, and his maddened brethren dragged his torn body in their struggle to escape from this turmoil and danger. A young soldier astride one of the leaders swore and fumed in his saddle and furiously jerked at the bridle. An officer screamed out an order so violently that his voice broke and ended the sentence in a falsetto shriek.

The leading company of infantry regiment was somewhat exposed, and the colonel ordered it moved more fully under the shelter of the hill. There was the clank of steel against steel.

A lieutenant of the battery rode down and passed them, holding his right arm carefully in his left hand. And it was as if this arm was not at all a part of him, but belonged to another man. His sober and reflective charger went slowly. The officer's face was grimy and perspiring, and his uniform was tousled as if he had been in direct grapple with an enemy. He smiled grimly when the men stared at him. He turned his horse toward the meadow.

Collins, of A Company, said: "I wisht I had a drink. I bet there's water in that there ol' well yonder!"

"Yes; but how you goin' to git it?"

For the little meadow which intervened was now suffering a terrible onslaught of shells. Its green and beautiful calm had vanished utterly. Brown earth was being flung in monstrous handfuls. And there was a massacre of the young blades of grass. They were being torn, burned, obliterated. Some curious fortune of the battle had made this gentle little meadow the object of the red hate of the shells, and each one as it exploded seemed like an imprecation in the face of a maiden.

The wounded officer who was riding across this expanse said to himself: "Why, they couldn't shoot any harder if the whole army was massed here!"

A shell struck the grey ruins of the house, and as, after the roar, the shattered wall fell in fragments, there was a noise which resembled the flapping of shutters during a wild gale of winter. Indeed, the infantry paused in the shelter of the bank appeared as men standing upon a shore contemplating a madness of the sea. The angel of calamity had under its glance the battery upon the hill. Fewer white-legged men labored about the guns. A shell had smitten one of the pieces, and after the flare, the smoke, the dust, the wrath of this blow were gone, it was possible to see white legs stretched horizontally upon the ground. And at that interval to the rear where it is the business of battery horses to stand with their noses to the fight, awaiting the command to drag their guns out of the destruction, or into it, or wheresoever these incomprehensible humans demanded with whip and spur—in this line of passive and dumb spectators, whose fluttering hearts yet would not let them forget the iron laws of man's control of them—in this rank of brute-soldiers there had been relentless and hideous carnage. From the ruck of bleeding and prostrate horses, the men of the infantry could see one animal raising its stricken body with its forelegs and turning its nose with mystic and profound eloquence toward the sky.

Some comrades joked Collins about his thirst. "Well, if yeh want a drink so bad, why don't yeh go git it?"

"Well, I will in a minnet, if yeh don't shut up!"

A lieutenant of artillery floundered his horse straight down the hill with as little concern as if it were level ground. As he galloped past the colonel of the infantry, he threw up his hand in swift salute. "We've got to get out of that," he roared angrily. He was a black-bearded officer and his eyes, which resembled beads, sparkled like those of an insane man. His jumping horse sped along the column of infantry.

The fat major, standing carelessly with his sword held horizontally behind him and with his legs far apart, looked after the receding horseman and laughed. "He wants to get back with orders pretty quick, or there'll be no batt'ry left," he observed.

The wise young captain of the second company hazarded to the lieutenant-colonel that the enemy's infantry would probably soon attack the hill, and the lieutenant-colonel snubbed him.

A private in one of the rear companies looked out over the meadow, and then turned to a companion and said, "Look there, Jim!" It was the wounded officer from the battery, who some time before had started to ride across the meadow, supporting his right arm carefully with his left hand. This man had encountered a shell, apparently, at a time when no one perceived him, and he could now be seen lying face downward with a stirruped foot stretched across the body of his dead horse. A leg of the charger extended slantingly upward, precisely as stiff as a stake. Around this motionless pair the shells still howled.

There was a quarrel in A Company. Collins was shaking his fist in the faces of some laughing comrades. "Dern yeh! I ain't afraid t' go. If yeh say much, I will go!"

"Of course, yeh will! You'll run through that there medder, won't yeh?"

Collins said, in a terrible voice: "You see now!"

At this ominous threat his comrades broke into renewed jeers.

Collins gave them a dark scowl, and went to find his captain. The latter was conversing with the colonel of the regiment.

"Captain," said Collins, saluting and standing at attention—in those days all trousers bagged at the knees—"Captain, I want t' get permission to go git some water from that there well over yonder!"

The colonel and the captain swung about simultaneously and stared across the meadow. The captain laughed. "You must be pretty thirsty, Collins?"

"Yes, sir, I am."

"Well—ah," said the captain. After a moment, he asked, "Can't you wait?"

"No, sir."

The colonel was watching Collins's face. "Look here, my lad," he said, in a pious sort of voice—"Look here, my lad"—Collins was not a lad—"don't you think that's taking pretty big risks for a little drink of water?"

"I dunno," said Collins uncomfortably. Some of the resentment toward his companions, which perhaps had forced him into this affair, was beginning to fade. "I dunno w'ether 'tis."

The colonel and the captain contemplated him for a time.

"Well," said the captain finally.

"Well," said the colonel, "if you want to go, why, go."

Collins saluted. "Much obliged t' yeh."

As he moved away the colonel called after him. "Take some of the other boys' canteens with you, an' hurry back, now."

"Yes, sir, I will."

The colonel and the captain looked at each other then, for it had suddenly occured that they could not for the life of them tell whether Collins wanted to go or whether he did not.

They turned to regard Collins, and as they perceived him surrounded by gesticulating comrades, the colonel said: "Well, by thunder! I guess he's going."

Collins appeared as a man dreaming. In the midst of the questions, the advice, the warnings, all the excited talk of his company mates, he maintained a curious silence.

They were very busy in preparing him for his ordeal. When they inspected him carefully, it was somewhat like the examination that grooms give a horse before a race; and they were amazed, staggered, by the whole affair. Their astonishment found vent in strange repetitions.

"Are yeh sure a-goin'?" they demanded again and again.

"Certainly I am," cried Collins at last, furiously.

He strode sullenly away from them. He was swinging five or six canteens by their cords. It seemed that his cap would not remain firmly on his head, and often he reached and pulled it down over his brow.

There was a general movement in the compact column. The long animal-like thing moved slightly. Its four hundred eyes were turned upon the figure of Collins.

"Well, sir, if that ain't th' derndest thing! I never thought Fred Collins had the blood in him for that kind of business."

"What's he goin' to do, anyhow?"

"He's goin' to that well there after water."

"We ain't dyin' of thirst, are we? That's foolishness."

"Well, somebody put him up to it, an' he's doin' it."

"Say, he must be a desperate cuss."

When Collins faced the meadow and walked away from the regiment, he was vaguely conscious that a chasm, the deep valley of all prides, was suddenly between him and his comrades. It was provisional, but the provision was that he return as a victor. He had blindly been led by quaint emotions, and laid himself under an obligation to walk squarely up to the face of death.

But he was not sure that he wished to make a retraction, even if he could do so without shame. As a matter of truth, he was sure of very little. He was mainly surprised.

It seemed to him supernaturally strange that he had allowed his mind to maneuver his body into such a situation. He understood that it might be called dramatically great.

However, he had no full appreciation of anything, excepting that he was actually conscious of being dazed. He could feel his dulled mind groping after the form and color of this incident. He wondered why he did not feel some keen agony of fear cutting his sense like a knife. He wondered at this, because human expression had said loudly for centuries that men should feel afraid of certain things, and that all men who did not feel that fear were phenomena—heroes.

He was, then, a hero. He suffered that disappointment which we would all have if we discovered that we were ourselves capable of those deeds which we most admire in history and legend. This, then, was a hero. After all, heroes were not much.

No, it could not be true. He was not a hero. Heroes had no shames in their lives, and, as for him, he remembered borrowing fifteen dollars from a friend and promising to pay it back the next day, and then avoiding that friend for ten months. When, at home, his mother had aroused him for the early labor of his life on the farm, it had often been his fashion to be irritable, childish, diabolical; and his mother had died since he had come to the war.

He saw that, in this matter of the well, the canteens, the shells, he was an intruder in the land of fine deeds.

He was now about thirty paces from his comrades. The regiment had just turned its many faces toward him.

From the forest of terrific noises there suddenly emerged a little uneven line of men. They fired fiercely and rapidly at distant foliage on which appeared little puffs of white smoke. The spatter of skirmish firing was added to the thunder of the guns on the hill. The little line of men ran forward. A color-sergeant fell flat with his flag as if he had slipped on ice. There was hoarse cheering from this distant field.

Collins suddenly felt that two demon fingers were pressed into his ears. He could see nothing but flying arrows, flaming red. He lurched from the shock of this explosion, but he made a mad rush for the house, which he viewed as a man submerged to the neck in a boiling surf might view the shore. In the air little pieces of shell howled, and the earthquake explosions drove him insane with the menace of their roar. As he ran the canteens knocked together with a rhythmical tinkling.

As he neared the house, each detail of the scene became vivid to him. He was aware of some bricks of the vanished chimney lying on the sod. There was a door which hung by one hinge.

Rifle bullets called forth by the insistent skirmishers came from the far-off bank of foliage. They mingled with the shells and the pieces of shells until the air was torn in all directions by hootings, yells, howls. The sky was full of fiends who directed all their wild rage at his head.

When he came to the well, he flung himself face downward and peered into its darkness. There were furtive silver glintings some feet from the surface. He grabbed one of the canteens and, unfastening its cap, swung it down by the cord. The water flowed slowly in with an indolent gurgle.

And now, as he lay with his face turned away, he was suddenly smitten with the terror. It came upon his heart like the grasp of claws. All the power faded from his muscles. For an instant he was no more than a dead man.

The canteen filled with a maddening slowness, in the manner of all bottles. Presently he recovered his strength and addressed a screaming oath to it. He leaned over until it seemed as if he intended to try to push water into it with his hands. His eyes as he gazed down into the well shone like two pieces of metal, and in their expression was a great appeal and a great curse. The stupid water derided him.

There was the blaring thunder of a shell. Crimson light shone through the swift-boiling smoke and made a pink reflection on part of the wall of the well. Collins jerked out his arm and canteen with the same motion that a man would use in withdrawing his head from a furnace.

He scrambled erect and glared and hesitated. On the ground near him lay the old well bucket, with a length of rusty chain. He lowered it swiftly into the well. The bucket struck the water and then, turning lazily over, sank. When, with hand reaching tremblingly over hand, he hauled it out, it knocked often against the walls of the well and spilled some of its contents.

In running with a filled bucket, a man can adopt but one kind of gait.

So, through this terrible field over which screamed practical angels of death, Collins ran in the manner of a farmer chased out of a dairy by a bull.

His face went staring white with anticipation—anticipation of a blow that would whirl him around and down. He would fall as he had seen other men fall, the life knocked out of them so suddenly that their knees were no more quick to touch the ground than their heads. He saw the long blue line of the regiment, but his comrades were standing looking at him from the edge of an impossible star. He was aware of some deep wheel-ruts and hoofprints in the sod beneath his feet.

The artillery officer who had fallen in this meadow had been making groans in the teeth of the tempest of sound. These futile cries, wrenched from him by his agony, were heard only by shells, bullets. When wild-eyed Collins came running, this officer raised himself. His face contorted and blanched from pain, he was about to utter some great beseeching cry. But suddenly his face straightened, and he called: "Say, young man, give me a drink of water, will you?"

Collins had no room amid his emotions for surprise. He was mad from the threats of destruction.

"I can't!" he screamed, and in his reply was a full description of his quaking apprehension. His cap was gone and his hair was riotous. His clothes made it appear that he had been dragged over the ground by the heels. He ran on.

The officer's head sank down, and one elbow crooked. His foot in its brass-bound stirrup still stretched over the body of his horse, and the other leg was under the steed.

But Collins turned. He came dashing back. His face had now turned grey, and in his eyes was all terror. "Here it is! Here it is!"

The officer was as a man gone in drink. His arm bent like a twig. His head drooped as if his neck were of willow. He was sinking to the ground, to lie face downward.

Collins grabbed him by the shoulder. "Here it is. Here's your drink. Turn over. Turn over, man, for God's sake!"

With Collins hauling at his shoulder, the officer twisted his body and fell with his face turned toward that region where lived the unspeakable noises of the swirling missiles. There was the faintest shadow of a smile on his lips as he looked at Collins. He gave a sigh, a little primitive breath like that from a child.

Collins tried to hold the bucket steadily, but his shaking hands caused the water to splash all over the face of the dying man. Then he jerked it away and ran on.

The regiment gave him a welcoming roar. The grimed faces were wrinkled in laughter.

His captain waved the bucket away. "Give it to the men!"

The two genial, skylarking young lieutenants were the first to gain possession of it. They played over it in their fashion.

When one tried to drink, the other teasingly knocked his elbow. "Don't Billie! You'll make me spill it," said the one. The other laughed.

Suddenly there was an oath, the thud of wood on the ground, and a swift murmur of astonishment among the ranks. The two lieutenants glared at each other. The bucket lay on the ground, empty.

Buddies

Giovanni Verga

"Malerba?"

"Here!"

"There's a button missing there, where is it?"

"I don't know, Corporal."

"Confined to the barracks!"

It was always that way: his overcoat was like a sack, his gloves bothered him, he didn't know what to do with his hands any more, his head was harder than a stone during instruction and on the drill field. And was he a clodhopper! In all the beautiful cities where he was stationed, he never went to see the streets, or the palaces, or the fairs—not even the side shows or the merry-go-rounds. He spent the time of his pass wandering along the streets in the outskirts of the city, his arms hanging down, or he watched the women who were squatted on the ground ripping up the grass in Castle Square; or he planted himself in front of the little chestnut cart, without ever spending a cent. His buddies laughed at him behind his back. Gallorini drew his picture on the wall with a piece of charcoal and put his name under it. He let them do it. But when, for a joke, they stole the cigar butts he kept hidden in the barrel of his gun, he flew into a rage, and once he went to the guardhouse on account of a punch that half blinded the Lucchese[1]—you could still see the black mark—and as stubborn as a mule he kept repeating:

"It's not true."

"Well then, who was it that punched the Lucchese?"

"I don't know."

1. *Lucchese* A person from the city of Lucca or the region surrounding it.

Then he would sit on his bed of hard boards, in his cell in the guard-house, his chin in his hands.

"When I get back to my home town . . ." That's all he said.

"Count the days then, go on. You've got a girl friend back home?" asked Gallorini. Malerba stared at him suspiciously and wagged his head. Neither yes nor no. Then he would look far away. With the stub of a pencil, every day he made a mark on a small calendar which he carried in his pocket.

But Gallorini had a girl friend. A great big woman with a mustache, who had been seen sitting with him at the café one Sunday, each one with a glass of beer, and she had been the one who wanted to pay. The Lucchese found out about it hanging around there with Gegia, who never cost him anything. With his smooth and pleasant line of chatter, he could find Gegias anywhere; and in order that they wouldn't get insulted by all being put in the same bunch even by name, he said it was the custom of his home town, when you love a girl, to call her Teresa, Assunta, or Bersabea.

At that time, the word was beginning to spread that there was going to be a war with the Germans. Soldiers coming and going, crowds on the streets, and people who came to see the exercises on the drill field. When the regiment filed by through the bands and the hand clapping, the Lucchese marched boldly and proudly as if the whole show were for him, and Gallorini never stopped greeting friends and acquaintances with his arm constantly in the air, and he wanted to come back either dead or an officer, he said.

"Aren't you glad you're going to war?" he asked Malerba when they stacked their guns at the station.

Malerba shrugged his shoulders, and continued watching the people who were shouting and yelling: "Hurrah!"

The Lucchese saw Gegia too; she was watching, curious, from a distance in the middle of the crowd, and she had at her side a crude-looking boy wearing a rough jacket and smoking a pipe.

"That's what you call being prepared!" muttered the Lucchese, who couldn't break ranks, and he asked Gallorini if his girl had joined the grenadiers in order not to leave him.

It was like a fiesta everywhere they went. Flags, towns all lit up, and peasants running to the railroad embankment to see the train go by packed with kepis[2] and guns. But sometimes in the evening, in the hour when the trumpets sounded taps, they felt overcome by nostalgia for Gegia, for their friends, for all the faraway things. As soon as the mail arrived at the camp, they ran up all together to stick their hands out.

2. *kepis* Soldiers wearing a type of military cap called a *kepi*.

Only Malerba stayed aside in a daze, like someone who didn't expect anything. He always made this mark on the calendar, day after day. And from a distance, he listened to the band, and thought of God knows what.

Finally one night, there was a lot of activity in the camp. Officers who were coming and going, wagons that were filing by toward the river. Reveille sounded two hours after midnight; nevertheless, they were already giving out the rations and pulling down the tents. Soon after, the regiment began to march.

The day was going to be hot. Malerba, who knew about these things, felt it by the gusts of wind that lifted up the dust. And then it rained big, scattered drops. From time to time, as soon as the shower stopped, and the rustle of the corn died down, the crickets began to chirp loudly in the fields on both sides of the road. The Lucchese, who was marching behind Malerba, amused himself at his buddy's expense:

"Up with your hoofs, buddy! What's wrong, why don't you talk? Thinking of your will maybe?"

With a twist of his shoulders, Malerba arranged his knapsack and muttered:

"Shut up!"

"Leave him alone," said Gallorini, "he's thinking of his girl who'll get somebody else if the Germans kill him."

"You shut up, too!" answered Malerba.

Suddenly in the night, the trotting of a horse and the tinkle of a saber passed between the two ranks of the regiment, which were marching on either side of the road.

"Have a good trip!" said the Lucchese, who was the company clown. "And say hello to the Germans if you meet them."

To the right, a group of houses made a patch of white in a huge dark spot. And the watchdog barked furiously, running along the hedge.

"That's a German dog," observed Gallorini, who wanted to joke like the Lucchese. "Can't you tell from the barking?"

It was still deep night. On the left, sticking out above a black cloud that must have been a hill, there was a shining star.

"What time do you think it is?" asked Gallorini. Malerba lifted his nose in the air, and answered immediately:

"It must be at least an hour before sunrise."

"What fun!" muttered the Lucchese. "They make us get up in the middle of the night for no reason at all!"

"Halt!" a curt voice ordered.

The regiment was still stamping, like a flock of sheep gathering close together.

"What are we waiting for?" muttered the Lucchese after a while.

Another group of cavalrymen went by. Now in the dawn that was beginning to break, you could see the banners of the lancers waving in the air, and a general, up front, his hat with gold braid all the way to the top and his hands stuck in the pockets of his field jacket. The road began to grow white, stretching straight ahead in the middle of the fields which were still dark. The hills seemed to rise one by one in the dim twilight; and you could see a fire burning below—made by some woodcutters, perhaps, or by peasants who had run away in front of that flood of soldiers. At the murmur of voices, the birds woke up and began to twitter on the branches of the mulberry trees, which outlined themselves against the dawn.

Shortly afterward, as daylight began to increase, you heard a deep rumble toward the left, where the horizon spread out in a glow of gold and pink; it was like thunder, and coming from that cloudless sky, it startled you. It could be the murmur of the river or the sound of marching artillery. All of a sudden they said:

"Cannon fire!"

And everyone turned to look toward the golden horizon.

"I'm tired!" muttered Gallorini.

"By now they should call a halt!" agreed the Lucchese.

The chatter was dying out as the soldiers marched on in the hot day, between stripes of dark earth, green wheat fields, vineyards prospering on the hills, rows of mulberry trees, stretching straight ahead as far as the eye could see. Here and there were abandoned houses and stables. As they drew near a well to get a sip of water, they saw some tools on the ground beside the door of a farmhouse and a cat that stuck his nose out between the ramshackle door leaves, miaowing.

"Look!" remarked Malerba. "Their wheat's ripe, poor people!"

"You want to bet that you won't eat any of that bread?" said the Lucchese.

"Shut up, hoodoo!" answered Malerba. "I've got the scapular of the Virgin[3] on me." And he crossed his fingers.

At that moment you could hear thundering on the left too, toward the plain. At first, rare shots that echoed from the mountain, and then a crackling like rockets, as if there were a fiesta in the village. Above the green that crowned the summit, you could see the bell tower, calm against the blue sky.

"No, it's not the river," said Gallorini.

"And it's not wagons going by either."

"Listen! Listen!" exclaimed Gallorini. "The fiesta's started down there."

"Halt!" was ordered again. The Lucchese listened, arching his

3. *scapular of the Virgin* A medal worn in place of the cloth squares worn under the clothing on the breast as a sacramental.

brows, and didn't say anything else. Malerba was near a road post and had sat down on it, with his gun between his legs.

The cannon bombardment must have been down on the plain. You could see the smoke of every shot, like a dense little cloud rising just above the rows of mulberry trees and breaking apart slowly. The quiet meadows sloped down toward the plain, while the quail sang among the clods.

The colonel, on horseback, looking toward the plain from time to time with a telescope, was talking with a group of officers at a standstill at the side of the road. As soon as his horse began to trot away, all the trumpets of the regiment blared out together:

"Forward march!"

To the right and to the left you could see bare fields. Then some more patches of corn. Then vineyards, ditches full of water, and finally some dwarf trees. The first houses of a village began to appear; the road was packed full of wagons and carts. A maddening confusion and clamor of voices.

At a gallop a courier came up, white with dust. His horse, a squat black animal all hair, had red and smoking nostrils. Then an officer of the general staff passed, shouting, as if possessed, to clear the road, hitting out left and right with his saber at the poor civilian mules. Through the elms on the edge of the road, you could see the black *bersaglieri*[4] run by with their plumes in the wind.

Now they were walking on a little road that turned to the right. The soldiers broke into the wheat—and so Malerba's heart wept. On the slope of a little mountain they saw a group of officers on horseback with an escort of lancers behind them, and the pointed hats of the *carabinieri*.[5] Three or four steps ahead, on horseback and with his fist on his hip, there was a big shot, whom the generals answered with their hands on their visors, and the officers passing by saluted with their sabers.

"Who's that?" asked Malerba.

"Vittorio," answered the Lucchese. "Haven't you ever seen him on money, you fool?"

The soldiers turned to look as long as they could see him. Then Malerba observed to himself:

"That's the King!"

A little farther on, there was a small dry creek. The bank on the far side, covered with bushes, climbed up toward the mountain which was scattered with topped elms. The bombardment wasn't heard any more. In that peacefulness of the clear morning, a blackbird began to whistle.

4. *bersaglieri* An elite combat group.
5. *carabinieri* Members of a para-military national police force.

Suddenly it all exploded like a tornado. The summit, the bell tower, everything was wrapped in smoke. Tree branches creaked and dust rose from the earth here and there at every cannon ball. A grenade swept away a group of soldiers. At the top of the hill, from time to time you heard immense shouts, like hurrahs.

"Blessed Virgin!" stammered the Lucchese. The sergeants ordered the soldiers to put their knapsacks on the ground. Malerba obeyed reluctantly because he had two new shirts and all his other things in his.

"Hurry up! Hurry up!" the sergeants were saying. Artillery guns arrived at a gallop from the stony little road, with an uproar, as if there were an earthquake: the officers ahead, the soldiers bent over the rigid manes of the smoking animals and whipping with all their might, the cannoneers grabbing the axles and spokes of the wheels and pushing them up the steep grade.

In the middle of the violent noise of the bombardment, you could see a wounded horse with hanging traces rolling down the slope, neighing, topping vines, shooting out desperate kicks. Farther below, there were groups of soldiers, bloody, their clothes torn, without kepis, waving their arms. Finally, whole platoons backing up step by step, stopping to open scattered fire among the trees. Trumpets and drums sounded the charge. The regiment plunged up the steep grade at a run, like a torrent of men.

The Lucchese felt it coming:

"Why all this rush for what's in store for us up there?"

Gallorini shouted:

"*Savoia!*"[6]

And to Malerba, who had a heavy step:

"Up with your hoofs, buddy!"

"Shut up!" said Malerba.

As soon as they got to the summit, to a rocky little meadow, they found themselves facing the Germans who were advancing in close ranks. A long flash of light ran over those swarming masses; the gunfire crackled from one end to the other. A young officer, fresh from the academy, fell at that moment, saber in hand. The Lucchese groped in the air a little with his hands, as if stumbling, and he fell too. Then you could no longer see what was going on. The men fought hand to hand, with blood in their eyes.

"*Savoia! Savoia!*"

At last the Germans had enough, and began to retreat step by step. Bands of gray-coats ran after them. Malerba, in the rush, felt something

6. *Savoia* The House of Savoy, which ruled Italy from 1861 to 1946. It is used here as a battle cry, signifying liberty, independence, and unity.

like a stone that hit him and made him limp. But soon he noticed that blood was dripping down his pants. Then, furious as an ox, he plunged forward with his head low and struck right and left with his bayonet. He saw a big blond devil who was coming at him with his saber overhead and Gallorini who was aiming the mouth of his gun at his back.

The trumpet sounded muster. In bands and in groups, all that remained of the regiment now ran toward the village which was smiling under the sun, in the green. However, at the first houses, you could see the slaughter that had taken place there. Cannons, horses, wounded *bersaglieri*, everything upside down. Doors broken in, window shutters hanging like rags in the sun. At the end of a courtyard there were a bunch of wounded men on the ground and a cart, still loaded with firewood, with its shafts in the air.

"And the Lucchese?" asked Gallorini out of breath.

Malerba had seen him fall; nevertheless, he turned around instinctively, toward the mountain that was swarming with men and horses. The weapons were glistening in the sun. In the center of an esplanade you could see some officers on foot looking far away with a telescope. The companies were coming down the slope one by one and flashes of light ran along the ranks.

It might have been ten o'clock—ten o'clock in the month of June, under the sun. As if burning, an officer had thrown himself on the water in which they were washing the breechblocks of the cannons. Gallorini was lying on his stomach against the wall of the cemetery, his face in the grass; at least there in the thick grass, a little coolness came from the nearby ditches. Malerba, seated on the ground, was trying his best to tie his leg with a handkerchief. He was thinking of the Lucchese, poor fellow, who had remained along the way spread out flat on his back.

"They're coming again! They're coming again!" somebody shouted. The trumpet sounded the call to arms. Ah! This time Gallorini was really fed up! Not even a minute to rest! He got up like a wild animal, his clothes all torn, and grabbed his gun. The company rushed into position at the first houses of the village, behind the walls, behind the windows. Two cannons stretched their black throats out in the middle of the road. You could see the Germans coming in close ranks, endlessly, one battalion after the other.

There Gallorini was hit. A bullet broke his arm. Malerba wanted to help him:

"What's the matter?"

"Nothing, leave me alone."

The lieutenant, too, was firing away like a private, and you had to run and give him a hand, and Malerba said at every shot:

"Let me do it, it's my job!"

The Germans disappeared again. Then retreat was ordered. The regiment couldn't stand any more of it. Lucky Gallorini and the Lucchese who were resting. Gallorini was sitting on the ground against the wall, and didn't want to move. It was about four o'clock; they had been in that heat more than eight hours with their mouths burned by the dust. Malerba, however, had begun to enjoy it all and asked:

"Now what do we do?"

But nobody listened to him. They were going down toward the little creek, still accompanied by the music that the cannon shots were making on the mountain. Later, from far away, they saw the village swarm with canvas uniforms. You couldn't figure anything out, neither where they were going nor what was happening. At the turn of an embankment, they ran into the hedge behind which the Lucchese had fallen. Gallorini wasn't with them any more either. They were coming back in disorder behind the limping officers—faces that didn't know one another, grenadiers and front-line infantry, their clothes torn, dragging their feet, the heavy guns on their shoulders.

Evening drifted down calmly in a great silence, everywhere.

You kept meeting wagons, cannons, and soldiers, going along in the dark, without trumpets and without drums. When they were beyond the river, they found out that they had lost the battle.

"What?" said Malerba. "What?" And he couldn't figure it out.

Then, at the end of his enlistment, he went back to his home town and found Martha already married, tired of waiting for him. He didn't have any time to waste either and married a widow with property. Some time later Gallorini, who worked on the nearby railroad, came by, and he had a wife and children too.

"Look! Malerba! What're you doing here? I'm doing contract jobs. I learned my business abroad, in Hungary, when they took me prisoner, remember? My wife brought me a little money . . . It's a hell of a world, eh? Did you think I got rich?. And we've done our duty for sure. But we aren't the ones to wallow in luxury. We've got to have a good clean up and start all over again."

On Sundays at the tavern, he preached the same thing to his workmen too. The poor men listened and nodded, sipping the bitter, cheap wine, resting their backs in the sun, like brutes, like Malerba, who didn't know anything more than how to sow, to reap, and to breed children. He nodded his head just to be polite, when his buddy spoke, but he didn't open his mouth. Gallorini, instead, had seen the world and knew all about everything, what was right and what was wrong; above all, he knew the wrong they were doing him, driving him crazy by forcing him to wander around and work in any old place, with a brood of children and a wife on his hands, while so many wallowed in luxury.

"You don't know anything about the way the world goes! If they have a demonstration and shout long live this and death to that, you don't know what to say. You don't understand at all what we need!"

And Malerba always nodded yes.—He needed rain for the wheat fields now. This coming winter he needed a new roof for the stable.

War

Luigi Pirandello

The passengers who had left Rome by the night express had had to stop until dawn at the small station of Fabriano in order to continue their journey by the small old-fashioned local joining the main line with Sulmona.

At dawn, in a stuffy and smoky second-class carriage in which five people had already spent the night, a bulky woman in deep mourning was hoisted in—almost like a shapeless bundle. Behind her, puffing and moaning, followed her husband—a tiny man, thin and weakly, his face death-white, his eyes small and bright and looking shy and uneasy.

Having at last taken a seat he politely thanked the passengers who had helped his wife and who had made room for her; then he turned round to the woman trying to pull down the collar of her coat, and politely inquired:

"Are you all right, dear?"

The wife, instead of answering, pulled up her collar again to her eyes, so as to hide her face.

"Nasty world," muttered the husband with a sad smile.

And he felt it his duty to explain to his traveling companions that the poor woman was to be pitied, for the war was taking away from her her only son, a boy of twenty to whom both had devoted their entire life, even breaking up their home at Sulmona to follow him to Rome, where he had to go as a student, then allowing him to volunteer for war with an assurance, however, that at least for six months he would not be sent to the front and now, all of a sudden, receiving a wire saying that he was due to leave in three days' time and asking them to go and see him off.

The woman under the big coat was twisting and wriggling, at times growling like a wild animal, feeling certain that all those explanations would not have aroused even a shadow of sympathy from those people who—most likely—were in the same plight as herself. One of them, who had been listening with particular attention, said:

"You should thank God that your son is only leaving now for the front. Mine has been sent there the first day of the war. He has already come back twice wounded and been back again to the front."

"What about me? I have two sons and three nephews at the front," said another passenger.

"Maybe, but in our case it is our *only* son," ventured the husband.

"What difference can it make? You may spoil your only son with excessive attentions, but you cannot love him more than you would all your other children if you had any. Paternal love is not like bread that can be broken into pieces and split amongst the children in equal shares. A father gives *all* his love to each one of his children without discrimination, whether it be one or ten, and if I am suffering now for my two sons, I am not suffering half for each of them but double. . . ."

"True . . . true . . ." sighed the embarrassed husband, "but suppose (of course we all hope it will never be your case) a father has two sons at the front and he loses one of them, there is still one left to console him . . . while . . ."

"Yes," answered the other, getting cross, "a son left to console him but also a son left for whom he must survive, while in the case of the father of an only son if the son dies the father can die too and put an end to his distress. Which of the two positions is the worse? Don't you see how my case would be worse than yours?"

"Nonsense," interrupted another traveler, a fat, red-faced man with blood shot eyes of the palest gray.

He was panting. From his bulging eyes seemed to spurt inner violence of an uncontrolled vitality which his weakened body could hardly contain.

"Nonsense," he repeated, trying to cover his mouth with his hand so as to hide the two missing front teeth. "Nonsense. Do we give life to our children for our own benefit?"

The other travelers stared at him in distress. The one who had had his son at the front since the first day of the war sighed: "You are right. Our children do not belong to us, they belong to the Country. . . ."

"Bosh," retorted the fat traveler. "Do we think of the Country when we give life to our children? Our sons are born because . . . well, because they must be born and when they come to life they take our own life with them. This is the truth. We belong to them but they never belong to us. And when they reach twenty they are exactly what we were at their age. We too had a father and mother, but there were so many other things as well . . . girls, cigarettes, illusions, new ties . . . and the Country, of course, whose call we would have answered—when we were twenty—even if father and mother had said no. Now at our age, the love of our Country is still great, of course, but stronger than it is the love for our children. Is there any one of us here who wouldn't gladly take his son's place at the front if he could?"

There was a silence all round, everybody nodding as to approve.

"Why then," continued the fat man, "shouldn't we consider the feelings of our children when they are twenty? Isn't it natural that at their age they should consider the love for their Country (I am speaking of decent boys, of course) even greater than the love for us? Isn't it natural that it should be so, as after all they must look upon us as upon old boys who cannot move any more and must stay at home? If Country exists, if Country is a natural necessity, like bread, of which each of us must eat in order not to die of hunger, somebody must go to defend it. And our sons go, when they are twenty, and they don't want tears, because if they die, they die inflamed and happy (I am speaking, of course, of decent boys). Now, if one dies young and happy, without having the ugly sides of life, the boredom of it, the pettiness, the bitterness of disillusion . . . what more can we ask for him? Everyone should stop crying; everyone should laugh, as I do . . . or at least thank God—as I do— because my son, before dying, sent me a message saying that he was dying satisfied at having ended his life in the best way he could have wished. That is why, as you see, I do not even wear mourning. . . ."

He shook his light fawn coat as to show it; his livid lip over his missing teeth was trembling, his eyes were watery and motionless, and soon after he ended with a shrill laugh which might well have been a sob.

"Quite so . . . quite so . . ." agreed the others.

The woman who, bundled in a corner under her coat, had been sitting and listening had—for the last three months—tried to find in the words of her husband and her friends something to console her in her deep sorrow, something that might show her how a mother should resign herself to send her son not even to death but to a probably dangerous life. Yet not a word had she found amongst the many which had been said . . . and her grief had been greater in seeing that nobody—as she thought —could share her feelings.

But now the words of the traveler amazed and almost stunned her. She suddenly realized that it wasn't the others who were wrong and could not understand her but herself who could not rise up to the same height of those fathers and mothers willing to resign themselves, without crying, not only to the departure of their sons but even to their death.

She lifted her head, she bent over from her corner trying to listen with great attention to the details which the fat man was giving to his companions about the way his son had fallen as a hero, for his King and his Country, happy and without regrets. It seemed to her that she had stumbled into a world she had never dreamt of, a world so far unknown to her and she was so pleased to hear everyone joining in congratulating that brave father who could so stoically speak of his child's death.

Then suddenly, just as if she had heard nothing of what had been said and almost as if waking up from a dream, she turned to the old man, asking him:

"Then . . . is your son really dead?"

Everybody stared at her. The old man, too, turned to look at her, fixing his great, bulging, horribly watery light gray eyes, deep in her face. For some little time he tried to answer, but words failed him. He looked and looked at her, almost as if only then—at that silly, incongruous question—he had suddenly realized at last that his son was really dead—gone for ever—for ever. His face contracted, became horribly distorted, then he snatched in haste a handkerchief from his pocket and, to the amazement of everyone, broke into harrowing, heart-rending, uncontrollable sobs.

POETRY

The Hero in Peace and War

The transition of an entire nation from peace to war, from one kind of life to another, from one state of mind and heart to another, is the subject of Whitman's "Beat! Beat! Drums!" In the offing, war is only a dim threat, vaguely fearful, vaguely thrilling. But when it comes, it comes with the inexorable force of an army marching to the beat of a thousand drums. This awesome rhythm reverberates through every human life as it reverberates through every line of Whitman's poem.

At the beginning of a war both sides are confident of victory, especially the young on both sides who will actually do the fighting. "All wars are boyish, and are fought by boys," as Herman Melville observes in "The March into Virginia." All wars are thus "children's crusades," in which the young, "champions and enthusiasts of the state," march off as if they were going on a picnic. They are fledgling worshippers of the god of war. Their innocent beliefs will inevitably be transformed into wiser, perhaps even bitter and ironic feelings through the experience of bloody battle. Historically, this is what happened at First Manassas, one of the earliest major battles of the Civil War and the occasion of Melville's poem.

Robert Lowell in his poem "Christmas Eve Under Hooker's Statue" reflects on the effects of wars on man from the Civil War to World War II. He establishes his own point in time in the first line, "Tonight a blackout," and bridges the gap between wars by his references to the rusting statue of the "heroic" Union general Joseph Hooker on the Boston Common and to Melville's poem "The March into Virginia."

Beat! Beat! Drums!

Walt Whitman

Beat! beat! drums! blow! bugles! blow!
Through the windows—through doors—burst like a ruthless
  force,
Into the solemn church, and scatter the congregation,
Into the school where the scholar is studying;
Leave not the bridegroom quiet—no happiness must he have
  now with his bride,   5
Nor the peaceful farmer any peace, ploughing his field or
  gathering his grain,
So fierce you whirr and pound you drums—so shrill you bugles
  blow.

Beat! beat! drums!—blow! bugles! blow!
Over the traffic of cities—over the rumble of wheels in the
  streets;
Are beds prepared for sleepers at night in the houses? no
  sleepers must sleep in those beds,   10
No bargainers' bargains by day—no brokers or speculators—
  would they continue?
Would the talkers be talking? would the singer attempt to
  sing?
Would the lawyer rise in the court to state his case before the
  judge?
Then rattle quicker, heavier drums—you bugles wilder blow.
Beat! beat! drums!—blow! bugles! blow!   15
Make no parley—stop for no expostulation,
Mind not the timid—mind not the weeper or prayer,
Mind not the old man beseeching the young man,
Let not the child's voice be heard, nor the mother's entreaties,
Make even the trestles to shake the dead where they lie
  awaiting the hearses,   20
So strong you thump O terrible drums—so loud you bugles
  blow.

The March into Virginia Ending in the First Manassas (July, 1861)

Herman Melville

Did all the lets and bars appear
   To every just or larger end,
Whence should come the trust and cheer?
   Youth must its ignorant impulse lend—
Age finds place in the rear.   5
   All wars are boyish, and are fought by boys,
The champions and enthusiasts of the state:
   Turbid ardours and vain joys
      Not barrenly abate—
   Stimulants to the power mature,   10
      Preparatives of fate.

Who here forecasteth the event?
What heart but spurns at precedent
And warnings of the wise,
Contemned foreclosures of surprise?   15
The banners play, the bugles call,
The air is blue and prodigal.
   No berrying party, pleasure-wooed,
No picnic party in the May,
Ever went less loth than they   20
   Into that leafy neighbourhood.
In Bacchic glee they file toward Fate,
Moloch's[1] uninitiate;
Expectancy, and glad surmise
Of battle's unknown mysteries.   25

All they feel is this: 'tis glory,
A rapture sharp, though transitory,
Yet lasting in belaureled story.
So they gaily go to fight,
Chatting left and laughing right.   30

---

1. *Moloch* A god of the Ammonites to whom children were sacrificed.

But some who this blithe mood present,
  As on in lightsome files they fare,
Shall die experienced ere three days are spent—
  Perish, enlightened by the volleyed glare;
Or shame survive, and, like to adamant,   35
  The throe of Second Manassas share.

Christmas Eve Under Hooker's Statue

Robert Lowell

Tonight a blackout.   Twenty years ago
I hung my stocking on the tree, and hell's
Serpent entwined the apple in the toe
To sting the child with knowledge.   Hooker's heels
Kicking at nothing in the shifting snow,   5
A cannon and a cairn of cannon balls
Rusting before the blackened Statehouse, know
How the long horn of plenty broke like glass
In Hooker's gauntlets.   Once I came from Mass;

Now storm-clouds shelter Christmas, once again   10
Mars meets his fruitless star with open arms,
His heavy saber flashes with the rime,
The war-god's bronzed and empty forehead forms
Anonymous machinery from raw men;
The cannon on the Common cannot stun   15
The blundering butcher as he rides on Time—
The barrel clinks with holly.   I am cold:
I ask for bread, my father gives me mould;

His stocking is full of stones.   Santa in red
Is crowned with wizened berries.   Man of war,   20
Where is the summer's garden?   In its bed
The ancient speckled serpent will appear,
And black-eyed susan with her frizzled head.
When Chancellorsville[1] mowed down the volunteer,

1. *Chancellorsville* A Civil War battle in which Hooker's forces were defeated.

"All wars are boyish," Herman Melville said;   25
But we are old, our fields are running wild:
Till Christ again turn wanderer and child.

Initiation

It is in military training camp that most ordinary men first face the
dangerous and bitter realities of heroism. Stanzas 1 through 4 of
Henry Reed's World War II poem "Unarmed Combat" consist of a
training talk on hand-to-hand combat by a British army sergeant to a
group of recruits. The sergeant's concluding statement—a probably
unintentional quote from *Hamlet*—initiates an interior monologue on
heroism by one of his trainees.

The awful routineness with which death occurs in training as well as
in combat is the theme of Randall Jarrell's poem "Losses." The
speaker of this poem, however, unlike the heroes of Tennyson's
"Charge of the Light Brigade," asks to know "the reason why."

The bitter pun concealed in the title of "Base Details" is, like the
poem as a whole, indicative of the feelings front line soldiers have
toward the fire-breathing "heroes" who remain safely behind in the
rear echelons. Bitterness is also the prevailing tone of Wilfred Owen's
"Dulce et Decorum Est." Owen's title is taken from a famous line of
the Roman poet Horace; given in full at the end of the poem, this
line can be translated: "How sweet and fitting it is to die for one's
country"—a statement which Owen calls "the old Lie."

Unarmed Combat
Henry Reed

In due course of course you will all be issued with
Your proper issue; but until tomorrow,
You can hardly be said to need it; and until that time,
We shall have unarmed combat.   I shall teach you
The various holds and rolls and throws and breakfalls   5
    Which you may sometimes meet.

And the various holds and rolls and throws and breakfalls
Do not depend on any sort of weapon,

But only on what I might coin a phrase and call
The ever-important question of human balance,   10
And the ever-important need to be in a strong
      Position at the start.

There are many kinds of weakness about the body
Where you would least expect, like the ball of the foot.
But the various holds and rolls and throws and breakfalls   15
Will always come in useful.   And never be frightened
To tackle from behind: it may not be clean to do so,
      But this is global war.

So give them all you have, and always give them
As good as you get; it will always get you somewhere.   20
(You may not know it, but you can tie a Jerry
Up without rope; it is one of the things I shall teach you.)
Nothing will matter if only you are ready for him.
      The readiness is all.

The readiness is all.   How can I help but feel   25
I have been here before?   But somehow then,
I was the tied-up one.   How to get out
Was always then my problem.   And even if I had
A piece of rope I was always the sort of person
      Who threw the rope aside.   30

And in my time I have given them all I had,
Which was never as good as I got, and it got me nowhere.
And the various holds and rolls and throws and breakfalls
Somehow or other I always seemed to put
In the wrong place.   And as for war, my wars   35
      Were global from the start.

Perhaps I was never in a strong position,
Or the ball of my foot got hurt, or I had some weakness
Where I had least expected.   But I think I see your point.
While awaiting a proper issue, we must learn the lesson   40
Of the ever-important question of human balance.
      It is courage that counts.

Things may be the same again; and we must fight
Not in the hope of winning but rather of keeping
Something alive: so that when we meet our end,   45

It may be said that we tackled wherever we could,
That battle-fit we lived, and though defeated,
   Not without glory fought.

Losses

Randall Jarrell

It was not dying: everybody died.
It was not dying: we had died before
In the routine crashes—and our fields
Called up the papers, wrote home to our folks,
And the rates rose, all because of us.   5
We died on the wrong page of the almanac,
Scattered on mountains fifty miles away;
Diving on haystacks, fighting with a friend,
We blazed up on the lines we never saw.
We died like aunts or pets or foreigners.   10
(When we left high school nothing else had died
For us to figure we had died like.)

In our new planes, with our new crews, we bombed
The ranges by the desert or the shore,
Fired at towed targets, waited for our scores—   15
And turned into replacements and woke up
One morning, over England, operational.[1]
It wasn't different: but if we died
It was not an accident but a mistake
(But an easy one for anyone to make).   20
We read our mail and counted up our missions—
In bombers named for girls, we burned
The cities we had learned about in school—
Till our lives wore out; our bodies lay among
The people we had killed and never seen.   25
When we lasted long enough they gave us medals;
When we died they said, "Our casualties were low."
They said, "Here are the maps"; we burned the cities.

1. *operational* Cleared for combat duty.

It was not dying—no, not ever dying;
But the night I died I dreamed that I was dead,   30
And the cities said to me: "Why are you dying?
We are satisfied, if you are; but why did I die?"

Base Details
Siegfried Sassoon

If I were fierce, and bald, and short of breath,
    I'd live with scarlet Majors at the Base,
And speed glum heroes up the line to death.
    You'd see me with my puffy petulant face,
Guzzling and gulping in the best hotel,   5
    Reading the Roll of Honor.   "Poor young chap,"
I'd say—"I used to know his father well;
    Yes, we've lost heavily in this last scrap."
And when the war is done and youth stone dead,
I'd toddle safely home and die—in bed.   10

Dulce et Decorum Est
Wilfred Owen

Bent double, like old beggars under sacks,
Knock-kneed, coughing like hags, we cursed through sludge,
Till on the haunting flares we turned our backs,
And towards our distant rest began to trudge.
Men marched asleep.   Many had lost their boots,   5
But limped on, blood-shod.   All went lame, all blind;
Drunk with fatigue; deaf even to the hoots
Of gas-shells dropping softly behind.

Gas!   GAS!   Quick, boys!—An ecstasy of fumbling
Fitting the clumsy helmets just in time,   10
But someone still was yelling out and stumbling
And flound'ring like a man in fire or lime.—

Dim through the misty panes and thick green light,
As under a green sea, I saw him drowning.
In all my dreams before my helpless sight   15
He plunges at me, guttering, choking, drowning.

If in some smothering dreams, you too could pace
Behind the wagon that we flung him in,
And watch the white eyes writhing in his face,
His hanging face, like a devil's sick of sin,   20
If you could hear, at every jolt, the blood
Come gargling from the froth-corrupted lungs
Bitten as the cud
Of vile, incurable sores on innocent tongues,—
My friend, you would not tell with such high zest   25
To children ardent for some desperate glory,
The old Lie: *Dulce et decorum est*
Pro patria mori.

Pro Patria Mori

When death comes to the soldier who has not distinguished himself as a hero, that death becomes, not legendary, but merely statistical. The quality of anonymity which unites those who have paid the supreme price for victory also unites the next two poems. The American airman of Randall Jarrell's "The Death of the Ball Turret Gunner" died six miles above Europe in a machine gun turret hung beneath the belly of a heavy bomber. He is as anonymous as the single fallen soldier and the single fallen leaf of Wallace Stevens' poem "The Death of a Soldier."

Wholesale death and oblivion have been brought even to civilians by modern technological warfare. In Tim Reynolds' poem "A Hell of a Day" certain citizens of the city of Hiroshima are named, only to be obliterated instantaneously in the atomic explosion which spelled defeat for Japan and victory for the Allies in World War II.

Victory can be short-lived, and its taste is not always sweet. The speaker of Emily Dickinson's poem has survived and even triumphed, but now he must live with the bloody past he has helped to create. The sense this poem conveys of how the seeming romance of war is transformed into something quite different after victory has been won is also in evidence in Wilfred Owen's World War I poem "Disabled" and in Louis Simpson's World War II poem "The Heroes."

The Death of the
Ball Turret Gunner

Randall Jarrell

From my mother's sleep I fell into the State,
And I hunched in its belly till my wet fur froze.
Six miles from earth, loosed from its dream of life,
I woke to black flak and the nightmare fighters.
When I died they washed me out of the turret with a hose.

The Death of a Soldier

Wallace Stevens

Life contracts and death is expected,
As in a season of autumn.
The soldier falls.

He does not become a three-days personage,
Imposing his separation,   5
Calling for pomp.

Death is absolute and without memorial,
As in a season of autumn,
When the wind stops,

When the wind stops and, over the heavens,   10
The clouds go, nevertheless,
In their direction.

A Hell of a Day

Tim Reynolds

This was a day of fumbling and petty accidents,
as though the population had grown all thumbs
at once.   Watering her chrysanthemums,
Mrs. Kamei was surprised to see the plants

blacken, water turn to steam. Both Dote and Michiko 5
noted the other's absence but not her own.
Mr. Kime lifted his hat, but his head was gone.
Mr. Watanabe rolled a double zero.
Photographing her son by the river bridge
Mrs. Ume pressed the shutter and overexposed her film. 10
Her son's yawn swallowed him. And everything turned on
when pretty Miss Mihara snapped the light switch.
Then old Mr. Ekahomo struck a match
to light his pipe, and the town caught, and dissolved in flame.

My Triumph Lasted
Emily Dickinson

My Triumph lasted till the Drums
Had left the Dead alone
And then I dropped my Victory
And chastened stole along
To where the finished Faces   5
Conclusion turned on me
And then I hated Glory
And wished myself were They.

What is to be is best descried
When it has also been—   10
Could Prospect taste of Retrospect
The tyrannies of Men
Were Tenderer—diviner
The Transitive toward.
A Bayonet's contrition   15
Is nothing to the Dead.

Disabled
Wilfred Owen

He sat in a wheeled chair, waiting for dark,
And shivered in his ghastly suit of grey,
Legless, sewn short at elbow. Through the park

Voices of boys rang saddening like a hymn,
Voices of play and pleasure after day,   5
Till gathering sleep had mothered them from him.

About this time Town used to swing so gay
When glow-lamps budded in the light-blue trees
And girls glanced lovelier as the air grew dim,
—In the old times, before he threw away his knees.   10
Now he will never feel again how slim
Girls' waists are, or how warm their subtle hands,
All of them touch him like some queer disease.

There was an artist silly for his face,
For it was younger than his youth, last year.   15
Now he is old; his back will never brace;
He's lost his colour very far from here,
Poured it down shell-holes till the veins ran dry,
And half his lifetime lapsed in the hot race,
And leap of purple spurted from his thigh.   20
One time he liked a bloodsmear down his leg,
After the matches carried shoulder-high.
It was after football, when he'd drunk a peg,
He thought he'd better join.   He wonders why . . .
Someone had said he'd look a god in kilts.   25

That's why; and maybe, too, to please his Meg,
Aye, that was it, to please the giddy jilts,
He asked to join.   He didn't have to beg;
Smiling they wrote his lie; aged nineteen years.
Germans he scarcely thought of; and no fears   30
Of Fear came yet.   He thought of jewelled hilts
For daggers in plaid socks; of smart salutes;
And care of arms; and leave; and pay arrears;
Esprit de corps; and hints for young recruits.
And soon, he was drafted out with drums and cheers.   35

Some cheered him home, but not as crowds cheer Goal.
Only a solemn man who brought him fruits
Thanked him; and then inquired about his soul.
Now, he will spend a few sick years in Institutes,
And do what things the rules consider wise,   40
And take whatever pity they may dole.
To-night he noticed how the women's eyes

Passed from him to the strong men that were whole.
How cold and late it is!   Why don't they come
And put him into bed?   Why don't they come?   45

The Heroes

Louis Simpson

I dreamed of war-heroes, of wounded war-heroes
With just enough of their charms shot away
To make them more handsome.   The women moved nearer
To touch their brave wounds and their hair streaked with
    gray.

I saw them in long ranks ascending the gang-planks;   5
The girls with the doughnuts were cheerful and gay.
They minded their manners and muttered their thanks;
The Chaplain advised them to watch and to pray.

They shipped these rapscallions, these sea-sick battalions
To a patriotic and picturesque spot;   10
They gave them new bibles and marksmen's medallions,
Compasses, maps, and committed the lot.

A fine dust has settled on all that scrap metal.
The heroes were packaged and sent home in parts
To pluck at a poppy and sew on a petal   15
And count the long night by the stroke of their hearts.

In Memoriam

The glory won by the hero lends him a kind of immortality—that which comes from his continuing to live in the memories of those who benefited from his victory.   It is the purpose, not only of monuments of marble or brass, but of commemorative poems as well, to keep such memories alive.   Ralph Waldo Emerson's "Concord Hymn," written for the dedication of a monument to those who fought at Lexington and Concord, is itself a poetic monument to the heroic spirit of the Revolutionary War.   Monuments, poetic and otherwise, assert the fallen hero's ultimate victory over mortality and oblivion.   But it is also possible to assert, as does Carl Sandburg's poem "Grass" that the world and all people will little note nor long remember either the victories or the victors. Calling the roll of the greatest battles of the Napoleanic Wars, the American Civil War, and World War I, Sandburg painfully records the eventual obliteration of the hero and his victories by nature and time.

Concord Hymn
Ralph Waldo Emerson

By the rude bridge that arched the flood,
    Their flag to April's breeze unfurled,
Here once the embattled farmers stood
    And fired the shot heard round the world.

The foe long since in silence slept;   5
    Alike the conqueror silent sleeps;
And Time the ruined bridge has swept
    Down the dark stream which seaward creeps.

On this green bank, by this soft stream,
    We set to-day a votive stone;   10
That memory may their dead redeem,
    When, like our sires, our sons are gone.

Spirit, that made those heroes dare
    To die, and leave their children free,
Bid Time and Nature gently spare   15
    The shaft we raise to them and thee.

Grass
Carl Sandburg

Pile the bodies high at Austerlitz and Waterloo.
Shovel them under and let me work—
    I am the grass; I cover all.

And pile them high at Gettysburg
And pile them high at Ypres and Verdun.   5
Shovel them under, and let me work.
Two years, ten years, and passengers ask the conductor:
        What place is this?
        Where are we now?

        I am the grass.   10
        Let me work.

DRAMA

The Straw Man

In our time the question of glory appears to have lost some of its relevance. For glory, whether won by an individual hero or by a nation, increasingly seems too costly, too ephemeral, perhaps even too self-serving, to be held up as one of the higher ideals. Indeed it has become commonplace to ask, not only what price glory, but even what price victory? Although victory, compared to glory, seems somehow more real and simple—someone loses, someone wins—the history of the twentieth century makes one wonder how simple and real victory actually is. The Allied victory in World War I, for example, "the war to end all wars," seemed simple and real at the time. But the victory of the Allies in World War II was immediately followed by a cold war between the Russians and their former comrades. Meanwhile, the defeated countries of Germany and Japan rose to new heights of prosperity, but victorious England declined in power and prestige. The Korean War ended in ambiguity, not victory, and to talk of victory in connection with Viet Nam now seems cruelly ironic. Finally, since 1945 we have lived in the shadow of World War III, Atomic War I, in which no real victory could be possible.

In such an age there would seem to be little place for the traditional hero. At the conclusion of the play which follows, both sides claim victory—and thus neither side can claim it. The heroes who paid for these hollow victories with their lives, "The Green Man" and "The Violet Man," have made their quests in vain. At the beginning of this allegorical drama these two characters are nonheroes, perhaps even anti-heroes. Each of them is a twentieth-century Everyman propelled against his will into the quest for victory, not by religion, but by politics-become-religion. And each comes to accept the patterns of thinking, feeling, and action which his politics have imposed upon him. Ironically, these turn out to be almost identical patterns.

The *Straw Man* is comic, but no comedy, tragic, but no tragedy. Though it has its "heroes," its "quests," and its "victories," all of these cancel each other out. And in spite of its broadly humorous moments, the play ends in negation, whereas true comedy ends in affirmation. At best, *The Straw Man* might be called "black comedy"—a play in which the laughable and the serious, the satiric and the humanitarian, are so mixed as to produce a deeply ironic theatrical experience. In this typically modern form of tragi-comedy there can be no heroes, only humanity, and no victory, only survival.

The Straw Man

Antonio Martínez Ballesteros

CHARACTERS

THE GREEN MAN
THE HIDDEN GREEN MAN
THE GREEN WOMAN
5 GREEN SOLDIERS
THE VIOLET MAN
THE HIDDEN VIOLET MAN
THE VIOLET WOMAN
5 VIOLET SOLDIERS

[*The set consists of a curtain in the background with warlike illustrations: tanks, planes, soldiers fighting with bayonets, etc. One small tree on the left and another on the right. And nothing more. Moments before the curtain is raised on an empty stage, a patriotic hymn is heard. After a few seconds two men enter with a placard on which is written: "Civil War." The two remain still for a moment in the center of the stage, each with one end of the placard, in order to give the public time to read it. Suddenly, from left and right, sounds of heavy fighting are heard. The men, frightened, abandon the placard and flee. They don't know where to hide. One of them falls to the ground, face down, putting his hands over the nape of his neck, in the center of the stage. The other tries to hide behind the tree on the right, but is pushed away by a violet-colored arm which belongs to someone already hidden there.*]

HIDDEN VIOLET MAN. Traitor! Get over there with the greens!

168

[*The man—we shall call him the first man—falls to the ground. The fighting noises increase and the first man puts his hands over his head. After a moment, very frightened, he continues looking for a place to hide, and reaches the tree on the left. But another arm from a second hidden man, this one dressed in green, pushes him away, shouting:*]

HIDDEN GREEN MAN. Traitor! Get over there with the violets!

[*The first man moves away and remains stretched out in the center of the stage, next to the other man, the second one, putting his hands over the nape of his neck. The sounds of fighting cease little by little. The men raise their heads to look around. The* HIDDEN VIOLET MAN *comes out from behind the tree and goes toward the right side, foreground, with a placard on his shoulder. He sticks it in the ground and we can read on it: "Violets. War Zone." Then he speaks to someone offstage.*]

HIDDEN VIOLET MAN. Come out now! [*Five soldiers dressed in violet come out, carrying their rifles.*] Fall in! At ease!

[*The soldiers remain in the indicated position. In the meantime, the* HIDDEN GREEN MAN *has come out from behind his tree with another placard, and goes to the left side of the stage, where he sticks it in the ground. One can read on it: "Greens. War Zone." Then he calls to someone inside.*]

HIDDEN GREEN MAN. You can come out now! [*Five other soldiers dressed in green appear.*] Fall in! At ease! [*The soldiers remain in the indicated position.*]

HIDDEN VIOLET MAN [*to his soldiers*]. This is our most advanced position. Defend it to the death.

HIDDEN GREEN MAN [*to his soldiers*]. This is the most advanced position we have been able to obtain. You must defend it with your lives.

HIDDEN VIOLET MAN. Aim! [*The violet soldiers raise their weapons to to the ordered position. The* HIDDEN VIOLET MAN *goes to his tree to hide.*]

HIDDEN GREEN MAN. Aim! [*The green soldiers obey. And the* HIDDEN GREEN MAN *goes to hide behind his tree.*]

HIDDEN VIOLET MAN [*sticking his head out from behind the tree.*] Fire! [*The violet soldiers fire. Two green soldiers fall. The men run from one side to the other, without knowing where to hide.*]

HIDDEN GREEN MAN [*sticking his head out from behind the tree*]. Fire! [*The green soldiers fire and two violet soldiers fall. The men, more and more frightened, throw themselves to the ground again, face down, between the two zones.*]

HIDDEN VIOLET MAN [*same as before*]. Fire! [*Another volley. Two green soldiers fall.*]

HIDDEN GREEN MAN. Fire! [*Volley. A violet soldier falls.*]

The Quest for Victory   169

HIDDEN VIOLET MAN & HIDDEN GREEN MAN [*at the same time*]. Fire! [*All the remaining soldiers fall. The hidden men remain behind their trees. After a moment of silence, the men sit up. They look at each other without understanding anything; then to the left and right, frightened.*]

HIDDEN VIOLET MAN [*sticking his head out from behind his tree, to the first man*]. Psst! Psst! . . .

FIRST MAN [*looking at him astonished*]. Who, me?

HIDDEN VIOLET MAN. Yes, come here. [*The* FIRST MAN *approaches the* HIDDEN VIOLET MAN, *who commands him to:*] Salute!

FIRST MAN [*disconcerted*]. Yes, sir. Good morning.

HIDDEN VIOLET MAN. Don't you know how to distinguish a person's rank? I am a Gorilla First Class! So you'd better look sharp and act respectful! See that you don't forget it! [*The* HIDDEN VIOLET MAN *is much smaller than the first man.*]

FIRST MAN [*disconcerted*]. Yes, sir. Good morning.

HIDDEN VIOLET MAN. That's better. Put this on. [*He gives him a violet jersey that the man puts on, which transforms him into a violet man, since his pants were violet.*]

VIOLET MAN. Done, Master.

HIDDEN VIOLET MAN. Now take away those bodies.

VIOLET MAN. Where to?

HIDDEN VIOLET MAN. Where do you think? To the ditch.

VIOLET MAN [*motionless, not knowing what to do*]. To the ditch?

HIDDEN VIOLET MAN. Haven't they taught you that it's a sacred duty to bury the dead? Well, those bodies are dead! The martyrs of submission! Submission to the past! You have to bury them!

VIOLET MAN [*preparing to obey*]. Yes, sir.

HIDDEN VIOLET MAN [*calling him*]. Hey, you.

VIOLET MAN [*stopping*]. What, sir?

HIDDEN VIOLET MAN. Don't ever forget proper respect! When a Gorilla speaks to you, you should always say, "Yes, Master! Whatever you command, Master."

VIOLET MAN [*at attention*]. Yes, Master! Whatever you command, Master!

HIDDEN VIOLET MAN. And now say: "Long live submission!"

VIOLET MAN. Long live submission!

HIDDEN VIOLET MAN [*dismissing him*]. To work!

VIOLET MAN. Whatever you command, Master! [*He moves away and begins to carry the bodies of the violet soldiers offstage. In the meantime, the* HIDDEN GREEN MAN *calls to the second man.*]

HIDDEN GREEN MAN. Ssss!

SECOND MAN. Who, me?

HIDDEN GREEN MAN. Look, who do you think I mean? Come here!

[*The* SECOND MAN *comes over to him.*] Put that on. [*He gives him a green jersey that the man puts on, which converts him into a green man, since his pants were this color.*]

GREEN MAN [*at attention*]. At your service!

HIDDEN GREEN MAN. Okay, okay, don't overdo it. We're all equal here. The hour of the revolution has arrived.

GREEN MAN [*without understanding anything*]. Yes, of course.

HIDDEN GREEN MAN. Don't you know what the revolution is?

GREEN MAN. Well, ah . . .

HIDDEN GREEN MAN. The revolution is . . . that's it, the revolution! Is that clear?

GREEN MAN. Very clear! It's the revolution. [*Pointing to the other side.*] But if there they say "Long live submission," what do we say here?

HIDDEN GREEN MAN. Very simple, just the opposite. Is that understood?

GREEN MAN. Yes, sir! Long live the opposite!

HIDDEN GREEN MAN. No! No! Not "the opposite"!

GREEN MAN. But that's what you just finished telling me.

HIDDEN GREEN MAN. Yes, yes, but you didn't understand me. The opposite does not mean that you have to say the opposite, but . . . the opposite! [*Noting the confused look of the man.*] Do you understand?

GREEN MAN [*pretending*]. Yes, yes, of course.

HIDDEN GREEN MAN. Good, then say "Long live Modacracy!", which is the opposite of theirs, and let's not split hairs.

GREEN MAN. Well . . . long live Modacracy!

HIDDEN GREEN MAN. And let's not waste any more time! Do you know why I've called you?

GREEN MAN. I can guess, Captain Gorilla, sir. To bury the dead.

HIDDEN GREEN MAN [*with emphasis*]. Our dead! The martyrs of Modacracy! Bury them!

GREEN MAN. Whatever you command, Captain Gorilla. [*He moves away and begins to drag the bodies of the green soldiers offstage. The* VIOLET MAN, *who has already finished his job, goes over to the* HIDDEN VIOLET MAN, *who, next to his tree, has set up a folding chair, in which he has sat down to smoke a pipe.*]

VIOLET MAN. Do you have something else for me to do, Master?

HIDDEN VIOLET MAN. Have you finished already?

VIOLET MAN. Yes, Master.

HIDDEN VIOLET MAN. Now pick up the rifle of one of our soldiers. Don't let the enemy surprise us.

VIOLET MAN. Whatever you command, Master. [*He goes and picks up one of the rifles from the bodies.*] Ready, Master!

HIDDEN VIOLET MAN. Now keep a close watch. And when you see a suspicious movement by the enemy, notify me.

The Quest for Victory   171

VIOLET MAN. Yes, Master. [*He settles down comfortably in his position. The* GREEN MAN, *who has also dragged off the bodies, picks up a rifle and stations himself in the same position as the other. The* HIDDEN GREEN MAN *has also seated himself in a folding chair and has begun to smoke an enormous cigar. Silence. Then, the roar of airplanes. The* GREEN MAN *puts the gun to his shoulder and fires upward. A duck falls from the sky and he picks it up.*]

HIDDEN GREEN MAN. What's that, soldier?

GREEN MAN. An enemy airplane, Captain Gorilla, sir. Shot down.

HIDDEN GREEN MAN. How do you know that it's an enemy one?

GREEN MAN. It has violet feathers.

HIDDEN GREEN MAN. Then there's no doubt. It's an enemy. [*He pauses. He takes a puff of his cigar. Suddenly, suspiciously:*] Feathers?

GREEN MAN [*hiding the duck with his body*]. I meant to say wings. They are wings.

HIDDEN GREEN MAN. Let's see, bring it here. [*The* GREEN MAN *hesitates.*] Obey. That's an order. [*The* GREEN MAN *brings the duck to him. The* HIDDEN GREEN MAN *takes it and examines it carefully.*] I would say that it has feathers.

GREEN MAN [*defending the booty*]. Nevertheless it also has two wings.

HIDDEN GREEN MAN [*examining it in greater detail*]. Do you think so? To be sure, we'll send it to the laboratory so they can analyze it.

GREEN MAN [*disconsolately*]. To the laboratory?

HIDDEN GREEN MAN. That way we will know what it's all about. Cook! [*He disappears to the left carrying the duck. The* GREEN MAN, *greatly disappointed, sits down on the ground, thoughtfully resting his chin on his hands. The sounds of fighting begin to be heard again. Suddenly there is a tremendous explosion. A ham falls from the sky on top of the* VIOLET MAN, *who staggers from the blow.*]

HIDDEN VIOLET MAN. What happened?

VIOLET MAN [*picking up the ham*]. A shell, your Highness.

HIDDEN VIOLET MAN. Bring it here. [*The* VIOLET MAN *pretends not to hear.*] Didn't you hear me? Bring that shell here. [*The man brings him the ham which the* HIDDEN VIOLET MAN *smells avidly.*] It appears that it hasn't exploded. A technician will have to examine it. Cook! [*He goes off to the right carrying the ham. The* VIOLET MAN *sits down in the same manner as the* GREEN MAN. *A green woman enters from the left, pushing a little cart. From the right, another woman, dressed in violet, with another little cart.*]

GREEN WOMAN [*approaching the* GREEN MAN *with her cart*]. Soldier, are you hungry? I have sandwiches of bread and sausage without sausage!

VIOLET WOMAN [*approaching the* VIOLET MAN]. Are you hungry, soldier? I have sandwiches of sausage and bread without bread!

GREEN MAN. Without sausage?

VIOLET MAN. Without bread?

VIOLET WOMAN & GREEN WOMAN [*in unison*]. That's what happens in wartime!

GREEN WOMAN. There's hunger!

VIOLET WOMAN. There's a scarcity!

GREEN MAN. I'm hungry!

VIOLET MAN. I suffer from scarcity!

GREEN WOMAN. We've been at war for four years.

VIOLET WOMAN. There are no men to work the land.

GREEN MAN. We all suffer.

VIOLET MAN. We all suffer, but . . .

GREEN WOMAN & VIOLET WOMAN [*in unison*]. May it all be for the cause!

GREEN MAN & VIOLET MAN [*in unison*]. Amen!

GREEN WOMAN. I have sandwiches of bread and sausage without sausage!

VIOLET WOMAN. I have sandwiches of sausage and bread without bread!

GREEN MAN. But that way it'll cost less.

GREEN WOMAN. Why?

GREEN MAN. Because it's only half a sandwich.

VIOLET WOMAN. So what? Everything has gone up!

GREEN WOMAN. I can't sell it cheaper. It costs the same as a whole sandwich.

GREEN MAN. But that's all the money I have.

VIOLET MAN. But that's all my money.

GREEN WOMAN. Take it or leave it.

GREEN MAN. But if I don't take, I don't eat.

VIOLET WOMAN. So what?

VIOLET MAN. And if I don't eat, I'll drop dead.

GREEN WOMAN. So what?

GREEN MAN [*after thinking about it a little, searching in his pocket*]. Okay, give me the sandwich.

VIOLET MAN. What can you do! Give me one. [*The women are ready to hand the sandwiches to the men, when the roar of planes begins to be heard.*]

GREEN WOMAN [*interrupting her actions, very frightened*]. An air raid!

VIOLET WOMAN. To shelter! Let's get to shelter! [*She begins to move around on the right side of the stage, as if fleeing from something. The* GREEN WOMAN *does the same on the left. The noises of planes and of exploding bombs become deafening. The women shriek, very frightened.*]

GREEN WOMAN [*running from one side to the other*]. Help! Planes!

VIOLET WOMAN. Help! Bombs! [*Two successive explosions, stronger than the previous ones, knock the two women to the ground, where they remain motionless, as though dead. The noise of the planes subsides little by little, until it disappears, leaving everything in the most absolute silence. The two men have observed what's happened with utter impassiveness, without stirring from their places. They remain this way for a few seconds more. A voice is heard through a loudspeaker.*]

VOICE. According to information from Supreme Headquarters of the Violet troops, the latest reports on the war could not be more encouraging. Our air force has bombed the enemy capital with great success. According to calculations, the number of victims of the bombardments of the current week are in excess of ten thousand. There is no doubt that we are now on the road to victory over the nefarious green Modacrats. [*The* VIOLET MAN *gives a sigh of satisfaction. Immediately a second voice is heard on another loudspeaker.*]

VOICE. Attention, please! Here is a news bulletin from the Supreme Headquarters of the Green Modacracy. Our air force has bombed various enemy cities with very satisfactory results during the past few hours. It is calculated that the number of enemy casualties during the past week already approaches twelve thousand. That is a clear indication that our triumph over the enemy is now very near. Long live Modacracy! [*Silence. When the two men are convinced that the news items have ended, they get up, in a very natural manner, and each one goes toward the woman's body in his zone. They grab them by their ankles and drag them offstage, each one to one side. Then they return to the little carts and examine the merchandise.*]

VIOLET MAN. Sausage without bread.

GREEN MAN. Bread without sausage.

VIOLET MAN. I'm sick of eating without bread. [*He walks around pensively with a piece of sausage in his hand.*]

GREEN MAN. I've had it up to here with dry bread. [*He wanders around pensively with a piece of bread in his hand. And, while walking, he suddenly finds himself face to face with the* VIOLET MAN.]

VIOLET MAN [*frightened*]. Halt! Who goes there?

GREEN MAN [*frightened also*]. Who are you?

VIOLET MAN [*immobilized by fear, guessing*]. You're one of the green ones!

GREEN MAN [*the same as the other*]. You're one of the violet ones!

VIOLET MAN. An enemy! Don't move! [*He points at him with a sausage, as if it were a weapon.*]

GREEN MAN. Hands up! [*He points at him with the piece of bread.*]

VIOLET MAN. Traitor!

GREEN MAN. Slave of the exploiters!

VIOLET MAN. Anarchist!

GREEN MAN. Capitalist pig!

VIOLET MAN. Drop that gun! [*Looking for the first time at the other's piece of bread.*] Hey, that's not a gun!

GREEN MAN. [*Almost at the same time*]: Drop that rifle! [*Noting the sausage for the first time.*] Hey, that's not a rifle!

VIOLET MAN [*astonished*]. I'm so hungry I'm seeing things!

GREEN MAN [*with astonishment*]. Same here!

VIOLET MAN. Do you know what I see in your hand instead of a gun?

GREEN MAN. Do you know what I see instead of a rifle?

VIOLET MAN. A piece of bread!

GREEN MAN. A sausage!

VIOLET MAN [*even more astonished*]. It *is* a piece of bread!

GREEN MAN [*extremely astonished*]. It *is* a sausage!

VIOLET MAN [*stepping back, and pointing at the other one with his rifle*]. Give me that piece of bread! I have to make myself a sandwich!

GREEN MAN [*stepping back and also pointing with his rifle*]. I'll do the sandwich making. Either give me the sausage or I shoot. [*The two men, now at a certain distance from each other, fire their rifles. They both fall backward.*]

VIOLET MAN [*putting one hand on his chest and holding on to the sausage with the other*]. Long live country, submission, and sausage! They got me!

GREEN MAN [*putting one hand on his chest and holding the piece of bread with the other*]. Long live country, Modacracy, and bread! They've killed me!

VIOLET MAN [*while he writhes on the ground, as if he were agonizing, to the other one*]. Assassin, green beast. . . .

GREEN MAN [*the same movements*]. Criminal, violet animal. . . .

VIOLET MAN. If you're insulting me, it means you aren't dead, green beast!

GREEN MAN. That's what you would like, you snivelling little violet animal! You only wounded me.

VIOLET MAN. The next time I'll finish you off!

GREEN MAN. The next time I'll kill you like a pig! Ambulance!

VIOLET MAN. Ambulance! [*He loses consciousness. A violet soldier approaches with a wheelbarrow, picks up his wounded man and carries him to the edge of their zone, where he unloads him by tipping up the wheelbarrow, as if he were dealing with cheap merchandise. Another green soldier does the same with his wounded man. The two soldiers disappear with their wheelbarrows. The VIOLET MAN and the GREEN MAN are on the ground, their shoulders leaning against their respective lateral walls, unconscious. The VIOLET WOMAN appears with a flag of the same color in her hand. She stoops down, gives the VIOLET MAN a kiss, and the latter regains consciousness. She puts the flag in his hand.*]

The Quest for Victory   175

VIOLET WOMAN. The flag of our country! [*And he remains very content. From the other side the* GREEN WOMAN *appears with another flag, this one green, of course. She repeats the same operation with the* GREEN MAN.]

GREEN WOMAN. The flag of our country! [*And he becomes very happy.*]

VIOLET WOMAN. Soon you will return to the front.

VIOLET MAN. Let's take advantage of the time.

GREEN WOMAN. Let's make love.

GREEN MAN. Yes, let's cover ourselves with the flag. That way no one will see us. [*The* VIOLET MAN *lies down with his wife and the* GREEN MAN *with his. Both pairs cover themselves with their flag, which, on being spread out, covers them completely. Only two humps can be seen on stage, one violet and the other green. Something moves beneath them. Suddenly the two humps become still. A voice is heard beneath the violet hump.*]

VOICE OF THE VIOLET WOMAN. We'll call him Francisco. [*And another voice beneath the green hump.*]

VOICE OF THE GREEN WOMAN. We'll call him Julian. [*The* HIDDEN VIOLET MAN *comes up to the violet hump and shouts gruffly. The* HIDDEN GREEN MAN *does the same in front of the green hump.*]

HIDDEN VIOLET MAN. Soldier! Your period of convalescence has ended!

HIDDEN GREEN MAN. Soldier! You are cured now! You must return to the line!

HIDDEN VIOLET MAN. To the front! Your country is calling you!

HIDDEN GREEN MAN. On to battle! For victory, soldier!

VIOLET MAN [*coming to attention*]. For submission!

GREEN MAN [*doing the same*]. For Modacracy!

HIDDEN VIOLET MAN [*to the* VIOLET WOMAN]. Woman! Say good-bye to your husband! [*The* VIOLET MAN & VIOLET WOMAN *embrace and thus remain motionless like two dolls.*]

HIDDEN GREEN MAN [*to the* GREEN MAN]. Husband! Say good-bye to your wife! [*The* GREEN MAN & GREEN WOMAN *embrace and also remain motionless like the others.*]

HIDDEN VIOLET MAN [*separating the pair*]. Let's go. That's enough.

HIDDEN GREEN MAN [*doing the same*]. Time's up. You have to leave. [*The* GREEN WOMAN & GREEN MAN *and the* VIOLET WOMAN & VIOLET MAN *separate like mechanical dolls with the respective hidden men in between.*]

HIDDEN VIOLET MAN [*to the* VIOLET WOMAN]. Now, woman, wife, and mother of the country!

HIDDEN GREEN MAN [*to the* GREEN WOMAN]. Wife at present, mother in the near future!

HIDDEN VIOLET MAN. The country thanks you! . . .

HIDDEN GREEN MAN. The country rewards you! . . .

HIDDEN VIOLET MAN. The services provided!

HIDDEN GREEN MAN. And the children engendered!

HIDDEN VIOLET MAN. Who one day will give their lives for submission!

HIDDEN GREEN MAN. Who one day will give their lives for Modacracy!

HIDDEN VIOLET MAN. Your country hasn't forgotten you!

HIDDEN GREEN MAN. Your country remembers you!

HIDDEN VIOLET MAN. Your country embraces you! [*He embraces the* VIOLET WOMAN.]

HIDDEN GREEN MAN. An embrace from your country! [*He embraces the* GREEN WOMAN. *The two women allow themselves to be embraced and fondled by the respective hidden men. They remain impassive, at attention, in spite of the shameless fondling by their "chiefs." Suddenly there sounds something which resembles the whistle of a locomotive.*]

HIDDEN VIOLET MAN [*releasing the woman*]. The train!

HIDDEN GREEN MAN [*releasing the other woman*]. We mustn't miss the train! [*The noise of a moving locomotive. The* HIDDEN VIOLET MAN *grabs the waist of the* VIOLET MAN; *the* HIDDEN GREEN MAN, *that of the* GREEN MAN. *And they begin to imitate a train in the way children do in their games. The women say good-bye to them with a wave of their handkerchiefs. The two "trains" reach their destination and stop at the moment that the noise of the locomotive ceases to be heard. The women go offstage.*]

HIDDEN VIOLET MAN [*in a shout which is a prologue to a patriotic harangue*]. Soldier!

HIDDEN GREEN MAN [*in the same manner*]. Soldier! [*The* GREEN MAN *same as the violet one before him, comes to attention.*]

HIDDEN VIOLET MAN. Your wound in battle . . .

HIDDEN GREEN MAN. . . . in the struggle for your country . . .

HIDDEN VIOLET MAN. . . . has made it possible . . .

HIDDEN GREEN MAN. . . . for you to be recommended to the High Command . . .

HIDDEN VIOLET MAN. . . . for you to be granted a medal . . .

HIDDEN GREEN MAN. . . . a decoration in recognition of demonstrated bravery . . .

HIDDEN VIOLET MAN. . . . in defense of the ideals of submission . . .

HIDDEN GREEN MAN. . . . of Modacracy.

HIDDEN VIOLET MAN. Well now . . .

HIDDEN GREEN MAN. Your wounds have already healed . . .

HIDDEN VIOLET MAN. And in recognition of your bravery . . .

HIDDEN GREEN MAN. . . . your country has awarded you . . .

HIDDEN VIOLET MAN. . . . a permit for convalescence . . .

HIDDEN GREEN MAN. . . . which has terminated . . .

HIDDEN VIOLET MAN. . . . which has expired . . .

HIDDEN GREEN MAN. Since you've recovered.

HIDDEN VIOLET MAN. You've recovered . . .

HIDDEN GREEN MAN. You've eaten . . .

HIDDEN VIOLET MAN. You've drunk . . .

HIDDEN GREEN MAN. You've been granted all the pleasures . . .

HIDDEN VIOLET MAN. . . . that are fitting for an honorable citizen.

HIDDEN GREEN MAN. But now . . .

HIDDEN VIOLET MAN. One must continue fighting . . .

HIDDEN GREEN MAN. . . . for Modacracy . . .

HIDDEN VIOLET MAN. . . . for submission . . .

HIDDEN GREEN MAN. Boom boom . . .

HIDDEN VIOLET MAN. Boom boom . . .

HIDDEN GREEN MAN [*while he takes out a handkerchief which he ties over the* GREEN MAN's *eyes*]. Remember the ideals we are fighting for.

HIDDEN VIOLET MAN [*doing the same with the* VIOLET MAN]. And in order that you always have them in mind . . .

HIDDEN GREEN MAN. . . . well carved in your mind . . .

HIDDEN VIOLET MAN. . . . screwed in . . .

HIDDEN GREEN MAN. . . . deeply engraved . . .

HIDDEN VIOLET MAN. . . . in your brain . . .

HIDDEN GREEN MAN. . . . of a good soldier . . .

HIDDEN VIOLET MAN. . . . repeat after me . . .

HIDDEN GREEN MAN. . . . the keypoints . . .

HIDDEN VIOLET MAN. . . . the ideals . . .

HIDDEN GREEN MAN. . . . that impel you . . .

HIDDEN VIOLET MAN. . . . that push you . . .

HIDDEN GREEN MAN. . . . to struggle . . .

HIDDEN VIOLET MAN. . . . until death . . .

HIDDEN GREEN MAN & HIDDEN VIOLET MAN. Are you ready?

GREEN MAN & VIOLET MAN. Ready!

HIDDEN GREEN MAN. Modacracy!

GREEN MAN. Modacracy!

HIDDEN VIOLET MAN. Submission!

VIOLET MAN. Submission!

HIDDEN GREEN MAN. Modacracy!

GREEN MAN. Modacracy!

HIDDEN VIOLET MAN. Submission!

VIOLET MAN. Submission!

HIDDEN GREEN MAN. Boom boom!

GREEN MAN. Boom boom!

HIDDEN VIOLET MAN. Boom boom!

VIOLET MAN. Boom boom! [*And, from this moment on, the four, in a progressively frenetic tone, continue to repeat the refrain.*]

EVERYONE [*at the same time*]. Modacracy! Submission! Modacracy!
Submission! Boom boom! Boom boom! Modacracy! Submis-
sion!, etc. . . . . [*Until the noise of a volley of machine-gun fire dis-
perses them.*]

HIDDEN VIOLET MAN. The enemy! To battle, soldier! [*He gives a rifle to
the* VIOLET MAN *and pushes him forward. He hides behind his
tree.*]

HIDDEN GREEN MAN. Start fighting! Let's defend our country! [*He gives
a rifle to the* GREEN MAN *and hides behind his tree after pushing him
to center stage. In this way the two men have come face to face,
each one with a rifle in his hand, but with their eyes bandaged.
They fire their rifles, blindly, of course. They change position, then
fire again. Thus several times, until, at last, they fall to the ground,
hit.*]

VIOLET MAN [*as he falls wounded*]. Submission!

GREEN MAN [*as he falls wounded*]. Modacracy!

VIOLET MAN. Liberty! Revolution! Agrarian Reform! [*He dies.*]

GREEN MAN. Agrarian Reform! Revolution! Liberty! [*He dies. An
absolute silence follows. Then, from behind his tree, the* HIDDEN
GREEN MAN *sticks out his hand, holding a little white flag. Immediately, the same operation from behind the other tree. While the
two little flags are being waved, the* GREEN WOMAN *and* VIOLET
WOMAN *appear, wearing black veils which reach the ground, each
from one side. They kneel before their dead men, with a sad and
static expression. A voice is heard through the loud speaker.*]

VOICE. Due to the almost total elmination of fighting forces, the general
headquarters of the violet troops and the general headquarters of
the green troops have decided to draw up a cease-fire, and to leave
for the moment their struggle for their ideals. Parallel 777 has
been established as the frontier between the two zones. [*As these
words are being spoken, the* HIDDEN VIOLET MAN *and the* HIDDEN
GREEN MAN *have each nailed into center-stage a sign on which can
be read:* "PARALLEL 777. Greens." *And:* "PARALLEL 777. Violets."] It is calculated that the number of casualties among the two
forces is in excess of three million, with civilian personnel included.
You have just heard the latest international news. [*The* HIDDEN GREEN
MAN *has gone to the sign that he nailed up at the beginning; the*
HIDDEN VIOLET MAN *to his. These signs designated the two war
zones. The hidden men turn them around and there appears clearly,
on each one of them, the following word: PEACE. The two
women, with their long veils, continue kneeling before the bodies.*]

[*Curtain*]

The
Quest for
Social Order

CHAPTER THREE

When the time comes, as it must, for the hero to face his antagonist, that antagonist will be one of four basic types. There is the personal enemy whose quarrel is with the hero himself and him alone. A second is the enemy without, who represents a community which is seen as a rival to the hero's community. A third is the enemy within, who threatens the well-being of the community of which both he and the hero are members. And finally, there is malign nature, which, in the form of an animal or of a natural force like a flood, threatens to destroy the hero or his community.

The first aim of any community, be it family, tribe, city, or nation, is self-preservation. Its second aim, of almost equal importance, is the maintaining of social order. In fact, both aims go together. If a community is unable to foster a high degree of stability and harmony in its daily life, it fails to justify its existence, and in fact its very existence may be threatened. For a community must not merely preserve itself and its members; it must, as much as possible, minimize the frictions among those members and maximize their contentment.

Normally the community carries out its aims "bureaucratically," through the routine services of its elected or appointed officials and their agencies. But when pressures from within cause those services to break down, the community has to call upon its individual heroes. Almost inevitably then the traditional or ideal hero is something of an establishment figure, for serving the communty in most cases means serving its leaders or officials and sharing their aims and ideals. Those aims and ideals may not always, of course, be identical to the aims and ideals of the general populace, but internal conflicts tend to be minimized when a community is threatened by an external enemy. Danger from without normally serves to strengthen the unity of those within. The familiar cry is "It's them or us," the "them" being the outsiders, the menacing strangers or foreigners.

From that first occasion on which some primitive man drove a wanderer from another tribe away from the communal circle of his campfire, to yesterday, when some nation or other responded to a real or imagined threat to its security with modern weaponry, mankind has usually operated upon the premise that human beings who are known, however unsatisfactory they might be, are preferable to human beings who are not known. Thus, throughout history, the community's instructions to its heroes usually have been variations upon the themes of "The only good stranger is a dead stranger" or "Shoot first, ask questions later." The more primitive heroes—the tribal champions, professional soldiers, or gunfighters—generally adhere to such policies because they identify closely with their communities. More complex heroes are capable of having doubts about those oversimplifications like "Remember the Maine!" or "America! Love it or leave it!" which emotionally bind the members of the community together. Such heroes tend to be philosophically as well as psychologically somewhat distanced from their communities.

Unless he is some type of policeman figure—a sheriff, detective, or espionage agent—the hero is less often called upon to combat an enemy within. When he is, his mission becomes more complicated, for the enemy is no longer a readily depersonalized foreigner. He is now one of the hero's own tribe, perhaps even a friend or relation. Though both the general populace and the establishment may cry for blood, may indeed be more vehement and violent toward an aberrant member of their community than toward a foreigner, the more complex hero often will have a deep sense of conflicting emotions and clashing loyalties.

It is such complications in questions of value and such intensifications of emotional stress that make civil war so profoundly disturbing. Such a war's transformation of friend into foe, of familiar into alien, takes its toll in psychic shock. Furthermore, as United States history amply demonstrates, those wounds in the body politic which have been inflicted by civil war are the ones that take the longest to heal. Even when social disorder does not flare into out-and-out warfare, its effects upon the community are far-reaching, as the present state of black-white relationships in the United States bears witness.

Social order can, of course, be imposed simply by force. Police states appear to be "quieter," more orderly, than democratic states, at least on the surface. If law and order are the only goals of the hero and the state, they can be achieved by police power. But if social order with justice and freedom is the goal, mere might is insufficient. If a community is not only to be preserved, but preserved to serve all of its members equally and with the least infringement of their personal freedoms, moral force must also be applied. To achieve social order with justice and freedom the hero must not only be the strongest, but the most fair-minded. He must serve not merely his community, right or wrong, but that which transcends his community, moral law itself.

SHORT STORIES

The Hero and Society

Since civil war and its aftermath are so profound in their effects on mankind, it is not surprising that they loom large in the imaginations of writers. Although the story by an American writer which follows is set in the twentieth century, the United States Civil War and the struggle for human rights which proceeded from it serve as an implied backdrop to the story. The second story, by an Irish writer, concerns the early years of a civil war whose consequences are to this day disrupting the social order of Northern Ireland and the Irish Free State.

That history makes heroes and heroes make history are two views which need not be mutually exclusive. The main character of Richard Wright's story "Fire and Cloud," the Reverend Daniel Taylor, is a case in point. Reverend Taylor eventually makes history, even though it is only local history, just as the once unknown black pastor Dr. Martin Luther King, Jr., made history during the Alabama bus boycott. And whether he is fully aware of it or not, Reverend Taylor is also acted upon by history, the history of black-white relations in a small Southern town and, in a sense, the whole history of the black man in America. A long chain of events places Reverend Taylor in a position where he has the opportunity for heroic action. The choice he finally makes, however, is determined by more than historical necessity. It proceeds out of his manhood, his sense of morality, and his religious faith. In this story, Reverend Taylor is a hero to most of the black community, while the white community might consider him a villain or an enemy within, since he is upsetting the established social order of the dominant white society. In his attempt to create a new social order that is just and moral for all he must temporarily disturb the status quo. Ultimately his action preserves the unity of the black community and enhances the integrity of the whole town. Realistically set in the Great Depression of the 1930's, Wright's story is at once dramatically powerful and prophetic. Reading its final paragraph, one cannot help but be struck by the fact that it was written, not in 1968, but in 1938.

Sean O'Faolain's story "The Patriot" takes place after the Anglo-Irish War (1916–1921), a war which officially concluded with the signing of a treaty dividing Ireland into independent Eire (the Irish Free State) and Ulster (the Northern Counties), politically a part of Great Britain. This division was unacceptable to those Irishmen who envisioned their country as a completely unified and fully independent republic. Mr. Bradley, the "patriot" of this story, is such a one, as is his young admirer, Bernard. Both have been associated with the organization most active in the cause of Irish unity, the Irish Republican Army (IRA)—Bernard, in his youth, as an irregular or guerilla, Mr. Bradley as a propagandist. Mr. Bradley attempts to inspire young men like Bernard with his visions of heroism, honor, glory, and victory for the Republican cause, even though the sporadic civil war which the IRA is fighting has not been going well and is eroding the morale of the country. Bernard wishes to become a hero and holds out hope of victory, but two events—one military, the other, personal—dim his patriotic vision. For Mr. Bradley the vision remains intact in spite of everything. Each character exhibits a different kind of heroism and illustrates a different way of mediating between the order of one's private life and the social order. The question the reader is left with is to what extent is the social order affected by each hero's visions of victory, glory, and happiness.

Fire and Cloud

Richard Wright

"*A naughts a naught . . .*"

As he walked his eyes looked vacantly on the dusty road, and the words rolled without movement from his lips, each syllable floating softly up out of the depth of his body.

"*N fives a figger . . .*"

He pulled out his pocket handkerchief and mopped his brow without lessening his pace.

"*All fer the white man . . .*"

He reached the top of the slope and paused, head down.

"*N none fer the nigger. . . .*"

His shoulders shook in half laugh and half shudder. He finished mopping his brow and spat, as though to rid himself of some bitter thing. He thought, Thas the way its awways been! Wistfully he turned and looked back at the dim buildings of the town lying sprawled mistily on the crest of a far hill. Seems like the white folks jus erbout own this whole worl! Looks like they done conquered *everything*. We black folks is jus los in one big white fog. . . . With his eyes still on the hazy buildings, he flexed his lips slowly and spoke under his breath:

"They could do something! They could do *something*, awright! Mabbe ef five er six thousan of us marched downtown we could *scare* em into doin something! Lawd knows, mabbe them Reds *is* right!"

He walked again and tucked his handkerchief back into his pocket. He could feel the heat of the evening over all his body, not strongly, but closely and persistently, as though he were holding his face over a tub of steaming suds. Far below him, at the bottom of the valley, lay a cluster of bleak huts with windowpanes red-lit from dying sunlight. Those huts were as familiar to his eyes as a nest is to the eyes of a bird, for he had lived among them all his life. He knew by sight or sound every black man, woman and child living within those huddled walls. For a moment an array of soft black faces hovered before his eyes. N whut kin Ah tell em? Whut kin Ah say t em? He stopped, looked at the ground and sighed. And then he saw himself as he had stood but a few minutes ago, facing the white woman who sat behind the brown, gleaming desk: her arms had been round, slender, snow-white, like cold marble; her hair had been the color of flowing gold and had glinted in the sunlight; her eyes had been wide and gray behind icily white spectacles. It seemed he could hear her saying in her dry, metallic voice: I'm sorry, Taylor. You'll just have to do the best you can. Explain it to them, make them understand that we cant do anything. Everybodys hongry, and after all, its no harder on your people than it is on ours. Tell them theyll just have to wait. . . .

He wagged his head and his lips broke in a slow sick smile. Whut she know erbout bein hongry? Whut she know erbout it? He walked again, thinking, Here Ah is a man called by Gawd t preach n whut kin Ah do? Hongry folks lookin t me fer hep n whut kin Ah do? Ah done tried everything n cant do *nuthin!* Shucks, mabbe Hadley n Greens right? They *might* be right. Gawd knows, they *might* be right.

He lifted his head and saw the wide fields plunging before him, down the hillside. The grass was dark and green. All this, he thought. All *this* n folks hongry! Good Gawd, whuts *wrong!* He saw the road running before him, winding, vanishing, the soft yellow dust filled with the ruts of wagon wheels and tiny threads of auto tires. He threw back his head and spoke out loud:

"The good Lawds gonna clean up this ol worl someday! Hes gonna make a new Heaven n a new Earth! N Hes gonna do it in a eye-twinkle change! Hes gotta do it! Things cant go on like this ferever! Gawd knows they cant!" He pulled off his coat and slung it under his left arm. "Waal, there ain nothin t do but go back n tell em. . . . Tell em the white folks wont let em eat. . . ."

The road curved, descending among the green fields that tumbled to a red sky. This was the land on which the Great God Almighty had first let him see the light of His blessed day. This was the land on which he had first taken unto himself a wife, leaving his mother and father to cleave to her. And it was on the green slopes of these struggling hills that his first-born son, Jimmy, had romped and played, growing to a strong, upright manhood. He wagged his head, musing, Lawd, them wuz the good ol days. . . . There had been plenty to eat; the blessings of God had been overflowing. He had toiled from sunup to sundown, and in the cool of the evenings his wife, May, had taught him to read and write. Then God had spoken to him, a quiet, deep voice coming out of the black night; God had called him to preach His word, to spread it to the four corners of the earth, to save His black people. And he had obeyed God and had built a church on a rock which the very gates of Hell could not prevail against. Yes, he had been like Moses, leading his people out of the wilderness into the Promised Land. He sighed, walking and taking his coat from his left arm and tucking it under his right. Yes, things had been clear-cut then. In those days there had stretched before his eyes a straight and narrow path and he had walked in it, with the help of a Gracious God. On Sundays he had preached God's Word, and on Mondays and Tuesdays and Wednesdays and Thursdays and Fridays and Saturdays he had taken old Bess, his mule, and his plow and had broke God's ground. For a moment while walking through the dust and remembering his hopes of those early years he seemed to feel again the plow handles trembling in his calloused hands and hear the earth cracking and breaking open, black, rich and damp; it seemed he could see old Bess straining forward with the plow, swishing her tail and tossing her head and snorting now and then. Yes, there had been something in those good old days when he had walked behind his plow, between the broad green earth and a blue sweep of sunlit sky; there had been in it all a surge of will, clean, full, joyful; the earth was his and he was the earth's; they were one; and it was that joy and will and oneness in him that God had spoken to when He had called him to preach His Word, to save His black people, to lead them, to guide them, to be a shepherd to His flock. But now the whole thing was giving way, crumbling in his hands, right before his eyes. And every time he tried to think of some way out, of some way to stop it, he saw wide gray eyes behind icily white spectacles. He mopped his brow again. Mabbe Hadley n Greens right. . . . Lawd, Ah don know what t do! Ef Ah fight fer things the white folk say Ahma bad nigger stirrin up trouble. N ef Ah don do nothin, we starve. . . . But somethings *gotta* be done! Mabbe ef we hada demonstration like Hadley n Green said, we could *scare* them white folks into doin something. . . .

He looked at the fields again, half wistfully, half curiously. Lawd, we could make them ol fiels bloom ergin. We could make em feed us. Thas whut Gawd put em there fer. Plows could break and hoes could chop and hands could pick and arms could carry. . . . On and on that could happen and people could eat and feel as he had felt with the plow handles trembling in his hands, following old Bess, hearing the earth cracking and breaking because he wanted it to crack and break; because he willed it, because the earth was his. And they could sing as he had sung when he and May were first married; sing about picking cotton, fishing, hunting, about sun and rain. They could . . . But whuts the usa thinkin erbout stuff like this? Its all gone now. . . . And he had to go and tell his congregation, the folks the Great God Almighty had called him to lead to the Promised Land—he had to tell them that relief would give them no food.

That morning he had sent a committee of ten men and a woman from his congregation to see the mayor. Wondah how they come out? The mayor tol em something, sho! So fer hes been pretty wid me even ef he is a white man. As his feet sank softly into the dust he saw Mayor Bolton; he saw the red chin that always had a short, black stubble of beard; he saw the cigar glowing red in front of a pink, fat face. But he needs something t scare im now, he thought. Hes been running over us too long. . . .

He reached the bottom of the slope, turned into a cinder path and approached the huts. N Lawd, when Ah do try t do somethin mah own folks wont stan by me, wont stick wid me. Theres ol Deacon Smith a-schemin n a-plottin, jus a-watchin me like a hawk, jus a-waitin fer me t take mah eyes off the groun sos he kin trip me up, sos he kin run t the white folks n tell em Ahm doin somethin wrong! A black snake in the grass! A black Judas! Thas all he is! Lawd, the Devils sho busy in this worl. . . .

He was walking among the crowded huts now.

hello, reveren

"How yuh tonight, sonny!" Let ol Deacon Smith tell it, no mattah whut Ah do Ahm wrong. . . .

good evenin, reveren

"Good evenin, Sistah!" Hes been a-tryin t cheat me outta mah church ever since hes been erroun here. . . .

how yuh tonight, reveren taylor?

"Jus fine. N how yuh tonight, Brother?" Hes awways a-whisperin berhin mah back, a-tryin t take mah congregation erway from me. . . . N when he ain doin tha hes a-tryin his bes t give me wrong advice, jus like the Devil a-tryin t tempt Jesus. But Ahm gonna march on wida hepa Gawd. . . . Yeah, Ah might preach a sermon erbout tha nex Sunday.

As he turned into the street leading to his home and church, he saw a tall brown-skinned boy hurrying toward him. Here comes Jimmy! Ah bet hes lookin fer me. . . . Lawd, Ah hope ain nothin wrong. . . .

II

"Pa!" said Jimmy breathlessly when he was some twenty feet away.
Taylor stopped.
"Whuts the mattah, son?"
Jimmy came close.
"The mayors at home, waitin t see yuh," he whispered.
"The *mayor?*"
"Yeah, n two mo white men. One of em is the chiefa police."
"They there *now?*"
"Yeah; in the parlor."
"How long they been there?"
"Bout two-three minutes, Ah reckon. N lissen, Pa . . . Sam wuz by jus now. He say the white folks is ridin up n down the streets in their cars warnin all the black folks t stay off the streets cause theres gonna be trouble. . . ."
"Sam say tha?"
"Thas whut he tol me. N lissen, Pa . . . Ahma git Sam n Pete n Bob n Jack n some mo boys together sos ef anything happens . . ."
Taylor gripped Jimmy's shoulders.
"Naw, son! Yuh fixin t git us *all* inter trouble now! Yuh cant do nothin like tha! Yuh gotta be careful! Ef them white folks jus *thought* we wuz doin something like tha theyd crack down on us! Wed hava riot!"
"But we cant let em ride erroun n talk big n we do nothin!"
"Lissen here, son! Yuh do whut Ah tell you t do!" He shook Jimmy's shoulders and his voice was husky. "Yuh go tell them boys t do *nuthin* till Ah see em, yuh hear me? Yuh young fools fixin t git us *all* murdered!"
"We just as waal git killed fightin as t git killed doin nothin," said Jimmy sullenly.
"Yuh go n do whut Ah tol yuh, *hear* me? Ah gotta go n see tha mayor. . . ."
"Hes here t see yuh erbout tha demonstration," said Jimmy.
"How yuh know?"
"Cause thas whut everybodys sayin."
"Who yuh hear say tha?"
"Deacon Smiths spreadin the word."
Taylor winced as though struck by a blow and looked at the dust.
"Hes tellin alla deacons n the church membahs tha the mayors here t stop yuh," said Jimmy. "Hes tellin em yuhs mixed up wid the Reds."
"Deacon Smith there now *too?*"

"Yeah; hes in the basement wida other deacons.   Theys waitin t see yuh."

"How long they been there?"

"Bout hafa hour.   N Hadley n Greens in the Bible Room, waitin t talk wid yuh too. . . ."

Fear gripped Taylor and he stammered:

"Ddddid the mmmmayor sssee em?"

"Naw, ain nobody seen em yit.   Ah brought em in thu the back do and tol em t wait fer yuh.   Ahm mighty scared wid them Reds waitin fer yuh in the Bible Room and tha chiefa police waitin fer yuh in the parlor.   Ef ol Deacon Smith knowed tha he sho would make a lotta trouble. . . ."

"Where yo ma?"

"She upstairs, sewin."

"She know whuts happenin?"

"Naw, Pa."

Taylor stood still, barely breathing.

"Whut yuh gonna do, Pa?"   asked Jimmy.

"Yuh go n tell them boys not t do nothin wrong, son.   Go on n tell em now!   Ah got too much on mah hans now widout yuh boys stirrin up mo trouble!"

"Yessuh."

"Yuh bettah go n do it *now!*"

"Yessuh."

He watched Jimmy hurry down the street.   Lawd, Ah hope tha boy don go n git inter trouble. . . .

"Yuh do whut Ah tol you, Jimmy!"   he yelled.

"Yessuh!"   Jimmy hollered back.

He saw Jimmy turn a dusty corner and go out of sight.   Hadley n Greens there in the Bible Room n the chiefa police is waitin in the parlor! Ah cant let them white folks see them Reds!   N ef Deacon Smith tells on me theyll lynch me. . . .   Ah gotta git em out of tha church widout em seein each other. . . .   Good Gawd, whut a mess!

III

No sooner had he opened the door of his church than he heard a crescendo of voices.   They back awready!   Tha committees back!   Aw, Ah bet the mayor followed em here. . . .   He walked down the hall, turned into the church's waiting room and saw a roomful of black faces.

"Reveren Taylor!   The mayor run us out!"

"He put the police on us!"

The black brothers and sisters ran to Taylor and surrounded him.

"The mayor tol us t git out n don come back no mo!"

A thin black woman swung onto Taylor's arm, crying:

"Whut Ahm gonna do? Ah ain gotta mouthful bread at home!"

"Sistahs n Brothers, jusa minute," said Taylor. "Firs, tell me whut the mayor said. . . ."

"He say he cant do *nuthin!* N say fer us not t come back t his office no *mo!* N say ef we do hes gonna put us in jail!"

"In *jail?*" asked Taylor.

"Thas whut he said."

"N he tol us not t march, Reveren. He said ef we demonstrated hed put us *all* in jail."

"Who tol em yuh wuz gonna march?" asked Taylor.

"Ah bet it wuz the ol Deacon Smith," said Sister Harris.

"The Bible says testify whut yuh see n speak whut yuh know," said Sister Davis to Sister Harris.

"Ah knows whut Ahm talkin erbout!" blazed Sister Harris.

"Sistahs n Brothers, les don start no fuss," said Taylor, sighing and dropping his shoulders.

"Whut they tell yuh at the relief station, Reveren Taylor?" asked Sister James.

"They say they cant do nothin," said Taylor.

The thin black woman came and knelt at Taylor's feet, her face in her hands.

"Reveren Taylor, it ain fer me Ahm astin! Its fer ma chillun! Theys hongry! It ain for me, its fer them! Gawd, have mercy, theys hongry. . . ."

Taylor stepped back, ran his hand into his pocket and pulled out a palmful of loose coins.

"Here, Sistahs n Brothers, split this up between yuh all. Its ever cent Ah got in this worl, so hep me Gawd!"

He laid the coins on a small table. Brother Booker divided them as far as they would go. Then they swarmed around him again.

"Reveren, whut we gonna do?"

"Cant we make the white folks do something fer us?"

"Ahm tireda bein hongry!"

"Reveren, mah babys sick n Ah cant git her no milk!"

"Reveren, whut kin Ah tell mah wife?"

"Lawd knows, Ahm just erbout sick of this!"

"Whut kin we do, Reveren?"

Taylor looked at them and was ashamed of his own helplessness and theirs.

"Sistahs n Brothers, les call on the great Gawd who made us n put us in this worl. . . ."

He clasped his hands in front of him, closed his eyes and bowed his head. The room grew still and silent.

"Lawd Gawd Awmighty, Yuh made the sun n the moon n the stars n the earth n the seas n mankind n the beasts of the fiels!"

yes jesus

"Yuh made em all, Lawd, n Yuh tol em whut t do!"

yuh made em lawd

"Yuhs strong n powerful n Yo will rules this worl!"

yuh rules it lawd

"Yuh brought the chillun of Israel outta the lan of Egypt!"

yuh sho did

"Yuh made the dry bones rise up outta the valley of death n live!"

yuh made em live lawd

"Yuh saved the Hebrew chillun in the fiery furnace!"

yes jesus

"Yuh stopped the storm n yuh made the sun stan still!"

yuh stopped it lawd

"Yuh knocked down the walls of Jericho n Yuh kept Jona in the belly of the whale!"

yuh kept im lawd

"Yuh let Yo son Jesus walk on watah n Yuh brought Im back from the dead!"

have mercy jesus

"Yuh made the lame walk!"

yuh did it lawd

"Yuh made the blin see!"

hep us now lawd

"Yuh made the deaf hear!"

glory t the mos high

"Lawd, Yuhs a rock in the tima trouble n Yuhs a shelter in the tima storm!"

he is he is

"Lawd, Yuh said Yuhd strike down the wicked men who plagued yo chillun!"

glory t gawd

"Yuh said Yuhd destroy this ol worl n create a new Heaven n a new Earth!"

wes waitin on yuh jesus

"Lawd, Yuh said call on Yo name n Yuhd answer!"

yuh said it lawd n now wes callin

"Yuh made us n put the breatha life in us!"

yuh did lawd

"Now look down on us, Lawd!   Speak t our hearts n let us know whut Yo will is!   Speak t us like Yuh spoke t Jacob!"

speak lawd n our souls will be clay in yo hans

"Lawd, ack in us n well obey!   Try us, lawd, try us n watch us move t Yo will!   Wes helpless at Yo feet a-waitin fer Yo sign!"

send it lawd

"The white folks say we cant raise nothin on Yo earth!   They done put the lans of the worl in their pockets!   They done fenced em off n nailed em down!   Theys a-tryin t take Yo place, Lawd!"

speak t em lawd

"Yuh put us in this worl n said we could live in it!   Yuh said this worl wuz Yo own!   Now show us the sign like Yuh showed Saul!   Show us the sign n well ack!   We ast this in the name of Yo son Jesus who died tha we might live!   Amen!"

amen amen

Taylor stopped and opened his eyes.   The room was quiet; he could hear the clock ticking softly above his head, and from the rear came the sound of children playing back of the church.   The sisters and brothers rose from their knees and began talking in subdued tones.

"But, Reveren, whut kin we *do?*"

"The issues wid Gawd now, Sistahs n Brothers."

"Is we gonna march?"

"Is yuh goin wid us t the mayor?"

"Have faith, Sistahs n Brothers.   Gawd takes care of His own."

"But Ahm hongry, Reveren. . . ."

"Now, Sistahs n Brothers, Ah got t go.   Ah got business t tend t. . . ."

He pushed ahead of the black hands that clung to his sleeve.

"Reveren Taylor. . . ."

The thin black woman wailed, kneeling:

"Please, Reveren, cant yuh do *somethin*. . . ."

He pushed through the door, closed it and stood for a moment with his eyes shut and with his fingers slowly loosening on the knob, his ears filled with the sound of wailing voices.

IV

How come all this gotta happen at *once?*   Folks a-beggin fer bread n the mayor here t see me n them Reds a-waitin in the Bible Room. . . .   Ef Deacon Smith knowed tha hed ruin me sho!   Ah cant let the mayor see them Reds. . . .   Naw, Gawd!   He looked at a door at the far end of the room, then hurried to it and opened it softly.

"May!"   he called in a hoarse whisper.

"Hunh?"

"C mere, quick!"

"Whutcha wan, Dan?"

"C mon in the *room*, May!"

She edged through the half-opened door and stood in front of him, wide-eyed.

"Whutcha wan, Dan?"

"Now, lissen. . . ."

"Ain nothin wrong, is it, Dan? Ain nothin happened, is it?"

He grabbed her arm.

"Naw, n don git scared!"

"Ah ain scared!"

"Yuh cant do whut Ah wan yuh t do ef yuhs scared!"

"Ah *ain* scared, Dan!"

"Lissen. . . ."

"Yeah?"

"The mayors here, in the parlor. N the chiefa police. . . ."

She stood stock still and seemed not to breathe.

"The *mayor?*"

"Yeah. . . ."

"*Ain* nothin wrong, is it, Dan?"

"There wont be ef yuh lissen n try t do right."

"Be careful, Dan!"

"Yeah," he said, his voice low and husky. "Go in and tell them white folks Ahm sick, hear?"

She stepped back from him and shook her head.

"Gawd *ain* wid yuh when yuh lie, Dan!"

"We *gotta* lie t white folks! Theys on our necks! They *make* us lie t them! Whut kin we do but lie?"

"*Dan!*"

"Lissen t whut Ahm tellin yuh, May! Tell the mayor Ahm gittin outta bed t see im. Tell im Ahm dressin, see? Tell im t wait a few minutes."

"Yeah?"

"Then go t the basement n tell Deacon Smith Ahm wid the mayor. Tell im n the other deacons t wait."

"Now?"

"Yeah; but Ah ain thu yit. Yuh know Hadley n Green?"

"Them *Reds?*"

"Yeah. . . ."

"Dan!" said May, her lungs suspiring in one gasp of amazed helplessness.

"May, fer Chrissakes!"

She began to cry.

"Don do nothin wrong, Dan, please! Don fergit Jimmy! Hes jus a young boy n hes gotta grow up in this town wid these white folks. Don go n do nothin n fix it so he wont hava chance. . . . Me n yuh don mattah, but thinka him, Dan, please. . . ."

Taylor swallowed and looked hard at her.

"May, yuh do whut *Ah* tell yuh t do! Ah know whut Ahm doin. Hadley n Greens downstairs, in the Bible Room. Tell em so nobody kin hear yuh, hear?—tell em aftah yuh done tol the others—tell em t come in here. Let em in thu *yo* room. . . ."

"Naw!"

She tried to get through the door. He ran to her and caught her hand again.

"Yuh do whut Ah tell yuh, May!"

"Ah ain gonna have them Reds in *here* wid the mayor n chiefa police out *there!* Ah *ain!*"

"Go on n do whut Ah tell yuh, May!"

"Dan!"

"Go *erhead*, May!"

He pushed her. She went through the door, slowly, looking back at him. When the door was closed he rammed his hands deep into his pants pockets, turned to the open window and looked out into the street. It was profoundly quiet, save for the silvery sound of children's voices back of the church. The air was soft, warm and full of the scent of magnolias and violets. Windowpanes across the street were blood-red from dying sunlight. A car sped past, lifting a great cloud of yellow-brown dust. He went to the center of the room and stood over a table littered with papers. He cocked his head, listening. He heard a door slam; footsteps echoed and ceased. A big eight-day clock above his head boomed six times; he looked and his eyes strayed up and rested on a gleaming brass cross. Gawd, hep me now! Jus hep me t go thu wid this! Again he heard a door slam. Lawd, Ah hope May do right now. . . . N Ah hope Jimmy don go n ack a fool. . . . He crossed the floor on tiptoe, opened the door and peeped into May's room. It was empty. A slender prism of dust-filled sunlight cut across the air. He closed the door, turned, pulled off his coat and threw it across the table. Then he loosened his collar and tie. He went to the window again and leaned with his back against the ledge, watching the door of May's room. He heard a hoarse voice rise and die. Footsteps again sounded and ceased. He frowned, listening. How come its takin May so long? He started when a timid knock came. He hurried to the door and cracked it.

v

"Hello, Reverend Taylor!" said Hadley, a white man.

"How yuh, Brother Hadley?"

"N how yuh, Reveren?" asked Green, a black man.

194

"Ahm fine, Brother Green.   C mon in, yuh all."

Hadley and Green edged through the door.

"Say, whuts alla mystery?"   asked Green.

"Ssssh!   Don talk so loud," cautioned Taylor.   "The mayor n the chiefa police is out there."

The Negro and the white man stood stone still.

"Do they know wes here?"   asked Green.

"Naw, n don git scared.   They done come t see me erbout tha demonstration. . . ."

Hadley and Green looked at each other.

"Pull down tha shade," whispered Green, pointing a shaking black finger.

Quickly Hadley moved to one side, out of range of the window.   His cheeks flushed pink.   Taylor lowered the shade and faced them in the semidarkness.   The eyes of the white man and the black man were upon him steadily.

"Waal?"   said Green.

"Ah spose yuh know whuts up," said Taylor.

"Theyre here to scare you," said Hadley.

"Ahm trustin Gawd," sighed Taylor.

"Whut yuh gonna tell em?"   asked Green.

"Thas whut Ah wanna see yuh all erbout," said Taylor.

"O.K.   Whut kin we do?"   asked Green.

Taylor looked around and motioned toward two chairs.

"Set down, Brothers."

"Naw, this is awright," said Green, still standing.

"Come on," said Hadley.   "What's on your mind?"

Taylor folded his arms and half sat and half leaned on the edge of the table.

"Yuh all think wes gonna have many folks out in the mawnin fer the demonstration?"

"Whut yuh mean?"   asked Green.

"When Ahm talkin wid the mayor and chiefa police Ah wanna know how many folks Ahm talkin fer.   There ain no use in us havin a demonstration ef ain but a few of us is gonna be out there.   The police will try t kill us then. . . ."

"How many folks we can get out tomorrow depends a great deal on you, Reverend," said Hadley.

"Hows tha?"   asked Taylor.

"If you had let us use your name on those handbills, we could say five thousand easily. . . ."

Taylor turned sharply to Hadley.

"Lissen, Brother, Ah done tol yuh Ah cant do tha! N there ain no use in us talkin erbout it no mo! Ah done tol yuh Ah cant let them white folks know Ahm callin folks t demonstrate. After all, Ahma preacher. . . ."

"Its yo duty, Reveren," said Green. "We owes it our black folks."

"Ahm doin mah duty as Gawd lets me see it," said Taylor.

"All right, Reverend," said Hadley. "Heres what happened: Weve covered the city with fifteen thousand leaflets. Weve contacted every organization we could think of, black and white. In other words, weve done all *we* could. The rest depends on the leaders of each group. If we had their active endorsement, none of us would have to worry about a crowd tomorrow. And if we had a crowd we would not have to worry about the police. If they see the whole town turning out, theyll not start any trouble. Now, youre known. White and black in this town respect you. If you let us send out another leaflet with your name on it, calling for . . ."

Taylor turned from them and drew his hand nervously across his face. Hadley and Green were silent, watching him. Taylor went to the window and pulled back the curtain slightly and peeped out. Without turning he said softly:

"Ah done tol yuh all Ah ain scareda lettin yuh use mah name."

"We don mean *tha*," said Green hastily.

"Ef it wuz jus me who wuz takin the chance," said Taylor, "Ah wouldn't care none. But Gawd knows it ain right fer me to send them po folks out inter the streets in fronta police. Gawd knows, Ah cant do tha!"

"Honest, Reveren," said Green touching Taylor's arm, "Ah don understan. Yuh done been thu harder things than this befo."

"N Ahll go thu wid em ergin," said Taylor proudly.

"All right!" said Hadley. "You can say the word that can make this thing a success. If you dont and we have no crowd, then youre to blame. . . ."

Taylor's eyes narrowed and when he spoke there was a note of anger in his voice.

"Gawd hep yuh ef yuhs a-tryin t say yuh gonna blame me ef things don go right!"

"Naw, Reveren!" said Green, coming hurriedly forward and spreading his black palms softly upon the air. "Don feel tha way! Wes all jus in a jam. We got t do either two things: Call off this demonstration and let the folks stay hongry, er git as many as we kin together n go downtown in the mawnin. Ef we git five thousan down there the police wont bother us. Ef yuh let us send out yo name tellin the black folks . . ."

"Naw, Brother!" said Taylor emphatically.

"Then the demonstrations going to be smashed," said Hadley. "*You* can stop it! You have the responsibility and the blame!"

Taylor sighed.

"Gawd knows Ah ain t blame. Ahm doin whut mah heart tells me t do. . . ."

"Then whats keeping you from working with us?" asked Hadley. "Im a white man and Im here willing to fight for your peoples rights!"

"Ahm wid yuh, Brother!" said Taylor in a voice which carried a deep note of pleading. "Ahm wid yuh no matter whut yuh *think!* But yuh *cant* use mah name! Ef them white folks knowed Ah wuz callin mah folks in the streets t demonstrate, they wouldnt never gimme a chance t git something fer mah folks ergin. . . ."

"Thats just it, Reverend," said Hadley. "Don't be afraid of their turning you down because youre fighting for your people. If they knew youd really fight, theyd dislike you; yes? But you can *make* them give something to *all* of your people, not just to *you.* Don't you see, Taylor, youre standing *between* your people and the white folks. You can make them give something to *all* of them. And the poor, hungry white folks will be with you."

"Ah can't lead mah folks t go ergin them white folks like tha," said Taylor. "Thas *war!*"

Hadley came close to Taylor.

"Reverend, cant you see thats just the way the white folks *want* you to feel? Are you leading your folks just because the white folks *say* you should, or are you leading them because you *want* to? Dont you believe in what youre doing? What kind of leaders are black people to have if the white folks pick them and tell them what to do?"

"Brothers, Ahma Christian, n whut yuhs astin fer is something tha makes blood!" thundered Taylor.

Hadley and Green looked at each other.

"Waal, whut yuh gonna tell the mayor?" asked Green.

Taylor stood in the center of the room with his hands in his pockets, looking down at his feet. His voice came low, as though he were talking to himself, trying to convince himself.

"Ahma tell em mah folks is hongry. Ahma tell em they wanna march. Ahma tell em ef they march Ahma march wid em. Ahma tell em they wan bread. . . ."

"Reverend," asked Hadley, "why do you feel that this is so different from all the other times youve gone straight to the white folks and *demanded* things for your people?"

"It is different!" said Taylor.

"You didnt say that when you saved Scott from that *mob!*"

"Tha wuz different, Brother Hadley."

"I dont see it."

Taylor's voice came low.

"Ah feels differently erbout it, Brothers."

"You saved Scotts life. All right, youre saving the lives of your con-gregation now. Scott was one man, but there are five hundred starving people in your church."

"We ain facin no mob now, Brother Hadley."

"Then what in Gods name are we facing, Reverend? If those police wholl be out there in the morning with their guns and clubs arent a *legal* mob, then what . . ."

"It more than a mob, Brother Hadley."

Hadley and Green shook their heads.

"Ah don understan yuh, Reveren," said Green.

"When Ah saved Scott from tha mob, Ah wuz going erginst *some* of the white folks. But this thing is going ergin em *all!* This is too much like war!"

"You mean youre going against the ones with *money* now!" said Hadley. "Over three thousand of the poor white folks will be with *us*. . . ."

"But, Brother Hadley, the white folks whos got moneys got *everthing!* This is jus like civil war!"

"Reverend," said Hadley, "cant you see that if they were not afraid they wouldn't be here asking to *talk* with you? Go in and talk with them, speak to them in the name of five thousand hungry people. Tell the mayor and the chief of police that if they dont give the relief back we will demonstrate."

"Ah cant do tha, Brothers. Ah cant let these white folks think Ahm leadin mah folks tha way. Ah tol yuh brothers when Ah ergreed t work wid you Ahd go as fer as Ah could. Waal, Ah done done tha. Now yuh here astin me t threaten this whole town n Ah ain gonna do that!" said Taylor.

"Yuh astin fer bread, Reveren," said Green.

"Its threatenin, Brothers," said Taylor. "N tha ain Gawds way!"

"So youll let your folks starve before youll stand up and talk to those white folks?" asked Hadley.

"Ahm ackin as Gawd gives me the light t see," said Taylor.

There was silence. Then Hadley laughed, noiselessly.

"Well," he said. "I didnt know you felt this way, Reverend. I thought we could count on you. You know the Party will stand behind you no matter what happens."

"Ahm sorry, Brother Hadley," said Taylor.

"When kin we see yuh t fin out whut the mayor n chiefa police say?" asked Green.

Taylor looked at his watch.

"Its a little aftah six now. Make it haf-pas six. Thall gimme time t see the Deacon Board."

Green sighed.

"O.K."

"O.K."

Taylor held the door for them. Then he stood in the center of the room and looked miles through the floor. Lawd, Ah hope Ahm doin right. N they think Ahm scared. . . . He flushed hot with shame and anger. He sat in a chair for a moment, then got right up. He drummed his fingers on the corner of the table. Shucks, Ah jus as waal see them white folks now n git it over wid. Ah knowed this wuz comin up! Ah knowed it! He went through May's room, walking slowly, softly, seeing in his mind the picture of the fat, pink face of Mayor Bolton and the lean, red face of Chief of Police Bruden. As he turned into the narrow hall that led to the parlor he heard children yelling in the playground. He went down a stairway, opened a door and walked through his hushed, dim-lit church. Pale rose light fell slantwise through stained windows and glinted on mahogany pews. He lifted his eyes and saw the figure of Christ on a huge snow-white cross. Gawd, hep me now! Lemme do the right thing! He followed a red carpet to a door that opened into the parlor. He paused and passed his tongue over his dry lips. He could feel his heart beating. Ahll let them do all the talkin. Ahll jus tell em mah folks is hongry. Thas all Ah kin do. Slowly he turned the knob, his lips half parted in dread.

VI

"Why, hello, Dan!"

"Good evenin, Mistah Mayor."

"Howve you been, Dan?"

"Fairly well, wid the hepa Gawd, suh."

Taylor shook hands with a tall, fat white man in a blue serge suit.

"Its been a long time since Ive seen you, Dan."

"Yessuh. It sho has, yo honah."

"Hows Jimmy?"

"Jus fine, suh."

"Thats a fine boy youve got, Dan."

"Ahm sho glad yuh think so, suh."

"If you raise that boy right he will be a leader of his people someday, Dan."

"Thas the one hope of mah life, suh," said Taylor with deep emotion.

"May was tellin me youre sick," said the mayor.

"Aw, it ain nothin, suh. Jusa summer col, suh."

"I didnt mean to bother you if youre sick, Dan."

"Thas awright, suh. Ahm feelin much bettah now, suh."

"Oh, youll pull through all right; itll take a lot more than a summer cold to kill old war horses like you and me, eh, Dan?"

The mayor laughed and winked.

"Ahm hopin Gawd spares me a few mo years, suh," said Taylor.

"But at least you look all right now," said the mayor. "Say, Dan, I want you to meet Chief Bruden. This is Dan, Chief, the boy I was telling you about."

"How yuh, Mistah Chief?" asked Taylor.

A black cigar burned red in Bruden's mouth. He shifted his thin body and growled:

"Hello, boy."

"And, Dan, this is Mr Lowe, head of our fine Industrial Squad."

"How yuh, suh?" asked Taylor.

Lowe nodded with half-closed eyes.

"Sit down, Dan," said the mayor.

"Yessuh."

Taylor sat on the edge of a chair and rested his palms lightly on his knees.

"Maybe our little visit is a surprise, hunh?" asked the mayor.

"Yessuh. It is. But Ahm glad to be of any hep Ah kin, suh."

"Good! I knew youd talk that way. Now, Dan, we want you to help us. Youre a responsible man in this community; thats why we are here."

"Ah tries t do mah duty as Gawd shows it t me, suh."

"Thats the spirit, Dan!" The mayor patted Taylor's knee. "Now Im going to be perfectly frank with you, Dan." The mayor peeled a wrapper from a black cigar. "Here, have one."

"Thank yuh, suh." Taylor put the cigar into his vest pocket. "Ahll smoke it aftah dinner, suh."

There was a silence during which the three white men looked at Taylor.

"Dan," began the mayor, "its not every nigger Id come to and talk this way. Its not every nigger Id trust as Im about to trust you." The mayor looked straight at Taylor. "Im doing this because Ive faith in you. Ive known you for twenty-five years, Dan. During that time I think Ive played pretty fair with you, havent I?"

Taylor swallowed.

"Ahll have t say yuh have, yo honah."

"Mister Lowe and the chief here had another plan," said the mayor.

"But I wouldnt hear of it. I told them Id work this thing *my* way. I thought *my* way would be much better. After all, Dan, you and I have worked together in the past and I dont see why we cant work together now. Ive backed you up in a lot of things, Dan. Ive backed you even when other white folks said you were wrong. But I believe in doing the right thing. After all, we are human beings, arent we?"

"Yessuh."

"What Ive done for you in the past Im willing to do again. You remember Scott, dont you?"

"Yessuh. Yuhs been a big hep t me n mah folks, suh."

"Well, Dan, my office is always open to you when you want to see me about any of your problems or the problems of your people," said the mayor.

"N Gawd knows Ah sho thanks yuh, suh!"

The mayor bit off the tip of his cigar and spat it into a brass spittoon.

"Im not going to beat about the bush, Dan."

The mayor paused again. There was silence. Taylor felt called upon to say something.

"Yessuh. Ah sho preciates tha, suh."

"You know these Goddam Reds are organizing a demonstration for tomorrow, dont you?" asked the mayor.

Taylor licked his lips before he answered.

"Yessuh. Ah done heard a lotta folks talkin erbout it, suh."

"Thats too bad, Dan," said the mayor.

"Folks is talking erbout it everwhere . . ." began Taylor.

"What *folks?*" interjected Bruden.

"Waal, mos everbody, suh."

Bruden leaned forward and shook his finger in Taylor's face.

"Listen, boy! I want you to get this straight! Reds aint *folks!* Theyre Goddam sonofabitching lousy bastard rats trying to wreck our country, see? Theyre stirring up race hate! Youre old enough to understand that!"

"Hes telling you straight, boy," said Lowe. "And furthermore . . ."

"Say, whats all this?" demanded the mayor, turning to Lowe and Bruden. "Wait a minute! Whats the big idea of talking to Dan like that? Hes not mixed up in anything like that. Save that kind of talk for bad niggers. . . ."

"The quicker all you niggers get sense enough in your Goddam thick skulls to keep away from them Reds the better off youll be!" said Bruden, ignoring the mayor.

"Aw, c mon," said the mayor. "Dans all right. Aint that right, Dan?"

Taylor looked down and saw at his feet a sharp jutting angle of sunshine falling obliquely through a window. His neck felt hot. This is the showdown, he thought. Theys tryin t trap me. . . . He cleared his throat and looked up slowly and saw the mayor gazing at him with cold gray eyes. He shifted his body slightly and saw the glint of Chief Bruden's police star; he saw Lowe's red lips twisted in half smile and half leer.

"Isnt that right, Dan?" the mayor asked again.

"Yessuh. Whut yuh white folks say is right. N Ah ergrees wid yuh. But Ah ain foolin wid nobody thas tryin t stir up race hate; naw *suh!* Ah ain never done nothin like tha n Ah never will, so hep me Gawd! Now erbout this demonstration: Yessuh, Ah heard erbout it. Thas all ever-bodys been talkin erbout erroun here fer a week, yo honah. Waal, suh, Ahll tell yuh. Theys jus hongry! Theys marchin cause they don know whut else t do, n thas the truth from here t Heaven! Mistah Mayor, theys hongry! Just plain *hongry!* Ah give mah las dime today t a woman wid eight chillun. . . ."

"We know all about that, Dan," said the mayor.

"Everybodys hungry," said Bruden.

"Boy, cant you see we are all in the *same* boat?" asked Lowe.

"Waal . . ." drawled Taylor.

"Thingsll be straightened out soon, Dan," interjected the mayor sooth-ingly. "We will see that nobody starves."

"Ah beg yo pardon, suh. A man died jus the other day from starva-tion. . . ."

Taylor's voice died in his throat and he looked at the floor. He knew that he had said too much.

"I reckon that makes you out a liar, dont it?" Bruden asked the mayor.

"Aw, naw suh!" said Taylor eagerly. "Ah ain disputin nobodys word, suh. Ah jus thought yuh hadn't heard erbout it. . . ."

"We know all about it," said Bruden, turning his head away and look-ing out of the window; as though he was through with the conversation, as though his mind was made up.

"What do they think theyre going to get by marching?" asked Lowe.

"They think they kin git some bread," said Taylor.

"It wont get em a Goddam crumb!" said Lowe.

There was silence. Taylor looked again at the jutting angle of sun-shine and heard the mayor's shoes shifting uneasily on the brown carpet. A match struck; he heard it drop with an angry hiss into the spittoon.

"I dont see why we cant get along, Dan," drawled the mayor.

"Ahm willin t git erlong, Mistah Mayor!" protested Taylor.

"Dan, here we all are, living in good old Dixie. There are twenty-five thousand people in this town. Ten thousand of those people are black, Dan. Theyre your people. Now its our job to keep order among the whites, and we would like to think of you as being a responsible man to keep order among the blacks. Lets get together, Dan. You know these black people better than we do. We want to feel we can depend on you. Why dont you look at this thing the right way? You know Ill never turn you down if you do the right thing. . . ."

"Mistah Mayor, as Gawds mah judge, Ahm doin right when Ah tell you mah folks is hongry. . . ."

"Youre not doing right when you act like a Goddam Red!" said Lowe.

"These niggers around here trust you, Dan," said the mayor. "Theyll do what you tell them to do."

"Speak to them," urged Lowe. "Tell them whats right."

"Mistah Mayor, Gawd in Heaven knows mah people is hongry," said Taylor humbly.

The mayor threw his body forward in the chair and rested his hands on his knees.

"Listen, Dan. I know just how you feel. We *all* feel that way. White people are hungry too. But weve got to be prudent and do this thing right. Dan, youre a leader and youve got great influence over your congregation here." The mayor paused to let the weight of his words sink in. "Dan, I helped you to get that influence by doing your people a lot of favors through *you* when you came into my office a number of times." The mayor looked at Taylor solemnly. "I'm asking you now to use that influence and tell your people to stay *off* the streets tomorrow!"

When Taylor spoke he seemed to be outside of himself, listening to his own words, aghast and fearful.

"Ahm sho thankful as Gawd knows fer all yuh done done fer me n mah people, suh. But mah word don go so fer in times like these, yo honah. These folks is lookin t me fer bread n Ah cant give it t em. They hongry n Ah cant tell em where t eat. Theys gonna march no mattah what Ah say. . . ."

"Youve got influence here, Dan, and you can use it!"

"They wouldnt be marchin ef they wuznt hongry, yo honah!"

"Thats Red talk, nigger!" said Lowe, standing.

"Aw, thats all right, Lowe," said the mayor placatingly.

"Im not going to sit here and let this Goddam nigger insult me to my face!" said Lowe.

Taylor stood up.

"Ahm sorry, suh!"

"You *will* be sorry when you find a Goddam rope around your neck!" said Lowe.

"Now, now," said the mayor, laying his hand on Lowe's arm. He turned to Taylor. "You dont mean you wont speak to em, do you, Dan?"

"There ain nothin Ah kin say t em, Mistah Mayor. . . ."

"Youre doing the wrong thing, Dan!"

"Ahm lettin Gawd be mah judge, suh!"

"If you dont do the right thing *we* will be your judges!" said Lowe.

"Ahm trustin Gawd, suh."

"Well, Goddammit, you better let Him guide you right!" said Bruden, jumping to his feet.

"But, white folks!" pleaded Taylor. "Mah folks cant plant nothin! Its erginst the law! They cant git no work! Whut they gonna do? They don want no trouble. . . ."

"Youre heading for aplenty right now!" said Bruden.

The mayor spoke and his voice was low and resigned.

"Ive done all I could, Dan. You wouldn't follow my advice, now the rest is up to Mister Lowe and Chief Bruden here."

Bruden's voice came with a shout:

"A niggers a nigger! I was against coming here talking to this nigger like he was a white man in the first place. He needs his teeth kicked down his throat!" Bruden poked the red tip of his cigar at Taylor's face. "Im the chief of police of this town, and Im here to see that orders kept! The Chamber of Commerce says therell be no demonstration tomorrow. Therell be three hundred police downtown in the morning to see that thats done! If you send them niggers down there, or if you let these Goddam Reds fool you into it, Ill not be responsible for whatll happen! Weve never had a riot in this town, but youre plotting one right now when you act like this! And you know wholl get the worst of it!"

"Cant yuh do something, Mistah Mayor? Cant yuh fix it sos we kin git some relief?"

The mayor did not answer; Lowe came close to him.

"We know youve been seeing Hadley and Green! We know whats going on! So watch yourself, nigger!"

"Suh?"

They went out. Taylor stood at the window and saw them get into their car and disappear in a cloud of dust around the corner. He sat down, feeling sweat over all his body. *Gawd knows whut t do. . . . He brought Lowe n Bruden here t threaten me. . . . N they know erbout Hadley n Green. . . . Somebody tol. . . .* He looked up, hearing the soft boom of a clock. *Hadley n Greens comin back here at six-thirty. . . .* He went down the hall, thinking, *Lawd, ef Ah only knowed whut t do. . . .*

VII

May met him in the hall.

"Whut they say, Dan?" she asked with suppressed hysteria.

"Don bother me now, May!"

"There wont be no trouble, will it, Dan?"

204

"Naw, May! Now please! Yuh worryin me!"

"Yuhll spoil things fer Jimmy, Dan! Don do nothin wrong! Its fer Jimmy Ahm astin!"

"Itll be awright! Now lemme go!"

He hurried down the hallway, leaving her crying. Good Gawd! How come she wont leave me erlone? Firs its Jimmy; then its her. . . . Ef it ain one its the other. . . . He went to the end of the hall, down the steps, turned and came to the door of the Deacon Room. He heard subdued voices. He knew that the deacons were waiting for him, waiting for some definite word. Shucks, Ahm willin t go thu wid tha march ef they is. Them white folks cant kill us *all*. . . . He pushed the door in. The voices ceased. He saw a dense cloud of tobacco smoke and a circle of black faces. He forced a wan smile.

"Good evenin, Brothers!" he said.

"How yuh, Reveren?" asked Deacon Bonds.

"Ahm sorry Ahm late," said Taylor.

"Wuz tha the mayor out there?" asked Deacon Williams.

Taylor paused and pulled out his handkerchief.

"Yeah, Brothers, it wuz the mayor. N the chiefa police n tha man Lowe from the Red Squad. . . ."

"RED SQUAD!" shouted Deacon Smith, jumping to his feet with an outraged look.

"Whut they say, Reveren?" asked Deacon Williams quickly, ignoring Deacon Smith.

Taylor sighed and looked at the floor. For a moment he loathed them because he knew they were expecting an answer to their questions. They were expecting him to speak now as he had always spoken, to the point, confidently, and finally. He had wanted them to do the talking, and now they were silent, waiting for him to speak. Lawd, Ah hope Ahm doin right. Ah don wanna lead these folks wrong. . . .

"They know all erbout tha demonstration," he said.

"But whut they *say?*" asked Deacon Bonds.

"Shucks, man! Yuh *know* whut they said!" said Deacon Smith. "Yuh *know* how them white folks feel erbout this thing!"

"They don wan us t march," said Taylor. "They said ef we march theyll put the police on us. . . ."

Deacon Smith leveled his forefinger at Taylor and intoned:

"AH TOL YUH SO!"

"They said therell be a riot," Taylor went on stubbornly.

"Yessuh! Brothers, wes gotta do *right!*" said Deacon Smith, banging his open palm down on the table. "Ah awways said wes gotta do *right*, Reveren!"

"Ahm prayin t Gawd t guide us right," said Taylor.

"Yuh sho don ack like it!" said Deacon Smith.

"Let the Reveren finish, will yuh?" asked Deacon Bonds.

"Wes gotta do right!" said Deacon Smith again, sitting down, folding his arms, crossing his legs and turning his face sternly away.

"Whut else they say, Reveren?" asked Deacon Bonds.

Taylor sighed.

"They say wes mixed up wid the Reds. . . ."

"N by Gawd we *is!*" bawled Deacon Smith. "At least *yuh* is! Ah tol yuh t leave them Reds erlone! They don mean *no*body *no* good! When men starts t deny Gawd, nothin good kin come from em!"

"Brother Smith, let the Reveren talk, will yuh?" asked Deacon Williams.

"He ain talkin *sense!*" said Deacon Smith.

"They say therell be three hundred police downtown in the mawnin," said Taylor, ignoring Smith. "They say only Washington kin do something erbout relief, n tha we must wait. . . ."

"N Gawd Awmighty knows thas all we kin do: wait!" said Deacon Smith.

"Fer Chrissakes, Brother Smith, let im talk!" said Deacon Williams. "We all knows *yuhs* scared!"

"Ah ain scared! Ah got sense! Ah . . ."

"Yuh sho don ack like it, the way yuh shoot off yo mouth!" said Deacon Williams.

Deacon Smith stood up.

"Yuh cant talk tha way t me!"

"Then keep yo big mouth shut!" said Deacon Williams.

"Whos gonna make me?"

"Brothers, please!" begged Taylor.

"A fool kin see tha the white folks is scared!" said Deacon Williams.

"N jus cause theys *scared*, theyll kill *any*body whuts fool ernuff t go downtown in the mawnin," said Deacon Smith.

"Shucks, Ahm willin t taka chance," said Deacon Hilton.

"Me too!"

"We ain got nothin t lose!"

"Any *fool* kin git his head busted!" said Deacon Smith.

"Brothers, fer the lova Gawd, quit fussin!" said Taylor.

They were silent. Taylor looked at them, letting his eyes rove from face to face.

"Brothers, this is the case," he said finally. "They threatenin us not t march, but they ain sayin our folks kin git no relief. Now Ah figgers ef we hada big crowd downtown in the mawnin they wont bother us. . . ."

"Thas whut *yuh* think," sneered Deacon Smith.

"N ef we don hava big crowd, theyll smash us. Now its up t us . . ."

"Reveren, do the *po* white folks say they gonna be *wid* us?" asked Deacon Jones.

"Brother Hadley tol me theys gonna be wid us," said Taylor.

"Tha Hadley is a lie n the trutha Gawd ain in im!" shouted Deacon Smith. "Tha white man is jus tryin t trick yuh, Ahm tellin yuh!"

"Waal, we kin never know less we try n see," said Deacon Bonds.

"Yeah, they ain gonna let yuh try but *once*," said Deacon Smith.

"Waal, Ah ain got but *one* time t die!" said Deacon Bonds.

"Ah think the white folksll be there," said Taylor. "Theys hongry too. . . ."

"Yuhll wake up *some* day!" said Deacon Smith.

"Whut yuh gonna do, Reveren?" asked Deacon Williams.

"Do the congregation wanna march?" asked Taylor.

"They say theys *gonna* march!"

"Waal, Ahll march wid em," said Taylor quietly. "They wont march erlone. . . ."

Deacon Smith waved his arms and screamed:

"Yeah, yuhll march! But yuhs scared t let me use yo name! Whut kinda leader *is* yuh? If yuh gonna ack a fool n be a *Red*, then how come yuh wont come on out n say so sos we kin all hear it? Naw, yuh ain man ernuff t say whut yuh is! Yuh wanna stan in wid the white folks! Yuh wanna stan in wid the Reds! Yuh wanna stan in wid the congregation! Yuh wanna stan in wid the Deacon Board! Yuh wanna stan in wid *ever*body n yuh stand in wid *no*body!"

"Ahm ackin accordin t mah lights!" said Taylor.

"Waal, they ain lettin yuh see fer!" said Deacon Smith.

"Ef yuh gotta plan bettah than mine, Brother Smith, tell us erbout it!"

"AH SAY WE OUGHTNT MARCH!"

"Then whut we gonna do?"

"Wait n see how things come out!"

"Ahm tireda waitin," said Taylor.

"How come yuh didnt send yo name out on them leaflets?" demanded Deacon Smith. Without waiting for Taylor to answer, he flared: "Ahll tell yuh why yuh didnt! Yuh *scared!* Yuh didnt wan them white folks t know yuhs mixed up in this demonstration. Yuh wanted em t think yuh wuz being pushed erlong by other folks n yuh couldnt hep whut wuz happenin! But, Reveren, as sho as theres a Gawd in Heaven yuh ain foolin nobody!"

Taylor stood up.

"Brother Smith, Ah knows whut yuhs up t! Yuh tryin t run me outta mah church, but yuh cant! Gawd Awmighty Himself put me here n

Ahm stayin till He says fer me t go! Yuh been schemin t git me out, but yuh cant do it this way! It ain right n Gawd knows it ain! Yeah; ef mah folks marches in the mawnin Ahm marchin wid em!"

"Thas the time, Reveren!"

"We kin show tha ol mayor something!"

"N therell be white folks wid us too!"

"Ahll go wid the Reveren n the congregation!"

"Ahll go!"

"N me too!"

"Gawd ain wid yuh when yuh ain in the right!" said Deacon Smith.

"Gawd didnt mean fer folks t be hongry!" said Deacon Bonds.

"But He ain wid yuh when yuh stirrin up trouble, makin blood n riots!" said Deacon Smith. "N any man whut sets here n calls himself a leader called by Gawd t preach n leads his folks the wrong way is a fool n the spirita Gawd ain in im!"

"Now wait a minute there, Brother Smith!" said Taylor. "Yuhs talkin *dangerous!*"

"Ah say any man whut leads his folks inter guns n police . . ."

"Ain nobody leadin us *nowhere!*" said Deacon Bonds.

"We gwine *ourselves!*" said Deacon Williams.

"Ah ain in this!" said Deacon Smith, jumping again to his feet. "Ah ain in this n Ahm gonna do whut Ah kin t hep mah people!"

The room grew quiet.

"Whut yuh mean, Brother Smith?" asked Taylor.

"Ah say Ahm gonna hep mah people!" said Deacon Smith again.

Taylor walked over to him.

"Is yuh gonna tell the white folks on us?"

Deacon Smith did not answer.

"Talk, Brother Smith!" said Taylor. "Tell us whut yuh mean!"

"Ah means whut Ah means!" said Deacon Smith; and he clamped his teeth tight, sat again, crossed his legs, folded his arms and stared at the blank wall.

Taylor swallowed and looked at the floor. Lawd, Ah don know whut t do! Ah wish this wuz over. . . . This niggers gonna tell on us! Hes gonna tell the white folks sos he kin stan in wid em. . . .

"Brother Smith . . ." began Taylor.

The door opened and Jimmy stepped into the room.

"Say, Pa!"

"Whut yuh wan, son?"

"Somebodys out front t see yuh. Theys in a car. Theys white folks."

"Scuse me, Brothers," said Taylor. "Ahll be right back."

"Wes gonna set right here till yuh git back," said Deacon Smith.

When outside the door, Taylor turned to Jimmy.

"Who is they, Jimmy? How come they wouldnt come in?"

"Ah dunno, Pa. The car drove up jus as Ah wuz comin thu the gate. They white men. They said fer yuh t come right out."

"Awright. N, son, yuh bettah go see bout yo ma."

"Whuts the mattah?"

"She jus upset erbout the demonstration."

"Is they gonna march, Pa?"

"Ah reckon so."

"Is many gonna be out?"

"Ah dunno, son. Ah hope so. Yuh bettah go see erbout yo ma now."

"Yessuh."

"Yuh tell them boys whut Ah tol yuh?"

"Yessuh."

Taylor paused at the front door and peeped out from behind a curtain. In front of his gate was a long black car. Who kin tha be? For a moment he thought the mayor had come back. But his cars gray. . . . He opened the door and walked slowly down the steps. Lawd, mabbe we oughtnt go thu wid this demonstration aftah all? We might all be sorry ef somebodys killed in the mawnin. . . . He walked along a flower-bordered path that smelt of violets and magnolias. Dust rested filmily on tree leaves. The sun was almost gone. As he came to the car a white face looked out.

"You Taylor?"

"Yessuh," answered Taylor, smiling.

The rear door of the car opened and the white man stepped to the ground.

"So youre Taylor, hunh?"

"Yessuh," said Taylor again, still smiling, but puzzled. "Kin Ah be of service t yuh, suh?"

Taylor saw it coming, but could do nothing. He remembered afterward that he had wanted to ask, Whut yuh doin? The blow caught him flush on the point of the jaw, sending him flying backward. His head struck the edge of the running board; a flash of red shot before his eyes. He rolled, face downward, into a bed of thick violets. Dazed, he turned his head, trying to speak. He felt a hand grab the back of his collar and jerk him up.

"Get in the car, nigger!"

"Say, whut yuh . . ."

"Shut up and get in the car, Goddam you!"

A blow came to his right eye. There were three white men now. They lifted him and rammed him down on the floor in the back of the car.

"Say, you cant do this!"

"Get your Goddam mouth shut, you bastard!"

A hard palm slapped him straight across his face. He struggled up, protesting.

"You . . ."

The heel of a shoe came hard into his solar plexus. He doubled up like a jackknife. His breath left, and he was rigid, half paralyzed.

"You think you can run this whole Goddam town, don't you? You think a nigger can run over white folks and get away with it?"

He lay still, barely breathing, looking at blurred white faces in the semidarkness of the roaring car.

VIII

The moment he tried to tell the direction in which the car was moving he knew he had waited too long. He remembered dimly that they had turned corners at least three times. He lay with closed eyes and wondered what they were going to do with him. She gonna be worried t death, he thought, thinking of May. And then he thought of Jimmy and said to himself, Ah hope he don go n ack a fool now. . . . The numbness which had deadened most of his stomach and chest was leaving. He felt sweat on his back and forehead. The car slowed, turned; then it ran fast again. He knew by the way the rocks crunched beneath the humming rubber tires that they were speeding over gravel. Whut roads this? He could not tell. There were so many gravel roads leading out of town. He tried to recall how long he had lain there half paralyzed from that kick in the solar plexus. He was confused; it might have been five minutes or it might have been an hour. The car slowed again, turning. He smelt the strong scent of a burning cigarette and heard the toll of a far-off church bell. The car stopped; he heard the sound of other cars, gears shifting and motors throbbing. We mus be at some crossroads. But he could not guess which one. He had an impulse to call for help. But there would not be any use in his doing that now. Mabbe they white folks anyhow. He would be better off as he was; even six white men were better than a mob of white men. The car was speeding again, lurching. He smelt dust, clay dust. Then he heard a hard, rasping voice:

"How is he?"

"O.K."

"Keep im quiet!"

"O.K."

He said nothing. He began to wonder how many of them were in the car. Yes, he should have been watching for something like this. They been threatenin me fer a long time. Now this is it. The car was gradually slowing with that long slow slowing preceding a final stop. He felt the rubber tires turning over rough ground; his head rocked from side to side, hitting against the lower back of the front seat. Then the car stopped; the motor stopped; for a moment there was complete silence. Then he heard wind sighing in trees. Wes out in the country somewhere. In the woods, he thought.

"O.K.?"

"O.K.!"

He heard a door open.

"C mon, nigger! Get up and watch yourself!"

He pulled up and caught a glimpse of starry sky. As his feet hit the ground his head began to ache. He had lain cramped so long the blood had left his limbs; he took a step, kicking out his legs to restore circulation. His arms were grabbed from behind and he felt the pressure of a kneecap in the center of his spine. He gasped and reeled backward.

"Where you think youre going?"

He rested on his knees, his body full of pain. He heard a car door slam.

"Awright, nigger! Lets go! Straight ahead!"

He got up and twisted his head about to see who had spoken. He saw four blurred white faces and then they were blotted out. He reeled backward again, his head striking the ground. A pain knotted in his temple.

"Get up, nigger! Keep your eyes in front, and walk, Goddammit!"

He pulled up and limped off, his head down. Mabbe they gonna shoot me? His feet and the feet behind him made a soft *cush-cush* in the dew-wet grass and leaves.

"All right, nigger!"

He stopped. Slowly he raised his eyes; he saw a tall white man holding a plaited leather whip in his hand, hitting it gently against his trousers leg.

"You know what this is, nigger?"

He said nothing.

"Wont talk, hunh? Well, this is a nigger lesson!"

The whip flashed in faint starlight. The blow numbed his lips. He tasted blood.

"You know what this is? Im asking you again, nigger?"

"Nawsuh," he whispered.

"This is a nigger whip!"

The leather whacked across his shoulders.

"Mistah, Ah ain done nothin!"

"Aw, naw! You aint done nothing! You aint never done a Goddam thing, have you?" White men were standing close around him now.

"All you ever do is play around with Reds, dont you? All you ever do is get crowds of niggers together to threaten white folks, dont you? When we get through with you tonight youll know how to stay in a niggers place! C mon! Get that Goddam vest off!"

He did not move. The whip wrapped itself around his neck, leaving a ring of fire.

"You want me to *beat* it off you?"

He pulled off the vest and held it in his hands.

"C mon! Get that shirt and undershirt off!"

He stripped to his waist. A night wind cooled his sweaty body; he was conscious of his back as he had never been before, conscious of every square inch of black skin there. One of the white men walked off a few paces and stopped.

"Bring im over here!"

"O.K.!"

They guided him with prods and kicks.

"On your knees, nigger!"

He did not move. Again his arms were caught from behind and a kneecap came into the center of his back. Breathless, he dropped, his hands and knees cooling in the wet grass. He lifted his fingers to feel his swelling lips; he felt his wrists being grabbed and carried around the trunk of a tree. He held stiffly and struggled against a rope.

"Let go!"

His arms went limp. He rested his face against a cold tree trunk. A rope cut into his wrists. They tied his feet together, drawing the rope tight about his ankles. He looked around; they stood watching.

"Well, nigger, what do you know?"

"Nothin, suh."

"Youre a preacher, aint you?"

"Yessuh."

"Well, lets hear you pray some!"

He said nothing. The whip lashed across his bare back, *whick!* He flinched and struggled against the rope that cut his wrists to the bone. The leather thong hummed again, *whick!* and his spine arched inward, like a taut bow.

"Goddam your black soul, pray!"

He twisted his face around, pleading:

"Please, mistah! Don whip me! Ah ain done nothin. . . ."

Another lash came across his half-turned cheek, *whick!* He jerked around and sheltered his face against the tree trunk. The lash hit his back, *whick!*

"*Hit* that black bastard, Bob!"

"Let me have that whip!"

"Naw, wait a minute!"

He said nothing. He clenched his teeth, his whole body quivering and waiting. A split second after each blow his body would lurch, as though absorbing the shock.

"You going to pray? You want me to beat you till you *cant* pray?"

He said nothing. He was expecting each blow now; he could almost feel them before they came, stinging, burning. Each flick came straight on his back and left a streak of fire, a streak that merged with the last streak, making his whole back a sheet of living flame. He felt his strength ebbing; he could not clench his teeth any more. His mouth hung open.

"Let me have it, Bob?"

"Naw, its my turn!"

There was a pause. Then the blows came again; the pain burned its way into his body, wave upon wave. It seemed that when he held his muscles taut the blows hurt less; but he could not hold taut long. Each blow weakened him; each blow told him that soon he would give out. Warm blood seeped into his trousers, ran down his thighs. He felt he could not stand it any longer; he held his breath, his lungs swelling. Then he sagged, his back a leaping agony of fire; leaping as of itself, as though it were his but he could not control it any longer. The weight of his body rested on his arms; his head dropped to one side.

"Ahhlll pppprray," he sobbed.

"Pray, then! Goddam you, pray!"

He tried to get his breath, tried to form words, hearing trees sighing somewhere. The thong flicked again, *whick!*

"Aint you going to pray?"

"Yyyyyessuh. . . ."

He struggled to draw enough air into his lungs to make his words sound.

"Ooour ffather . . ."

The whip cut hard, *whick!* pouring fire and fire again.

"Have mercy, Lawd!" he screamed.

"Pray nigger! Pray like you *mean* it!"

". . . wwwhich aaaaart in Hheaven . . . hhhallowed bbe Tttthy nname. . . ." The whip struck, *whick!* "Ahm prayin, mmmmistah!"

"Goddam your black heart, *pray!*"

". . . Ttthy kkkindom ccome . . . Ttthy wwill bbe ddddone. . . ."

He sobbed, his breath leaving his lungs, going out from him, not wanting to stay to give sound to his words. The whip brought more fire and he could not stand it any longer; his heart seemed about to burst. He screamed, stretched his knees out and twisted his arms till he lay sideways, half on his stomach. The whip came into his stomach, *whick!* He turned over; it came on his back again, *whick!* He stopped struggling and hung limply, his weight suspended on arms he could not feel. Then fire flamed over all his body; he stiffened, glaring upward, wild-eyed.

"Whats the matter, nigger? You hurt?"

"Awright, kill me! Tie me n kill me! Yuh white-trash cowards, kill me!"

"Youre tough, aint you? Just wait! We'll kill you, you black sonofabitch!"

"Lemme have that whip!"

"C mon, now! Its my turn!"

"Give me that whip, Ellis!"

He was taut, but not feeling the effort to be taut.

"Well git yuh white trash someday! So hep me Gawd, well git yuh!"
The whip stopped.

"Say that again, Goddam you!"

The whip lashed, *whick!* but there was no streak of fire now; there was only one sheet of pain stretching all over his body, leaping, jumping, blazing in his flesh.

"Say it!"

He relaxed and closed his eyes. He stretched his legs out, slowly, not listening, not waiting for the whip to fall. *say it whick! say it whick! say it whick!* He groaned. Then he dropped his head and could not feel any more.

IX

Moonlight pained his eyeballs and the rustle of tree leaves thundered in his ears. He seemed to have only a head that hurt, a back that blazed and eyes that ached. In him was a feeling that some power had sucked him deep down into the black earth, had drained all strength from him. He was waiting for that power to go away so he could come back to life, to light. His eyes were half open, but his lids did not move. He was thirsty; he licked his lips, wanting water. Then the thunder in his ears died, rolling away. He moved his hand and touched his forehead; his arm fell limply in the wet grass and he lay waiting to feel that he wanted to move. As his blood began to flow swiftly again he felt sweat breaking out over his body. It seemed he could hear a tiny, faraway sound whispering over and over like a voice in an empty room: Ah got fever. . . . His back rested on a bed of fire, the imprint of leaves and grass searing him with a scalding persistence. He turned over on his stomach and groaned. Then he jerked up, half sitting. He was fully conscious now, fighting for his strength, remembering the curses, the prayer and the whip. The voice whispered again, this time louder: Ah gotta git home. . . . With fumbling fingers he untied the rope from his wrists and ankles. They didnt kill me, he thought. He stood up and the dark earth swayed and the stars blurred. Lawd, have mercy! He found himself on his knees; he had not known when he had started falling; he just found himself on his knees. Lawd, Ahm weak! He stood up again, more slowly this time, holding onto a tree. He would have to get his shirt; he could not go through the streets with a naked and bleeding back. He put one foot in front of the other with conscious effort, holding his body stiffly. Each slight twist of his shoulders sent a wave of liquid metal over him. In the grass at his feet his shirt was smeared like a white blur. He touched it; it was wet. He held it, instinctively fearing to put it on. When it did touch, his whole back blazed with a pain so intense that it seemed to glow white hot. No, he could not put it on now. Stiffly he went among the trees, holding the shirt in his hands, looking at the ground.

He stopped at the edge of a dirt road, conscious of the cool steady stars and the fire that smoldered in his back. Whut roads this? He could not tell. Then he heard a clock striking so faintly that it seemed to be tolling in his own mind. He counted, Wun, tuh. . . . Its tuh erclock, he thought. He could not stay here all night; he had to go in one direction or another. He watched the brown dusty road winding away in the darkness, like a twisting ribbon. Then he ducked his head, being seared again with fire and feeling a slight rush of air brush across his face. A small bird wheeled past his eyes and fluttered dizzily in the starlight. He watched it veer and dip, then crash softly into a tree limb. It fell to the ground, flapping tiny wings blindly. Then the bird twittered in fright and sailed straight upward into the starlight, vanishing. He walked northward, not going anywhere in particular, but walked northward because the bird had darted in the direction.

The road curved, turned to gravel, crunching under his shoes. This mus be the way, he thought. There were fences along the sides of the road now. He went faster, holding his legs stiffly to avoid pulling the muscles in his back. A church steeple loomed in the starlight, slender and faint. Yeah, thas Houstons church. N Ah gotta go thu a white neighborhood, he thought with despair. He saw houses, white, serene and cool in the night. Spose Ah go to Houston? Naw, hes white. *White.* . . . Even tho he preaches the gospel Ah preaches, he might not take me in. . . . He passed a small graveyard surrounded by a high iron picket fence. A *white* graveyard, he thought and snickered bitterly. Lawd Gawd in Heaven, even the dead cant be together! He stopped and held his shirt in his hands. He dreaded trying to put it on, but he had to. Ah cant go thu the streets like this. Gingerly he draped the shirt over his shoulders; the whole mass of bruised and mangled flesh flamed, glowed white. With a convulsive movement he rammed his arms into the sleeves, thinking that the faster he did it the less pain there would be. The fire raged so he had a wild impulse to run, feeling that he would have no time then to suffer. But he could not run in a white neighborhood. To run would mean to be shot, for a burglar, or anything. Stiff-legged, he went down a road that turned from brown dust to black asphalt. Ahead street lamps glowed in round, rosy hazes.

Far down the shadow-dappled pavement he heard the sound of feet. He walked past a white man, then he listened to the white man's footsteps dying away behind him. He stopped at a corner and held onto a telephone pole. It would be better to keep in the residential district than to go through town. He would be stopped and questioned in town surely. And jailed maybe. Three blocks later on a white boy came upon him so softly and suddenly that he started in panic. After the boy had gone he turned to look; he saw the boy turning, looking at him. He walked on hurriedly. A block later a white woman appeared. When she was some fifty feet away she crossed to the other side of the street. Hate tightened his throat, then he emptied his lungs in a short, silent, bitter laugh. Ah ain gonna bother yuh, white lady. Ah only want t git home. . . .

Like a pillar of fire he went through the white neighborhood. Someday theys gonna burn! Someday theys gonna burn in Gawds Awmighty fire! How come they make us suffer so? The worls got too mucha everthing! Yit they bleed us! They fatten on us like leeches! There ain no groun yuh kin walk on tha they don own! N Gawd knows tha ain right! He made the earth fer us all! He ain tol no lie when He put us in this worl n said be fruitful n multiply. . . . Fire fanned his hate; he stopped and looked at the burning stars. "Gawd, ef Yuh gimme the strength Ahll tear this ol buildin down! Tear it down, Lawd! Tear it down like ol Samson tore the temple down!" He walked again, mumbling. "Lawd, tell me whut t do! Speak t me, Lawd!" He caught his breath; a dark figure came out of the shadows in front of him. He saw a glint of metal; it was a policeman. He held erect and walked rapidly. Ahll stop, he thought. He wont have t ast me t stop. . . . He saw the white face drawing closer. He stopped and waited.

"Put your hands up, nigger!"

"Yessuh."

He lifted his arms. The policeman patted his hips, his sides. His back blazed, but he bit his lips and held still.

"Who you work for?"

"Ahma preacher, suh."

"A *preacher?*"

"Yessuh."

"What you doing out here this time of night?"

"Ah wuz visitin a sick man, a janitah, suh, whut comes t mah church. He works fer Miz Harvey. . . ."

"Who?"

"Miz Harvey, suh."

"Never heard of her, and Ive been on this beat for ten years."

"She lives right back there, suh," he said, half turning and pointing.

"Well, you look all right.   You can go on.   But keep out of here at night."

"Yessuh."

He was near his own people now.   Across a grassy square he could see the top of the roundhouse glinting dully in the moonlight.   The black asphalt turned to cinders and the houses were low, close together, squatting on the ground as though hiding in fear.   He saw his church and relaxed.   He came to the steps, caught hold of a banister and rested a moment.

When inside he went quietly down a hall, mounted the stairs and came to the door of his room.   He groped in the dark and felt the bed. He tried to pull off the shirt.   It had stuck.   He peeled it.   Then he eased onto the bed and lay on his stomach.   In the darkness his back seemed to take new fire.   He went to the kitchen and wet a cloth with cold water.   He lay down again with the cloth spread over him.   That helped some.   Then he began to shake.   He was crying.

x

The door creaked.

"Tha yuh, Pa?"

"Son?"

"Good Gawd, wes been lookin all over fer yuh!   Where yuh been? Mas worried t death!"

"C mon in, son, n close the do."

"Don yuh wanna light?"

"Naw; close the do."

There was a short silence.

"Whuts the mattah, Pa?   Yuh sick?"

"Close the do n set down, son!"

Taylor could hear Jimmy's breathing, then a chair scraping over the floor and the soft rustle of Jimmy's clothes as he sat.

"Whuts the mattah, Pa?   What happened?"

Taylor stared in the darkness and slowly licked his swollen lips.   He wanted to speak, but somehow could not.   Then he stiffened, hearing Jimmy rise.

"Set *down,* son!"

"But, Pa . . ."

Fire seethed not only in Taylor's back, but all over, inside and out. It was the fire of shame. The questions that fell from Jimmy's lips burned as much as the whip had. There rose in him a memory of all the times he had given advice, counsel and guidance to Jimmy. And he wanted to talk to him now as he had in the past. But his impulses were deadlocked. Then suddenly he heard himself speaking, hoarsely, faintly. His voice was like a whisper rising from his whole body.

"They whipped me, son. . . ."

"Whipped yuh? Who?"

Jimmy ran to the bed and touched him.

"Son, set *down!*"

Taylor's voice was filled with a sort of tense despair. He felt Jimmy's fingers leaving him slowly. There was a silence in which he could hear only his own breath struggling in his throat.

"Yuh mean the *white* folks?"

Taylor buried his face in his pillow and tried to still the heaving in his chest.

"They beat me, son. . . ."

"Ahll git a doctah!"

"Naw!"

"But yuhs hurt!"

"Naw; lock the do! Don let May in here. . . ."

"Goddam them white bastards!"

"Set down, son!"

"Who wuz they, Pa?"

"Yuh cant do nothin, son. Yuhll have t wait. . . ."

"Wes been waitin too long! All we do is wait, *wait!*"

Jimmy's footsteps scuffed across the floor. Taylor sat up.

"Son?"

"Ahma git mah gun n git Pete n Bob n Joe n Sam! Theyll see they cant do this t us!"

Taylor groped in the darkness; he found Jimmy's shoulders.

"C mon, son! Ahm awright. . . ."

"Thas the reason why they kill us! We take everthing they put on us! We take everthing! *Everthing!*"

"Yuh cant do nothin *erlone,* Jimmy!"

Jimmy's voice was tense, almost hysterical.

"But we kin *make* em know they cant do this t us widout us doin some*thing*! Aw, hell, Pa! Is we gonna be dogs *all* the time?"

"But theyll kill yuh, son!"

"Somebody *has* t die!"

Taylor wanted to tell Jimmy something, but he could not find the words. What he wanted to say boiled in him, but it seemed too big to come out. He flinched from pain, pressing his fingers to his mouth, holding his breath.

"Pa?"

"Yeah, son?"

"Hadley n Green wuz here t see yuh three-fo times."

"Yeah?"

Jimmy said nothing. Taylor twisted around, trying to see his son's face in the darkness.

"Whut they say, son?"

"Aw, hell! It don mattah. . . ."

"Tell me whut they *said!*"

"Ttthey ssaid . . . Aw, Pa, they didn't know!"

"Whut they *say?*"

"They said yuh had done run out on em. . . ."

"Run *out?*"

"Everbody wuz astin where yuh wuz," said Jimmy. "Nobody knowed. So they tol em yuh run out. N Brother Smith had the Deacon Board t vote yuh outta the church. . . ."

"Vote me *out?*"

"They said they didn't wan yuh fer pastah no mo. It wuz Smith who made em do it. He tol em yuh had planned a demonstration n lef em holdin the bag. He fussed n stormed at em. They thought they wuz doin right. . . ."

Taylor lay on his bed of fire in the darkness and cried. He felt Jimmy's fingers again on his face.

"Its awright, Pa. Well git erlong somehow. . . ."

"Seems like Gawds done lef me! Ahd die fer mah people ef Ah only knowed how. . . ."

"Pa . . ."

"How come Ah cant ever do nothin? All mah life Ah done tried n cant do nothin! *Nothin!*"

"Its awright, Pa!"

"Ah done lived all mah life on mah knees, a-beggin n a-pleadin wid the white folks. N all they gimme wuz crumbs! All they did wuz kick me! N then they come wida gun n ast me t give mah own soul! N ef Ah so much as talk lika man they try t kill me. . . ."

He buried his face in the pillow, trying to sink himself into something so deeply that he could never feel again. He heard Jimmy turning the key in the lock.

"Son!"

Again he ran to Jimmy and held him.

"Don do tha, son!"

"Thingsll awways be like this less we *fight!*"

"Set down, son! Yo po ol pas a-*beggin* yuh to set down!"

He pulled Jimmy back to the bed. But even then it did not seem he could speak as he wanted to. He felt what he wanted to say, but it was elusive and hard to formulate.

"Son . . ."

"Ah ain gonna live this way, Pa!"

He groped for Jimmy's shoulders in the darkness and squeezed them till the joints of his fingers cracked. And when words came they seemed to be tearing themselves from him, as though they were being pushed upward like lava out of a mountain from deep down.

"Don be a fool, son! Don thow yo life erway! We cant do nothin erlone."

"But theys gonna treat us this way as long as we *let* em!"

He had to make Jimmy understand; for it seemed that in making him understand, in telling him, he, too, would understand.

"We gotta git wid the *people*, son. Too long we done tried t do this thing our way n when we failed we wanted t run out n pay off the white folks. Then they kill us up like flies. Its the *people*, son! Wes too much erlone this way! Wes los when wes erlone! Wes gotta be wid our folks. . . ."

"But theys killin us!"

"N theyll keep on killin us less we learn how t fight! Son, its the people we must git wid us! Wes empty n weak this way! The reason we cant do nothin is cause wes so much erlone. . . ."

"Them Reds wuz right," said Jimmy.

"Ah dunno," said Taylor. "But let nothin come tween yuh n *yo* people. Even the Reds cant do nothin ef yuh lose yo people. . . ." Fire burned him as he talked, and he talked as though trying to escape it. "Membah whut Ah told yuh prayer wuz, son?"

There was silence, then Jimmy answered slowly:

"Yuh mean lettin Gawd be so real in yo life tha everthing yuh do is cause of Im?"

"Yeah, but its different now, son. Its the *people!* Theys the ones whut mus be real t us! Gawds wid the people! N the peoples gotta be real as Gawd t us! We cant hep ourselves er the people when wes erlone. Ah been wrong erbout a lotta things Ah tol yuh, son. Ah tol yuh them things cause Ah thought they wuz right. Ah tol yuh t work hard n climb t the top. Ah tol yuh folks would lissen t yuh then. But they wont, son! All the will, all the strength, all the power, all the numbahs is in the people! Yuh cant live by yoself! When they beat me tonight, they beat *me. . . .* There wuznt nothing Ah could do but lay there n hate n pray n cry. . . . Ah couldnt *feel* mah people, Ah couldnt *see* mah people, Ah couldnt *hear* mah people. . . . All Ah could feel wuz tha whip cuttin mah blood out. . . ."

In the darkness he imagined he could see Jimmy's face as he had seen it a thousand times, looking eagerly, his eyes staring before him, fashioning his words into images, into life. He hoped Jimmy was doing that now.

"Ahll awways hate them bastards! Ahll *aw*ways hate em!"

"Theres other ways, son."

"Yuhs sick, Pa. . . ."

"Wes all sick, son. Wes gotta think erbout the people, night n day, think erbout em so hard tha our po selves is fergotten. . . . Whut they suffer is whut Ah suffered las night when they whipped me. Wes gotta keep the people wid us."

Jimmy was silent. A soft knock came at the door.

XI

"Dan!"

"Thas Ma," said Jimmy.

Taylor heard Jimmy rise to his feet; he gripped Jimmy's hands.

"Please, Pa! Let her come in n hep yuh!"

"Naw."

"Dan!"

Jimmy broke from him; he heard the key turn in the lock. The door opened.

"Dan! Fer Gawds sake, whuts the mattah?"

Jimmy switched on the light. Taylor lay blinking at May's anxious face. He felt shame again, knowing that he should not feel it, but feeling it anyway. He turned over and buried his face in his hands.

"Dan!"

She ran and knelt at the side of the bed.

"They tried t kill im, Ma! They beat im!" said Jimmy.

"Ah knowed them white folks wuz gonna do something like this! Ah knowed it," sobbed May.

Taylor sat up.

"Yuh be still! Lay down!" said May. She pushed him back onto the bed.

"Cant yuh do something fer im, Ma? Hes sufferin tha way."

Taylor heard May leave the room and come back.

"Hol still, Dan. This ain gonna hurt yuh. . . ."

He felt warm water laving him, then something cool that smelled of oil. He heard Jimmy moving to and fro, getting things for May. When his back was dressed he felt the bed sink as May sat on the edge of it. The heavy odors of violets and magnolias came to him; he was slowly coming back to the world again. He was the same man, but he was coming back somehow changed. He wondered at the strange peace that seeped into his mind and body there in the room with May and Jimmy, with the white folks far off in the darkness.

"Feel bettah, Dan?"

"Ahm awright."

"Yuh hongry?"

"Naw."

He wanted to talk to Jimmy again, to tell him about the black people. But he could not think of words that would say what he wanted to say. He would tell it somehow later on. He began to toss, moving jerkily, more now from restlessness of mind than from the dying fire that still lingered in his body.

XII

Suddenly the doorbell pealed. Taylor turned and saw May and Jimmy looking at each other.

"Somebody at the do," said Jimmy in a tense voice.

"Yuh reckon they white folks?" asked May.

"Yuh bettah go down, Jimmy," said Taylor.

"Ef its any white folks tell em Dans out," said May.

Jimmy's footsteps died away on the stairs. A door slammed. There were faint sounds of voices. Footsteps echoed, came on the stairs, grew loud. Taylor knew that more than one person was coming up. He lifted himself and sat on the edge of the bed.

"Dan, yuh cant git up! Yuhll make yoself sick!"

He ignored her. The door opened and Jimmy ran in.

"Its Brother Bonds, Pa!"

Bonds stood in the doorway with his head wrapped in blood-stained bandages. His face twitched and his eyes stared at something beyond the walls of the room, as though his attention had been riveted once and for always upon one fixed spot.

"Whut happened, Brother?" asked Taylor.

Bonds stared, dazed, with hunched and beaten shoulders. Then he sank to the floor, sobbing softly:

"They beat me! They beat mah chillun! They beat mah wife! They beat us all cause Ah tol em t git outta mah house! Lawd, how long Yuh gonna let em treat us this way? How long Yuh gonna let em make us suffer?"

May sobbed. Jimmy ran out of the room. Taylor caught him on the stairs.

"Don be a fool, boy! Yuh c mon back here, *now!*"

Jimmy flopped on the edge of a chair and mumbled to himself. The room was quiet save for the rustle of tree leaves that drifted in from the outside and the sound of Bonds sobbing on the floor. As Taylor stood his own suffering was drowned in a sense of widening horror. There was in his mind a vivid picture of all the little dingy huts where black men and women were crouched, afraid to stir out of doors. Bonds stopped crying and looked at Taylor; again that sense of shame spread over Taylor, inside and out. It stirred him to speech.

"Who else they beat, Brother?"

"Seem like everbody, Reveren! Them two Commoonists got beat something terrible n they put em in jail. N Ah heard they kilt one black man whut tried t fight back. They ketchin everbody they kin on the streets n lettin em have it. They ridin up n down in cars. . . ."

Jimmy cursed. The doorbell pealed again.

"Git me a shirt, May!"

"Dan, yuh ain able t do nothin!"

The doorbell pealed again, then again. Taylor started toward the dresser; but May got there before he did and gave him a shirt.

"Dan, be careful!"

"C mon downstairs, Brother Bonds. N yuh, too, Jimmy," said Taylor.

XIII

The church's waiting room was full. Black men and women sat and stood, saying nothing, waiting. Arms were in slings; necks were wrapped in white cloth; legs were bound in bloodstained rags.

"LOOK AT WHUT YUH DONE DONE!" a voice bawled.

It was Deacon Smith. Taylor's eyes went from face to face; he knew them all. Every Sunday they sat in the pews of his church, praying, singing and trusting the God he gave them. The mute eyes and silent lips pinned him to a fiery spot of loneliness. He wanted to protest that loneliness, wanted to break it down; but he did not know how. No parables sprang to his lips now to give form and meaning to his words; alone and naked, he stood ashamed. Jimmy came through the door and placed his hand on his shoulder.

"Its daylight, Pa. The folks is gatherin in the playgroun; theys waitin fer yuh. . . ."

Taylor went into the yard with the crowd at his heels. It was broad daylight and the sun shone. The men in their overalls and the women with children stood about him on all sides, silent. A fat black woman elbowed her way in and faced him.

"Well, Reveren, we done got beat up. Now is we gonna march?"

"Yuh wanna march?" asked Taylor.

"It don make no difference wid me," she said. "Them white folks cant do no more than theys aweady done."

The crowd chimed in.

"N Gawd knows they cant!"

"Ahll go ef the nex one goes!"

"Ah gotta die sometime, so Ah jus as waal die now!"

"They cant kill us but once!"

"Ahm tired anyhow! Ah don care!"

"The white folks says they gonna meet us at the park!"

Taylor turned to Jimmy.

"Son, git yo boys together n tell em t roun up everbody!"

"Yessuh!"

May was pulling at his sleeve.

"Dan, yuh *cant* do this. . . ."

Deacon Smith pushed his way in and faced him.

"Yuhll never set foot in a church ergin ef yuh lead them po black folks downtown t be killed!"

The crowd surged.

"Ain nobody leadin us nowhere!"

"We goin ourselves!"

"Is we gonna march, Reveren?"

"Yeah; soon as the crowd gits together," said Taylor.

"Ain nobody t blame but yuh ef yuh carry em t their *death!*" warned Deacon Smith.

"How come yuh don shut yo ol big mouth n let the Reveren talk?" asked the fat woman.

"Sistah, Ah got as much right t speak as yuh!"

"Well, don speak to me, yuh hear!"

"Somebody has t say something when ain *nobody* got no sense!"

"Man, don yuh tell me Ah ain got no sense!"

"Yuh sho don ack like it!"

"Ah got as much sense as yuh got!"

"How come yuh don use it?"

The fat sister slapped Deacon Smith straight across his face. Taylor ran between them and pried them apart. The crowd surged and screamed.

"Ef he touches Sistah Henry ergin Ahll kill im!"

"He ain got no bisness talkin tha way t a woman!"

Taylor dragged the fat woman toward the gate. The crowd followed, yelling. He stopped and faced them. They circled around, tightly, asking questions. May had hold of his sleeve. Jimmy came to him.

"Pa, theys comin!"

Taylor turned and walked across the yard with the crowd following. He took two planks and laid them upon the ends of two sawhorses and made a solid platform. He climbed up and stood in the quiet sunshine. He did not know exactly what it was he wanted to say, but whatever it was he would say it when they were quiet. He felt neither fear nor joy, just a humble confidence in himself, as though he were standing before his mirror in his room. Then he was conscious that they were quiet; he took one swift look over their heads, heads that stretched away to the street and beyond, a solid block of black, silent faces; then he looked down, not to the dust, but just a slight lowering of eyes, as though he were no longer looking at them, but at something within himself.

"Sistahs n Brothers, they tell me the Deacon Boards done voted me outta the church. Ef thas awright wid yuh, its awright wid me. The white folks says Ahma bad nigger n they don wanna have nothin else t do wid me. N thas awright, too. But theres one thing Ah wanna say. Ah knows how yuh feel erbout bein hongry. N how yuh feel is no different from how Ah feel. Yuh been waitin a week fer me t say whut yuh ought t do. Yuh been wonderin how come Ah didnt tell yuh what yuh oughta do. Waal . . ."

He paused and looked over the silent crowd; then again his eyes, his gaze, went inward.

"Sistahs n Brothers, the reason Ah didnt say nothin is cause Ah didnt know *whut* t say. N the only reason Ahm speakin now is cause Ah *do* know. Ah know whut t do. . . ."

He paused again, swallowing. The same feeling which had gripped him so hard last night when he had been talking to Jimmy seized him. He opened his mouth to continue; his lips moved several times before words came; and when they did come they fell with a light and hoarse whisper.

"Sistahs n Brothers, las night the white folks took me out t the woods. They took me out cause Ah tol em yuh wuz hongry. They ast me t tell yuh not t march, n Ah tol em Ah wouldnt. Then they beat me. They tied me t a tree n beat me till Ah couldnt feel no mo. They beat me cause Ah wouldnt tell yuh not t ast fer bread. They said yuhd blieve everthing Ah said. All the time they wuz hepin me, all the time they been givin me favors, they wuz doin it sos *they* could tell *me* t tell *yuh* how t ack! Sistahs n Brothers, as Gawds mah judge, Ah thought Ah wuz doin right when Ah did tha. Ah thought Ah wuz doin right when Ah tol yuh t do the things they said. N cause Ah wouldnt do it this time, they tied me t a tree n beat me till mah blood run. . . ."

Mist covered his eyes. He heard the crowd murmuring; but he did not care if they were murmuring for or against him; he wanted to finish, to say what he had been trying so hard to say for many long hours.

"Sistahs n Brothers, they whipped me n made me take the name of *Gawd* in vain! They made me say mah prayers n beat me n laughed! They beat me till Ah couldnt membah nothin! All las night Ah wuz lyin stretched out on the groun wid mah back burnin. . . . All this mawnin befo day Ah wuz limpin thu white folks streets. Sistahs n Brothers, Ah *know* now! Ah done seen the *sign!* Wes gotta git together. Ah know whut yo life is! Ah done felt it! Its *fire!* Its like the fire tha burned me las night! Its sufferin! Its hell! Ah cant bear this fire erlone! Ah know now whut t do! Wes gotta git close t one ernother! Gawds done spoke! Gawds done sent His sign. Now its fer us t *ack. . . .*"

The crowd started yelling:

"Well go ef yuh go!"

"Wes ready!"

"The white folks says theyll meet us at the park!"

The fat black woman started singing:

"*So the sign of the fire by night*

"*N the sign of the cloud by day*

"*A-hoverin oer*

"*Jus befo*

"*As we journey on our way. . . .*"

Taylor got down. He moved with the crowd slowly toward the street. May went with him, looking, wondering, saying nothing. Jimmy was at his side. They sang as they marched. More joined along the way. When they reached the park that separated the white district from the black, the poor whites were waiting. Taylor trembled when he saw them join, swelling the mass that moved toward the town. He looked ahead and saw black and white marching; he looked behind and saw black and white marching. And still they sang:

"*So the sign of the fire by night . . .*"

They turned into the street that led to town.

"*N the sign of the cloud by day . . .*"

Taylor saw blue-coated policemen standing lined along the curb.

"*A-hoverin oer . . .*"

Taylor felt himself moving between the silent lines of blue-coated white men, moving with a sea of placards and banners, moving under the sun like a pregnant cloud. He said to himself, They ain gonna bother us! They bettah *not* bother us. . . .

"*Jus befo . . .*"

Across a valley, in front of him, he could see the buildings of the town sprawled on a hill.

"As we journey on our way. . . ."

They were tramping on pavement now. And the blue-coated men stood still and silent. Taylor saw Deacon Smith standing on the curb, and Smith's face merged with the faces of the others, meaningless, lost. Ahead was the City Hall, white and clean in the sunshine. The autos stopped at the street corners while the crowd passed; and as they entered the downtown section people massed quietly on the sidewalks. Then the crowd began to slow, barely moving. Taylor looked ahead and wondered what was about to happen; he wondered without fear; as though whatever would or could happen could not hurt this many-limbed, many-legged, many-handed crowd that was he. He felt May clinging to his sleeve. Jimmy was peering ahead. A policeman came running up to him.

"You Taylor?"

"Yessuh," he said quietly, his gaze straight and steady.

"The mayors down front; he wants to see you!"

"Tell im Ahm back here," said Taylor.

"But he wants to see the leader up front!"

"Tell im Ahm back here," said Taylor again.

The man hesitated, then left; they waited, quiet, still. Then the crowd parted. Taylor saw Mayor Bolton hurrying toward him, his face beet-red.

"Dan, tell your people not to make any trouble! We dont want any trouble, Dan. . . ."

"There ain gonna be no trouble, yo honah!"

"Well, tell them they can get food if they go back home peacefully. . . ."

"Yuh tell em, yo honah!"

They looked at each other for a moment. Then the mayor turned and walked back. Taylor saw him mount the rear seat of an auto and lift his trembling hands high above the crowd, asking for silence, his face a pasty white.

A baptism of clean joy swept over Taylor. He kept his eyes on the sea of black and white faces. The song swelled louder and vibrated through him. This is the way! he thought. Gawd ain no lie! He ain no lie! His eyes grew wet with tears, blurring his vision: the sky trembled; the buildings wavered as if about to topple; and the earth shook. . . . He mumbled out loud, exultingly:

"Freedom belongs t the strong!"

The Patriot

Sean O'Faolain

It was doubtless because of the inevitable desire of man to recapture the past that they went to Youghal for their honeymoon. Their friends expected them to go at least to Dublin, if not to London or Paris, but they knew in their hearts that they had spent the gayest days of their lives in this little town, and so, as if to crown all those early happinesses, to Youghal they went, like true voluptuaries, deliberately creating fresh memories that would torment them when they were old.

Across there on the little stone promenade, when they were as yet little more than girl and boy, they had met for the first time. She was on holiday with her sister; he had come with his aunt for the day. In the train they had met Edward Bradley, his former teacher, and Mr. Bradley had walked about with him (in spite of his aunt) for a few hours, and given them tea. He had been flattered, he remembered, because old Bradley stayed with them so long, and afterwards he pretended to Norah that Mr. Bradley was really a great friend of his. Off there at the end of the promenade they had sat, the three of them, because his aunt was too old to walk far without a rest, and as they sat there, Norah and her sister came and halted opposite them to lean on the wall. A liner was passing slowly, almost imperceptibly, along the horizon and everybody was looking at it, and his aunt was asking him to tell them—he was young, God bless him, and had the better sight—was it two funnels or three it had. He had stood up, pretending to look at the liner, but he was really trying to look at Norah's black hair and her jet-black eyes without being seen, growing irritated because he and she could not be there alone, and growing more irritated still because he saw that she too was trying to look at him without being observed, turning her back frequently on the sea to look, as it were, up over their heads at the crowds on the cliffs, herself backwards over the wall and standing on her toes as if to show herself off to him. In the end her sister drew her away as the ship became too faint to be seen and Bernard became so disconsolate and silent that his aunt plucked at him and said:

"What on earth's wrong with you, Bernie? Are you tired, or what is it?"

But Mr. Bradley cocked his eye at him and winked without his aunt seeing. Old Bradley was a cute boyo, he had thought, and flushed because he felt he had been observed. After tea he and his aunt were alone again, and she, who had been so sweet to their companion, was now abusing him roundly for a firebrand who was leading all the young

228

men into wild politics. "Some day," Bernie defended, "that man will be Lord Mayor of Cork and then you'll sing a different song," but she would have none of it and as he just then caught sight again of his dark girl in the distance and wished to walk on and catch up with her he did not argue further. Alas! His aunt got tired once more, saying that the tea was like a load on her stomach, and they had to sit on another bench. His dark vision passed out of his sight and he felt she had merely floated before him and he would never meet her again.

When he did meet her again it was several years after and she was again on holiday in Youghal, and it was only by degrees they realized they had seen each other before. On this occasion he was an Irregular guerrilla—doubly a rebel—seated high up on a lorry, with his rifle across his back and his coat collar turned up, and his cap thrown back and upwards from his forehead to let his curls free to the wind. Seven other lorries were roaring along behind him through the streets and as they tore their way under the old clock archway, there on the pavement, smiling up at them, and waving her green handkerchief to them, was the loveliest dark-haired girl he had ever seen. Their lorry halted just beyond the arch to wait for the troops marching in from the railway, and he alighted and by virtue of being a soldier was able to approach her on the pretense of wanting matches or cigarettes. By the time the troops came into the town they were in a little teashop, and he was flirting away with all the bravado in the world. As the men passed outside, four by four, they sang their rebelly songs, waking, as he said to her, the ghosts of old Raleigh, who had once lived there, and of the stiff Earl of Cork from his tomb in Christ's Church, and the ghost of every Elizabethan sailorman who had cast a rope ashore by the crumbled quays they could see through the rear door of the shop, edging with their fallen stones the glittering blue of the bay.

There were descendants of those sea dogs in that town still, she told him, for having come there year after year on her holidays since she was a little child she knew Youghal as if she had been born there. She chanted the names to him, the Merricks, the Gurneys, the Boyles, the Brisketts, and at each name he swaggered his cup on high to curse them, so that it was a profane litany that finished their tea.

"The Yardleys too," she said, laughing at him.

"God damn them forever!" he swashbuckled.

"Of course the Townshends are Cromwellians," she smiled.

"Damn them forever!" he cried again.

Her eyes wandered to the bay. A brown-sailed yawl was floating past on the blue water as gracefully as a yacht.

"Isn't she lovely?" she cried, flushing with the delight of it.

"Not as lovely as you," he bantered.

"Oh! Come and watch her," she invited, and away they went.

When he found his way to the abandoned military barracks they had taken over, it was late night—discipline was a joke in those days—but he did not sleep for many hours, standing at the window of the deserted messroom watching where the moon poured down across the face of the shimmering ocean, into the little harbor. It lit up as if it were day the shouldering furze-bright hills, and the white edge of motionless surf at the base of the distant cliffs, and every sleeping roof in the town clustered beneath him.

It was curious that it was there in Youghal, too, that same summer, that Norah had first met Edward Bradley. There had been a public meeting in the market place while the guerrillas held the town and one of the chief speakers was Bradley. That day he had spoken with a terrible passion against England, and against the Irish traitors who had been cowed by her, and his passionate words caught and flared the temper of the people so that they cheered and cheered until their voices echoed across the smooth surface of the water into the woods beyond. Bernie had cheered like the rest where he stood beside Norah, proud to be that man's friend. After the meeting the three met, and the teacher, flushed with his success, walked between them along the tumble-down quays. He found that he knew Norah's people quite well, though he had not seen them for many years.

"But I'll call on them often now," he said, looking at Norah, and he began to take her arm, and then he remembered Bernie and he took his arm—like a grandfather, Bernie had said, jokingly, to him, and was angry with himself for saying it, for a deeper blush crept over the face of the older man and, halting, he had said:

"Maybe I am too old to be walking with the like of ye," and cocking his eye at the girl again he had laughed, half bitterly as Bernie thought, and with a "God bless ye, my children," turned and walked away. Wasn't he a very nice man, Norah had said, and stood looking after the teacher so long that Bernie almost thought he was going to be jealous; but he had not thought long of it. It was a warm autumn day, and so clear that they could see across the channel where the hay garnered in for the winter had left white patches on the clovered meadows. Tempted by the fields beyond they had rowed slowly cross the bay to spend the afternoon on the other side. The geese had cropped the grass of the foreshore until it was as close and clean as a golf course, except where a few odd straws lost to the granary lay strewn about and, with them, cast up by the tide, bits of reedy sea wrack, and here and there the dark gray droppings of the fowl. The air was so rarefied that as they crossed the low stone walls on their way into the oak woods the stones fell with a gurgling sound like water, and far away the ocean boomed deeply into the crannied rocks. They had gone deep into the woods to lie there while the misty darkness fell, bringing in the night wind a little rain, to lie there in their deep love as still as corpses, as still as fallen leaves. They returned late at night to the town whose yellow windows, bright across the channel, spoke to them of sanded floors in quayside pubs and the first fires before the winter.

But before that week was out the town was abandoned and Norah had to stand under the shelter of the old town walls watching the great barracks smoking against the fading sky and the distant mountains, themselves so faint that in their grayness they blended and were lost in the darkness and the smoke.

It was the way of that guerrilla life that for months on end a man never even thought of home or friends, and for months Bernard wandered among those gray mountains to the north of Youghal, as aimlessly as, and, he used to feel, more uselessly than, a lost sheep. Once only did he use his rifle in those seven months of guerrilla life and that was when sniping from fifteen hundred yards a village supposed to contain enemy troops. He slept in a different bed each night and never ate twice in succession from the same table so that most of his time was spent in going from place to place in search of food and rest. He did so less from a sense of danger than a sense of pity towards the farmers who had to feed and shelter him and his fellows, never thinking that as all his fellows did as he was doing, it saved nothing to the flour bin lying lightly on the loft, or the tea caddy on the high mantelshelf, emptied almost daily.

The days scarcely existed for him, the weeks flew over his head as *des*. unnoticed as birds homing at night, until as a human being he almost ceased to be, enveloped by the countryside as if he were a twig, a stone, an ear of corn. And then, without the slightest warning, as suddenly as the breaking of a thundershower, he remembered how lovely Youghal had been, and Norah, and he hated to look up at the cold and naked mountains. It was late February with the rain falling as by the clock, and for a month they had been hunted through it, day and night. Thinking of that and thinking of the summer his memory began to work on him like a goad. All about him on the night he thought of her, sitting alone by the embers of a turf fire after the family had gone to bed, the mountains lay black and silent, wet as if they had been dipped in the sea. Overhead a white path of stars more clear in the washed air than if there were a frost abroad. Out there, too, he felt, was danger; he was listening so intently that he almost leaped when a little cricket chirruped in the dark warmth of the hearth. He feared even to stir, so great a noise did every movement make—almost as great, it seemed, as the resounding *drop-drop* of the leaking thatch beyond the door.

In his pocketbook he had her one letter, reminding him of that little wood where they had loved:

I went specially to Youghal to see our wood again. The autumn is over it and over all the land. The days are shortening, farmers are threshing, thatching turf-ricks, digging potatoes, culling sheep from their flocks to barter in fair and market, fields are decaying with grief for the loss of their fruits, and grief is a brown and withered hag, nuts are ripening, blackberries are rotting, holly berries are reddening, leaves are dropping yellow. Mists cover the mountains like a hooded cloak, gray rocks ooze tears of desolation, green ferns on the hillside are withering, and purple heather is turning gray. Birds are silent, winds rustling in denuded boughs. In Youghal tourists are departed—no more the hum of the motor, nor the flash of fashionable attire. In my little hotel Mrs. M—— is resting and knitting, K—— turning over stacks of *McCall's Journals* and *Home Gossips*, the serving-girl is considering her return to her mother's home, P—— L—— wearing her shoes "going aisht and wesht," B—— twinkling with gestating jokes, and R—— counting the takings of the season. Norah is at the moment writing to Bernard; at other moments?—thinking, reading, peering into a dimly lit future. . . .

He smiled at that letter, so full of life as it was. Then he thought of the night outside and went to the door. He could hear the streams swirling down the dark *leaca* and as he listened their roar mingled with the desolation of the silence, and he wished passionately to be away from so lonely and cruel a place.

Three miles across the hills, in a little fishing hotel by a mountain lake, was the headquarters of the division. There, he hoped, he might get money—a few shillings would do—to help him on the road home, and maybe they would give him a clean shirt and collar, and a better hat and trousers than these guerrilla rags that, up to now, he had been flaunting as with a deliberate joy in their torn dirt. Above all he might meet Edward Bradley there. For he too had been hiding for several months in the mountains, not daring to stay in the city for fear of arrest. He felt he wanted to talk to somebody like Bradley, someone who would persuade him that this struggle of theirs was not hopeless, that all their humiliation of poverty and hunger was not, as he had long since begun to feel, a useless and wasted offering. Quietly he unbolted the door and stole through the yard into the sodden starlight.

It was midnight when he saw the lake below him and to his surprise every window in the little hotel was lit. He approached warily, alert for a sentry's challenge, an enemy patrol—he might, he knew, be shot as easily by either. But he continued to walk unaccosted past the sleeping farmhouses and the great strewn rocks until he came to the lakeside edge and the lighted windows. Inside the steamed window the room was filled with armed men, smoking, drinking, arguing in groups. He recognized the faces of three or four officers. There was the adjutant with his eyes swollen with too much drink and too little sleep—it was common knowledge that he lived like that. By the fire was Boyle, a great black-faced commandant from Kerry; under the lamp in the largest group he recognized Tom Carroll from East Cork—clearly a meeting of the officers of the division.

He entered unchallenged where a group of men were lounging in the dim candlelit hall. Three officers strode out of the room—it was the dining room—with empty glasses in each hand, returning gingerly when the glasses had been filled to the brim with black stout or porter. He saw the quartermaster coming out of the kitchen with a pair of black pint glasses dripping their froth about his wrists. He went over to tell him how dangerous it was to leave the back road unguarded. The quartermaster only growled:

"Well, what are you doing here then? Go up yourself and sentrify it," and passed on.

The column captain came out from the bar with a tray of divers-colored glasses and to him also Bernie told how the north road was unprotected. But the captain flew into a rage and glared at him over the tray.

"I've told off six men, there, to go," he said, jerking his head at the loungers in the hall.

One of them spoke back at him, a fellow with only two walrus teeth above and below in his gums.

"We won't go. Why should we go? Ye're all dhrinking. Why don't we get a dhrink?"

"Go into the kitchen and get it," said the captain.

"Where'll we get the money?"

"Ask the quartermaster."

"Damn the quartermaster."

"I want the quartermaster," said Bernie. "I want a couple of bob to get home."

The loungers scoffed at him in a loud chorus, and Buckteeth called him Sweet Innocence. Two more joined them, swaggering in their belted and ragged raincoats, out from the glow of the dining room into the dark hall. As they came they deliberately crushed against the captain's tray, all but upsetting his yellow and purple argosy. With a curse at them he raced like a waiter balancing his tray into the dining room, returning to grab Bernard and put him standing in the between passage outside the dining-room door.

"Stand there, you," he growled. "And let nobody into this room unless he has business there."

The loungers cheered.

"Will ye go up, for Christ's sake," the captain implored them, "to the north road and watch it or the whole division will be caught?"

"Oh! It's always deh division, aw!" piped up a little fair-haired sprat of a boy from the foot of the stairs. "What about deh men, aw? Dere's never any talk about deh men?"

"For God's sake, get us a drink, Jim," appealed the man with the walrus teeth.

"Go on, Jim," joined in three or four more. They seemed to have no sense of pride left.

With a sudden air of intimacy the captain stepped into the middle of them, bending his neck right and left among them like a pecking hen.

"Go in," he said, "and take it. Say the quartermaster will fix it up. They'll never know in the hotel."

Buckteeth turned away in disgust.

"No! They feed us, and they sleep us," he said, "and we're not going to soak drink from them as well."

"Well, I have no money for you," complained the captain.

"Deh quartermaster have buckets of it," declared Fair Hair.

"*Buckets* is deh word," sneered a tall man in spectacles from his dark corner at the door.

They laughed at the word in spite of their anger: it measured the quartermaster's thirst.

"Well, I can do no more for ye," said the captain in a temper, and left them.

Bernie stood where he had been placed by the dining-room door and everybody passed in and out without paying the slightest attention to him. The quartermaster, already flushed with drink, returned to fill his glasses once more, and timidly Bernie touched him on the shoulder.

"Well? Are you here still?" said the quartermaster.

Bernie had not the courage to face the refusal of a loan so he asked instead for cigarettes. The quartermaster thrust a package in his hand.

"Here," he said. "You fellows do nothing from morning to night but bum and soak for cigarettes. Why don't ye do something?"

As he passed by, a piece of black and white paper fluttered gently to the ground in his wake. Bernie picked it up. It was a hundred-pound note. For a moment he thought of rushing out to his fellows in the hall and waving it in the air before their eyes; for another moment he thought of using it himself to get home. Then he realized he could not steal money like that, and even if he did nobody would change so large a note for them or him. As the quartermaster returned he tapped his arm once again. A wave of whiskey belched into his face as the fellow turned on him and stuck his potato nose into his face. Bernie held up the note, saw him look stupidly at it, without a word thrust it into his vest pocket and stride into the dining room with his dripping glasses. What a hopeless sort of army they were, Bernie thought, and he made up his mind that he must at all costs go back into the city out of these mountains *wly?* where they did nothing for month after month but eat the substance of the people and lounge over the fire like sleepy dogs. Things were still happening occasionally in the city. If he could rest for a while and see Norah, he would become invigorated by her and be of some use again. *wly?* Suddenly there was a great stirring in the room and the captain returned to tell him to close and guard the outer door. Bernie did not have the energy to tell him that all this was foolery. Instead he begged a match from him and lit a cigarette and leaned into the corner of the passage to think. He had waited so long he could wait now another couple of hours until the dawn.

By the glow of the lamps in the room beyond the passageway he read Norah's letter again, scarcely hearing the talking and arguing rising hotter at the meeting, though he faintly gathered as he read the letter by the dim light that they were considering the whole military situation in the south and that some were for laying down their arms at once, and others for fighting on. He was hardly interested. He was thinking only of the summer that was gone and of every little incident of his last meeting with Norah in the woods beyond the bay at Youghal. Gradually the discussion in the room changed to an argument about men and ammunition and money and as the voices fell his thoughts wandered freely to the brown-sailed yawl they saw floating past the frame of the restaurant door, the sun shining on the blue and white sea in its wake and the curling foam at its bows. He remembered how he had whispered an old song to her as they lay among the leaves and to himself he hummed it over again:

> O beloved of my inmost heart,
> Come some night and soon,
> When my people are at rest,
> That we may talk together;
> My arms shall encircle you
> While I relate my sad tale
> That it was your pleasant soft voice
> That has stolen my heaven.
> The fire is unraked,

The light extinguished,
The key is under the door.
And do you softly draw it.
My mother is asleep,
But I am awake.
My fortune is in my hand
And I am ready.
I will go with you. . . .

He heard Edward Bradley's voice addressing the meeting. Why he should
be there he did not know, for he was not an army man. Afterwards he
told Bernie that because he was older than anybody there they wanted
to hear what the politicians had to say. He was imploring them not to
lay down their arms—far better to be defeated, at a blow or by degrees,
though that would be slow and terrible for them all. As on that day at
Youghal his passion carried the meeting with him and they cheered him
loudly when he finished. When he came into the passage he was flushed
and trembling, and when he saw Bernie he drew him with him into the
hall and, because the loungers were still there, out into the cool air by
the side of the lake. A sedge of broken reeds had been washed ashore
by the storms, reminding Bernie of the sedge of sea wrack on the foreshore across Youghal bay, but across the lake the mountain streams made
a ceaseless desolate moaning, and a night mist was blowing in their faces
so that they had to shelter in the darkness of a gable wall. He told
Bernie how terrible things were all over the country and Bernie told him
what he knew of the state of the men among those hills, all of them weak
and scabby and sore, not a penny in their pockets, not a pipeful to smoke,
nothing to do from one week to another but run when danger approached, never together, badly led, beaten all but in name.

"And in this hotel," said Bradley, "the officers taking their breakfast
at six o'clock in the evening and drinking in the dawn."

Suddenly Bradley said:

"Do you hear at all from that girl now?"

"What girl?"

"The girl in Youghal."

"A long time ago. I got a letter."

He hated to talk of Norah. It was as if she were a secret part of him
and he would not bare it.

"She is a very intelligent girl," said Bradley.

"Yes," said Bernie as if he were not really interested, but he felt his
breath come in heavy waves.

"Oh, yes!" said Bradley. "I saw a good deal of her before I came out here. I stayed at her house for safety several times before I took to the hills. A very nice girl."

Bernie shivered, his blood turning over in his body, but it was not from the cold.

"Well, I'm leaving in an hour or two," said Bradley. "This place won't be safe for twenty miles around after the news of this meeting gets to the military."

In the hall the candle was guttering out, but the loungers still remained. To say something to them as he passed in Bernie told them what Bradley had said of the conditions about the country and of the officers in the hotel.

"Puh!" taunted the tall bespectacled fellow. "And what does he do himself but hang over a book in the comfort of the hotel fire from morning to night?"

Bernie returned to his position in the passage. He was sick of these tauntings and tale bearings. He wondered how a man like Bradley could remain out there where he must hear them and notice them day after day. If Bradley chose he could go back to hide in the city any day— there would be many people glad to receive and shelter him, and Bernie wished he had asked for the loan of half a crown and a clean collar and tie. He must see Norah again, and the city, and his people, and friends. The quartermaster was talking now, in a thick but fierce voice.

" 'No surrender' must be our cry," he was saying. "I'd rather be shot any day than surrender. Let those that are tired of the fight go into the city and surrender!"

He peeped into the long room. One lamp was guttered low to a smoking circle of red wick. The other glowed like a yellow ball through the skeins of smoke woven in heavy layers from table to ceiling. Beer bottles and empty glasses were everywhere. The men were yawning and stretching themselves, some talking among themselves, paying no heed at all to the speaker, and the chairman was drawing idle circles with a pencil on the table before him.

Somebody silenced the quartermaster with a question and by degrees the talk fell again to a drone as they discussed men and money and ammunition. He leaned back into a corner of the passage and while he thought of the road home, of every wind and turn in it, of every side road and back road he could take, he fell into a doze where he stood. He awoke to hear Boyle from Kerry cry out in a fury at somebody:

"Let them that want to rat, do it. Myself and John Jo Sheehan will hold Kerry anyway. Won't we, John Jo?"

The meeting seemed to be ending. Sheehan was standing huge against the window with his back to them all; in spite of the lamp, black-shouldered against the pale glimmer of the dawn hanging over the mists on the lake outside. In taunting and utter disbelief he cursed over his shoulder at Boyle.

"Hold Kerry, how are you? You and Kerry may go to hell!"

The meeting broke up in laughter, men standing and talking in little groups, edging around their chief to discuss private questions of their own. It seemed as if they would never come out and Bernie sat on the ground to sleep. The first few officers leaving the room poked his stomach with their boots in mockery of their sleeping sentry. He made his way out to the kitchen, where the loungers were strewn asleep on the settle, the table, on chairs or about the floor near the gray embers of the fire. He rolled a porter barrel in from the bar and sat on it and through the sounds of the departing officers, horses stamping, carts trundling out, searchings in the dark for last drinks, calls and farewells, he slept in the corner of the cooling hearth. When he awoke the morning had come and the loungers were, like him, shivering together over the grate, where Buckteeth was blowing the seed of fire into a fresh sod of turf. Seeing him open his eyes they asked him:

"Well? What was deh end of deh meeting, aw? Are we to go home or stay here? Aw?"

"Fight on!" said Bernie.

They looked at him too tired to mock the phrase.

"Stay here, he means," said Buckteeth. "Stay bloody well here."

Bernie shared his cigarettes about and they smoked in silence while the fowl awakened by the echoing crow of the cock began to clatter and cackle in the rain water of the yard, for the rain was now darkening the window, pouring straight down into the dung-filled haggard.[1] Looking out at it Bernie saw again the mist hanging in the woods of Youghal, and Norah running down the slip to the ferry, her black curls swinging as she ran. Their hunger began to stir in them, but they could not find a scrap of food in the house—it had all been eaten by the crowd just departed. In their search they found the quartermaster snoring on the sofa of the dining room, a roll of bank notes hanging from his pocket. At once they grabbed them, sharing out the smaller notes, leaving the twenty-fives and the fifties and the hundreds, but as they argued over the division the quartermaster awoke and in a fury he demanded the money. Buckteeth, who held the fistful of notes, showered them over the furious man's head, and while he clambered under the tables and the chairs to collect them they mocked at him. Beside himself with rage he cursed them for lazy, useless louts and rushing off to tackle his horse and sidecar in the yard

1. *haggard* An open area between the house and the barn for keeping cattle or storing grain.

238

he left through the blowing rain while in a crowd they cheered him from the door. But money would not buy them food and they went about draining the ebb of porter in every glass, then wandering over the hotel from floor to attic to see what they could find. There was not a soul there but the people of the house sleeping heavily after the long hours of work the day before, so they returned to the kitchen to wait.

At last the girls of the house came down the ladderlike stairs, their legs thrust bare into their dung-covered boots. They sat on the settle by the fire, bowed over their knees until their mother followed.

"A bad morning, Mrs. O'Rourke," said Bernie to the mother.

She stood by the low window and looked sadly at the rain.

"Isn't it a bad morning, thanks be to God?" she sighed.

Not a word of reproach was said, or of inquiry about the meeting, or of complaint at their long labor. The girls sat looking at the fire or out at the rain. There was nothing for them to eat, and nothing to do on such a wet day. The mother began to scrape the bins and the bags for flour and when the boy of the house came in he milked the cows. The dough was dampened with spring water and fresh milk. It was kneaded and shaped and put into the bastable while they all looked on. Through the open door they could see the rain splashing the causeway outside and a duck poked his eye in by the jamb. Buckteeth spat at the cocked eye and the duck clattered out, but nobody laughed. The bastable was over the fire and they had all turned to it to watch while the cake baked. While they waited six other men came to the house, sodden with rain, arm and thigh and chest, searching for a breakfast and news of the meeting, but when they found the others before them they moved on patiently to the next farmhouse a mile off. They said they must be in Millstreet, twenty miles away, before night. Then they would walk on into Limerick along the Feale. For Limerick, they declared, bare and open though it was, was safer now than Cork. One of them, a Kerry lad, had no socks and his feet were torn by the bare leather of his boots. He had no overcoat, his very shirt clung to his back with wet, and he coughed ceaselessly. The woman of the house took pity on him and asked him to stay, and when he heard the others argue that Limerick was a far more dangerous place than Cork he sat down wearily by the fire and began to cry, telling his companions between his tears that he was afraid to go on with them and would hide here among the mountains. All the while Buckteeth and the others looked awkwardly at him. They offered him cigarettes and tried to cheer him by assuring him that this place was as safe as a house, and while he and they drank the scalding tea and ate soft hot cake the girls searched him out a pair of socks and a dry, if torn, shirt.

But while they ate they were less sure about the safety of the glens and they argued and argued as to what they should do next. The Kerry lad could say nothing but "We must hide. We must hide in the holes of the mountains," and the little fair-haired city gamin kept whining plaintively "But where are our officers? Where are our officers from us now? Aw?" At intervals the boy of the house assured them again and again that it was madness to stay here another day with the valleys filled, as he said, with "people taking the heels from one another with the news of the meeting to the military in the next village." So when the rain lightened they scattered, some going to the north, one declaring that the safest thing was to skirt the village to the east, and Bernie found he had lost courage to attempt the journey home. Tomorrow he would go, he thought, and with Buckteeth and Kerry, as they christened him, he went up among the cliffs in search of a cave to hide in. The boy of the house, though he kept assuring them it was madness to stay there, showed them a dump that had been made in a cleft between the rocks, a gravelike place dug out of the earth and covered with a sheet of corrugated tin and hidden by stones and withered brushwood. There was barely room for the three to lie in this dark, damp tomb, but as Kerry implored them to go into it at once, they lay down there, shoulder to shoulder, peering up and out all day long at the gray spears of the falling rain.

At dark, in spite of their hunger and the cold, they slept. They slept past the rising of the sun, past the late morning, and all the while it rained and the whistling of the rain seemed to lull and keep them asleep in spite of encircling danger. They were awakened by the shattering echoes of machine-gun fire and the impact of hundreds of bullets tearing at the rock above their heads. When the first volley ceased, the echoes carried its *rat-a-tat-tat* across the clifftop to where another echoing air seized upon it and reduplicated it fainter and fainter into the heart of the mountains before it finally died into silence. There was such a long interval that it seemed as if everybody were listening to that last faint replication so high up and so far away. Then they heard the shouts below them:

"Come out! Come out, ye snipes! Come out or we'll bomb ye out. Come out!"

These cries were echoed, and then a brief silence followed. The next minute the gun seemed to tear the tin roof from over their heads where they crouched helpless, their faces to the clay. They had placed their boots to dry, the night before, on the ledge before their dump and these now shot in on their foreheads torn to pieces by bullets. Again the echoes were reduplicated to the farthest uttermost glen and again the shouts came, mingling with those echoes and their own that followed after.

"Yeer last chance! Come out!"

The Kerry boy began to weep again.

"O God!" he shouted. "Leave us out. Leave us out."

"Throw down yeer guns," cried the echoing voices below.

They did so, and Buckteeth, tearing a sleeve from his shirt, raised it before him as he crawled out into the rain. Below them was a score sturdy green-clad riflemen and in a minute the three were among them, shivering with fear and excitement—broken, timid as children.

They passed through Youghal as prisoners, standing high on a lorry, conspicuous in their rags, and as it roared its way under the old clock archway, there across the wind-blown bay Bernie glimpsed his woods shrouded in mist, growing, as it seemed, out of the gray-green bay. Never did anything seem so definitely past to him as his summer flirting under those trees. It might have happened to him in another life, it might have been something he read of in a novel, so distant did it seem.

They drove him to Cork that night and there he remained in prison until the winter was passed and another winter had come again. Norah wrote to him many times while he was in jail—at first briefly but kindly, sending him gifts as she might to any other prisoner, later on long letters at greater length, as to a special friend. After a while she brought herself to reproach him for his long silence of that lonely winter, a winter in which she had tried hard, and vainly, to be, as he had been, forgetful of the sweetness of their summer and autumn love. It was Christmas when he received a letter from her confessing how miserable and unhappy those months had been, and he was glad of the confession though it was a torment to him to be reminded, in the place where he was, of this foolishness when he had been free. When she wrote that Edward Bradley often stayed with them, and spoke kindly of him, it was a double torment—that worst torment of all prisoners—to think what lovely things life could have given him, too, if he were out in the world and part of it. When he was freed he was very ill and weak and the doctor ordered him to the sea and he went, as a matter of course, to Youghal. It was February again, just a year since he had passed through it as a prisoner, and the woods and the bay were again shrouded in haze, but because Norah came to see him, and walked with him there, and showed him the rain in the cobwebs among the branches, and—it was so mild there by the sea—an early celandine hiding under a root, he thought those woods even more beautiful than they had been almost two years before when they watched the red globe of the autumn sun sinking behind its black branches.

Small wonder then that they should come back to the little seaside town for their honeymoon. It was Easter and late in the spring—the fifteenth of April had been Easter Sunday—so that the catkins' furry paws were already raised to the sun, and the long tails and the tiny wet noses of the lambs protruded from the red and blue creels rumbling in to the lamb fair. The yellow furze was ranged high against the blue sky along the slopes of the hills, and over the surface of the sea beneath there was a cold layer of air that made the waves break with a brittle noise such as one never hears in the soft, dead heat of summer. They went about that first day, their wedding day, noticing everything with new delight— the spears of green grass shooting through the dead fields, the primroses and the violets clustered near the gray stones in the ditches, the beech buds swollen red, the patches of hawthorn green lighting the withered hedges.

The long country lanes were empty; they had the ocean to themselves. The summer visitors had not yet even thought of coming and all the length of the old stone promenade was bare. They even felt a delight in the shuttered windows and the bathing boxes nailed up since last autumn. On the sands stretching for miles in front of them, lost in the end in the spume of the incoming waves far off in the distance, they saw only a sandpiper or two strutting by the skirts of the spreading sea, or peewits in their swoop turning as if to command on their white bellies, then turning again on dark wings, low over the thunderous waves. When they lay under an early blossoming blackthorn high above that singing sea and in the long silences of love gazed over the empty horizon, or back at the clustered smoking chimneys on the farther shore, Bernard felt, and knew that his young wife felt, that if another gull should wheel through the blue air, another distant lamb call out to its dam, their cups of ecstasy must overflow and roll upon the ground. They crossed back then, as of old, to the points of light that marked the town through an early sea haze and sought out that little restaurant where so long ago they had cursed the Elizabethans and the Cromwellians, and there they had their tea, watching back through the open door at the rear of the shop the channel darkening with the fall of night. As they ate they suddenly saw beside them a little green poster bearing that day's name and date. They read it with interest:

SINN FEIN ABU
A Public Meeting
will be addressed
in the Town Hall
at 7 P.M.
by
EDWARD BRADLEY

"Shall we go?" asked Bernard.

It was almost the hour as they made their way down the wandering side lanes that led to the wharves and the town hall. There, hidden deep in the crowd, they stood by an open window through which they could see the ever-present channel and the waters of the bay. The gaslights in the hall hummed like flies, huge green luminous flies that had floated in from the half night outside, so blue and lovely where it sank down, darker and darker, over the masts and the brown sails of the fishing smacks in the harbor, and far in the distance the peaked mountains that Bernard knew so well. It was so lovely to watch the hollow night fall outside, and through it now and again a green light climbing up a mast, and to turn from it to the pale pink-washed green-lit room within, that they paid but little heed to the speakers until their friend the teacher rose.

The years between that night and the day in the market square had not dulled his eloquence, and though his temples were gone quite white now—premature for his years—the terrible passion of the man blazed like the fire of burning youth. Yet as he talked the lovers did not join in the cheers of the audience. The night had fallen now and nothing showed beyond but the eyes of green or red on mast and poop. The mountains had vanished. The far woods were gone. They barely heard the lapping of the bay. As by one thought they moved quietly out through the cheering crowd into the darkness. But, shyly, they did not go back directly to their hotel. Wrapped in their own silence and the silence of the night they wandered about the quays or in and out among the lanes as if prolonging the night to the very last moment. The meeting was over before they returned to their hotel, and the lights of the houses in that street, and doubtless of every street in the town, were gone up to the second story. When they entered their room they saw that the pale light of the gas lamp outside the window fell on the high old-fashioned ceiling and from there glimmered down on the wide, carved bridal-bed, and needing no other light they used none. Across the street was another row of sleeping houses, and beyond that the bay, widening to the ocean, and when they stood without stirring they could hear the low boom of the waves on the cliffs and across the bar. As they undressed, the faint hum of a motor rose in the distance and approached along the street.

"Bernard," she whispered.

Over his shoulder he could see her pale body in the dim light, but where he stood by the window with one hand raised to draw down the blind his eyes fell on the passing car. He saw the white hair of their orator friend, the old bachelor, the patriot, driving out of the town into the country and the dark night. The hedges would race past him; the rabbits skip before his headlights on the road; the moths in the cool wind would fly around his flushed face and his trembling hands. But that wind would not for many miles cool the passion in him to which he had given his life.

"Bernard," she whispered again, and her voice trembled a little.

He drew the blind down slowly. The lamp shadowed the framework of the window on it. Slowly he turned to her where she gleamed even in the dark.

POETRY

O Brave New World

During the Renaissance English poets envisioned a heroic future for those of their countrymen engaged in the quest to establish a new social order in the New World. In "To the Virginian Voyage," his ode to the courageous colonizers of America, Michael Drayton foresees not merely the founding of another England but a new England, a second Paradise amid the Edenic beauty and fertility of the New World. In his poem "Bermudas" Andrew Marvell sees the Puritan émigrés as spiritual heroes, new Adams in quest of a new Garden of Eden and a perfected social order.

The mystique of the New World, which transformed transplanted Englishmen into Americans and created a new social order, is the subject of Robert Frost's "The Gift Outright." For this transformation to become complete, however, the active, even heroic, participation of the colonists themselves was eventually required: "The deed of gift was many deeds of war." This poem was recited by Robert Frost at the inauguration of John F. Kennedy as President of the United States on January 20, 1961.

That special relationship between the land and its people which is uniquely American is implicit in the myth of the frontier and finds its most complete symbolic embodiment in the figure of Daniel Boone. In his poem "For the Grave of Daniel Boone" William Stafford suggests that the questing spirit of this hero is still an aspect of our national character, that even today, "in a barbwire time," there is something of the frontiersman in every American.

To the Virginian Voyage

Michael Drayton

You brave heroic minds
Worthy your country's name,
    That honor still pursue,
    Go, and subdue,

Whilst loit'ring hinds[1]
Lurk here at home, with shame.

Britons, you stay too long;
Quickly aboard bestow you,
   And with a merry gale
   Swell your stretched sail,
With vows as strong
As the winds that blow you.

Your course securely steer,
West and by south forth keep,
   Rocks, lee shores, nor shoals,
   When Aeolus[2] scowls,
You need not fear,
So absolute the deep.

And cheerfully at sea,
Success you still entice,
   To get the pearl and gold,
   And ours to hold,
Virginia,
Earth's only paradise,

Where nature hath in store
Fowl, venison, and fish,
   And the fruitful'st soil
   Without your toil
Three harvests more,
All greater than your wish.

And the ambitious vine
Crowns with his purple mass
   The cedar reaching high
   To kiss the sky,
The cypress, pine,
And useful sassafras.

To whose the golden age
Still nature's laws doth give,
   No other cares that tend,
   But them to defend

5

10

15

20

25

30

35

40

1. *hinds* Rustics.   2. *Aeolus* The wind god.

From winter's age,
That long there doth not live.

Whenas the luscious smell
Of that delicious land,
   Above the seas that flows,   45
   The clear wind throws,
Your hearts to swell
Approaching the dear strand,

In kenning of the shore,
Thanks to God first given,   50
   Oh you, the happiest men,
   Be frolic then,
Let cannons roar,
Frighting the wide heaven.

And in regions far   55
Such heroes bring ye forth
   As those from whom we came,
   And plant our name
Under that star
Not known unto our north.   60

And as there plenty grows
Of laurel everywhere,
   Apollo's sacred tree,
   You it may see
A poet's brows   65
To crown, that may sing there.

Thy voyages attend,
Industrious Hakluyt,[3]
   Whose reading shall enflame
   Men to seek fame,   70
And much commend
To after times thy wit.

3. *Hakluyt* The historian who chronicled the Elizabethan voyages of discovery of the New World.

Bermudas

Andrew Marvell

Where the remote Bermudas ride,
In th' ocean's bosom unespied,
From a small boat that rowed along,
The listening winds received this song:
   "What should we do but sing His praise,   5
That led us through the watery maze
Unto an isle so long unknown,
And yet far kinder than our own?
Where He the huge sea monsters wracks,[1]
That lift the deep upon their backs;   10
IIe lands us on a grassy stage,
Safe from the storms, and prelate's rage.[2]
He gave us this eternal spring
Which here enamels everything,
And sends the fowls to us in care,   15
On daily visits through the air;
He hangs in shades the orange bright,
Like golden lamps in a green night,
And does in the pomegranates close
Jewels more rich than Ormus[3] shows;   20
He makes the figs our mouths to meet,
And throws the melons at our feet;
But apples[4] plants of such a price,
No tree could ever bear them twice;
With cedars, chosen by His hand,   25
From Lebanon, He stores the land;
And makes the hollow seas, that roar,
Proclaim the ambergris on shore;
He cast (of which we rather boast)
The Gospel's pearl upon our coast,   30
And in these rocks for us did frame
A temple, where to sound His name.
O! let our voice His praise exalt,

1. *wracks* Casts ashore.
2. *prelate's rage* The Prelates were the high priests of the Church of England whose persecution of the Puritans forced them to seek escape by emigration to the New World.   3. *Ormus* An island off the coast of Persia.
4. *apples* Here, this means pineapples.

Till it arrive at heaven's vault,
Which, thence (perhaps) rebounding, may   35
Echo beyond the Mexique Bay."[5]
    Thus sung they in the English boat,
An holy and a cheerful note;
And all the way, to guide their chime,
With falling oars they kept the time.   40

The Gift Outright

Robert Frost

The land was ours before we were the land's.
She was our land more than a hundred years
Before we were her people.   She was ours
In Massachusetts, in Virginia,
But we were England's, still colonials,   5
Possessing what we still were unpossessed by,
Possessed by what we now no more possessed.
Something we were withholding made us weak
Until we found out that it was ourselves
We were withholding from our land of living   10
And forthwith found salvation in surrender.
Such as we were we gave ourselves outright
(The deed of gift was many deeds of war)
To the land vaguely realizing westward,
But still unstoried, artless, unenhanced,   15
Such as she was, such as she would become.

For the Grave of Daniel Boone

William Stafford

The farther he went the farther home grew.
Kentucky became another room;
the mansion arched over the Mississippi;

5. *Mexique Bay* The Gulf of Mexico.

flowers were spread all over the floor.
He traced ahead a deepening home,   5
and better, with goldenrod:

Leaving the snakeskin of place after place,
going on—after the trees
the grass, a bird flying after a song.
Rifle so level, sighting so well   10
his picture freezes down to now,
a story-picture for children.

They go over the velvet falls
into the tapestry of his time,
heirs to the landscape, feeling no jar: 15
it is like evening; they are the quail
surrounding his fire, coming in for the kill;
their little feet moved sacred sand.

Children, we live in a barbwire time
but like to follow the old hands back—   20
the ring in the light, the knuckle, the palm,
all the way to Daniel Boone,
hunting our own kind of deepening home.
From the land that was his I heft this rock.

Here on his grave I put it down.   25

One Nation Indivisible

Unlike the quest of the frontiersman Daniel Boone, John Brown's
was more than a private one.   Brown, a white man, was an abolitionist,
passionately dedicated to the liberation of the black race in America.
Langston Hughes' poem on the anniversary of Brown's raid on Harpers
Ferry (October 16, 1859) is addressed to his fellow black citizens, but
is pertinent to all Americans, especially those who have forgotten how
the heroes of the past have helped to shape the present.

Frederick Douglass was, like John Brown, an abolitionist, but he was
also a writer, an orator, and a black man.   In his poem on Douglass,
Robert Hayden sees this man as a hero whose quest for social order
with justice will one day be completed by others, for it is as yet an
unrealized dream.

October 16

Langston Hughes

Perhaps
You will remember
John Brown.

John Brown
Who took his gun,   5
Took twenty-one companions
White and black,
Went to shoot your way to freedom
Where two rivers meet
And the hills of the   10
North
And the hills of the
South
Look slow at one another—
And died   15
For your sake.
Now that you are
Many years free,
And the echo of the Civil War
Has passed away,   20
And Brown himself
Has long been tried at law,
Hanged by the neck,
And buried in the ground—
Since Harpers Ferry   25
Is alive with ghosts today,
Immortal raiders
Come again to town—

Perhaps
You will recall   30
John Brown.

Frederick Douglass

Robert Hayden

When it is finally ours, this freedom, this liberty, this beautiful
and terrible thing, needful to man as air,
usable as earth; when it belongs at last to all,
when it is truly instinct, brain matter, diastole, systole,
reflex action; when it is finally won; when it is more   5
than the gaudy mumbo jumbo of politicians:
this man, this Douglass, this former slave, this Negro
beaten to his knees, exiled, visioning a world
where none is lonely, none hunted, alien,
this man, superb in love and logic, this man   10
shall be remembered.   Oh, not with statues' rhetoric,
not with legends and poems and wreaths of bronze alone,
but with the lives grown out of his life, the lives
fleshing his dream of the beautiful, needful thing.

I Have a Dream . . .

Like Dr. Martin Luther King, Jr., Malcolm X became a martyr to the quest for social order with justice.   According to Don L. Lee's poem "Malcolm Spoke/who listened?" this charismatic and militant hero of the black community was also a prophet, but he was assassinated before his message of black consciousness, black pride, and black power was fully understood by those to whom it was addressed—including the poet himself, as the poem's subtitle indicates.   Another such martyr was the civil rights leader Medgar Evers who was assassinated in 1963. Gwendolyn Brooks' poem on Evers, dedicated to the brother who has carried on his quest, employs a series of symbols to suggest the effects the rebel-hero has upon the established social order which opposes him.

That the United States has produced heroes both black and white in appreciable numbers is not a chauvinistic claim but a fact of history. That our need for heroes continues and is likely to do so in the foreseeable future would seem to be a reasonable inference from present-day realities.   The heroes of our past can be called upon to serve our spiritual and psychological needs, but real crises demand action from live heroes.   Rhetoric, especially jingoistic rhetoric of the kind satirized by e. e. cummings in his poem "next to of course god america i" will not suffice. The quest for social order with justice and freedom can go on only so long as America produces the heroes to undertake it.

Malcolm Spoke/who listened?

(this poem is for my consciousness too)
Don L. Lee

he didn't say
wear yr/blackness in
outer garments
& blk/slogans fr/the top 10.
he was fr a long   5
line of super-cools,
    doo-rag[1] lovers &
    revolutionary pimps.
u are playing that
high-yellow[2] game in blackface   10
minus the straighthair.
now
it's nappy-black[3]
&   air conditioned volkswagens
with undercover whi   15
te girls who studied faulkner at
smith
& are authorities on "militant"
knee/grows
selling u at jew town rates: 20
    niggers with wornout tongues
    three for a quarter/or will consider a trade

the double-breasted hipster
has been replaced with a
dashiki wearing rip-off   25
who went to city college
majoring in physical education.

1. *doo-rag* A scarf worn by blacks who have chemically straightened hair.
2. *high-yellow* Light-skinned blacks.   3. *nappy-black* Tightly curled hair of blacks.

animals come in all colors.
dark meat will roast as fast as whi-te meat
especially in   30
the unitedstatesofamerica's
new
self-cleaning ovens.
if we don't listen.

Medgar Evers

For Charles Evers
Gwendolyn Brooks

The man whose height his fear improved he
arranged to fear no further.   The raw
intoxicated time was time for better birth or
a final death.

Old styles, old tempos, all the engagement of   5
the day—the sedate, the regulated fray—
the antique light, the Moral rose, old gusts,
tight whistlings from the past, the mothballs
in the Love at last our man forswore.

Medgar Evers annoyed confetti and assorted   10
brands of businessmen's eyes.
The shows came down: to maxims and surprise.
And palsy.

Roaring no rapt arise-ye to the dead, he
leaned across tomorrow.   People said that   15
he was holding clean globes in his hands.

next to of course
god america i

e. e. cummings

"next to of course god america i
love you land of the pilgrims' and so forth oh
say can you see by the dawn's early my
country 'tis of centuries come and go
and are no more what of it we should worry   5
in every language even deafanddumb
thy sons acclaim your glorious name by gorry
by jingo by gee by gosh by gum
why talk of beauty what could be more beautiful than these heroic happy dead   10
who rushed like lions to the roaring slaughter
they did not stop to think they died instead
then shall the voice of liberty be mute?"

He spoke. And drank rapidly a glass of water

DRAMA

The Devil in the Dark

Television drama is obviously the most popular form of entertainment in our time. It is in fact the most popular form of theater the world has ever known. Although television as a viable electronic medium is hardly more than a quarter of a century old, the dramas it presents are seen regularly by more people than could have attended the legitimate theater in the thousands of years of that theater's existence. Not even movies can consistently lay claim to such large audiences. Nonetheless, as a form of literature television drama has much in common with its predecessors, for much of it will be found to conform to one of the traditional literary modes—most often to comedy or romance, less often to tragedy, satire, or realism. Thus most television dramas feature plots and types of characters which would have been familiar enough to Shakespeare's audience and even to the audiences in the amphitheaters of ancient Greece and Rome.

The Devil in the Dark is an edited version of an original script for a program in the popular series *Star Trek*. Like most of the dramas in that series it is a science fiction romance. Although *The Devil in the Dark* is set in the twenty-third century, this drama's literary lineage can be traced back to such classic works as Edmund Spenser's epic poem of the sixteenth century *The Faerie Queene*. In *The Devil in the Dark*, as in *The Faerie Queene*, the focus is upon the hero figures. Spencer's romance-epic deals with the several quests of a number of heroes; whereas *Star Trek* treats a single quest, an exploration of outer space, by several heroes, including a "nonhuman," Mr. Spock, a large-eared native of the planet Vulcan.

The heroes of *The Faerie Queene* encounter a wide variety of villains and monsters, and so do the heroes of *Star Trek*. In *The Devil in the Dark*, however, the three featured heroes—Captain Kirk, Mr. Spock, and Dr. McCoy—find friends turning into enemies, at least temporarily; discover that there are more kinds of community and social order than are dreamt of in their philosophies; and learn that "monster" is a relative term. An interesting difference between a classic romance such as *The Faerie Queene* and *The Devil in the Dark* is the sharply defined distinction between good and evil, which is characteristic of Spenser's poem and of most of the romances read today as examples of "serious" literature, and the complexity and ambiguity of good and evil in this particular example of "popular" literature.

Since *The Devil in the Dark*, like so many television dramas, has the potential for achieving some kind of impact upon a very large audience, the kinds of heroes, villains, and monsters it portrays and the views and values it embodies may not only reflect but influence society's attitudes. The premise upon which the *Star Trek* series is based is that of a quest for social order, or more precisely, a quest for cosmic order. *The Devil in the Dark* presents an interesting example of the kind of threat to social order that our own futures could contain. But it may also be read as a dramatization of the forms of behavior man has historically exhibited in his past quests for social order, in his encounters with new worlds and new races.

The Devil in the Dark

Gene Coon

CHARACTERS

CAPTAIN JAMES KIRK, *Commander of the Starship "Enterprise" during its five-year mission to explore outer space*

MR. SPOCK, *Captain Kirk's second-in-command and Science Officer of the "Enterprise"; a native of the planet Vulcan*

DR. McCOY, *Chief Medical Officer of the "Enterprise"*

MR. SCOTT, *Engineering Officer of the "Enterprise"; Captain Kirk's third-in-command*

COMMANDER GIOTTO, *in charge of the "Enterprise" Security Force*

VANDERBERG, *Chief Engineer of the pergium production station of the planet Thetis Six*

APPEL, *one of Vanderberg's engineers*

SCHMITTER, *another engineer*

SECURITY GUARDS *and* ENGINEERS

THE TIME.   the twenty-third century.

THE PLACE.   beneath the hostile surface of the planet Thetis Six.   Because of its rich deposits of pergium and other valuable minerals, Thetis Six has been colonized.   All of the action takes place underground, in the tunnels and rooms of the man-made mining complex.

PROLOGUE

SCENE 1

[*On Camera: a finished tunnel outside a large room; some engineers, wearing coveralls, are herding a small crowd of frightened women and children through the tunnel and into the large room.*]

APPEL. That's all of them. . . .

VANDERBERG. Good.

APPEL. But we can't keep them there indefinitely.

VANDERBERG. We've called for help.   The Starship "Enterprise" is on its way.

APPEL. Can we hold out until then?

VANDERBERG [*angrily*]. How do I know?

APPEL. This thing—whatever it is—

VANDERBERG. We fight it!

APPEL. Fight it? We can't even find it! But it finds us! Ten men dead in the last two weeks!

VANDERBERG. What do you want from me? A miracle?

APPEL. All I know is we can't go on. Machinery is being eaten away—key personnel murdered—worse than murdered!

VANDERBERG. What do you want to do, Appel? Lock yourself up in a closet somewhere?

APPEL. If I thought it might be safe! But nothing's safe!

[*Enter four engineers armed with Phaser #1, a hand-carried weapon which emits a beam of energy. The engineers, one of whom is* SCHMITTER, *are obviously apprehensive.*]

VANDERBERG. All right, Appel. It won't do any good to cry about it. We'll just have to hold out.

APPEL. For how long?

VANDERBERG. Until we get help! Until we find out what's doing it—and kill it! In the meantime we hold out—the way we've been doing. [*to the engineers*] All right. Let's go.

[*He turns his back on the angry* APPEL *and leaves. The four engineers follow him out.*]

SCENE 2

[*On Camera: an unfinished tunnel, cluttered with ruined pieces of mining machinery; a nervous guard stands by; hearing a sound down the tunnel he stiffens, whipping his phaser around in the direction of the noise.*]

GUARD. Who's there?

VOICE OF VANDERBERG. It's your relief, Sam.

[*The guard is visibly relieved; enter four men led by* VANDERBERG; SCHMITTER *steps out to take the guard's place.*]

SCHMITTER. Quiet?

GUARD. I didn't see a thing. But this place—

SCHMITTER. All right! I don't like it any more than you do.

VANDERBERG. Schmitter, keep your phaser in your hand. If you hear anything, see anything—anything at all—call in immediately.

SCHMITTER. You don't have to worry about me, chief.

VANDERBERG. All right. I'll see you in four hours. Good luck.

[*Exit* VANDERBERG *and the four guards;* SCHMITTER *watches them depart rather wistfully; alone, he looks around nervously, hefting the phaser in his hand.*]

On Camera: something large, dark, and shapeless is seen near SCHMIT-
TER; *it is slug-like, shaggy, knobby; it makes a scuffling sound which*
SCHMITTER *hears; he turns slowly, the thing rushes; he screams and fires
his phaser; the huge thing envelops* SCHMITTER, *cutting off his scream.*

On Camera: hearing the scream, VANDERBERG *and his men freeze; he
turns, then signals them back.]*

VANDERBERG. Come on!

[*On Camera: the guard post in the tunnel; all that remains is a black
blotch on the floor, seen with horror by* VANDERBERG *and the others as
they enter.]*

VANDERBERG. Schmitter—like the rest of them—burned to a crisp.

[*On Camera: the horrified faces of the men. Fade Out.]*

ACT I

SCENE 1

VOICE OF CAPTAIN KIRK. Captain's Log, Star Date 3196.1 A distress call
from the pergium production station on Thetis Six has brought the
"Enterprise" to that long-established colony. . . . Mr. Spock and I,
and a party of specialists from the "Enterprise," have beamed down
to meet with Chief Engineer Vanderberg, administrative head of
Thetis Six.

[*On Camera:* VANDERBERG's *office; he stands behind his large desk, in
front of which are arrayed* KIRK, SPOCK, MCCOY, *and* GIOTTO.]

VANDERBERG [*urgently, rapidly*]. I tell you, you have to do something!
We've been brought to an absolute stop! Production nil! Almost
fifty murders—
KIRK. Slow down, Mr. Vanderberg. You haven't even told us what it's
all about yet.
VANDERBERG. It's a monster—something—horrible, lashing out—
SPOCK. There are very few "monsters" in the universe, Mr. Vanderberg.
VANDERBERG. Well, there's one here!

[KIRK *and* SPOCK *exchange glances. This is a very overwrought man.]*

KIRK. All right. Let's assume there's a monster. What has it done?
When did it start?
VANDERBERG [*pulling himself together; he presses a button on his desk
communicator*]. Send Ed Appel in here. [*to* KIRK] About three
months ago we opened a new level. Sensors gave us an unusually

rich pergium reading—not only pergium—anything you want: gold, platinum, cerium, uranium. The whole planet's like that. A treasure house.

KIRK. We're aware of that. If mining conditions weren't so difficult Thetis Six could supply a thousand planets' mineral needs. But what happened?

VANDERBERG. First, the automatic machinery. It started to—almost— disintegrate. Corrode. Metal began to dissolve away. No reason for it. Nothing has changed. There's nothing in the soil to account for it!

SPOCK. Nevertheless, sir, I am sure that there is a reason. It simply has not been discovered yet.

VANDERBERG. Yes it has. I don't know *what* it is, but I know what it's doing.

KIRK. You said "murders."

VANDERBERG. First, our maintenance engineers—sent down into the drifts to repair the corroded machinery. We found them—burned to a crisp. Seared beyond recognition.

KIRK. Flame? Lava, perhaps?

SPOCK. There is no current volcanic activity on the planet, Captain.

VANDERBERG. He's right. None. At first the murders were down deep, but they've been moving toward our levels. The last man died two days ago, three levels below this.

KIRK. The same way? Burned?

MCCOY. I'd like to examine the body.

VANDERBERG. We kept it for you. It isn't pretty.

KIRK. You've posted sentries? Guards?

[*Enter Engineer* APPEL.]

VANDERBERG. Of course. And five of them have died.

KIRK. Has anybody seen this—this "monster" of yours?

APPEL. I have.

VANDERBERG [*introducing*]. Ed Appel. Chief Processing Engineer.

SPOCK. Describe it, please.

APPEL. I can't. I only got a glimpse of it. Big. Shaggy—

VANDERBERG. Ed shot it.

KIRK. Oh? You mean, shot at it.

APPEL. No! I mean I shot it! With this! [*indicates his phaser*] A good, clean shot. It didn't even slow it down.

[KIRK *and* SPOCK *register surprise.*]

SPOCK. Gentlemen. A phaser is effective against any known form of life in the galaxy.

APPEL. It's a pea-shooter. I only got away by the skin of my teeth. Poor Bill Andersen—the man who was with me—we had to scrape him up.

SPOCK. Fascinating.

VANDERBERG. I've already made my report to you. Production is shut down. Nobody will go into the levels—and I don't blame them. If the Federation wants pergium, do something about it!

KIRK. That's what we're here for, Mr. Vanderberg. . . . Mr. Spock, I'll want a complete computer-bank evaluation. Interview everyone who knows anything about this. Mr. Vanderberg, I'll want a complete subsurface chart of all drifts, tunnels, and adits.

VANDERBERG. You'll get it.

[SPOCK, *curious, steps forward and touches a large, glossy, round object on* VANDERBERG's *desk.*]

SPOCK. This, Mr. Vanderberg. What is it?

VANDERBERG. It's a silicon nodule. There are a million of them down there. No commercial value.

SPOCK. But a geological oddity, to say the least. Pure silicon?

VANDERBERG. A few trace elements. Look, we didn't call you here so you could collect rocks. I've assigned you rooms down the hall. If you've got equipment to set up—

KIRK. Thank you, Mr. Vanderberg. We'll need your complete cooperation.

VANDERBERG. You'll have it. Just find this creature, whatever it is. I've got a quota to meet.

SCENE 2

[*On Camera:* KIRK's *headquarters, with a small medical lab and a few items of furniture;* KIRK *and* SPOCK *are examining a map of the tunnel system of Thetis Six;* MCCOY *is looking into a microscope and making entries in his medical log.*]

KIRK. An incredible number of tunnels. Even in fifty years, even with automated equipment . . .

SPOCK. They are not man-made, Captain. They seem to be lava tubes— or so I am informed. I plan to examine them as soon as possible. A network of them extends throughout the entire interior of the planet. Geologically, most unusual.

KIRK. They won't make hunting any easier. [*turns to* DR. MCCOY] Doc?

MCCOY. Schmitter wasn't burned to death, Jim. Not in the usual sense, at least.

KIRK. Explain.

MCCOY. A chemical corrosion. Almost as if he had been thrown into a vat of an incredibly corrosive acid.

KIRK. An acid strong enough to eat away machinery?

MCCOY. Or anything else you can think of.

KIRK. Mr. Spock?

SPOCK. Yes, Captain?

KIRK. Does the acid tie in with what you have learned?

SPOCK. Not specifically. Mr. Vanderberg maintains that the creature lives beneath the surface, using the network of lava tubes to move through. I disagree. I have charted the positions of the deaths and the acts of sabotage. [*Moves to a chart and points out several places, marked with X's, which are not crossed by the labyrinthian lines marking the tunnels*] Here, and here, and here. Now, unless the sensor readings of the tunnels are in error, the creature could not possibly have appeared at these points. Yet it did.

KIRK. How recent are those tunnel charts?

SPOCK. They were made last year.

KIRK. Before the appearance of this—whatever it is.

SPOCK. Yes, sir.

KIRK. Run another sensor check, Mr. Spock. Compare.

SPOCK. I have already ordered it, Captain.

KIRK. Good. Report on life beneath the surface?

SPOCK. There is no life, other than the accountable human residents of the colony, under the surface. At least—not life as we know it.

KIRK [*staring at the chart*]. We can't just start covering tunnel by tunnel on foot. We've got to get production going again. We must have this pergium!

SPOCK. Indeed, Captain. The task would take years. I suggest that another appearance by the creature—

KIRK. When this creature appears, men die.

SPOCK. Yes, I know. [*They stare at one another.*]

SCENE 3

[*On Camera: the tunnel outside the Fusion Reaction Chamber; a large metal door blocks the tunnel at the far end; a posted sign reads: CAUTION! RADIATION CHAMBER. ONLY AUTHORIZED PERSONS BEYOND THIS POINT! A guard, armed with Phaser #1, stands uneasily at his post. A scuffling noise; from behind the guard a huge shaggy figure emerges; he whirls, screams, throws his phaser up to fire; the figure envelops him and then moves off toward the metal door; it tracks smoke. It moves through the metal door, leaving a gaping hole*] *that looks as if it had been created by burning; inside the Fusion Reaction Chamber there are noises—metallic, mechanical; a hissing sound, and then a clank of metal on stone.*]

SCENE 4

[*On Camera:* KIRK's *headquarters;* DR. MCCOY *is still at work;* KIRK *and* SPOCK *are going over stacks of papers.*]

KIRK. Too many tunnels. We couldn't possibly— Mr. Spock, what kind of life form would not register on our sensors?

SPOCK. Our sensors can pick up normal life functions at a distance of nearly a parsec. I cannot conceive—

KIRK. Normal life functions. How about abnormal life functions?

[SPOCK *looks thoughtful. Suddenly there is a distant boom, the room shakes, its lights flicker, an alarm bell begins to clang. The door flies open and* VANDERBERG *rushes in, pale and frightened.*]

VANDERBERG. Something's happened in the Main Reaction Chamber!

KIRK. Let's go!   [*All exit.*]

SCENE 5

[*On Camera: the tunnel outside the Fusion Reaction Chamber; visible are the remains of the guard and the gaping hole in the door; but now something else is visible—a large, almost perfectly circular hole in one wall; enter* KIRK *and party, who stop to stare at the remains of the guard;* MCCOY *begins a medical examination;* VANDERBERG *looks at the door, recoils.*]

VANDERBERG. Look at that!

[VANDERBERG, KIRK, *and* SPOCK *hurry toward the ruined door;* VANDERBERG *moves on inside;* SPOCK *and* KIRK *look intently at the hole;* KIRK *is about to touch it.*]

SPOCK. Don't touch it, Captain!   —Some extremely active corrosive. Traces may linger.

VANDERBERG'S VOICE [*from within*]. Kirk! Quickly!

SCENE 6

[*On Camera: the interior of the Main Reactor Room, with pipes, control panels, etc.; an appalled* VANDERBERG *is staring at one of the pipes, where a section is missing*]

262

KIRK. I didn't know anyone still used fusion for power.

VANDERBERG. We're not going to either. Not for long.

KIRK. Explain.

VANDERBERG. The central retarding mechanism—the safety valve for the entire reactor. It's gone!

[SPOCK *examines the break in the pipe.*]

SPOCK. The same indications shown by the door, Captain. A very strong corrosive.

KIRK [*to* VANDERBERG]. You have a replacement for this?

VANDERBERG. None. It's outdated—but we never had any trouble with it.

KIRK. Spock? On board?

SPOCK. Nothing for a device this antiquated, Captain.

VANDERBERG. Without the control mechanism, the reactor will go critical. It could blow up half the planet. [*panicky*] And we can't shut it down! It provides heat and air and life support for the whole colony!

KIRK. Well, Mr. Spock? We seem to have a choice of asphixiation or a nuclear fusion explosion.

SPOCK. Indeed, Captain. It is a very narrow choice. [*He is not being facetious; they stare at one another. Fade Out.*]

ACT II

SCENE 1

[*On Camera: the interior of the Main Reactor Room;* VANDERBERG *is examining the damage;* KIRK *is making contact with* SCOTT, *on board the orbiting "Enterprise."*]

KIRK. Scotty, this is the Captain.

SCOTT. Yes, Captain.

KIRK. Do we have a spare retarding mechanism for the PXK pergium reactor?

SCOTT. Not a chance, Captain. Haven't seen one of them in twenty years.

KIRK. We need one. Can you rig one up? It's vital.

SCOTT. Well sir, I could put together some odds and ends. But they wouldn't hold for long.

KIRK. How long?

SCOTT. Forty-eight hours, maybe, with a bit of luck. Those old pergium reactors lay out a lot of stress and strain.

KIRK. Forty-eight hours is better than nothing. Get together what you need and beam down here with it. Top priority.

SCOTT. Aye, aye, Captain. I'll be right there. Scott out.

KIRK [*to* VANDERBERG]. My chief engineer can rig up a temporary retarder.

VANDERBERG. I heard him. What happens when it breaks down?

KIRK. Hopefully we'll have found the missing part by then.

VANDERBERG. Hopefully! Small chance!

KIRK. If we haven't, we'll beam up all colonists and evacuate.

VANDERBERG. And there goes your precious pergium. A dozen planets already screaming for it. Reactors closing down, life support systems failing. [*intensely*] You've got to find it! And find the monster! Get us back in production, man, or it means disaster for billions of people!

KIRK. I'm aware of that, Chief. We'll do what we can.   [*Exit* KIRK.]

SCENE 2

[*On Camera: the tunnel outside the Main Reactor Room; enter* KIRK; *enter* SPOCK *from the newly formed tunnel in the side of the main tunnel.*]

SPOCK. Most curious, Captain. This tunnel is not indicated on any of the charts we were provided. I have made inquiries. It simply was not there before.

KIRK. Maybe it had been there all along, undiscovered, abutting up against this tunnel, but not breaking through into it.

SPOCK. Possibly. But it is most strange.

KIRK. A lava tube?

SPOCK. I suppose it is possible, but it is unlike any in my experience. A lava tube should have certain random irregularities. This has none. It is as straight as a phaser beam.

KIRK [*examining the tunnel*]. The edges. Almost glassy.

SPOCK. Yes. Too glassy. It joins a charted tunnel back there about fifty yards.

KIRK. Have a Security team check it out—as far as you can. Examine every tunnel on this level. In the meantime, let's see if Doc has come up with anything.

SCENE 3

[*On Camera:* KIRK's *headquarters.*]

MCCOY. I think it's mass hysteria.

KIRK. Hysteria? Dozens of people have been killed.

MCCOY. Some—natural cause. A phenomenon—

SPOCK [*who has been examining the round silicon object he got from* VANDERBERG]. Surely, Doctor. A natural cause. But not hysteria.

MCCOY. All right. You asked my opinion. I gave it to you. How do I know? Maybe there is some kind of a "monster"—

SPOCK. Not a "monster," Doctor. A "creature." And an intelligent one.

MCCOY. What makes you think so?

SPOCK. The missing retarder mechanism was not taken by accident. It was the one piece of portable equipment absolutely essential to the operation of the reactor.

KIRK. You think this creature is trying to drive the colonists off the planet?

SPOCK. It seems logical.

KIRK. Why just now, Mr. Spock? This production facility was established here fifty years ago.

SPOCK. I do not know, sir— [staring at the round object] There is a possibility—

KIRK. What, Mr. Spock?

SPOCK. The fact that Mr. Appel claimed to have hit the creature with his phaser.

KIRK. He could have been mistaken.

SPOCK. Mr. Appel strikes me as being a capable, unimaginative man. If he said he hit it, I tend to believe he did. That being the case, why wasn't the creature affected?

KIRK. I can't explain it.

SPOCK. Perhaps I can—though Dr. McCoy will accuse me of creating fantasies.

MCCOY. You? I doubt it.

SPOCK. A phaser—Number One or Number Two—is designed to affect any life form as we know it.

KIRK. Of course.

SPOCK. Life, as we know it, is universally based on some combination of carbon compounds. Phasers are designed to destroy carbon compounds. But what if life exists using another element for a base— [staring at the round object]—for instance, silicon?

MCCOY. You're right, Mr. Spock. You're creating fantasies.

KIRK. Is it possible?

MCCOY. Of course not.

SPOCK. You mean, not in our experience, Doctor. But the possibility of silicon being used as a life building block has been hypothesized.

KIRK. Silicon-based life would be of an entirely different order. Maybe our phasers wouldn't affect it.

SPOCK. Certainly not Phaser #1, Captain, which is considerably less powerful than Phaser #2. [becoming excited; pacing back and forth] In addition, let us hypothesize a creature which lives in the depths of a planet, under extreme pressure. Such a creature— especially if silicon-based—would have to develop a form of armor-plating to survive.

KIRK. Armor plate—silicon-based—naturally phaser-resistant. And these colonists are armed only with Phaser #1.

SPOCK. Yes, Captain. It could explain much.

KIRK. But *our* people have #2 Phasers—

SPOCK. And I could make an adjustment on them—to affect silicon.

MCCOY. I still think you're imagining things. Silicon-based life is physiologically impossible.

KIRK. You may be right—but it's something to go on. Spock. Assemble the security forces, with Phasers #2. Make the required adjustments. [SPOCK *is fingering the round object thoughtfully*.] You seem fascinated by that rock, Mr. Spock.

SPOCK. Yes, Captain. You will recall that Chief Engineer Vanderberg commented that there were thousands of these on a lower level— the level the machinery had opened just before the first appearance of the creature.

KIRK. Do they tie in?

SPOCK. I don't know.

KIRK. Speculate.

SPOCK. I have already provided Doctor McCoy with sufficient cause for amusement. If you don't mind, Captain, I would prefer to cogitate on the possibilities for a time.

KIRK. A short time, Mr. Spock. We have very little.

SCENE 4

[*On Camera: the interior of the Main Reactor Chamber;* SCOTT, *with an assistant, is at work replacing the retardation mechanism; enter* KIRK.]

KIRK. Well, Scotty?

SCOTT [*drawing back, showing a complicated array of pipes, lines, and valves occupying the place of the missing retardation mechanism*]. It's a plumber's nightmare, Captain, but it'll hold for a bit.

KIRK. It may have to hold longer than a bit.

SCOTT. I'm sorry, Captain, that's the best I can do—and I guarantee you it's not good enough. [*a signal from* KIRK's *communications device is heard; he opens it*] Kirk here.

VOICE OF SPOCK. Captain, the Security officers have gathered in Chief Vanderberg's office.

KIRK. I'll be right there. Kirk out. [*to* SCOTT] Ride herd on it, Scotty. Kind words and tender, loving care. Baby it. Flatter it. Kiss it if you have to. But keep it working.

SCOTT. I'll do what I can sir. [*exit* KIRK; SCOTT *looks at the results of his labor*] Well, you're an ugly little devil, but you're all mine and I love you.

[*On Camera: interior of* VANDERBERG's *office; several* SECURITY OFFICERS *and* VANDERBERG *are present; enter* KIRK, *facing them.*]

KIRK. Gentlemen, as soon as this briefing is over you will report to Mr. Spock, who will make certain adjustments on your phasers.   I assume your details are complete?   [*They nod affirmatively.*]   You will each be given a complete chart of all tunnels and diggings under this installation.   You will proceed from level to level, checking out every foot of opening.   You will be searching for some variety of creature which apparently is highly resistant to phaser fire.   You will have your phasers set on maximum.   And remember this: fifty people have been killed.   I want no more deaths—

VANDERBERG. Except the bloody thing!

[KIRK *looks at him, nods.*]

KIRK. The creature may or may not attack on sight.   However, *you* must. A great deal depends on getting this installation back into production.

SPOCK. Mr. Vanderberg, may I ask at which level you discovered the nodules of silicon?

VANDERBERG. The twenty-third.   Why?

KIRK. Commander Giotto, you will take your detail directly to the twenty-third level and start your search from there.

GIOTTO. Aye, aye, sir.   May I ask if you have reason to suspect this— creature—may be on that level?

KIRK. It is one of the possibilities we have discussed.   [*to* VANDERBERG] Chief, have any of your people volunteered to join in the search?

VANDERBERG. A dozen or so.   Mr. Appel has them outside.

KIRK. Equip them with Phasers #2, Commander.

GIOTTO. Yes, sir.

KIRK [*to* VANDERBERG]. I want all the rest of your people to stay on the top level, together, in a safe place.

VANDERBERG. I don't know any safe place, Captain, the way this thing comes and goes.

KIRK. We'll see what we can do about that.   All right, gentlemen.   You have your instructions.   Let's get at it.   [*All exit.*]

SCENE 6

[*On Camera: in the tunnel complex; numerous members of the "Enterprise" Security Detachment are fanning out, searching the tunnels.*]

Scene 7

[*On Camera:* *the interior of a tunnel on the twenty-third level; enter* SPOCK, KIRK, *and two* SECURITY GUARDS; SPOCK *is taking an instrument reading;* KIRK *and* GIOTTO *are examining a map.*]

KIRK [*pointing*]. We are here. You will have your men fan out through these tunnels. They converge up ahead. We'll rendezvous at this point.

GIOTTO. Aye aye, sir. [*turning to leave, turning back*] Captain—just the two of you here. Maybe just a couple more men—

KIRK. We've got a lot of territory to cover, Commander. Assign your men as I told you.

GIOTTO. Aye aye, sir.   [*Exit* GIOTTO *and his men.*]

SPOCK. Captain.

KIRK. Yes, Mr. Spock.

SPOCK. This is most interesting. My tricorder indicates that there are far more tunnels on this level than indicated on Chief Vanderberg's charts.

KIRK. This is a recently opened level.

SPOCK. Of course. But it is not logical that all the tunnels I read are lava tubes. Not at this great depth.

KIRK. All right. Let's go take a look.

[*They both draw phasers and move down the tunnel.* SPOCK *pauses as they are about to pass another, smaller tunnel, like the one outside the Main Reactor Chamber; he takes a reading.*]

KIRK. What are you doing, Mr. Spock?

SPOCK. None of our instruments had picked up any signs of life down here, Captain. That might possibly be because they were set to pick up carbon-based traces only. I am adjusting my tricorder to register for silicon. [*He makes the adjustment and checks the readings.*] Most interesting.

KIRK. Traces?

SPOCK. Many traces, Captain. A great many. But they are all extremely old. Many thousands of years old.

KIRK. That doesn't make sense. Nothing fresh?

SPOCK. Not at this point.

KIRK [*touching the rim of the tunnel*]. Glassy. Smooth. Almost as if it had been fused.

SPOCK. The same as the other. However, it does not relate.

KIRK. Perhaps it does, Mr. Spock.

SPOCK. How, Captain?

268

KIRK. Not tunnels. Not adits. —Highways. Roads. Thoroughfares. [*puzzled*] Yet you say the traces you found were thousands of years old.

SPOCK. There is no question of that.

KIRK. Mr. Spock, give me an environmental reading—for a thousand yards in any direction.

[SPOCK *takes the reading, suddenly reacts.*]

SPOCK. Captain. A life form—azimuth 111 degrees.

KIRK. One of our people?

SPOCK. No sir—silicon.

KIRK. Come on! [*Both exit along the tunnel.*]

SCENE 8

[*On Camera: another tunnel; an "Enterprise" Security Guard is moving along the tunnel; he pauses to inspect a smaller tunnel opening into it, sees nothing, and moves on; behind him, out of the smaller tunnel comes an indistinct object, large and low to the ground; the guard hears slithering noises behind him, turns, screams, and raises his phaser; he is engulfed before he has a chance to fire; the creature disappears;* KIRK *and* SPOCK *enter on the run and stop, horrified, as they see the remains of the guard;* SPOCK *picks up the guard's phaser.*]

SPOCK. He did not have a chance to fire, Captain.

KIRK. It's only been seconds since we heard him scream. The creature must still be around.

SPOCK. Indeed. [*He takes a reading on his tricorder, moves along the tunnel, then stops at a secondary tunnel opening.*] Captain!

KIRK. What is it?

SPOCK. This tunnel. It is not only not on the charts Chief Vanderberg gave us, but my readings indicate that it has been made within the hour—moments ago, in fact.

KIRK [*staring incredulously at him, then inside the tunnel opening*]. Are you certain?

SPOCK. Positive.

KIRK. But it goes back as far as the eye can see. The best machinery we have couldn't cut a tunnel that fast. Phaser beams couldn't do it.

SPOCK. Indeed, Captain. I am quite at a loss—

[*There is a sudden noise; they whirl, phasers raised, a shape appears in the wall; it makes a hard noise, as if rocks were being shaken together; it moves toward the incredulous* KIRK *and* SPOCK. *Fade Out.*]

The Quest for Social Order   269

ACT III

SCENE 1

[*On Camera: the same scene as before; it is only a second later; the thing is motionless now, pointed at* KIRK *and* SPOCK, *who cover it with their phasers.*]

VOICE OF KIRK [*heard as background*]. Captain's Log, Star Date 3196.8. Deep beneath the surface of Thetis Six, Mr. Spock and I have come face to face with the mysterious creature which has killed dozens of colonists. . . .   It seems to be bracing itself for a charge.

[*The creature suddenly lurches forward, both men fire their phasers, the creature roars in agony and leaps back into the hole from which it came;* SPOCK *and* KIRK *run up to the hole, but it appears to be empty; they stare at one another.*]

KIRK. Gone.

SPOCK. Astonishing, Captain, that anything of that bulk could move so rapidly.

KIRK [*touching the walls of the tunnel*]. Mr. Spock!   These walls are hot.

SPOCK [*taking a reading*]. Indeed, Captain.   Though it seems impossible, this tunnel has been cut within the last two minutes.   [*They stare at one another as* COMMANDER GIOTTO *and a guard enter on the run.*]

GIOTTO. Are you all right, Captain?

KIRK. Perfectly, Commander.

GIOTTO [*looking with revulsion at the remains of the guard*]. Poor Kelly.
      [*to* KIRK] Did you see it, sir?

KIRK. We saw it.   Mr. Spock, where does this new tunnel go?

SPOCK. My readings indicate a maze of tunnels in that direction—of this general category.

GIOTTO. Did you get a shot at it?

KIRK. We took a bite out of it.

SPOCK [*bending over and picking up what looks like a tuft of shaggy hair*]. Captain.

[KIRK *comes over and examines the tuft.*]

KIRK. It looks like hair.   But it's not, is it?

SPOCK. No, sir.   The closest approximation I could come to is a fibrous asbestos.   A mineral, Captain.

KIRK. Then your guess was right.

SPOCK. It would appear to be.   Silicon-based.

KIRK. Summation.

SPOCK. We are dealing with a creature of the deep rocks, silicon-based, capable of moving through solid rock as easily as we move through air. I should say this is due to a powerful corrosive, secreted from the creature's body. Such a substance would explain these tunnels, the door into the reactor chamber, and the murdered men.

KIRK. And it is definitely phaser-resistant. Our weapons were set for silicon and were on full power, but we only damaged it. It still lives.

GIOTTO. You mean it's impossible to kill?

KIRK. Not at all, Commander. It may require massed phasers—

SPOCK. Or a single phaser with much longer contact.

KIRK. Pass the word to your men, Commander. [*He looks again at the tunnel, his face grim.*] We already knew it was a killer. Now it's wounded—in pain—back in there somewhere. There's nothing more dangerous than a wounded animal. Keep that in mind. Mr. Spock.

SPOCK [*who has been taking readings*]. One moment, Captain.

KIRK. Commander Giotto, reinstruct your men to concentrate their search in this sector—and remind them that the creature is wounded.

GIOTTO. Aye aye, sir.   [*Exit* GIOTTO.]

KIRK [*moving to* SPOCK]. What is it, Mr. Spock?

SPOCK. I have just run a complete life form check, 360 degrees, set at one hundred miles. I located our men—all of them—and I located the creature, which is moving rapidly through native rock at azimuth 201, 1100 yards. But nothing else.

KIRK. Did you expect to find anything else?

SPOCK. There are literally hundreds of thousands of these glassy tunnels in this general area alone. Far too many to be cut by the one creature in an ordinary lifetime.

KIRK. You read earlier that you found traces of ancient life. Perhaps there used to be more of them—and this one somehow survived.

SPOCK. Or perhaps there never has been more than one; for hundreds of thousands of years, one creature, haunting these depths.

KIRK. You are speaking of immortality. It does not exist.

SPOCK. As far as we know. I do not close my mind to the possibility. Perhaps silicon as a life base enables a creature to live almost indefinitely.

KIRK. Perhaps. But I fail to see where it has a bearing upon our problem.

SPOCK. I mention it, Captain, because if this is the only survivor of a dead race, to kill it would be a crime against science.

KIRK. Our concern is the protection of this colony, Mr. Spock. To get pergium moving again. This is not a zoological expedition. [*pause*] Keep your tricorder active. Maintain a constant reading on the creature. We'll try to use existing tunnels to cut it off. If we have to, we'll use our phasers to cut our own tunnels. [*pause*] I'm sorry, Mr. Spock. I'm afraid it must die.

SPOCK. I see no alternative myself. It merely seems a pity. [*reading his tricorder*] The search forces are gathering in the main tunnel, Captain.

KIRK. Good. I want to talk to them.   [*They exit.*]

SCENE 2

[*On Camera: a large tunnel, at a point where several tunnels come together; some corroded machinery is lying about;* KIRK *and* SPOCK *are addressing* GIOTTO *and his* SECURITY GUARDS.]

KIRK. So it is wounded, and therefore twice as dangerous as it was before. Stay in pairs. If you find it, concentrate both phasers on what appears to be its head. Maintain it. Concentrate it. It's definitely resistant, but it can be hurt. And if it can be hurt, it can be killed. Mr. Spock?

SPOCK. Examine your charts, please. I last located the creature in the area marked adit 26, moving at azimuth 201. Extend beyond that area, on all sides. We hope to surround it. [*pause*] Perhaps capture it.

KIRK. No, Mr. Spock. [*to the others*] The orders are shoot to kill! Protect yourselves at all times. Commander Giotto, disperse your search parties.

[*The* SECURITY GUARDS *exit, leaving* KIRK *and* SPOCK.]

KIRK [*staring at* SPOCK, *scowling slightly*]. Capture it, Mr. Spock? I don't recall giving any such order.

SPOCK. You did not, Captain. I only thought that if the opportunity arose—

KIRK. I will lose no more men, Mr. Spock. The creature will be killed on sight. That's the end of it.

SPOCK. Very well, sir.

KIRK [*his face softening a trifle*]. Mr. Spock, I want you to return to the upper level, to assist Mr. Scott in the maintenance of his makeshift retardation mechanism.

SPOCK [*surprised*]. I beg your pardon, Captain?

KIRK. You heard me. It's vital that we keep that reactor in operation. Your scientific knowledge—

SPOCK. —will be far more valuable down here, when we catch up with that which we seek.

KIRK. Mr. Spock, I—

SPOCK. Jim. You are Commander of the "Enterprise," and I am second in command. You are afraid of both of us being engaged in this dangerous hunt. You wonder what would happen if we were both killed.

KIRK. This Vulcan telepathic ability can be annoying, Mr. Spock.

SPOCK. I did not read your mind, Captain. But I do know the way you think.

KIRK. All right. It's true, isn't it? Either one of us is expendable. Not both.

SPOCK. My presence here is of utmost importance, Captain. We are dealing with the scientifically unknown—and I am obviously the one person on board the "Enterprise" best qualified for such dealings.

KIRK. Logically.

SPOCK. Of course, Captain.

KIRK. Your logic can be very troublesome.

SPOCK. Logic is frequently troublesome.

KIRK. Very well, Mr. Spock. We'll continue our search together. [*A signal is heard from* KIRK's *communications device; he opens it.*] Kirk here.

VOICE OF SCOTT. Scotty, Captain. My brilliant improvisation just gave up the ghost. It couldn't take the strain.

KIRK. Can you fix it again?

SCOTT. Negative, Captain; it's gone for good.

KIRK. Very well. Start immediate evacuation of all colonists to the "Enterprise."

VOICE OF VANDERBERG. Not all of them, Captain. Me and some of my key personnel are staying. We'll be down to join you.

KIRK. We don't have phasers enough for all of you.

VANDERBERG. Then we'll use clubs. We won't be chased away from here.

KIRK. I could order you.

VANDERBERG. Save your orders for your crew, Captain. My people take orders from me. We're staying.

KIRK. Very well. Get everybody else on board the "Enterprise." The fewer people we have breathing the air, the longer the rest of us can hold out. How long, Scotty?

SCOTT. The reactor will go critical in about ten hours. You've got that long to find the mechanism, Captain.

KIRK. We'll do our best. Feed us constant status reports, Scotty. Vanderberg, you and your men assemble on level 23, Checkpoint "Tiger." Kirk out.

[*On Camera: the tunnel complex;* KIRK *is giving orders to* VANDERBERG *and his* ENGINEERS.]

KIRK. Team up with the "Enterprise" security personnel. They're better armed than you are. Keep in sight of someone else at all times. Vanderberg, take two men, go through that tunnel and rendezvous with Commander Giotto. Appel, take the rest of the men, go that way, tie up with Lieutenant Osborne's detail. Mr. Spock and I will control all operations from a central point. That's all.

[*Exit all except* SPOCK *and* KIRK. *Suddenly* SPOCK *reacts, grows tense, almost as if he senses something.* KIRK *observes this reaction.*]

KIRK. Mr. Spock?
SPOCK [*softly*]. Captain—we are being watched.
KIRK. Are you sure? [SPOCK *nods*]. Intuition, Spock?
SPOCK. No sir. We are being watched. [*He takes a quick reading and focuses on one wall.*] Amazing. The creature has been here—but is fleeing. Apparently it recognized my tricorder as a potential danger. [*pause*] A highly intelligent creature, Captain.
KIRK. And a highly dangerous one. Let's go, Mr. Spock. [*They exit.*]

SCENE 4

[*On Camera:* KIRK *and* SPOCK, *moving through one tunnel, encounter* GIOTTO *and* VANDERBERG, *coming from another; all are startled, raising their phasers; then they relax, somewhat sheepishly.*]

GIOTTO. I'm sorry, Captain.
KIRK. That's all right. We're all getting a little jumpy. Anything?
GIOTTO. Nothing fresh, Captain. Some week-old traces.
SPOCK. From my last reading, I have reason to believe that we have encircled the creature. It is somewhere within our search lines. I remind you, however, that it has the ability to move through solid rock.
GIOTTO. My tricorders are working, Mr. Spock. We'll keep tabs on it.
KIRK. Very well, Commander. Proceed. [*Exit* GIOTTO *and* VANDERBERG.] How much time do we have left, Mr. Spock?
SPOCK. Eight hours, thirty-two minutes, forty-seven seconds. [*They exchange glances and move on to where the main tunnel splits into*

separate tunnels. SPOCK *takes readings, suddenly reacts.*] Captain! Fresh readings. Within the hour—in each of these tunnels.

KIRK [*looking at his chart*]. The chart says these two tunnels converge a few thousand yards further. Take the left one, Mr. Spock. I'll go to the right.

SPOCK. Should we separate?

KIRK. Two tunnels. Two of us. We separate.

SPOCK [*dubiously*]. Very well, Captain.

[*They exit into their respective tunnels.*]

SCENE 5

[*On Camera:* KIRK *is moving slowly through the tunnel; he comes upon a stratum in the rock in which are imbedded dozens of the round, silicon objects such as* VANDERBERG *had in his office; he pries one out and then opens his communications device.*]

KIRK. Mr. Spock.

VOICE OF SPOCK. Yes, Captain?

KIRK. I've found a whole layer of those silicone nodules of yours. Hundreds of them.

SPOCK. Indeed, Captain. I find that most illuminating. Captain, be absolutely sure you do not damage any of them.

KIRK. Explain.

SPOCK. It is only a theory, Captain, but— [*With a roar, a part of the main tunnel collapses, bringing down tons of rock and debris.*] Captain! Are you all right? Captain!

KIRK [*who has not been near the collapse*]. Yes, Mr. Spock. Quite all right. [*Moving to the rock fall.*] We seem to have had a cave in.

SPOCK. I can phaser you out.

KIRK. No, even from here I can see it's delicately balanced. Any disturbance would bring the rest of the wall down. Anyway, it isn't necessary. The charts said our tunnels meet further on. There's no danger. I can just walk out.

SPOCK. Very well. But I find it disquieting that your roof chose that moment to collapse. Please proceed with extreme caution, Captain. I shall double my pace.

KIRK. Very well, Mr. Spock. I'll meet you at the end of the tunnel. Kirk out.

[*He is about to go on his way, but stops and freezes. In plain sight for the first time, the creature is seen blocking* KIRK's *path; it is huge, shaggy, and makes a low, threatening sound, like pebbles being shaken together. It begins to move toward* KIRK. *Fade Out.*]

The Quest for Social Order   275

Act IV

Scene 1

[*On Camera: the same scene as previously; it is only a second later;* KIRK *whips his phaser up to fire; the creature stops, shuffles backward.* KIRK *stares, puzzled, then lowers his phaser a trifle. The creature moves forward again, making its low sound, which to our ears sounds threatening.* KIRK *raises his phaser again. The creature stops, moves backward. Keeping his phaser at the ready,* KIRK *tries to move around the creature, but, without making any threatening moves, it keeps its massive body between him and the open end of the tunnel.* KIRK *is plainly puzzled by the creature's actions; he keeps his phaser ready, but is not quite certain whether or not he should fire. A signal is heard from his communications device.*]

KIRK. Kirk here.

VOICE OF SPOCK. Captain, I have just read fresh signs. The creature is in this area now. I'll take a life form reading—

KIRK. Not necessary, Mr. Spock. I know exactly where the creature is.

SPOCK. Where, Captain?

KIRK. Standing about ten feet away from me.

SPOCK [*alarmed*]. Kill it, Captain! Quickly!

KIRK. It's—not making any threatening moves, Mr. Spock.

SPOCK. You don't dare take the chance! Kill it!

KIRK. I thought you were the one who wanted it kept alive. Captured, if possible.

SPOCK. Your life is in danger, Captain. You can't take the risk!

KIRK. It's just standing there. It seems to be—waiting, Spock.

SPOCK. Captain, Please. Full power phaser—

KIRK. Not yet, Mr. Spock.

SPOCK. Very well, Captain. If it moves, please shoot it. I will hurry through my tunnel and approach you from the rear. I remind you that it is a proven killer. Spock out.

Scene 2

[*On Camera: another tunnel;* VANDERBERG *appears from one end,* APPEL *and some of his men from the other;* APPEL *is greatly excited.*]

APPEL. Chief! I just picked it up on my communicator. Kirk's found it!

VANDERBERG. Where?

APPEL. I'm headed there. I'm going to get myself a piece of that murdering devil. Come on! [*All hurry off in* APPEL's *original direction.*]

[*On Camera: the blocked tunnel, with* KIRK *and the creature; it is silent now and seemingly waiting;* KIRK *lowers his phaser a trifle; the creature does not move.*]

KIRK. All right. What do we do now? Talk it over? [*No reaction.* KIRK *takes a step forward and to one side; the creature moves to block him. As it does so, a wound can be seen in its side.*] Well, you can be hurt, can't you? [*He lifts his phaser. The creature makes its sound again—and backs off; obviously it is afraid of the phaser, and yet it is not fleeing. It is standing its ground.* KIRK *lowers his phaser, moves back against the nearest wall, and slowly assumes a squatting position, his phaser held loosely in his hand. The creature watches silently.*]

KIRK. All right. Your move. Or do we just sit and wait for something to happen? [*Silence. Then rapidly approaching footsteps are heard and* SPOCK *emerges from the open end of the tunnel. He takes the whole scene in quickly and, almost involuntarily, raises his phaser.*] Don't shoot! [SPOCK *stops, watches. The creature turns from* KIRK *to* SPOCK, *then moves back, leaving a space for* SPOCK *to move to* KIRK.] Come on over, Mr. Spock. [*Very cautiously, his highly interested eyes fastened on the creature,* SPOCK *moves to* KIRK's *side.*]

SPOCK. Fascinating, Captain. It's made no move against you?

KIRK. None. It seems to be waiting. I tried talking to it, but it did no good. [SPOCK *observes the silicon nodules embedded in the wall of the tunnel.*] They're all through here—embedded in that light stratum. Thousands of them.

SPOCK. Yes. It is logical.

KIRK. They mean something to you?

SPOCK. I believe—the answer, Captain. But I cannot be sure. [*pause*] Captain, you are aware that we Vulcans are capable of limited telepathy?

KIRK. Of course, but—

SPOCK. There is a technique I have never told you about. A joining of minds. Painful—and—terribly—personal, for a Vulcan, since it entails the complete lowering of the mental barriers, a complete mental exposure.

KIRK. You mean, there's a possibility that you could get through to this thing?

SPOCK. Possibly. If I could touch it— [SPOCK *extends his hand, and moves slowly towards the creature; it lurches back, making an angry sound.* SPOCK *stops, as does the creature. They wait.*] It would be better if I could touch it. However, if you will be patient, Captain. [SPOCK *closes his eyes and begins to concentrate intensely. The creature reacts nervously. Suddenly* SPOCK'S *face contorts in agony; he cries out.*] Pain! Pain! Pain! [*With a great shudder, contact is broken.* SPOCK, *ashen-faced, almost falls;* KIRK *steadies him.*] That's all I got, Captain. Waves and waves of searing pain. It's in agony.

[*Suddenly the creature hurls itself full-length on the wall, clings there a moment, and then slips back down. Etched into the wall, in English letters which are still smoking, are the words, "NO KILL I."*]

KIRK. "No Kill I." What is it? A plea that we don't kill it? Or a promise it won't kill us?

SPOCK. I don't know. Obviously it gained an immediate knowledge of us from its empathy with me. In my brief contact with the creature's mind, I learned that it is a highly sophisticated, extremely intelligent creature. In great agony because of its wound, of course, but not reacting at all like a wounded animal. [*pause*] It calls itself a "Horta."

KIRK. "Horta." [*louder*] "Horta!" [*The creature reacts, with its peculiar sound.*] Mr. Spock, we have to find that retardation mechanism which the "Horta" took. You'll have to re-establish communications.

SPOCK. Of course, Captain. But it has no reason to give us the device, and apparently every reason to wish us off this planet.

KIRK. I'm aware of that. If we can win its confidence— [*Takes out his communications device.*] Doctor McCoy. This is the captain.

VOICE OF MCCOY. Yes, Captain.

KIRK. Get your medical kit and get down here on the double. We've got a patient for you!

MCCOY. Somebody injured? How?

KIRK. Never mind, Doctor, just come. Twenty-third level. You'll be directed to us by tricorder readings. And hurry. Kirk out.

SPOCK. I remind you, Captain, if this is a silicon-based form of life, as we suspect, Doctor McCoy's medical knowledge will be totally useless.

KIRK. He's a healer. Let him heal. [*pause*] Go ahead, Mr. Spock. Try to contact it again. And try to find out why it suddenly took to murder.

SPOCK [*Moving forward, hand outstretched. The creature is nervous, but this time remains still.* SPOCK'S *hand touches it; it quivers, makes its warning sound, but does nothing more.* SPOCK *concentrates; then his face shows signs of pain, but this time he speaks more softly*]. Pain—pain—

[*A signal is heard from* KIRK's *communications device.*]

KIRK. Kirk here.

VOICE OF GIOTTO. Giotto, Captain. Are you all right?

KIRK. Perfectly all right.

GIOTTO. We're at the end of the tunnel. Mr. Vanderberg and his men are here. They're pretty ugly. I thought I'd check with you first.

KIRK. Hold them there, Giotto. Under no circumstances allow them in here yet. The minute Doctor McCoy gets there, send him through.

GIOTTO. Aye aye, sir. Giotto out.

[SPOCK *is sinking deeper and deeper into total empathy with the creature.*]

SPOCK [*as in a trance*]. Murder—the thousands—devils. Eternity ends— horrible, horrible. In the Chamber of the Ages—the Altar of To- morrow—horrible. Murderers—murderers—

KIRK. Mr. Spock! The mechanism—

SPOCK. Stop them—kill—strike back—monsters—

[*There is the sound of rapidly approaching footsteps and* DOCTOR MCCOY *enters, then stops, stunned at what he sees.* KIRK *motions for* MCCOY *to join him.*]

MCCOY [*whispering*]. What in the name of—

KIRK [*also whispering*]. It's wounded—badly. You've got to help it.

MCCOY. Help—this?

KIRK. Take a look at it.

[MCCOY *moves to the creature.*]

SPOCK. The end of Life—the murderers—killing—the dead children—

[MCCOY, *examining the creature, looks incredulous, takes an instrument reading and examines the results with disbelief. Almost indignantly he returns to* KIRK.]

MCCOY. You can't be serious. That thing is virtually made out of stone!

KIRK. Help it. Treat it.

MCCOY. I'm a doctor, not a bricklayer!

KIRK. You're a healer. That's your patient. That's an order, Doctor.

[MCCOY *shakes his head in wonder and returns to the creature.*]

KIRK. Spock. Tell it we're trying to help. A doctor.

SPOCK. Understood. Understood. It is the end of Life. Eternity stops. Go out. Out of the gateway. To the Tunnel of Immortality. To the Chamber of the Ages. Cry for the children. Walk carefully in the Vault of Tomorrow. Sorrow for the murdered children. Weep for the crushed ones. Tears for the stolen ones. The thing you search for is there. Go. Go. Sadness for the end of things. [KIRK, *listening, considers, hesitates, looks at the tunnel opening.*] Go! It is over. Quickly. Quickly. Sorrow. Such sorrow. Sadness. Pain. [*Tears are running down* SPOCK's *cheeks.*] Sorrow. The dead. Sorrow. The children.

[KIRK *hesitates, then exits quickly through the open end of the tunnel.*]

SCENE 4

[*On Camera: a tunnel, through which* KIRK *is searching; he finds an opening, half hidden in the wall. He enters into what appears to be a vast chamber, whose walls are lined with the bright strata which contain the silicon nodules. Many of the nodules are on the ground, most of them broken.* KIRK *stops, taking it all in; gradually he realizes what he is seeing and a great sadness comes over him. He looks around, sees the retardation mechanism on the ground, picks it up and exits.*]

SCENE 5

[*On Camera: back in the blocked tunnel;* MCCOY, *kneeling near the "Horta," is speaking into his communications device.*]

MCCOY. That's right, Lieutenant. Beam it down to me immediately. Don't ask questions. Never mind what I want it for. I just want it! Now move!

SPOCK [*tears still running down his cheeks*]. The ages die. Sadness. Pain. It is time to sleep. It is over. Failure. The murderers have won. Death is welcome. Let it end here, with the murdered children—

[KIRK *enters, carrying the retardation unit; he calls.*]

KIRK. Mr. Spock! Come back! Spock! [SPOCK *reels, making an effort to disengage himself. He is weak with the effort.*] Are you all right?

SPOCK. I—yes, Captain. I am all right.

KIRK. Those silicon nodules—they're eggs, aren't they?

SPOCK. Yes, Captain. They are eggs.

SCENE 6

[*On Camera: at the entrance to a tunnel;* GIOTTO *is holding back a crowd of furious civilians, including* APPEL, *with a club in his hand, and* VANDERBERG.]

GIOTTO. The captain said for you to stay out here, and this is where you're going to stay!

VANDERBERG. That murdering monster's in there! We're going to kill it!

GIOTTO. You're going to stay here!

APPEL [*suddenly pointing into the dark tunnel behind* GIOTTO]. There! They're coming out! [GIOTTO *whirls to see and* APPEL *clubs him down.*] All right, let's go!

[*Armed, furious, and dangerous, the civilians flood into the tunnel.*]

SCENE 7

[*On Camera: back in the blocked tunnel;* SPOCK *has just finished talking.*]

KIRK [*nodding gravely*]. I see. All these centuries—

SPOCK. Yes, Captain. The "Horta" was defending her race—against, what were to her, murdering "monsters."

KIRK [*to* MCCOY]. How are you doing, Doctor?

MCCOY [*ministering to the "Horta"*]. I'll let you know.

[*There is a sound of many running footsteps.* VANDERBERG, APPEL, *and the armed civilians burst into the area; seeing the creature, those armed with phasers raise them. Kirk rushes between them and the "Horta."*]

KIRK. No! Don't shoot!

APPEL. Kill it! Kill it!

KIRK [*pulling out his phaser*]. I'll kill any man who shoots!

[*The civilians are stunned. They stare at* KIRK *in dismay.*]

VANDERBERG. That thing has killed fifty of my men!

KIRK. And you've killed thousands of its children!

VANDERBERG. What?

KIRK. Those round silicon nodules you've been collecting and destroying are eggs. [*pause*] Tell them, Mr. Spock.

SPOCK. There have been millions of "Horta" on this planet. Every fifty thousand years the entire race dies—all but one—like this one. But the eggs live. She protects them, cares for them, and when they hatch, she is the mother to them, millions of them. This creature is the mother of her race.

KIRK. She's intelligent, peaceful, and mild. She had no objection to sharing the planet with you people—until you broke into the "nursery" and started destroying her eggs. Then she fought back, in the only way she could—as any mother would, when her children were endangered.

VANDERBERG [*chastened*]. How were we to know? But—you mean if

The Quest for Social Order   281

those eggs hatch, there'll be millions of them crawling around down here?

KIRK. It's where they live. They digest the rock. They tunnel for nourishment.

SPOCK. And they are the mildest and most inoffensive of creatures. They harbor ill will toward no one.

APPEL. We've got pergium to deliver.

KIRK. You've complained that this planet is a minerological treasure house —if only you had the equipment to get at everything. The "Horta" moves through rock the way we move through air—and leaves a tunnel. The greatest natural miners in the universe. I don't see why we can't make an agreement, reach a *modus vivendi*. They tunnel; you collect and process. You get along together. Your processing operation would be a thousand times more profitable than it is now.

[*The miners look at each other with delight slowly appearing on their faces.* VANDERBERG, *however, still shows a little doubt.*]

VANDERBERG. Sounds all right—but how do you know the thing will go for it?

SPOCK. Why shouldn't it? It is logical. [*pause*] Except for one thing. The "Horta" is badly wounded. It may die.

MCCOY. It won't die. By golly, I'm beginning to think I can cure a rainy day.

KIRK. You helped it?

MCCOY. Helped it? I cured it.

KIRK. How?

MCCOY. I had the ship beam down a hundred pounds of thermo-concrete —the kind we build emergency shelters out of. I just troweled it into the wound. Take a look—good as new.

KIRK. Well, Mr. Spock, I'll have to ask you to get in contact with the "Horta" again. Tell it our proposition: she and her children dig all the tunnels they want, our people will remove the minerals, and each side will leave the other alone. Think she'll go for it?

SPOCK. As I said, Captain, it seems logical. The "Horta" has a very logical mind—and after years of close association with humans, I find it curiously refreshing.

EPILOGUE

[*On Camera: the bridge of the "Enterprise";* KIRK *is in the Captain's chair;* SPOCK *and other personnel are preparing to take the Starship out of its Thetis Six orbit.*]

SPOCK. All space details ready, Captain. Course laid in.

KIRK. Very good, Mr. Spock.

SPOCK. Chief Engineer Vanderberg is standing by on Channel One.

KIRK. Kirk here, Chief.

VOICE OF VANDERBERG. Just wanted to tell you the eggs have started to hatch, Captain, and the first thing the little devils do is start to tunnel. We've already hit huge new pergium deposits—and I'm afraid to tell you how much gold, platinum, and rare earths we've uncovered.

KIRK. Delighted, Chief. Once the mother "Horta" tells all her kids what to look for, you people are going to be embarrassingly rich.

VANDERBERG. The "Horta" aren't so bad—once you get used to their appearance. All right, Kirk. Drop in the next time you're in the vicinity.

KIRK. Right, Chief. Kirk out.

SPOCK. Interesting Chief Vanderberg should have said that, Captain.

KIRK. Said what?

SPOCK. That the "Horta" weren't so bad, once you got used to their appearance.

KIRK. Why so interesting?

SPOCK. It was precisely what the mother "Horta" said to me—about you, and the rest of us: our appearance is revolting. But she thought she could get used to it.

KIRK. Oh, did she? She didn't happen to make any comment about your ears?

SPOCK. Uh—not specifically, Captain. But I got the distinct impression she thought they were the most attractive human characteristic of all. I didn't have the heart to tell her that only I—

KIRK [*interrupting*]. All right, Mr. Spock. Would you mind putting us out into space?

SPOCK. It would be my pleasure, Captain. Helmsman: on set course, Warp Factor One.

KIRK. She really liked those ears, did she?

SPOCK. The "Horta" is a remarkably selective and intelligent animal—with impeccable taste.

KIRK. We should have left you there, Mr. Spock. You and the "Horta" would have made a lovely couple.

SPOCK. Hardly, Captain. I don't believe I could have stood her cooking.

The
Quest for
Love

CHAPTER FOUR

For the poet Robert Graves, beneath the surface of every work of the human imagination "there is one story and one story only"—that of the hero's quest for love in the person of "the Lady." While it is possible to disagree with Graves that this quest, "from woman back to woman," from mother to lover, lies behind all art, myth, and dream, its importance to both literature and life is obvious enough. So universal a quest can be expected to figure in the lives of most heroes, for most heroes, be they gods or humans, possess some kind of sexual identity. That identity may be stressed or suppressed in the story of any particular hero, but it always will be felt somehow, even though the hero's quest may not be specifically directed toward love.

John Dryden wrote, "Only the brave deserve the fair," thereby expressing in one line a traditional conception of the hero as lover; but there is another side to the tradition of the hero which implies that even the fair may not deserve the brave. For in some fictions, the male hero, regardless of his manliness, is expected to be not only "above" sex, but "above" romantic love itself. Love is an emotion which the "chaste" hero is supposed to reserve for God, for country, and for his comrades.

In other fictions, the hero may love, but only "from afar," or he may love and lose. Only in comedy and in some romance does he love and live happily ever after. Marriage and heroism, in fact, seem to mix only indifferently well. Although the hero is by definition a purveyor of stability, which is a necessary quality of family as well as of community life, it is amid instability that he fulfills himself as a hero. Those virtues which serve the hero well in crises—physical prowess, courage, and the highest idealism—are not necessarily the qualities most needed for successful domesticity. This is particularly evident in the case of the female hero. A woman becomes a hero by exhibiting pretty much the same qualities as a male hero, but traditionally she must do so without compromising what is thought of as her "feminine nature." Otherwise she runs the risk of being regarded as some kind of biological freak or cultural misfit. And for her, moreso even than for the male hero, love and marriage seem to require that she abandon heroic action for quiet domesticity. In a male-dominated society, being wed to a female hero is somehow seen as compromising the "masculinity" of a nonheroic spouse.

Less godlike heroes (the Leader, the Common Man, and the Lowly Man in our classification system) are more likely to undertake the quest for love than the Super Man and Supreme Man, for such a quest is usually more in the nature of a private than a public one, one which fulfills the hero's personal desires rather than those of his community. It is a more "human" quest, perhaps, but because love is associated more closely with man's biological nature than his spiritual side, the quest for love may be deemed somewhat less "worthy," less "noble." Yet the violence amid which the hero often fulfills himself can have its sexual and soulless side, whereas the quest for love can make heavy demands on the hero's moral as well as emotional resources. Although such a quest may call for a more human and less godlike hero—gods, after all, can transcend emotion and dictate values—like other kinds of quests it can take the measure of a human being, as the works which follow make clear.

SHORT STORIES

The Power of Love: Heroism in Everyday Life

The frequency with which the hero of the quest for love turns out to be a person pretty much like ourselves is suggested by the following stories: in none of them is the hero any more than a Common Man or Lowly Man. This may also be due in part to the relative modernity of the short story, which did not emerge as a distinct literary form until the early nineteenth century. The flowering of this form during the last hundred years coincided with the gradual dissolution of consensus about values in the Western world, and when consensus about values disappears, it becomes difficult to write about the more idealized type of hero. The old tradition of the idealized military hero as lover *par excellence* is a case in point. This tradition goes back beyond even the Age of Chivalry, when a knight was expected to be as accomplished in the arts of love as he was in the arts of war.

Anton Chekhov's story "The Kiss" takes place in Russia during the latter part of the nineteenth century, when the traditions of chivalry were not yet dead and when every officer was expected to be not only a gentleman but a lover. The latter expectation weighs heavily upon Chekhov's hero, Staff-Captain Riabovitch, who finds it difficult to play the hero when it comes to the ladies. But he is content with the routine of all-male existence of military life until its safe monotony is disrupted by a remarkable and romantic incident. That incident, however, is less the subject of Chekhov's concern than are the frustrations and even the pathos of the quest for love.

John Updike's story "A&P" also revolves about one unexpected incident, like Riabovitch's kiss, a minor affair to an outside observer, but important to the person involved in it. It takes place in an unlikely setting for a drama of heroism, a grocery store, and its central figure, Sammy, a young clerk, is almost as unlikely a candidate for hero status as Captain Riabovitch. But the quest for love is open to all and can begin anywhere. It also has a number of ramifications, as Sammy finds out. His feelings about his "lady" lead him into a personal crisis. Whether those feelings are merely a young man's momentary and physical attraction to a girl, whether he exhibits courage or only bravado, whether his action is idealistic or merely compulsive—in short, whether Sammy is hero or fool—can be determined only by a careful reading of Updike's spare and realistic story.

Leo Finkle is the unheroic-sounding name of the hero of Bernard Malamud's story "The Magic Barrel." Leo initiates his quest for love more out of practical than romantic considerations. The further that quest takes him, however, the more deeply human it becomes. And finally, it begins to take on genuine romantic overtones, the more Leo begins to feel and act like the lonely young man he is and less like the ascetic religious figure he aspires to be. The fact that he is steeped in the manners and mores of his orthodox Jewish culture makes Leo's acceptance of the romantic challenge he faces more heroic, and also gives moral and spiritual dimensions to his quest even when it seems that he is wholly disregarding such factors.

The Kiss

Anton Chekhov

On the twentieth of May, at eight o'clock in the evening, six batteries of the N Artillery Brigade arrived at the village of Miestetchki to spend the night, before going to their camp.

The confusion was at its height—some officers at the guns, others in the church square with the quartermaster—when a civilian upon a re-markable horse rode from the rear of the church. The small cob with well-shaped neck wobbled along, all the time dancing on its legs as if someone were whipping them. Reaching the officers, the rider doffed his cap with ceremony and said—

"His Excellency, General von Rabbek, requests the honor of the offi-cers' company at tea in his house near by . . ."

The horse shook its head, danced, and wobbled backwards; its rider again took off his cap, and turning around disappeared behind the church.

"The devil!" the general exclaimed, the officers dispersing to their quarters. "We are almost asleep, yet along comes this von Rabbek with his tea! That tea! I remember it!"

The officers of the six batteries had vivid recollections of a past invita-tion. During recent maneuvers they had been asked, with their Cossack comrades, to tea at the house of a local country gentleman, a Count, re-tired from military service; and this hearty old Count overwhelmed them with attentions, fed them like gourmands, poured vodka into them and made them stay the night. All this, of course, was fine. The trouble was that the old soldier entertained his guests too well. He kept them up till daybreak while he poured forth tales of past adventures and pointed out valuable paintings, engravings, arms, and letters from celebrated men. And the tired officers listened, perforce, until he ended, only to find out that the time for sleep had gone.

Was von Rabbek another old Count? It might easily be. But there was no neglecting his invitation. The officers washed and dressed, and set out for von Rabbek's house. At the church square they learnt that they must descend the hill to the river, and follow the bank till they reached the general's gardens, where they would find a path direct to the house. Or, if they chose to go uphill, they would reach the general's barns half a *verst* from Miestetchki. It was this route they chose.

"But who is this von Rabbek?" asked one. "The man who com-manded the N Cavalry Division at Plevna?"

"No, that was not von Rabbek, but simply Rabbe—without the von."

"What glorious weather!"

At the first barn they came to, two roads diverged; one ran straight forward and faded in the dusk; the other, turning to the right, led to the general's house. As the officers drew near they talked less loudly. To right and to left stretched rows of red-roofed brick barns, in aspect heavy and morose as the barracks of provincial towns. In front gleamed the lighted windows of von Rabbek's house.

"A good omen, gentlemen!" cried a young officer. "Our setter runs in advance. There is game ahead!"

On the face of Lieutenant Lobuitko, the tall stout officer referred to, there was not one trace of hair though he was twenty-five years old. He was famed among comrades for the instinct which told him of the presence of women in the neighborhood. On hearing his comrade's remark, he turned his head and said—

"Yes. There are women there. My instinct tells me."

A handsome, well-preserved man of sixty, in mufti, came to the hall door to greet his guests. It was von Rabbek. As he pressed their hands, he explained that though he was delighted to see them, he must beg pardon for not asking them to spend the night; as guests he already had his two sisters, their children, his brother, and several neighbors—in fact, he had not one spare room. And though he shook their hands and apologized and smiled, it was plain that he was not half as glad to see them as was the last year's Count, and that he had invited them merely because good manners demanded it. The officers climbing the soft-carpeted steps and listening to their host understood this perfectly well; and realized that they carried into the house an atmosphere of intrusion and alarm. Would any man—they asked themselves—who had gathered his two sisters and their children, his brother and his neighbors, to celebrate, no doubt, some family festival, find pleasure in the invasion of nineteen officers whom he had never seen before?

A tall elderly lady, with a good figure, and a long face with black eyebrows, who resembled closely the ex-Empress Eugénie, greeted them at the drawing-room door. Smiling courteously and with dignity, she affirmed that she was delighted to see the officers, and only regretted that she could not ask them to stay the night. But the courteous, dignified smile disappeared when she turned away, and it was quite plain that she had seen many officers in her day, that they caused not the slightest interest, and that she had invited them merely because an invitation was dictated by good breeding and by her position in the world.

In a big dining room, at a big table, sat ten men and women, drinking tea. Behind them, veiled in cigar smoke, stood several young men, among them one, red-whiskered and extremely thin, who spoke English loudly with a lisp. Through an open door the officers saw into a brightly lighted room with blue wallpaper.

"You are too many to introduce singly, gentlemen!" said the general loudly, with affected joviality. "Make one another's acquaintance, please —without formalities!"

The visitors, some with serious, even severe faces, some smiling constrainedly, all with a feeling of awkwardness, bowed, and took their seats at the table. Most awkward of all felt Staff-Captain Riabovitch, a short, round-shouldered, spectacled officer, whiskered like a lynx. While his brother officers looked serious or smiled constrainedly, his face, his lynx whiskers, and his spectacles seemed to explain: "I am the most timid, modest, undistinguished officer in the whole brigade." For some time after he took his seat at the table he could not fix his attention on any single thing. Faces, dresses, the cut-glass cognac bottles, the steaming tumblers, the molded cornices—all merged in a single, overwhelming sentiment which caused him intense fright and made him wish to hide his head. Like an inexperienced lecturer he saw everything before him, but could distinguish nothing, and was in fact the victim of what men of science diagnose as "psychical blindness."

But, slowly conquering his diffidence, Riabovitch began to distinguish and observe. As became a man both timid and unsocial, he remarked first of all the amazing temerity of his new friends. Von Rabbek, his wife, two elderly ladies, a girl in lilac, and the red-whiskered youth (who, it appeared, was a young von Rabbek) sat down among the officers as unconcernedly as if they had held rehearsals, and at once plunged into various heated arguments in which they soon involved their guests. That artillerists have a much better time than cavalrymen or infantrymen was proved conclusively by the lilac girl, while von Rabbek and the elderly ladies affirmed the converse. The conversation became desultory. Riabovitch listened to the lilac girl fiercely debating themes she knew nothing about and took no interest in, and watched the insincere smiles which appeared on and disappeared from her face.

While the von Rabbek family with amazing strategy inveigled their guests into the dispute, they kept their eyes on every glass and mouth. Had everyone tea, was it sweet enough, why didn't one eat biscuits, was another fond of cognac? And the longer Riabovitch listened and looked, the more pleased he was with this disingenuous, disciplined family.

After tea the guests repaired to the drawing room. Instinct had not cheated Lobuitko. The room was packed with young women and girls, and ere a minute had passed the setter-lieutenant stood beside a very young, fair-haired girl in black, and, bending down as if resting on an invisible sword, shrugged his shoulders coquettishly. He was uttering, no doubt, most unentertaining nonsense, for the fair girl looked indulgently at his sated face, and exclaimed indifferently, "Indeed!" And this indifferent "Indeed!" might have quickly convinced the setter that he was on a wrong scent.

Music began. As the notes of a mournful valse throbbed out of the open window, through the heads of all flashed the feeling that outside that window it was springtime, a night of May. The air was odorous of young poplar leaves, of roses and lilacs—and the valse and the spring were sincere. Riabovitch, with valse and cognac mingling tipsily in his head, gazed at the window with a smile; then began to follow the movements of the women; and it seemed that the smell of roses, poplars, and lilacs came not from the gardens outside, but from the women's faces and dresses.

290

They began to dance. Young von Rabbek valsed twice round the room with a very thin girl; and Lobuitko, slipping on the parqueted floor, went up to the girl in lilac, and was granted a dance. But Riabovitch stood near the door with the wallflowers, and looked silently on. Amazed at the daring of men who in sight of a crowd could take unknown women by the waist, he tried in vain to picture himself doing the same. A time had been when he envied his comrades their courage and dash, suffered from painful heart-searchings, and was hurt by the knowledge that he was timid, round-shouldered, and undistinguished, that he had lynx whiskers, and that his waist was much too long. But with years he had grown reconciled to his own insignificance, and now looking at the dancers and loud talkers, he felt no envy, but only mournful emotions.

At the first quadrille von Rabbek junior approached and invited two non-dancing officers to a game of billiards. The three left the room, and Riabovitch, who stood idle, and felt impelled to join in the general movement, followed. They passed the dining room, traversed a narrow glazed corridor and a room where three sleepy footmen jumped from a sofa with a start; and after walking, it seemed, through a whole houseful of rooms, entered a small billiard room.

Von Rabbek and the two officers began their game. Riabovitch, whose only game was cards, stood near the table and looked indifferently on, as the players, with unbuttoned coats, wielded their cues, moved about, joked, and shouted obscure technical terms. Riabovitch was ignored, save when one of the players jostled him or nudged him with the cue, and turning towards him said briefly, "Pardon!" so that before the game was over he was thoroughly bored, and, impressed by a sense of his superfluity, resolved to return to the drawing room and turned away.

It was on the way back that his adventure took place. Before he had gone far he saw that he had missed his way. He remembered distinctly the room with the three sleepy footmen; and after passing through five or six rooms entirely vacant, he saw his mistake. Retracing his steps, he turned to the left, and found himself in an almost dark room which he had not seen before; and after hesitating a minute, he boldly opened the first door he saw, and found himself in complete darkness. Through a clink of the door in front peered a bright light; from afar throbbed the dullest music of a mournful mazurka. Here, as in the drawing room, the windows were open wide, and the smell of poplars, lilacs, and roses flooded the air.

Riabovitch paused in irresolution. For a moment all was still. Then came the sound of hasty footsteps; then, without any warning of what was to come, a dress rustled, a woman's breathless voice whispered "At last!" and two soft, scented, unmistakably womanly arms met round his neck, a warm cheek impinged on his, and he received a sounding kiss. But hardly had the kiss echoed through the silence when the unknown shrieked loudly, and fled away—as it seemed to Riabovitch—in disgust. Riabovitch himself nearly screamed, and rushed headlong towards the bright beam in the door chink.

As he entered the drawing room his heart beat violently, and his hands trembled so perceptibly that he clasped them behind his back. His first emotion was shame, as if everyone in the room already knew that he had just been embraced and kissed. He retired into his shell, and looked fearfully around. But finding that hosts and guests were calmly dancing or talking, he regained courage, and surrendered himself to sensations experienced for the first time in his life. The unexampled had happened. His neck, fresh from the embrace of two soft, scented arms, seemed anointed with oil; near his left mustache, where the kiss had fallen, trembled a slight, delightful chill, as from peppermint drops; and from head to foot he was soaked in new and extraordinary sensations, which continued to grow and grow.

He felt that he must dance, talk, run into the garden, laugh unrestrainedly. He forgot altogether that he was round-shouldered, undistinguished, lynx-whiskered, that he had an "indefinite exterior"—a description from the lips of a woman he had happened to overhear. As Madame von Rabbek passed him he smiled so broadly and graciously that she came up and looked at him questioningly.

"What a charming house you have!" he said, straightening his spectacles.

And Madame von Rabbek smiled back, said that the house still belonged to her father, and asked were his parents still alive, how long he had been in the Army, and why he was so thin. After hearing his answers she departed. But though the conversation was over, he continued to smile benevolently, and think what charming people were his new acquaintances.

At supper Riabovitch ate and drank mechanically what was put before him, heard not a word of the conversation, and devoted all his powers to the unraveling of his mysterious, romantic adventure. What was the explanation? It was plain that one of the girls, he reasoned, had arranged a meeting in the dark room, and after waiting some time in vain had, in her nervous tension, mistaken Riabovitch for her hero. The mistake was likely enough, for on entering the dark room Riabovitch had stopped irresolutely as if he, too, were waiting for someone. So far the mystery was explained.

"But which of them was it?" he asked, searching the women's faces. She certainly was young, for old women do not indulge in such romances. Secondly, she was not a servant. That was proved unmistakably by the rustle of her dress, the scent, the voice . . .

When at first he looked at the girl in lilac she pleased him; she had pretty shoulders and arms, a clever face, a charming voice. Riabovitch piously prayed that it was she. But, smiling insincerely, she wrinkled her long nose, and that at once gave her an elderly air. So Riabovitch turned his eyes on the blonde in black. The blonde was younger, simpler, sincerer; she had charming kiss-curls, and drank from her tumbler with inexpressible grace. Riabovitch hoped it was she—but soon he noticed that her face was flat, and bent his eyes on her neighbor.

"It is a hopeless puzzle," he reflected. "If you take the arms and shoulders of the lilac girl, add the blonde's curls, and the eyes of the girl on Lobuitko's left, then—"

He composed a portrait of all these charms, and had a clear vision of the girl who had kissed him. But she was nowhere to be seen.

Supper over, the visitors, sated and tipsy, bade their entertainers good-by. Both host and hostess apologized for not asking them to spend the night.

"I am very glad, gentlemen!" said the general, and this time seemed to speak sincerely, no doubt because speeding the parting guest is a kindlier office than welcoming him unwelcomed. "I am very glad indeed! I hope you will visit me on your way back. Without ceremony, please! Which way will you go? Up the hill? No, go down the hill and through the garden. That way is shorter."

The officers took his advice. After the noise and glaring illumination within doors, the garden seemed dark and still. Until they reached the wicket gate all kept silence. Merry, half tipsy, and content as they were, the night's obscurity and stillness inspired pensive thought. Through their brains, as through Riabovitch's, sped probably the same question: "Will the time ever come when I, like von Rabbek, shall have a big house, a family, a garden, the chance of being gracious—even insincerely—to others, of making them sated, tipsy, and content?"

But once the garden lay behind them, all spoke at once, and burst into causeless laughter. The path they followed led straight to the river, and then ran beside it, winding around bushes, ravines, and overhanging willow trees. The track was barely visible; the other bank was lost entirely in gloom. Sometimes the black water imaged stars, and this was the only indication of the river's speed. From beyond it sighed a drowsy snipe, and beside them in a bush, heedless of the crowd, a nightingale chanted loudly. The officers gathered in a group and swayed the bush, but the nightingale continued his song.

"I like his cheek!" they echoed admiringly. "He doesn't care a *kopek!* The old rogue!"

Near their journey's end the path turned up the hill, and joined the road not far from the church enclosure; and there the officers, breathless from climbing, sat on the grass and smoked. Across the river gleamed a dull red light, and for want of a subject they argued the problem, whether it was a bonfire, a window light, or something else. Riabovitch looked also at the light, and felt that it smiled and winked at him as if it knew about the kiss.

On reaching home, he undressed without delay, and lay upon his bed. He shared the cabin with Lobuitko and a Lieutenant Merzliakoff, a staid, silent little man, by repute highly cultivated, who took with him everywhere *The Messenger of Europe* and read it eternally. Lobuitko undressed, tramped impatiently from corner to corner, and sent his servant for beer. Merzliakoff lay down, balanced the candle on his pillow, and hid his head behind *The Messenger of Europe.*

"Where is she now?" muttered Riabovitch, looking at the soot-blacked ceiling.

His neck still seemed anointed with oil, near his mouth still trembled the speck of peppermint chill. Through his brain twinkled successively the shoulders and arms of the lilac girl, the kiss-curls and honest eyes of the girl in black, the waists, dresses, brooches. But though he tried his best to fix these vagrant images, they glimmered, winked, and dissolved; and as they faded finally into the vast black curtain which hangs before the closed eyes of all men, he began to hear hurried footsteps, the rustle of petticoats, the sound of a kiss. A strong, causeless joy possessed him. But as he surrendered himself to this joy, Lobuitko's servant returned with the news that no beer was obtainable. The lieutenant resumed his impatient march up and down the room.

"The fellow's an idiot," he exclaimed, stopping first near Riabovitch and then near Merzliakoff. "Only the worst numbskull and blockhead can't get beer! *Canaille!*"

"Everyone knows there's no beer here," said Merzliakoff, without lifting his eyes from *The Messenger of Europe.*

"You believe that!" exclaimed Lobuitko. "Lord in heaven, drop me on the moon, and in five minutes I'll find both beer and women! I will find them myself! Call me a rascal if I don't!"

He dressed slowly, silently lighted a cigarette, and went out.

"Rabbek, Grabbek, Labbek," he muttered, stopping in the hall. "I won't go alone, devil take me! Riabovitch, come for a walk! What?"

As he got no answer, he returned, undressed slowly, and lay down. Merzliakoff sighed, dropped *The Messenger of Europe,* and put out the light. "Well?" muttered Lobuitko, puffing his cigarette in the dark.

Riabovitch pulled the bedclothes up to his chin, curled himself into a roll, and strained his imagination to join the twinkling images into one coherent whole. But the vision fled him. He soon fell asleep, and his last impression was that he had been caressed and gladdened, that into his life had crept something strange, and indeed ridiculous, but uncommonly good and radiant. And this thought did not forsake him even in his dreams.

When he awoke the feeling of anointment and peppermint chill was gone. But joy, as on the night before, filled every vein. He looked entranced at the window panes gilded by the rising sun, and listened to the noises outside. Someone spoke loudly under the very window. It was Lebedietsky, commander of his battery, who had just overtaken the brigade. He was talking to the sergeant-major, loudly, owing to lack of practice in soft speech.

"And what next?" he roared.

"During yesterday's shoeing, your honor, *Golubtchik* was picked. The regimental doctor ordered clay and vinegar. And last night, your honor, mechanic Artemieff was drunk, and the lieutenant ordered him to be put on the limber of the reserve gun carriage."

The sergeant-major added that Karpoff had forgotten the tent pegs and the new lanyards for the friction tubes, and that the officers had spent the evening at General von Rabbek's. But here at the window appeared Lebedietsky's red-bearded face. He blinked his short-sighted eyes at the drowsy men in bed, and greeted them.

"Is everything all right?"

"The saddle wheeler galled his withers with the new yoke," answered Lobuitko.

The commander sighed, mused a moment, and shouted—

"I am thinking of calling on Alexandra Yegorovna. I want to see her. Good-by! I will catch you up before night."

Fifteen minutes later the brigade resumed its march. As he passed von Rabbek's barns, Riabovitch turned his head and looked at the house. The Venetian blinds were down; evidently all still slept. And among them slept she—she who had kissed him but a few hours before. He tried to visualize her asleep. He projected the bedroom window opened wide with green branches peering in, the freshness of the morning air, the smell of poplars, lilacs, and roses, the bed, a chair, the dress which rustled last night, a pair of tiny slippers, a ticking watch on the table—all these came to him clearly with every detail. But the features, the kind, sleepy smile—all, in short, that was essential and characteristic—fled his imagination as quicksilver flees the hand. When he had covered half a *verst* he again turned back. The yellow church, the house, gardens, and river were bathed in light. Imaging an azure sky, the green-banked river specked with silver sunshine flakes was inexpressibly fair; and, looking at Miestetchki for the last time, Riabovitch felt sad, as if parting forever with something very near and dear.

By the road before him stretched familiar, uninteresting scenes; to the right and left, fields of young rye and buckwheat with hopping rooks; in front, dust and the napes of human necks; behind, the same dust and faces. Ahead of the column marched four soldiers with swords—that was the advance guard. Next came the bandsmen. Advance guard and bandsmen, like mutes in a funeral procession, ignored the regulation intervals and marched too far ahead. Riabovitch, with the first gun of Battery No. 5, could see four batteries ahead.

To a laymen, the long, lumbering march of an artillery brigade is novel, interesting, inexplicable. It is hard to understand why a single gun needs so many men; why so many, such strangely harnessed horses are needed to drag it. But to Riabovitch, a master of all these things, it was profoundly dull. He had learned years ago why a solid sergeant-major rides beside the officer in front of each battery; why the sergeant-major is called the *unosni,* and why the drivers of leaders and wheelers ride behind him. Riabovitch knew why the near horses are called the saddle horses, and why the off horses are called led horses—and all of this was uninteresting beyond words. On one of the wheelers rode a soldier still covered with yesterday's dust, and with a cumbersome, ridiculous guard on his right leg. But Riabovitch, knowing the use of this leg guard, found it in no way ridiculous. The drivers, mechanically and with occasional cries, flourished their whips. The guns in themselves were unimpressive. The limbers were packed with tarpaulin-covered sacks of oats; and the guns themselves, hung round with teapots and satchels, looked like harmless animals, guarded for some obscure reason by men and horses. In the lee of the gun tramped six gunners, swinging their arms, and behind each gun came more *unosniye,* leaders, wheelers; and yet more guns, each as ugly and uninspiring as the one in front. And as every one of the six batteries in the brigade had four guns, the procession stretched along the road at least half a *verst.* It ended with a wagon train, with which, its head bent in thought, walked the donkey Magar, brought from Turkey by a battery commander.

Dead to his surroundings, Riabovitch marched onward, looking at the napes ahead or at the faces behind. Had it not been for last night's event, he would have been half asleep. But now he was absorbed in novel, entrancing thoughts. When the brigade set out that morning he had tried to argue that the kiss had no significance save as a trivial though mysterious adventure; that it was without real import; and that to think of it seriously was to behave himself absurdly. But logic soon flew away and surrendered him to his vivid imaginings. At times he saw himself in von Rabbek's dining room, *tête-à-tête* with a composite being, formed of the girl in lilac and the blonde in black. At times he closed his eyes, and pictured himself with a different, this time quite an unknown, girl of cloudy feature; he spoke to her, caressed her, bent over her shoulders; he imagined war and parting . . . then reunion, the first supper together, children . . .

"To the brakes!" rang the command as they topped the brow of each hill.

Riabovitch also cried "To the brakes!" and each time dreaded that the cry would break the magic spell, and recall him to realities.

They passed a big country house. Riabovitch looked across the fence into the garden, and saw a long path, straight as a ruler, carpeted with yellow sand, and shaded by young birches. In an ecstasy of enchantment, he pictured little feminine feet treading the yellow sand; and, in a flash, imagination restored the woman who had kissed him, the woman he had visualized after supper the night before. The image settled in his brain and never afterward forsook him.

The spell reigned until midday, when a loud command came from the rear of the column.

"Attention! Eyes right! Officers!"

In a *calèche* drawn by a pair of white horses appeared the general of the brigade. He stopped at the second battery, and called out something which no one understood. Up galloped several officers, among them Riabovitch.

"Well, how goes it?" The general blinked his red eyes, and continued, "Are there any sick?"

Hearing the answer, the little skinny general mused a moment, turned to an officer, and said—

"The driver of your third-gun wheeler has taken off his leg guard and hung it on the limber. *Canaille!* Punish him!"

Then raising his eyes to Riabovitch, he added—

"And in your battery, I think, the harness is too loose."

Having made several other equally tiresome remarks, he looked at Lobuitko, and laughed.

"Why do you look so downcast, Lieutenant Lobuitko? You are sighing for Madame Lopukhoff, eh? Gentlemen, he is pining for Madame Lopukhoff!"

Madame Lopukhoff was a tall, stout lady, long past forty. Being partial to big women, regardless of age, the general ascribed the same taste to his subordinates. The officers smiled respectfully; and the general, pleased that he had said something caustic and laughable, touched the coachman's back and saluted. The *calèche* whirled away.

"All this, though it seems to me impossible and unearthly, is in reality very commonplace," thought Riabovitch, watching the clouds of dust raised by the general's carriage. "It is an everyday event, and within everyone's experience . . . This old general, for instance, must have loved in his day; he is married now, and has children. Captain Wachter is also married, and his wife loves him, though he has an ugly red neck and no waist . . . Salmanoff is coarse, and a typical Tartar, but he has had a romance ending in marriage . . . I, like the rest, must go through it all sooner or later."

And the thought that he was an ordinary man, and that his life was ordinary, rejoiced and consoled him. He boldly visualized *her* and his happiness, and let his imagination run mad.

Towards evening the brigade ended its march. While the other officers sprawled in their tents, Riabovitch, Merzliakoff, and Lobuitko sat round a packing case and supped. Merzliakoff ate slowly, and, resting *The Messenger of Europe* on his knees, read on steadily. Lobuitko, chattering without cease, poured beer into his glass. But Riabovitch, whose head was dizzy from uninterrupted daydreams, ate in silence. When he had drunk three glasses he felt tipsy and weak; and an overmastering impulse forced him to relate his adventure to his comrades.

"A most extraordinary thing happened to me at von Rabbek's," he began, doing his best to speak in an indifferent, ironical tone. "I was on my way, you understand, from the billiard room. . . ."

And he attempted to give a very detailed history of the kiss. But in a minute he had told the whole story. In that minute he had exhausted every detail; and it seemed to him terrible that the story required such a short time. It ought, he felt, to have lasted all the night. As he finished, Lobuitko, who as a liar himself believed in no one, laughed incredulously. Merzliakoff frowned, and, with his eyes still glued to *The Messenger of Europe,* said indifferently—

"God knows who it was! She threw herself on your neck, you say, and didn't cry out! Some lunatic, I expect!"

"It must have been a lunatic," agreed Riabovitch.

"I, too, have had adventures of that kind," began Lobuitko, making a frightful face. "I was on my way to Kovno. I traveled second-class. The carriage was packed, and I couldn't sleep. So I gave the guard a *rouble,* and he took my bag, and put me in a *coupé.* I lay down, and pulled my rug over me. It was pitch dark, you understand. Suddenly I felt someone tapping my shoulder and breathing in my face. I stretched out my hand, and felt an elbow. Then I opened my eyes. Imagine! A woman! Coal-black eyes, lips red as good coral, nostrils breathing passion, breasts—buffers!"

"Draw it mild!" interrupted Merzliakoff in his quiet voice. "I can believe about the breasts, but if it was pitch dark how could you see the lips?"

By laughing at Merzliakoff's lack of understanding, Lobuitko tried to shuffle out of the dilemma. The story annoyed Riabovitch. He rose from the box, lay on his bed, and swore that he would never again take anyone into his confidence.

Life in camp passed without event. The days flew by, each like the one before. But on every one of these days Riabovitch felt, thought, and acted as a man in love. When at daybreak his servant brought him cold water, and poured it over his head, it flashed at once into his half-awakened brain that something good and warm and caressing had crept into his life.

At night when his comrades talked of love and of women, he drew in his chair, and his face was the face of an old soldier who talks of battles in which he has taken part. And when the rowdy officers, led by setter Lobuitko, made Don Juanesque raids upon the neighboring "suburb," Riabovitch, though he accompanied them, was morose and conscience-struck, and mentally asked *her* forgiveness. In free hours and sleepless nights, when his brain was obsessed by memories of childhood, of his father, his mother, of everything akin and dear, he remembered always Miestetchki, the dancing horse, von Rabbek, von Rabbek's wife, so like the ex-Empress Eugénie, the dark room, the chink in the door.

On the thirty-first of August he left camp, this time not with the whole brigade but with only two batteries. As an exile returning to his native land, he was agitated and enthralled by daydreams. He longed passionately for the queer-looking horse, the church, the insincere von Rabbeks, the dark room; and that internal voice which so often cheats the lovelorn whispered an assurance that he should see *her* again. But doubt tortured him. How should he meet her? What must he say? Would she have forgotten the kiss? If it came to the worst—he consoled himself—if he never saw her again, he might walk once more through the dark room, and remember . . .

Towards evening the white barns and well-known church rose on the horizon. Riabovitch's heart beat wildly. He ignored the remark of an officer who rode by, he forgot the whole world, and he gazed greedily at the river glimmering afar, at the green roofs, at the dove-cote, over which fluttered birds dyed golden by the setting sun.

As he rode towards the church, and heard again the quartermaster's raucous voice, he expected every second a horseman to appear from behind the fence and invite the officers to tea. . . . But the quartermaster ended his harangue, the officers hastened to the village, and no horseman appeared.

"When von Rabbek hears from the peasants that we are back he will send for us," thought Riabovitch. And so assured was he of this, that when he entered the hut he failed to understand why his comrades had lighted a candle, and why the servants were preparing the samovar.

A painful agitation oppressed him. He lay on his bed. A moment later he rose to look for the horseman. But no horseman was in sight. Again he lay down; again he rose; and this time, impelled by restlessness, went into the street and walked towards the church. The square was dark and deserted. On the hill stood three silent soldiers. When they saw Riabovitch they started and saluted, and he, returning their salute, began to descend the well-remembered path.

Beyond the stream, in a sky stained with purple, the moon slowly rose. Two chattering peasant women walked in a kitchen garden and pulled cabbage leaves; behind them their log cabins stood out black against the sky. The river bank was as it had been in May; the bushes were the same; things differed only in that the nightingale no longer sang, that it smelt no longer of poplars and young grass.

When he reached von Rabbek's garden Riabovitch peered through the wicket gate. Silence and darkness reigned. Save only the white birch trunks and patches of pathway, the whole garden merged in a black, impenetrable shade. Riabovitch listened greedily, and gazed intent. For a quarter of an hour he loitered; then hearing no sound, and seeing no light, he walked wearily towards home.

He went down to the river. In front rose the general's bathing box; and white towels hung on the rail of the bridge. He climbed on to the bridge and stood still; then, for no reason whatever, touched a towel. It was clammy and cold. He looked down at the river which sped past swiftly, murmuring almost inaudibly against the bathing-box piles. Near the left bank glowed the moon's ruddy reflection, overrun by ripples which stretched it, tore it in two, and it seemed, would sweep it away as twigs and shavings are swept.

"How stupid! How stupid!" thought Riabovitch, watching the hurrying ripples, "How stupid everything is!"

Now that hope was dead, the history of the kiss, his impatience, his ardor, his vague aspirations and disillusion appeared in a clear light. It no longer seemed strange that the general's horseman had not come, and that he would never again see *her* who had kissed him by accident instead of another. On the contrary, he felt, it would be strange if he did ever see her again . . .

The water flew past him, whither and why no one knew. It had flown past in May; it had sped a stream into a great river; a river, into the sea; it had floated on high in mist and fallen again in rain; it might be, the water of May was again speeding past under Riabovitch's eyes. For what purpose? Why?

And the whole world—life itself—seemed to Riabovitch an inscrutable, aimless mystification . . . Raising his eyes from the stream and gazing at the sky, he recalled how Fate in the shape of an unknown woman had once caressed him; he recalled his summer fantasies and images—and his whole life seemed to him unnaturally thin and colorless and wretched . . .

When he reached the cabin his comrades had disappeared. His servant informed him that all had set out to visit "General Fonrabbkin," who had sent a horseman to bring them . . . For a moment Riabovitch's heart thrilled with joy. But that joy he extinguished. He cast himself *why?* upon his bed, and wroth with his evil fate, as if he wished to spite it, ignored the invitation.

A & P

John Updike

In walks these three girls in nothing but bathing suits. I'm in the third checkout slot, with my back to the door, so I don't see them until they're over by the bread. The one that caught my eye first was the one in the plaid green two-piece. She was a chunky kid, with a good tan and a sweet broad soft-looking can with those two crescents of white just under it, where the sun never seems to hit, at the top of the backs of her legs. I stood there with my hand on a box of HiHo crackers trying to remember if I rang it up or not. I ring it up again and the customer starts giving me hell. She's one of those cash-register-watchers, a witch about fifty with rouge on her cheekbones and no eyebrows, and I know it made her day to trip me up. She'd been watching cash registers for fifty years and probably never seen a mistake before.

By the time I got her feathers smoothed and her goodies into a bag—she gives me a little snort in passing, if she'd been born at the right time they would have burned her over in Salem—by the time I get her on her way the girls had circled around the bread and were coming back, without a pushcart, back my way along the counters, in the aisle between the checkouts and the Special bins. They didn't even have shoes on. There was this chunky one, with the two-piece—it was bright green and the seams on the bra were still sharp and her belly was still pretty pale so I guessed she just got it (the suit)—there was this one, with one of those chubby berry-faces, the lips all bunched together under her nose, this one, and a tall one, with black hair that hadn't quite frizzed right, and one of these sunburns right across under the eyes, and a chin that was too long—you know, the kind of girl other girls think is very "striking" and "attractive" but never quite makes it, as they very well know, which is why they like her so much—and then the third one, that wasn't quite so tall. She was the queen. She kind of led them, the other two peeking around and making their shoulders round. She didn't look around, not this queen, she just walked straight on slowly, on these long white prima-donna legs. She came down a little hard on her heels, as if she didn't walk in her bare feet that much, putting down her heels and then letting the weight move along to her toes as if she was testing the floor with every step, putting a little deliberate extra action into it. You never know for sure how girls' minds work (do you really think it's a mind in there or just a little buzz like a bee in a glass jar?) but you got the idea she had talked the other two into coming in here with her, and now she was show-ing them how to do it, walk slow and hold yourself straight.

She had on a kind of dirty-pink—beige maybe, I don't know—bathing suit with a little nubble all over it and, what got me, the straps were down. They were off her shoulders looped loose around the cool tops of her arms, and I guess as a result the suit had slipped a little on her, so all around the top of the cloth there was this shining rim. If it hadn't been there you wouldn't have known there could have been anything whiter than those shoulders. With the straps pushed off, there was nothing be-tween the top of the suit and the top of her head except just *her,* this clean bare plane of the top of her chest down from the shoulder bones like a dented sheet of metal tilted in the light. I mean, it was more than pretty.

She had sort of oaky hair that the sun and salt had bleached, done up in a bun that was unravelling, and a kind of prim face. Walking into the A & P with your straps down, I suppose it's the only kind of face you *can* have. She held her head so high her neck, coming up out of those white shoulders, looked kind of stretched, but I didn't mind. The longer her neck was, the more of her there was.

She must have felt in the corner of her eye me and over my shoulder Stokesie in the second slot watching, but she didn't tip. Not this queen. She kept her eyes moving across the racks, and stopped, and turned so slow it made my stomach rub the inside of my apron, and buzzed to the other two, who kind of huddled against her for relief, and then they all three of them went up the cat-and-dog-food-breakfast-cereal-macaroni-rice-raisins-seasonings-spreads-spaghetti-soft-drinks-crackers-and-cookies aisle. From the third slot I look straight up this aisle to the meat counter, and I watched them all the way. The fat one with the tan sort of fumbled with the cookies, but on second thought she put the package back. The sheep pushing their carts down the aisle—the girls were walking against the usual traffic (not that we have one-way signs or anything)—were pretty hilarious. You could see them, when Queenie's white shoulders dawned on them, kind of jerk, or hop, or hiccup, but their eyes snapped back to their own baskets and on they pushed. I bet you could set off dynamite in an A & P and the people would by and large keep reaching and checking oatmeal off their lists and muttering "Let me see, there was a third thing, began with A, asparagus, no, ah, yes, applesauce!" or whatever it is they do mutter. But there was no doubt, this jiggled them. A few houseslaves in pin curlers even looked around after pushing their carts past to make sure what they had seen was correct.

You know, it's one thing to have a girl in a bathing suit down on the beach, where what with the glare nobody can look at each other much anyway, and another thing in the cool of the A & P, under the fluorescent lights, against all those stacked packages, with her feet paddling along naked over our checkerboard green-and-cream rubber-tile floor.

"Oh Daddy," Stokesie said beside me. "I feel so faint."

"Darling," I said. "Hold me tight." Stokesie's married, with two babies chalked up on his fuselage already, but as far as I can tell that's the only difference. He's twenty-two, and I was nineteen this April.

"Is it done?" he asks, the responsible married man finding his voice. I forgot to say he thinks he's going to be manager some sunny day, maybe in 1990 when it's called the Great Alexandrov and Petrooshki Tea Company or something.

What he meant was, our town is five miles from a beach, with a big summer colony out on the Point, but we're right in the middle of town, and the women generally put on a shirt or shoes or something before they get out of the car into the street. And anyway these are usually women with six children and varicose veins mapping their legs and nobody, including them, could care less. As I say, we're right in the middle of town, and if you stand at our front doors you can see two banks and the Congregational church and the newspaper store and three real-estate offices and about twenty-seven old freeloaders tearing up Central Street because the sewer broke again. It's not as if we're on the Cape; we're north of Boston and there's people in this town haven't seen the ocean for twenty years.

The girls had reached the meat counter and were asking McMahon something. He pointed, they pointed, and they shuffled out of sight behind a pyramid of Diet Delight peaches. All that was left for us to see was old McMahon patting his mouth and looking after them sizing up their joints. Poor kids, I began to feel sorry for them, they couldn't help it.

Now here comes the sad part of the story, at least my family says it's sad, but I don't think it's so sad myself. The store's pretty empty, it being Thursday afternoon, so there was nothing much to do except lean on the register and wait for the girls to show up again. The whole store was like a pinball machine and I didn't know which tunnel they'd come out of. After a while they come around out of the far aisle, around the light bulbs, records at discount of the Caribbean Six or Tony Martin Sings or some such gunk you wonder they waste the wax on, sixpacks of candy bars, and plastic toys done up in cellophane that fall apart when a kid looks at them anyway. Around they come, Queenie still leading the way, and holding a little gray jar in her hand. Slots Three through Seven are unmanned and I could see her wondering between Stokes and me, but Stokesie with his usual luck draws an old party in baggy gray pants who stumbles up with four giant cans of pineapple juice (what do these bums *do* with all that pineapple juice? I've often asked myself) so the girls come to me. Queenie puts down the jar and I take it into my fingers icy cold. Kingfish Fancy Herring Snacks in Pure Sour Cream: 49¢. Now her hands are empty, not a ring or a bracelet, bare as God made them, and I wonder where the money's coming from. Still with that prim look she lifts a folded dollar bill out of the hollow at the center of her nubbed pink top. The jar went heavy in my hand. Really, I thought that was so cute.

Then everybody's luck begins to run out. Lengel comes in from haggling with a truck full of cabbages on the lot and is about to scuttle into that door marked MANAGER behind which he hides all day when the girls touch his eye. Lengel's pretty dreary, teaches Sunday school and the rest, but he doesn't miss that much. He comes over and says, "Girls, this isn't the beach."

Queenie blushes, though maybe it's just a brush of sunburn I was noticing for the first time, now that she was so close. "My mother asked me to pick up a jar of herring snacks." Her voice kind of startled me, the way voices do when you see the people first, coming out so flat and dumb yet kind of tony, too, the way it ticked over "pick up" and "snacks." All of a sudden I slid right down her voice into her living room. Her father and the other men were standing around in ice-cream coats and bow ties and the women were in sandals picking up herring snacks on toothpicks off a big glass plate and they were all holding drinks the color of water with olives and sprigs of mint in them. When my parents have somebody over they get lemonade and if it's a real racy affair Schlitz in tall glasses with "They'll Do It Every Time" cartoons stencilled on.

"That's all right," Lengel said. "But this isn't the beach." His repeating this struck me as funny, as if it had just occurred to him, and he had been thinking all these years the A & P was a great big dune and he was the head lifeguard. He didn't like my smiling—as I say he doesn't miss much—but he concentrates on giving the girls that sad Sunday-school-superintendent stare.

Queenie's blush is no sunburn now, and the plump one in plaid, that I liked better from the back—a really sweet can—pipes up, "We weren't doing any shopping. We just came in for the one thing."

"That makes no difference," Lengel tells her, and I could see from the way his eyes went that he hadn't noticed she was wearing a two-piece before. "We want you decently dressed when you come in here."

"We *are* decent," Queenie says suddenly, her lower lip pushing, getting sore now that she remembers her place, a place from which the crowd that runs the A & P must look pretty crummy. Fancy Herring Snacks flashed in her very blue eyes.

"Girls, I don't want to argue with you. After this come in here with your shoulders covered. It's our policy." He turns his back. That's policy for you. Policy is what the kingpins want. What the others want is juvenile delinquency.

All this while, the customers had been showing up with their carts but, you know, sheep, seeing a scene, they had all bunched up on Stokesie, who shook open a paper bag as gently as peeling a peach, not wanting to miss a word. I could feel in the silence everybody getting nervous, most of all Lengel, who asks me, "Sammy, have you rung up their purchase?"

I thought and said "No" but it wasn't about that I was thinking. I go through the punches, 4, 9, GROC, TOT––it's more complicated than you think, and after you do it often enough, it begins to make a little song, that you hear words to, in my case "Hello (*bing*) there, you (*gung*) hap-py pee-pul (*splat*)!"—the *splat* being the drawer flying out. I un-crease the bill, tenderly as you may imagine, it just having come from between the two smoothest scoops of vanilla I had ever known were there, and pass a half and a penny into her narrow pink palm, and nestle the herring in a bag and twist its neck and hand it over, all the time thinking.

The girls, and who'd blame them, are in a hurry to get out, so I say "I quit" to Lengel quick enough for them to hear, hoping they'll stop and watch me, their unsuspected hero. They keep right on going, into the electric eye; the door flies open and they flicker across the lot to their car. Queenie and Plaid and Big Tall Goony-Goony (not that as raw material she was so bad), leaving me with Lengel and a kink in his eyebrow.

"Did you say something, Sammy?"

"I said I quit."

"I thought you did."

"You didn't have to embarrass them."

"It was they who were embarrassing us."

I started to say something that came out "Fiddle-de-doo." It's a say-ing of my grandmother's, and I know she would have been pleased.

"I don't think you know what you're saying," Lengel said.

"I know you don't," I said. "But I do." I pull the bow at the back of my apron and start shrugging it off my shoulders. A couple customers that had been heading for my slot begin to knock against each other, like scared pigs in a chute.

Lengel sighs and begins to look very patient and old and gray. He's been a friend of my parents for years. "Sammy, you don't want to do this to your Mom and Dad," he tells me. It's true, I don't. But it seems to me that once you begin a gesture it's fatal not to go through with it. I fold the apron, "Sammy" stitched in red on the pocket, and put it on the counter, and drop the bow tie on top of it. The bow tie is theirs, if you've ever wondered. "You'll feel this for the rest of your life," Lengel says, and I know that's true, too, but remembering how he made that pretty girl blush makes me so scrunchy inside I punch the No Sale tab and the machine whirs "pee-pul" and the drawer splats out. One advantage to this scene taking place in summer, I can follow this up with a clean exit, there's no fumbling around getting your coat and galoshes, I just saunter into the electric eye in my white shirt that my mother ironed the night before, and the door heaves itself open, and outside the sunshine is skating around on the asphalt.

I look around for my girls, but they're gone, of course. There wasn't anybody but some young married screaming with her children about some candy they didn't get by the door of a powder-blue Falcon station wagon. Looking back in the big windows, over the bags of peat moss and aluminum lawn furniture stacked on the pavement, I could see Lengel in my place in the slot, checking the sheep through. His face was dark gray and his back stiff, as if he'd just had an injection of iron, and my stomach kind of fell as I felt how hard the world was going to be to me hereafter.

The Magic Barrel

Bernard Malamud

Not long ago there lived in uptown New York, in a small, almost meager room, though crowded with books, Leo Finkle, a rabbinical student in the Yeshivah University. Finkle, after six years of study, was to be ordained in June and had been advised by an acquaintance that he might find it easier to win himself a congregation if he were married. Since he had no present prospects of marriage, after two tormented days of turning it over in his mind, he called in Pinye Salzman, a marriage broker, whose two-line advertisement he had read in the *Forward*.

The matchmaker appeared one night out of the dark fourth-floor hallway of the graystone rooming house, grasping a black, strapped portfolio that had been worn thin with use. Salzman, who had been long in the business, was of slight but dignified build, wearing an old hat and an overcoat too short and tight for him. He smelled frankly of fish, which he loved to eat, and although he was missing a few teeth, his presence was not displeasing, because of an amiable manner curiously contrasted by mournful eyes. His voice, his lips, his wisp of beard, his bony fingers were animated, but give him a moment of repose and his mild blue eyes soon revealed a depth of sadness, a characteristic that put Leo a little at ease although the situation, for him, was inherently tense.

He at once informed Salzman why he had asked him to come, explaining that his home was in Cleveland, and that but for his parents, who had married comparatively late in life, he was alone in the world. He had for six years devoted himself entirely to his studies, as a result of which, quite understandably, he had found himself without time for a social life and the company of young women. Therefore he thought it the better part of trial and error—of embarrassing fumbling—to call in an experienced person to advise him in these matters. He remarked in passing that the function of the marriage broker was ancient and honorable, highly approved in the Jewish community, because it made practical the necessary without hindering joy. Moreover, his own parents had been brought together by a matchmaker. They had made, if not a financially profitable marriage— since neither had possessed any worldly goods to speak of—at least a successful one in the sense of their everlasting devotion to one another. Salzman listened in embarrassed surprise, sensing a sort of apology. Later, however, he experienced a glow of pride in his work, an emotion that had left him years ago, and he heartily approved of Finkle.

The two men went to their business. Leo had led Salzman to the only clear place in the room, a table near a window that overlooked the lamplit city. He seated himself at the matchmaker's side but facing him, attempting by an act of will to suppress the unpleasant tickle in his throat. Salzman eagerly unstrapped his portfolio and removed a loose rubber band from a thin packet of much handled cards. As he flipped through them, a gesture and sound that physically hurt Leo, the student pretended not to see and gazed steadfastly out the window. Although it was still February, winter was on its last legs, signs of which he had for the first time in years begun to notice. He now observed the round white moon, moving high in the sky through a cloud menagerie, and watched with half-open mouth as it penetrated a huge hen, and dropped out of her like an egg laying itself. Salzman, though pretending through eyeglasses he had just slipped on to be engaged in scanning the writing on the cards, stole occasional glances at the young man's distinguished face, noting with pleasure the long, severe scholar's nose, brown eyes heavy with learning, sensitive yet ascetic lips, and a certain almost hollow quality of the dark cheeks. He gazed around at shelves upon shelves of books and let out a soft but happy sigh.

When Leo's eyes fell upon the cards, he counted six spread out in Salzman's hand.

"So few?" he said in disappointment.

"You wouldn't believe me how much cards I got in my office," Salzman replied. "The drawers are already filled to the top, so I keep them now in a barrel, but is every girl good for a new rabbi?"

Leo blushed at this, regretting all he had revealed of himself in a curriculum vitae he had sent to Salzman. He had thought it best to acquaint him with his strict standards and specifications, but in having done so now felt he had told the marriage broker more than was absolutely necessary.

He hesitantly inquired, "Do you keep photographs of your clients on file?"

"First comes family, amount of dowry, also what kind promises," Salzman replied, unbuttoning his tight coat and settling himself in the chair. "After comes pictures, rabbi."

"Call me Mr. Finkle. I'm not a rabbi yet."

Salzman said he would, but instead called him doctor, which he changed to rabbi when Leo was not listening too attentively.

Salzman adjusted his horn-rimmed spectacles, gently cleared his throat and read in an eager voice the contents of the top card:

"Sophie P. Twenty-four years. Widow for one year. No children. Educated high school and two years college. Father promises eight thousand dollars. Has wonderful wholesale business. Also real estate. On the mother's side comes teachers, also one actor. Well known on Second Avenue."

Leo gazed up in surprise. "Did you say a widow?"

"A widow don't mean spoiled, rabbi. She lived with her husband maybe four months. He was a sick boy, she made a mistake to marry him."

"Marrying a widow has never entered my mind."

"This is because you have no experience. A widow, specially if she is young and healthy like this girl, is a wonderful person to marry. She will be thankful to you the rest of her life. Believe me, if I was looking now for a bride, I would marry a widow."

Leo reflected, then shook his head.

Salzman hunched his shoulders in an almost imperceptible gesture of disappointment. He placed the card down on the wooden table and began to read another:

"Lily H. High school teacher. Regular. Not a substitute. Has savings and new Dodge car. Lived in Paris one year. Father is successful dentist thirty-five years. Interested in professional man. Well Americanized family. Wonderful opportunity.

"I know her personally," said Salzman. "I wish you could see this girl. She is a doll. Also very intelligent. All day you could talk to her about books and theyater and what not. She also knows current events."

"I don't believe you mentioned her age?"

"Her age?" Salzman said, raising his brows in surprise. "Her age is thirty-two years."

Leo said after a while, "I'm afraid that seems a little too old."

Salzman let out a laugh. "So how old are you, rabbi?"

"Twenty-seven."

"So what is the difference, tell me, between twenty-seven and thirty-two? My own wife is seven years older than me. So what did I suffer? —Nothing. If Rothschild's a daughter wants to marry you, would you say on account her age, no?"

"Yes," Leo said dryly.

Salzman shook off the no in the yes. "Five years don't mean a thing. I give you my word that when you will live with her for one week you will forget her age. What does it mean five years—that she lived more and knows more than somebody who is younger? On this girl, God bless her, years are not wasted. Each one that it comes makes better the bargain."

"What subject does she teach in high school?"

"Languages. If you heard the way she reads French, you will think it is music. I am in the business twenty-five years, and I recommend her with my whole heart. Believe me, I know what I'm talking, rabbi."

"What's on the next card?" Leo said abruptly.

Salzman reluctantly turned up the third card:

"Ruth K. Nineteen years. Honor student. Father offers thirteen thousand dollars cash to the right bridegroom. He is a medical doctor. Stomach specialist with marvelous practice. Brother-in-law owns own garment business. Particular people."

Salzman looked up as if he had read his trump card.

"Did you say nineteen?" Leo asked with interest.

"On the dot."

"Is she attractive?" He blushed. "Pretty?"

Salzman kissed his fingertips. "A little doll. On this I give you my word. Let me call the father tonight and you will see what means pretty."

But Leo was troubled. "You're sure she's that young?"

"This I am positive. The father will show you the birth certificate."

"Are you positive there isn't something wrong with her?" Leo insisted.

"Who says there is wrong?"

"I don't understand why an American girl her age should go to a marriage broker."

A smile spread over Salzman's face.

"So for the same reason you went, she comes."

Leo flushed. "I am pressed for time."

Salzman, realizing he had been tactless, quickly explained. "The father came, not her. He wants she should have the best, so he looks around himself. When we will locate the right boy he will introduce him and encourage. This makes a better marriage than if a young girl without experience takes for herself. I don't have to tell you this."

"But don't you think this young girl believes in love?" Leo spoke uneasily.

Salzman was about to guffaw but caught himself and said soberly, "Love comes with the right person, not before."

Leo parted dry lips but did not speak. Noticing that Salzman had snatched a quick glance at the next card, he cleverly asked, "How is her health?"

"Perfect," Salzman said, breathing with difficulty. "Of course, she is a little lame on her right foot from an auto accident that it happened to her when she was twelve years, but nobody notices on account she is so brilliant and also beautiful."

Leo got up heavily and went to the window. He felt curiously bitter and upbraided himself for having called in the marriage broker. Finally, he shook his head.

"Why not?" Salzman persisted, the pitch of his voice rising.

"Because I hate stomach specialists."

"So what do you care what is his business? After you marry her, do you need him? Who says he must come every Friday night to your house?"

Ashamed of the way the talk was going, Leo dismissed Salzman, who went home with melancholy eyes.

Though he had felt only relief at the marriage broker's departure, Leo was in low spirits the next day. He explained it as arising from Salzman's failure to produce a suitable bride for him. He did not care for his type of clientele. But when Leo found himself hesitating over whether to seek out another matchmaker, one more polished than Pinye, he wondered if it could be—his protestations to the contrary, and although he honored his father and mother—that he did not, in essence, care for the matchmaking institution. This thought he quickly put out of mind yet found himself still upset. All day he ran around in a fog—missed an important appointment, forgot to give out his laundry, walked out of a Broadway cafeteria without paying and had to run back with the ticket in his hand;

had even not recognized his landlady in the street when she passed with a friend and courteously called out, "A good evening to you, Doctor Finkle." By nightfall, however, he had regained sufficient calm to sink his nose into a book and there found peace from his thoughts.

Almost at once there came a knock on the door. Before Leo could say enter, Salzman, commercial cupid, was standing in the room. His face was gray and meager, his expression hungry, and he looked as if he would expire on his feet. Yet the marriage broker managed, by some trick of the muscles, to display a broad smile.

"So good evening. I am invited?"

Leo nodded, disturbed to see him again, yet unwilling to ask him to leave.

Beaming still, Salzman laid his portfolio on the table. "Rabbi, I got for you tonight good news."

"I've asked you not to call me rabbi. I'm still a student."

"Your worries are finished. I have for you a first-class bride."

"Leave me in peace concerning this subject." Leo pretended lack of interest.

"The world will dance at your wedding."

"Please, Mr. Salzman, no more."

"But first must come back my strength," Salzman said weakly. He fumbled with the portfolio straps and took out of the leather case an oily paper bag, from which he extracted a hard seeded roll and a small smoked whitefish. With one motion of his hand he stripped the fish out of its skin and began ravenously to chew. "All day in a rush," he muttered.

Leo watched him eat.

"A sliced tomato you have maybe?" Salzman hesitantly inquired.

"No."

The marriage broker shut his eyes and ate. When he had finished he carefully cleaned up the crumbs and rolled up the remains of the fish in the paper bag. His spectacled eyes roamed the room until he discovered, amid some piles of books, a one-burner gas stove. Lifting his hat he humbly asked, "A glass tea you got, rabbi?"

Conscience-stricken, Leo rose and brewed the tea. He served it with a chunk of lemon and two cubes of lump sugar, delighting Salzman.

After he had drunk his tea, Salzman's strength and good spirits were restored.

"So tell me, rabbi," he said amiably, "you considered any more the three clients I mentioned yesterday?"

"There was no need to consider."

"Why not?"

"None of them suits me."

"What, then, suits you?"

Leo let it pass because he could give only a confused answer.

Without waiting for a reply, Salzman asked, "You remember this girl I talked to you—the high school teacher?"

"Age thirty-two?"

But, surprisingly, Salzman's face lit in a smile. "Age twenty-nine."

Leo shot him a look. "Reduced from thirty-two?"

"A mistake," Salzman avowed. "I talked today with the dentist. He took me to his safety deposit box and showed me the birth certificate. She was twenty-nine years last August. They made her a party in the mountains where she went for her vacation. When her father spoke to me the first time I forgot to write the age and I told you thirty-two, but now I remember this was a different client, a widow."

"The same one you told me about? I thought she was twenty-four?"

"A different. Am I responsible that the world is filled with widows?"

"No, but I'm not interested in them, nor for that matter, in school-teachers."

Salzman passionately pulled his clasped hands to his breast. Looking at the ceiling he exclaimed, "Jewish children, what can I say to somebody that he is not interested in high school teachers? So what then you are interested?"

Leo flushed but controlled himself.

"In who else you will be interested," Salzman went on, "if you not interested in this fine girl that she speaks four languages and has personally in the bank ten thousand dollars? Also her father guarantees further twelve thousand. Also she has a new car, wonderful clothes, talks on all subjects, and she will give you a first-class home and children. How near do we come in our life to paradise?"

"If she's so wonderful, why wasn't she married ten years ago?"

"Why?" said Salzman with a heavy laugh "—Why? Because she is *partikler*. This is why. She wants only the *best*."

Leo was silent, amused at how he had trapped himself. But Salzman had aroused his interest in Lily H., and he began seriously to consider calling on her. When the marriage broker observed how intently Leo's mind was at work on the facts he had supplied, he felt positive they would soon come to an agreement.

Late Saturday afternoon, conscious of Salzman, Leo Finkle walked with Lily Hirschorn along Riverside Drive. He walked briskly and erectly, wearing with distinction the black fedora he had that morning taken with trepidation out of the dusty hatbox on his closet shelf, and the heavy black Saturday coat he had thoroughly whisked clean. Leo also owned a walking stick, a present from a distant relative, but had decided not to use it. Lily, petite and not unpretty, had on something signifying the approach of spring. She was *au courant*,[1] animatedly, with all subjects, and he weighed her words and found her surprisingly sound—score another for Salzman, whom he uneasily sensed to be somewhere around, hiding perhaps high in a tree along the street, flashing the lady signals; or perhaps a cloven-hoofed Pan, piping nuptial ditties as he danced his invisible way before them, strewing wild buds on the walk and purple summer grapes in their path, symbolizing fruit of a union, of which there was yet none.

Lily startled Leo by remarking, "I was thinking of Mr. Salzman, a curious figure, wouldn't you say?"

Not certain what to answer, he nodded.

She bravely went on, blushing, "I for one am grateful for his introducing us. Aren't you?"

He courteously replied, "I am."

"I mean," she said with a little laugh—and it was all in good taste, or at least gave the effect of being not in bad—"do you mind that we came together so?"

He was not afraid of her honesty, recognizing that she meant to set the relationship aright, and understanding that it took a certain amount of experience in life, and courage, to want to do it quite that way. One had to have some sort of past to make that kind of beginning.

He said that he did not mind. Salzman's function was traditional and honorable—valuable for what it might achieve, which, he pointed out, was frequently nothing.

Lily agreed with a sigh. They walked on for a while and she said after a long silence, again with a nervous laugh, "Would you mind if I asked you something a little bit personal? Frankly, I find the subject fascinating." Although Leo shrugged, she went on half embarrassedly, "How was it that you came to your calling? I mean was it a sudden passionate inspiration?"

Leo, after a time, slowly replied, "I was always interested in the Law."

"You saw revealed in it the presence of the Highest?"

He nodded and changed the subject. "I understand you spent a little time in Paris, Miss Hirschorn?"

"Oh, did Mr. Salzman tell you, Rabbi Finkle?" Leo winced but she went on, "It was ages and ages ago and almost forgotten. I remember I had to return for my sister's wedding."

But Lily would not be put off. "When," she asked in a trembly voice, "did you become enamored of God?"

He stared at her. Then it came to him that she was talking not about

1. *au courant* up to date.

Leo Finkle, but a total stranger, some mystical figure, perhaps even passionate prophet that Salzman had conjured up for her—no relation to the living or dead. Leo trembled with rage and weakness. The trickster had obviously sold her a bill of goods, just as he had him, who'd expected to become acquainted with a young lady of twenty-nine, only to behold, the moment he laid eyes upon her strained and anxious face, a woman past thirty-five and aging very rapidly. Only his self-control, he thought, had kept him this long in her presence.

"I am not," he said gravely, "a talented religious person," and in seeking words to go on, found himself possessed by fear and shame. "I think," he said in a strained manner, "that I came to God not because I loved him, but because I did not."

This confession he spoke harshly because its unexpectedness shook him.

Lily wilted. Leo saw a profusion of loaves of bread sailing like ducks high over his head, not unlike the loaves by which he had counted himself to sleep last night. Mercifully, then, it snowed, which he would not put past Salzman's machinations.

He was infuriated with the marriage broker and swore he would throw him out of the room the moment he reappeared. But Salzman did not come that night, and when Leo's anger had subsided, an unaccountable despair grew in its place. At first he thought this was caused by his disappointment in Lily, but before long it became evident that he had involved himself with Salzman without a true knowledge of his own intent. He gradually realized—with an emptiness that seized him with six hands —that he had called in the broker to find him a bride because he was incapable of doing it himself. This terrifying insight he had derived as a result of his meeting and conversation with Lily Hirschorn. Her probing questions had somehow irritated him into revealing—to himself more than her—the true nature of his relationship with God, and from that it had come upon him, with shocking force, that apart from his parents, he had never loved anyone. Or perhaps it went the other way, that he did not love God so well as he might, because he had not loved man. It seemed to Leo that his whole life stood starkly revealed and he saw himself, for the first time, as he truly was—unloved and loveless. This bitter but somehow not fully unexpected revelation brought him to a point of panic controlled only by extraordinary effort. He covered his face with his hands and wept.

The week that followed was the worst of his life. He did not eat, and lost weight. His beard darkened and grew ragged. He stopped attending lectures and seminars and almost never opened a book. He seriously considered leaving the Yeshivah, although he was deeply troubled at the thought of the loss of all his years of study—saw them likes pages from a book strewn over the city—and at the devastating effect of this decision upon his parents. But he had lived without knowledge of himself, and never in the Five Books and all the Commentaries—mea culpa[2]—had the truth been revealed to him. He did not know where to turn, and in all this desolating loneliness there was no *to whom*, although he often thought of Lily but not once could bring himself to go downstairs and make the call. He became touchy and irritable, especially with his landlady, who asked him all manner of questions; on the other hand, sensing his own disagreeableness, he waylaid her on the stairs and apologized abjectly, until, mortified, she ran from him. Out of this, however, he drew the consolation that he was yet a Jew and that a Jew suffered. But gradually, as the long and terrible week drew to a close, he regained his composure and some idea of purpose in life: to go on as planned. Although he was imperfect, the ideal was not. As for his quest of a bride, the thought of continuing afflicted him with anxiety and heartburn, yet perhaps with this new knowledge of himself he would be more successful than in the past. Perhaps love would now come to him and a bride to that love. And for this sanctified seeking who needed a Salzman?

The marriage broker, a skeleton with haunted eyes, returned that very night. He looked, withal, the picture of frustrated expectancy—as if he had steadfastly waited the week at Miss Lily Hirschorn's side for a telephone call that never came.

Casually coughing, Salzman came immediately to the point: "So how did you like her?"

Leo's anger rose and he could not refrain from chiding the matchmaker: "Why did you lie to me, Salzman?"

Salzman's pale face went dead white, as if the world had snowed on him.

"Did you not state that she was twenty-nine?" Leo insisted.

"I give you my word—"

"She was thirty-five. *At least* thirty-five."

"Of this I would not be too sure. Her father told me—"

"Never mind. The worst of it was that you lied to her."

"How did I lie to her, tell me?"

"You told her things about me that weren't true. You made me out to be more, consequently less than I am. She had in mind a totally different person, a sort of semi-mystical Wonder Rabbi."

"All I said, you was a religious man."

"I can imagine."

Salzman sighed. "This is my weakness that I have," he confessed. "My wife says to me I shouldn't be a salesman, but when I have two fine

---

2. *mea culpa* my fault.

people that they would be wonderful to be married, I am so happy that I talk too much." He smiled wanly. "This is why Salzman is a poor man."

Leo's anger went. "Well, Salzman, I'm afraid that's all."

The marriage broker fastened hungry eyes on him.

"You don't want any more a bride?"

"I do," said Leo, "but I have decided to seek her in a different way. I am no longer interested in an arranged marriage. To be frank, I now admit the necessity of premarital love. That is, I want to be in love with the one I marry."

"Love?" said Salzman, astounded. After a moment he said, "For us, our love is our life, not for the ladies. In the ghetto they—"

"I know, I know," said Leo. "I've thought of it often. Love, I have said to myself, should be a by-product of living and worship rather than its own end. Yet for myself I find it necessary to establish the level of my need and to fulfill it."

Salzman shrugged but answered, "Listen, rabbi, if you want love, this I can find for you also. I have such beautiful clients that you will love them the minute your eyes will see them."

Leo smiled unhappily. "I'm afraid you don't understand."

But Salzman hastily unstrapped his portfolio and withdrew a manila packet from it.

"Pictures," he said, quickly laying the envelope on the table.

Leo called after him to take the pictures away, but as if on the wings of the wind, Salzman had disappeared.

March came. Leo had returned to his regular routine. Although he felt not quite himself yet—lacked energy—he was making plans for a more active social life. Of course it would cost something, but he was an expert in cutting corners; and when there were no corners left he could make circles rounder. All the while Salzman's pictures had lain on the table, gathering dust. Occasionally as Leo sat studying, or enjoying a cup of tea, his eyes fell on the manila envelope, but he never opened it.

The days went by and no social life to speak of developed with a member of the opposite sex—it was difficult, given the circumstances of his situation. One morning Leo toiled up the stairs to his room and stared out the window at the city. Although the day was bright his view of it was dark. For some time he watched the people in the street below hurrying along and then turned with a heavy heart to his little room. On the table was the packet. With a sudden relentless gesture he tore it open. For a half-hour he stood there, in a state of excitement, examining the photographs of the ladies Salzman had included. Finally, with a deep sigh he put them down. There were six, of varying degrees of attractiveness, but look at them long enough and they all became Lily Hirschorn: all past their prime, all starved behind bright smiles, not a true personality in the lot. Life, despite their anguished struggles and frantic yoohoo-ings, had passed them by; they were photographs in a briefcase that stank of fish. After a while, however, as Leo attempted to return the pictures into the envelope, he found another in it, a small snapshot of the type taken by a machine for a quarter. He gazed at it a moment and let out a cry.

Her face deeply moved him. Why, he could at first not say. It gave him the impression of youth—all spring flowers, yet age—a sense of hav-ing been used to the bone, wasted; this all came from the eyes, which were hauntingly familiar, yet absolutely strange. He had a strong im-pression that he had met her before, but try as he might he could not place her, although he could almost recall her name, as if he had read it written in her own handwriting. No, this couldn't be; he would have remembered her. It was not, he affirmed, that she had an extraordinary beauty—no, although her face was attractive enough; it was that *some-thing* about her moved him. Feature for feature, even some of the ladies of the photographs could do better; but she leaped forth to the heart— had lived, or wanted to—more than just wanted, perhaps regretted it— had somehow deeply suffered it: it could be seen in the depths of those reluctant eyes, and from the way the light enclosed and shone from her, and within her, opening whole realms of possibility: this was her own. Her he desired. His head ached and eyes narrowed with the intensity of his gazing, then, as if a black fog had blown up in the mind, he experi-enced fear of her and was aware that he had received an impression, somehow, of filth. He shuddered, saying softly, it is thus with us all. Leo brewed some tea in a small pot and sat sipping it, without sugar, to calm himself. But before he had finished drinking, again with excite-ment he examined the face and found it good: good for him. Only such a one could truly understand Leo Finkle and help him to seek whatever he was seeking. How she had come to be among the discards in Salz-man's barrel he could never guess, but he knew he must urgently go find her.

Leo rushed downstairs, grabbed up the Bronx telephone book, and searched for Salzman's home address. He was not listed, nor was his office. Neither was he in the Manhattan book. But Leo remembered having written down the address on a slip of paper after he had read Salzman's advertisement in the "personals" column of the *Forward*. He ran up to his room and tore through his papers, without luck. It was exasperating. Just when he needed the matchmaker he was nowhere to be found. Fortunately Leo remembered to look in his wallet. There on a card he found his name written and a Bronx address. No phone num-ber was listed, which, Leo now recalled, was the reason he had originally communicated with Salzman by letter. He got on his coat, put a hat on over his skull cap and hurried to the subway station. All the way to the far end of the Bronx he sat on the edge of the seat. He was more than once tempted to take out the picture and see if the girl's face was as he remembered it, but he refrained, allowing the snapshot to remain in his inside coat pocket, content to have her so close. When the train pulled into the station he was waiting at the door and bolted out. He quickly located the street Salzman had advertised.

The building he sought was less than a block from the subway, but it was not an office building, nor even a loft, nor a store in which one could rent office space. It was an old and grimy tenement. Leo found Salzman's name in pencil on a soiled tag under the bell and climbed three dark flights to his apartment. When he knocked, the door was opened by a thin, asthmatic, gray-haired woman, in felt slippers.

"Yes?" she said, expecting nothing. She listened without listening. He could have sworn he had seen her somewhere before but knew it was illusion.

"Salzman—does he live here? Pinye Salzman," he said, "the match-maker?"

She stared at him a long time. "Of course."

He felt embarrassed. "Is he in?"

"No." Her mouth was open, but she offered nothing more.

"This is urgent. Can you tell me where his office is?"

"In the air." She pointed upward.

"You mean he has no office?" Leo said.

"In his socks."

He peered into the apartment. It was sunless and dingy, one large room divided by a half-open curtain, beyond which he could see a sagging metal bed. The near side of the room was crowded with rickety chairs, old bureaus, a three-legged table, racks of cooking utensils, and all the apparatus of a kitchen. But there was no sign of Salzman or his magic barrel, probably also a figment of his imagination. An odor of frying fish made Leo weak to the knees.

"Where is he?" he insisted. "I've got to see your husband."

At length she answered, "So who knows where he is? Every time he thinks a new thought he runs to a different place. Go home, he will find you."

"Tell him Leo Finkle."

She gave no sign that she had heard.

He went downstairs, deeply depressed.

But Salzman, breathless, stood waiting at his door.

Leo was overjoyed and astounded. "How did you get here before me?"

"I rushed."

"Come inside."

They entered.   Leo fixed tea and a sardine sandwich for Salzman.

As they were drinking he reached behind him for the packet of pictures and handed them to the marriage broker.

Salzman put down his glass and said expectantly, "You found maybe somebody you like?"

"Not among these."

The marriage broker turned sad eyes away.

"Here's the one I like."   Leo held forth the snapshot.

Salzman slipped on his glasses and took the picture into his trembling hand.   He turned ghastly and let out a miserable groan.

"What's the matter?"   cried Leo.

"Excuse me.   Was an accident this picture.   She is not for you."

Salzman frantically shoved the manila packet into his portfolio.   He thrust the snapshot into his pocket and fled down the stairs.

Leo, after momentary paralysis, gave chase and cornered the marriage broker in the vestibule.   The landlady made hysterical outcries but neither of them listened.

"Give me back the picture, Salzman."

"No."   The pain in his eyes was terrible.

"Tell me who she is then."

"This I can't tell you.   Excuse me."

He made to depart, but Leo, forgetting himself, seized the matchmaker by his tight coat and shook him frenziedly.

"Please," sighed Salzman.   *"Please."*

Leo ashamedly let him go.   "Tell me who she is," he begged.   "It's very important for me to know."

"She is not for you.   She is a wild one—wild, without shame.   This is not a bride for a rabbi."

"What do you mean wild?"

"Like an animal.   Like a dog.   For her to be poor was a sin.   This is why she is dead now."

"In God's name, what do you mean?"

"Her I can't introduce to you," Salzman cried.

"Why are you so excited?"

"Why he asks," Salzman said, bursting into tears.   "This is my baby, my Stella, she should burn in hell."

Leo hurried up to bed and hid under the covers.   Under the covers he thought his whole life through.   Although he soon fell asleep he could not sleep her out of his mind.   He woke, beating his breast.   Though he prayed to be rid of her, his prayers went unanswered.   Through days of torment he struggled endlessly not to love her; fearing success, he escaped it.   He then concluded to convert her to goodness, himself to God.   The idea alternately nauseated and exalted him.

He perhaps did not know that he had come to a final decision until he encountered Salzman in a Broadway cafeteria. He was sitting alone at a rear table, sucking the bony remains of a fish. The marriage broker appeared haggard, and transparent to the point of vanishing.

Salzman looked up at first without recognizing him. Leo had grown a pointed beard and his eyes were weighted with wisdom.

"Salzman," he said, "love has at last come to my heart."

"Who can love from a picture?" mocked the marriage broker.

"It is not impossible."

"If you can love her, then you can love anybody. Let me show you some new clients that they just sent me their photographs. One is a little doll."

"Just her I want," Leo murmured.

"Don't be a fool, doctor. Don't bother with her."

"Put me in touch with her, Salzman," Leo said humbly. "Perhaps I can do her a service."

Salzman had stopped chewing, and Leo understood with emotion that it was now arranged.

Leaving the cafeteria, he was, however, afflicted by a tormenting suspicion that Salzman had planned it all to happen this way.

Leo was informed by letter that she would meet him on a certain corner, and she was there one spring night, waiting under a street lamp. He appeared, carrying a small bouquet of violets and rosebuds. Stella stood by the lamppost, smoking. She wore white with red shoes, which fitted his expectations, although in a troubled moment he had imagined the dress red, and only the shoes white. She waited uneasily and shyly. From afar he saw that her eyes—clearly her father's—were filled with desperate innocence. He pictured, in hers, his own redemption. Violins and lit candles revolved in the sky. Leo ran forward with the flowers outthrust.

Around the corner, Salzman, leaning against a wall, chanted prayers for the dead.

POETRY

The Hero as Lover

"The General Prologue" to Geoffrey Chaucer's great poem *The Canterbury Tales* is, among other things, a magnificent portrait gallery of human types. On its literal level "The General Prologue" is intended to identify and characterize the various pilgrims who will be making the journey to Canterbury and telling their tales along the way.

The first pilgrim to be portrayed is the Knight, who emerges as the classic martial hero; next to be described is the Knight's son, the Squire, who perfectly exemplifies the traditional hero-lover.

The Squire

From "The General Prologue" to
The Canterbury Tales, lines 79–100

Geoffrey Chaucer

With him[1] ther was his sone, a yong Squier,[2]
A lovere and a lusty bacheler,   80
With lokkes crulle[3] as they were leyd in presse.
Of twenty yeer of age he was, I gesse.
Of his stature he was of evene lengthe,[4]
And wonderly delyvere,[5] and of greet strengthe.
And he hadde been som tyme in chivachye[6]   85
In Flaundres, in Artoys, and Picardye,
And born[7] him wel as of so litel space,
In hope to stonden[8] in his lady grace.
Embrouded[9] was he as it were a meede,[10]
Al ful of fresshe floures whyte and reede.   90
Syngynge he was, or floytynge,[11] al the day;
He was as fressh as is the month of May.
Short was his gowne, with sleves longe and wyde.
Wel koude he sitte on hors and faire ryde;
He koude songes make[12] and wel endite,[13]   95
Juste[14] and eek daunce, and wel purtreye[15] and write.
So hote[16] he lovede that by nyghtertale[17]
He slepte namoore than dooth a nyghtyngale.
Curteis he was, lowely, and servysable,
And carf biforn[18] his fader at the table.   100

---

1. *him* The knight.   2. *Squier* One in training to become a knight.
3. *lokkes crulle* Curly hair.   4. *evene lengthe* Average height.
5. *delyvere* Agile.   6. *chivachye* Cavalry expedition.   7. *born* Bore.
8. *stonden* Stand.   9. *Embrouded* Embroidered.   10. *meede* Meadow.
11. *floytynge* Whistling.   12. *make* Sing.   13. *endite* Compose lyrics.
14. *Juste* Joust.   15. *purtreye* Draw.   16. *hote* Passionately.
17. *nyghtertale* Nighttime.   18. *carf biforn* Carve before (and for).

Although Chaucer characteristically adds a touch of humor to his portrait of the Squire, he allows the youth his integrity as a man and a hero and his charm as a boy and a lover. He has proved himself in combat and in service to his father and is now ready (and eager) to enter the gentler battle of the sexes and the service of his lady. Physically attractive, dressed in the latest of fashions, accomplished in the arts of music, drawing, and courtly manners, he is born and bred to become the hero of a love story.

The following sonnet could have been "endited" by the Squire had he lived in sixteenth-century England. It was in fact written by one who was a hero in real life, Sir Philip Sidney (1554–1586). Like Chaucer's Squire, Sidney was accomplished in the fine arts as well as in the arts of war, but it was war that cut this excellent poet's life short at the age of thirty-two. While he lived, Sidney exemplified what was even then the old-fashioned tradition of chivalry, a tradition which he consciously sought to revive in England. Sidney's poem, the forty-first in the cycle of sonnets on the quest for love which he entitled *Astrophel and Stella*, takes as its occasion a day on which Astrophel has acquitted himself well in a jousting match with French knights. With the ultimate gallant gesture, however, he declines to play the hero, and instead transforms his victory into a celebration of Stella, his "lady fair."

Sonnet 41

Sir Philip Sidney

Having this day my horse, my hand, my lance
Guided so well that I obtained the prize,
Both by the judgment of the English eyes
And of some sent from that sweet enemy, France,
Horsemen my skill in horsemanship advance,   5
Town-folks my strength; a daintier[1] judge applies
His praise to sleight which from good use[2] doth rise;
Some lucky wits impute it but to chance;
Others, because of both sides I do take
My blood from them who did excel in this,   10
Think nature me a man of arms did make.

---

1. *daintier* More discriminating.   2. *good use* Hard practice.

How far they shoot awry!   The true cause is,
Stella looked on, and from her heavenly face
Sent forth the beams which made so fair my race.

The Lady as Hero and Heroine

Compared to the lady, the hero in literature is a fairly comprehensible figure.   She is a creature of "infinite variety," of many roles, many moods, many meanings.   If the hero has a "thousand faces," the lady, it would appear, has ten thousand.   Her mystery and her mystique resist simple classification particularly because she may serve one of two main functions: she can be either a hero in her own right, performing the same kinds of deeds that elevate the male to hero status; or she may function as a "heroine"—the object, deliberate or accidental, of the hero's quest.   What she is, her very nature as heroine, ultimately helps to define the nature of both the hero himself and of his quest.   One way of clarifying the complex nature and function of the lady is by classifying her (like the hero) according to her power of action.

As exemplified by Robert Grave's poem "The White Goddess" she can be a goddess-figure—the Virgin Mary, Venus-Aphrodite, mother and lover—ultimate woman, whose very existence impels the heroic quest for love on the part of the male.   This quest can transcend even religion, rationality, and morality, but in essence it is creative and life-affirming.

Another heroine type is the demigoddess, the woman who possesses more beauty, more grace, more innate wisdom than ordinary mortals. Though human, she has about her the aura of divinity.   Like the heroines of E. L. Mayo's poem "The Sleeping Beauty" and William Butler Yeats's poem "Her Triumph," she seems to have the power to elevate the hero and his quest from the mundane to the mythic.   Her presence and power prove to be the salvation of the hero.

A third kind of heroine is the woman who is recognizably human, but who is a figure of considerable authority.   That authority can be the result of her social status: Helen, of Yeats's poem "No Second Troy," was the wife of a king, and the title-figure of Thomas Merton's poem "Ariadne" was a princess.   The essential source of this type of heroine's power over the male, however, resides in her femininity—her beauty, grace, and spirit.   It is this feminine power of hers which, as both these poems suggest, is able to transform heroes into lovers and lovers into heroes.

The ordinary woman may not seem a likely candidate for heroine status yet, as suggested by William Shakespeare's "Sonnet 130," John Frederick Nims' "Love Poem," and John Ciardi's "Men Marry What They Need. I Marry You," her lover perceives more in her than the world does. For him, and perhaps only for him, she is capable of elevating reality into romance, a mere male into a kind of hero.

The Lowly Heroine, like the Lowly Hero, is a person of marked powerlessness. Her lack of control over her life may be due to her age, her character, her socio-economic status, or simply her sex. In the eyes of most males she may be merely a sex object, a servant, or a slave. The title figure of Robert Hayden's "The Ballad of Sue Ellen Westerfield" has been all three and is thus a traditional Lowly Heroine. But her pride in her blackness, her integrity as a human being, and her capacity for self-sacrifice clearly designate her as a hero as well.

The White Goddess

Robert Graves

All saints revile her, and all sober men
Ruled by the God Apollo's golden mean—
In scorn of which we sailed to find her
In distant regions likeliest to hold her
Whom we desired above all things to know,   5
Sister of the mirage and echo.

It was a virtue not to stay,
To go our headstrong and heroic way
Seeking her out at the volcano's head,
Among pack ice, or where the track had faded   10
Beyond the cavern of the seven sleepers:
Whose broad high brow was white as any leper's,
Whose eyes were blue, with rowan-berry lips,
With hair curled honey-coloured to white hips.

Green sap of Spring in the young wood a-stir   15
Will celebrate the Mountain Mother,
And every song-bird shout awhile for her;
But we are gifted, even in November
Rawest of seasons, with so huge a sense
Of her nakedly worn magnificence   20
We forget cruelty and past betrayal,
Heedless of where the next bright bolt may fall.

The Sleeping Beauty

E. L. Mayo

In a place where hunchbacks and old women
Quarrelled in their thin voices all the day
This temporizing grew intolerable:
I knew that here the Sleeping Beauty lay.

(Had they known it all the time and been   5
Sly servitors where I could only seize
Bad temper and distorted images?)
Sight ended the argument.   I saw

Her tower clear against the star-picked blue
Over their hovels.   It was no affair   10
Of a cloud and the moon's subtle conjunction; thorns
Hatched me all criss-cross as I hacked my way through

And stumbled bloody still and breathing still
Into a country where no footsteps fall
And where from moat, to keep, to citadel   15
Spider-webs lie like water.

I silvered as I entered through the door
Where time cannot prevail
But howls outside forever where I found her
Asleep, beautiful, the cobwebs round her.   20

Her Triumph

William Butler Yeats

I did the dragon's will until you came
Because I had fancied love a casual
Improvisation, or a settled game
That followed if I let the kerchief fall:
Those deeds were best that gave the minute wings   5
And heavenly music if they gave it wit;
And then you stood among the dragon-rings.

I mocked, being crazy, but you mastered it
And broke the chain and set my ankles free,
Saint George or else a pagan Perseus;[1]   10
And now we stare astonished at the sea,
And a miraculous strange bird shrieks at us.

No Second Troy
William Butler Yeats

Why should I blame her that she filled my days
With misery, or that she would of late
Have taught to ignorant men most violent ways,
Or hurled the little streets upon the great,
Had they but courage equal to desire?   5
What could have made her peaceful with a mind
That nobleness made simple as a fire,
With beauty like a tightened bow, a kind
That is not natural in an age like this,
Being high and solitary and most stern?   10
Why, what could she have done, being what she is?
Was there another Troy for her to burn?

Ariadne
Thomas Merton

All through the blazing afternoon
The hand drums talk together like locusts;
The flute pours out its endless, thin stream,
Threading it in and out the clatter of sticks upon wood-blocks.
Drums and bells exchange handfuls of bright coins,   5
Drums and bells scatter their music, like pennies, all over the
    air,

1. *Perseus* A mythological figure who slew the Medusa and with the aid of the
Medusa's head rescued Andromeda from a sea monster.

And see, the lutanist's thin hand
Rapidly picks the spangling notes off from his wires
And throws them about like drops of water.

Behind the bamboo blinds,   10
Behind the palms,
In the green, sundappled apartments of her palace
Redslippered Ariadne,[1] with a tiny yawn,
Tosses a ball upon her roulette wheel.

Suddenly, dead north,   15
A Greek ship leaps over the horizon, skips like a colt, paws the
   foam.
The ship courses through the pasture of bright amethysts
And whinnies at the jetty.
The whole city runs to see:
Quick as closing your hand   20
The racing sail's down.
Then the drums are stunned, and the crowd, exalted, cries:
O Theseus!   O Grecian hero!

Like a thought through the mind
Ariadne moves to the window.   25
Arrows of light, in every direction,
Leap from the armor of the black-eyed captain.
Arrows of light
Resound within her like the strings of a guitar.

Sonnet 130

William Shakespeare

My mistress' eyes are nothing like the sun;
Coral is far more red than her lips' red;
If snow be white, why then her breasts are dun;
If hairs be wires, black wires grow on her head.
I have seen roses damasked,[1] red and white,   5

1. *Ariadne* A mythological figure, she was the daughter of King Minos of Crete.
1. *damasked* A damasked rose is a large, hardy, fragrant pink rose.

But no such roses see I in her cheeks;
And in some perfumes is there more delight
Than in the breath that from my mistress reeks.
I love to hear her speak, yet well I know
That music hath a far more pleasing sound;   10
I grant I never saw a goddess go;
My mistress, when she walks, treads on the ground.
And yet, by heaven, I think my love as rare
As any she belied with false compare.

Love Poem

John Frederick Nims

My clumsiest dear, whose hands shipwreck vases,
At whose quick touch all glasses chip and ring,
Whose palms are bulls in china, burs in linen,
And have no cunning with any soft thing

Except all ill-at-ease fidgeting people: 5
The refugee uncertain at the door
You make at home; deftly, you steady
The drunk clambering on his undulant floor.

Unpredictable dear, the taxi drivers' terror,
Shrinking from far headlights pale as a dime   10
Yet leaping before red apoplectic streetcars—
Misfit in any space.   And never on time.

A wrench in clocks and the solar system.   Only
With words and people and love you move at ease.
In traffic of wit expertly maneuver   15
And keep us, all devotion, at your knees.

Forgetting your coffee spreading on our flannel,
Your lipstick grinning on our coat,
So gayly in love's unbreakable heaven
Our souls on glory of spilt bourbon float.   20

Be with me darling, early and late.   Smash glasses—
I will study wry music for your sake,
For should your hands drop white and empty
All the toys of the world would break.

Men marry what they need.
I marry you
John Ciardi

Men marry what they need.   I marry you,
morning by morning, day by day, night by night,
and every marriage makes this marriage new.

In the broken name of heaven, in the light
that shatters granite, by the spitting shore,   5
in air that leaps and wobbles like a kite,

I marry you from time and a great door
is shut and stays shut against wind, sea, stone,
sunburst, and heavenfall.   And home once more

inside our walls of skin and struts of bone,   10
man-woman, woman-man, and each the other,
I marry you by all dark and all dawn

and learn to let time spend.   Why should I bother
the flies about me?   Let them buzz and do.
Men marry their queen, their daughter, or their mother   15

by names they prove, but that thin buzz whines through:
when reason falls to reasons, cause is true.
Men marry what they need.   I marry you.

The Ballad of
Sue Ellen Westerfield

(for Clyde)

Robert Hayden

She grew up in bedeviled southern wilderness,
but had not been a slave, she said,
because her father wept and set her mother free.
She hardened in perilous rivertowns
and after The Surrender,   5
went as maid upon the tarnished Floating Palaces.
Rivermen reviled her for the rankling cold
sardonic pride
that gave a knife-edge to her comeliness.

When she was old, her back still straight,   10
her hair still glossy black,
she'd talk sometimes
of dangers lived through on the rivers.
But never told of him,
whose name she'd vowed she would not speak again   15
till after Jordan.
Oh, he was nearer nearer now
than wearisome kith and kin.
His blue eyes followed her
as she moved about her tasks upon the *Memphis Rose.*   20
He smiled and joshed, his voice quickening her.
She cursed the circumstance. . . .

The crazing horrors of that summer night,
the swifting flames, he fought his way to her,
the savaging panic, and helped her swim to shore.   25
The steamer like besieged Atlanta blazing,
the cries, the smoke and bellowing flames,
the flamelit thrashing forms in hellmouth water,
and he swimming out to them,
leaving her dazed and lost.   30
A woman screaming under the raddled trees—
Sue Ellen felt it was herself who screamed.

The moaning of the hurt, the terrified—
she held off shuddering despair
and went to comfort whom she could.   35
Wagons torches bells
and whimpering dusk of morning
and blankness lostness nothingness for her
until his arms had lifted her
into wild and secret dark.   40

How long how long was it they wandered,
loving fearing loving,
fugitives whose dangerous only hidingplace
was love?
How long was it before she knew   45
she could not forfeit what she was,
even for him—could not, even for him,
forswear her pride?
They kissed and said farewell at last.
He wept as had her father once.   50
They kissed and said farewell.
Until her dying-bed,
she cursed the circumstance.

Lovers as Heroes

To become lovers, ordinary people frequently have to act in a
fashion that approaches the heroic: they have to overcome obstacles of
time and space, as in Josephine Miles' poem "Meeting," or parental ob-
jections, as in A. D. Hope's poem "Crossing the Frontier." In the latter
poem, it should be noted that the woman's action clearly certifies her
as an authentic hero-figure. Her action also demonstrates the power
of love to transform human beings into heroes, to change the world—
even if it is only the world of the lovers themselves. That world, as
John Donne's poem "The Sun Rising" illustrates, is one over which the
lovers rule and from which they exclude the world of everyday.

Meeting
Josephine Miles

One there lived on the east side of the city
One who wished to meet
One who lived on the west side of the city,
A thousand miles away.

A thousand years went by.   5

Then the one who lived on the east side of the city
Set out on the main street
And met the one who lived on the west side of the city
Coming that way.

A thousand years.   10

Miraculous life!   that in its brief and mortal
Progress achieved this union of intents,
Inevitability sprung from the improbable,
Volition moving in the paths of chance.

Crossing the Frontier
A. D. Hope

Crossing the frontier they were stopped in time,
Told, quite politely, they would have to wait:
Passports in order, nothing to declare,
And surely holding hands was not a crime;
Until they saw how, ranged across the gate,   5
All their most formidable friends were there.

Wearing his conscience like a crucifix,
Her father, rampant, nursed the Family Shame;
And, armed with their old-fashioned dinner-gong,
His aunt, who even when they both were six,   10
Had just to glance towards a childish game
To make them feel that they were doing wrong.

And both their mothers, simply weeping floods,
Her head-mistress, his boss, the parish priest,
And the bank manager who cashed their cheques;   15
The man who sold him his first rubber-goods;
Dog Fido, from whose love-life, shameless beast,
She first observed the basic facts of sex.

They looked as though they had stood there for hours;
For years; perhaps for ever.   In the trees   20
Two furtive birds stopped courting and flew off;
While in the grass beside the road the flowers
Kept up their guilty traffic with the bees.
Nobody stirred.   Nobody risked a cough.

Nobody spoke.   The minutes ticked away;   25
The dog scratched idly.   Then, as parson bent
And whispered to a guard who hurried in,
The customs-house loudspeakers with a bray
Of raucous and triumphant argument
Broke out the wedding march from *Lohengrin*.   30

He switched the engine off: "We must turn back."
She heard his voice break, though he had to shout
Against a din that made their senses reel,
And felt his hand, so tense in hers, go slack.
But suddenly she laughed and said: "Get out!   35
Change seats!   Be quick!"   and slid behind the wheel.

And drove the car straight at them with a harsh,
Dry crunch that showered both with scraps and chips,
Drove through them; barriers rising let them pass;
Drove through and on and on, with Dad's moustache   40
Beside her twitching still round waxen lips
And Mother's tears still streaming down the glass.

The Sun Rising
John Donne

Busy old fool, unruly sun,
    Why dost thou thus,
Through windows and through curtains call on us?

Must to thy motions lovers' seasons run?
    Saucy pedantic wretch, go chide   5
    Late school boys and sour prentices,[1]
Go tell court huntsmen that the king will ride,
Call country ants to harvest offices;
Love, all alike, no season knows nor clime,
Nor hours, days, months, which are the rags of time.   10

    Thy beams, so reverend and strong
    Why shouldst thou think?
I could eclipse and cloud them with a wink,
But that I would not lose her sight so long;
    If her eyes have not blinded thine,   15

    Look, and tomorrow late tell me,
Whether both th' Indias[2] of spice and mine[3]
Be where thou leftst them, or lie here with me.
Ask for those kings whom thou saw'st yesterday,
And thou shalt hear, All here in one bed lay.   20

    She's all states, and all princes, I,
    Nothing else is.
Princes do but play us; compared to this,
All honor's mimic, all wealth alchemy.[4]
    Thou, sun, art half as happy as we,   25
    In that the world's contracted thus;
    Thine age asks ease, and since thy duties be
    To warm the world, that's done in warming us.
Shine here to us, and thou art everywhere;
This bed thy center is, these walls, thy sphere.   30

Love and Loss

All lovers eventually are losers. The lady may be captured by a rival, as in Sir Thomas Wyatt's sonnet "Whoso List To Hunt," or, as in his poem "They Flee from Me," she may simply turn her affections toward someone else. Implicit in the first stanza of "They Flee from

1. *prentices* Apprentices.   2. *Indias* The East and West Indies.
3. *mine* Treasure mines.
4. *alchemy* The pseudo-science of turning base metal into precious metal.

Me" is the possibility that the lover-hero himself has lost some of the dynamism required for pursuing the quest for love or even to be its object—for the lady herself can, of course, be a quester.

Ultimately the quest for love must end in death. The separation of lovers is a metaphor for death, the fading of love is a form of death, and, in any case, even though their love may be eternal, lovers themselves are not. Orpheus and Eurydice in Robert Hillyer's poem "The Lost Music" point the way. Orpheus was the fabled musician who lost his Eurydice to death. He heroically ventured into the underworld to win her back, but then lost her again when, violating the edict of Hades, he anxiously looked back to see if she were following him to the upper world. Even the lover-hero is no match for the ultimate enemy, death.

Whoso List To Hunt

Sir Thomas Wyatt

Whoso list to hunt, I know where is an hind,[1]
   But as for me, alas, I may no more;
   The vain travail[2] hath wearied me so sore,
   I am of them that furthest come behind.
Yet may I by no means my wearied mind   5
   Draw from the deer, but as she fleeth afore
   Fainting I follow; I leave off therefore,
   Since in a net I seek to hold the wind.
Who list her hunt, I put him out of doubt,
   As well as I, may spend his time in vain.   10
   And graven with diamonds in letters plain,
There is written her fair neck round about,
   "*Noli me tangere*,[3] for Caesar's I am,
   And wild for to hold, though I seem tame."

1. *hind* Deer.   2. *travail* Effort.   3. *"Noli me tangere"* "Touch me not."

They Flee from Me

Sir Thomas Wyatt

They flee from me, that sometime did me seek,
With naked foot stalking in my chamber.
I have seen them, gentle, tame, and meek,
That now are wild, and do not remember
That sometime they put themselves in danger   5
To take bread at my hand; and now they range,
Busily seeking with a continual change.

Thanked be Fortune it hath been otherwise,
Twenty times better; but once in special,
In thin array, after a pleasant guise,   10
When her loose gown from her shoulders did fall,
And she me caught in her arms long and small,
And therewith all sweetly did me kiss
And softly said, "Dear heart, how like you this?"

It was no dream, I lay broad waking.   15
But all is turned, thorough my gentleness,
Into a strange fashion of forsaking;
And I have leave to go, of her goodness,
And she also to use newfangleness.[1]
But since that I so kindely am served,   20
I fain would know what she hath deserved.

The Lost Music

Robert Hillyer

In the underworld, O Orpheus,
How strangely sounded string and voice
Before the midnight throne of Dis.[1]
In gardens of Persephone[2]

1. *newfangleness* Fickleness.

1. *Dis* Another name for Pluto, King of the Underworld.
2. *Persephone* The wife of Dis.

Where ghosts of flowers that bloomed above   5
Blossom again all winter long,
How strangely living was your song!
The Queen embraced Eurydice,
Homesick for summer and for love,
And both stood unbelieving there   10
To hear your music from afar.

O Orpheus, on your return
How strangely sounded voice and string
Along the beams of living spring.
Those were your lyre when you were young;   15
But birds and beasts now shunned the sound
That once had charmed them, for the tone
Held echoes from a world unknown.
Eurydice, still lost among
The wandering shadows underground,   20
Heard nothing now; and daylight spurned
Dead music from the past returned.

Anyone as Hero

If it is not the only story, the quest for love is one of the oldest of
stories. And it is one that is continually retold, yet never loses its
power to enthrall in the retelling. Perhaps this is because, of all the
quests of the hero, the quest for love is the most familiar, the one to
which every human being has been witness at one time or another,
and the one in which every human being has a chance to play a
starring role—to become, as it were, the Hero or the Lady. As R. G.
Vliet's "After the Lone Ranger Died" and e. e. cummings' "anyone
lived in a pretty how town" imply, it is a universal quest whose mythic
dimensions are visible in even the most ordinary lives of the most
ordinary people.

After The
Lone Ranger Died

R. G. Vliet

After the Lone Ranger died, they put him away in a cave.
For eight weeks Tonto carried the series;
then the Masked Rider resurrected, a mite slower
than Jesus, perhaps, but just as reliable.   The world
unloosed its bindings and straps and I slapped my horse's   5
rump through the sweet grass and the sour grass.
Such hoof poundings 'til my feet hurt.
I reared and neighed with the sweet iron bit
in my mouth.   I was sexual and the sky turned blue;
the white light of a slake desert hurt my eyes.   10
I rode up the hill to the hanging tree and the bound
leather-skirted maiden until I was called in to dinner.

anyone lived in a pretty
how town

e. e. cummings

anyone lived in a pretty how town
(with up so floating many bells down)
spring summer autumn winter
he sang his didn't he danced his did.

Women and men(both little and small)   5
cared for anyone not at all
they sowed their isn't they reaped their same
sun moon stars rain

children guessed(but only a few
and down they forgot as up they grew   10
autumn winter spring summer)
that noone loved him more by more

338

when by now and tree by leaf
she laughed his joy she cried his grief
bird by snow and stir by still   15
anyone's any was all to her

someones married their everyones
laughed their cryings and did their dance
(sleep wake hope and then)they
said their nevers they slept their dream   20

stars rain sun moon
(and only the snow can begin to explain
how children are apt to forget to remember
with up so floating many bells down)

one day anyone died i guess   25
(and noone stooped to kiss his face)
busy folk buried them side by side
little by little and was by was

all by all and deep by deep
and more by more they dream their sleep   30
noone and anyone earth by april
wish by spirit and if by yes.

Women and men(both dong and ding)
summer autumn winter spring
reaped their sowing and went their came   35
sun moon stars rain

DRAMA

Marty

The title-figure of the television play *Marty* could be dramatist Paddy Chayefsky's embodiment of e. e. cummings' "anyone." "I'm a little, short, fat fellow, and girls don't go for me, that's all," is Marty Pilletti's pained self-appraisal. And indeed, this thirty-six-year-old butcher does not seem to be the stuff of which lovers—or heroes—are made. Yet, though he would not have recognized it as such, Marty has been on a quest, a quest which, early in the play, he seems about to abandon: "I chased enough girls in my life," he says, "I went to enough dances."

To weaken during the trials which the quest for love imposes, to fail under pressure, is the mark of the nonhero or the anti-hero. And Marty *is* under considerable pressure. Constantly badgered by his mother, his friends, even his customers, to find a girl and get married, he has to discover the true nature of the terms they have imposed upon him and which he has unquestioningly accepted for so long. By himself, however, he is unable to do so. It is only with the appearance of "the Lady," in the modest person of Clara Davis, a school teacher, that Marty begins to realize what the quest for love is really all about and what its true values are. Once he has gained this insight, he must either act or revert to the deadening security of passivity.

In such a situation, a dime would seem to be an unlikely weapon for a hero and a telephone an unlikely object to represent the traditional hero's traditional challenge or obstacle. Yet anyone who has been confronted with the seemingly easy act of picking up a telephone—or of waiting for one to ring—can understand the importance and the meaning, perhaps even the heroic nature, of Marty's choice.

Marty

Paddy Chayefsky

CHARACTERS

MARTY PILLETTI
CLARA DAVIS
ANGIE
MOTHER
AUNT CATHERINE
VIRGINIA
THOMAS
YOUNG MAN
CRITIC

BARTENDER
TWENTY-YEAR-OLD
ITALIAN WOMAN
SHORT GIRL
GIRL
YOUNG MOTHER
STAG
FORTY-YEAR-OLD

ACT I

[FADE IN: *A butcher shop in the Italian district of New York City. Actually, we fade in on a close-up of a butcher's saw being carefully worked through a side of beef, and we dolly back to show the butcher at work, and then the whole shop. The butcher is a mild-mannered, stout, short, balding young man of thirty-six. His charm lies in an almost indestructible good-natured amiability.*

The shop contains three women customers. One is a YOUNG MOTHER *with a baby carriage. She is chatting with a second woman of about forty at the door. The customer being waited on at the moment is a stout, elderly* ITALIAN WOMAN *who is standing on tiptoe, peering over the white display counter, checking the butcher as he saws away.*]

ITALIAN WOMAN. Your kid brother got married last Sunday, eh, Marty?

MARTY [*Absorbed in his work*]. That's right, Missus Fusari. It was a very nice affair.

ITALIAN WOMAN. That's the big tall one, the fellow with the mustache.

MARTY [*Sawing away*]. No, that's my other brother Freddie. My other brother Freddie, he's been married four years already. He lives down on Quincy Street. The one who got married Sunday, that was my little brother Nickie.

ITALIAN WOMAN. I thought he was a big, tall, fat fellow. Didn't I meet him here one time? Big, tall, fat fellow, he tried to sell me life insurance?

MARTY [*Sets the cut of meat on the scale, watches its weight register*]. No, that's my sister Margaret's husband Frank. My sister Margaret, she's married to the insurance salesman. My sister Rose, she married a contractor. They moved to Detroit last year. And my other sister, Frances, she got married about two and a half years ago in Saint John's Church on Adams Boulevard. Oh, that was a big affair. Well, Missus Fusari, that'll be three dollars, ninety-four cents. How's that with you?

[*The* ITALIAN WOMAN *produces an old leather change purse from her pocketbook and painfully extracts three single dollar bills and ninety-four cents to the penny and lays the money piece by piece on the counter.*]

YOUNG MOTHER [*Calling from the door*]. Hey, Marty, I'm inna hurry.

MARTY [*Wrapping the meat, calls amiably back*]. You're next right now, Missus Canduso.

[*The old* ITALIAN WOMAN *has been regarding* MARTY *with a baleful scowl.*]

ITALIAN WOMAN. Well, Marty, when you gonna get married? You should be ashamed. All your brothers and sisters, they all younger than you, and they married, and they got children. I just saw your mother inna fruit shop, and she says to me: "Hey, you know a nice girl for my boy Marty?" Watsa matter with you? That's no way. Watsa matter with you? Now, you get married, you hear me what I say?

MARTY [*Amiably*]. I hear you, Missus Fusari.

[*The old lady takes her parcel of meat, but apparently feels she still hasn't quite made her point.*]

ITALIAN WOMAN. My son Frank, he was married when he was nineteen years old. Watsa matter with you?

MARTY. Missus Fusari, Missus Canduso over there, she's inna big hurry, and . . .

ITALIAN WOMAN. You be ashamed of yourself.

[*She takes her package of meat, turns, and shuffles to the door and exits.* MARTY *gathers up the money on the counter, turns to the cash register behind him to ring up the sale.*]

YOUNG MOTHER. Marty, I want a nice big fat pullet, about four pounds. I hear your kid brother got married last Sunday.

MARTY. Yeah, it was a very nice affair, Missus Canduso.

YOUNG MOTHER. Marty, you oughtta be ashamed. All your kid brothers and sisters, married and have children. When you gonna get married?

[CLOSE-UP: MARTY. *He sends a glance of weary exasperation up to the ceiling. With a gesture of mild irritation, he pushes the plunger of the cash register. It makes a sharp ping.*

DISSOLVE TO: *Close-up of television set. A baseball game is in progress. Camera pulls back to show we are in a typical neighborhood bar—red leatherette booths—a jukebox, some phone booths. About half the bar stools are occupied by neighborhood folk.* MARTY *enters, pads amiably to one of the booths where a young man of about thirty-odd already sits. This is* ANGIE. MARTY *slides into the booth across from* ANGIE. ANGIE *is a little wasp of a fellow. He has a newspaper spread out before him to the sports pages.* MARTY *reaches over and pulls one of the pages over for himself to read. For a moment the two friends sit across from each other, reading the sports pages. Then* ANGIE, *without looking up, speaks.*]

ANGIE. Well, what do you feel like doing tonight?

MARTY. I don't know, Angie. What do you feel like doing?

ANGIE. Well, we oughtta do something. It's Saturday night. I don't wanna go bowling like last Saturday. How about calling up that big girl we picked up inna movies about a month ago in the RKO Chester?

MARTY [*Not very interested*]. Which one was that?

ANGIE. That big girl that was sitting in front of us with the skinny friend.

MARTY. Oh, yeah.

ANGIE. We took them home alla way out in Brooklyn. Her name was Mary Feeney. What do you say? You think I oughtta give her a ring? I'll take the skinny one.

MARTY. It's five o'clock already, Angie. She's probably got a date by now.

ANGIE. Well, let's call her up. What can we lose?

MARTY. I didn't like her, Angie. I don't feel like calling her up.

ANGIE. Well, what do you feel like doing tonight?

MARTY. I don't know. What do you feel like doing?

ANGIE. Well, we're back to that, huh? I say to you: "What do you feel like doing tonight?" And you say to me: "I don't know, what do you feel like doing?" And then we wind up sitting around your house with a couple of cans of beer, watching Sid Caesar on television. Well, I tell you what I feel like doing. I feel like calling up this Mary Feeney. She likes you.

[MARTY *looks up quickly at this.*]

MARTY. What makes you say that?

ANGIE. I could see she likes you.

MARTY. Yeah, sure.

ANGIE [*Half rising in his seat*]. I'll call her up.

MARTY. You call her up for yourself, Angie. I don't feel like calling her up.

[ANGIE *sits down again. They both return to reading the paper for a moment. Then* ANGIE *looks up again.*]

ANGIE. Boy, you're getting to be a real drag, you know that?

MARTY. Angie, I'm thirty-six years old. I been looking for a girl every Saturday night of my life. I'm a little, short, fat fellow, and girls don't go for me, that's all. I'm not like you. I mean, you joke around, and they laugh at you, and you get along fine. I just stand around like a bug. What's the sense of kidding myself? Everybody's always telling me to get married. Get married. Get married. Don't you think I wanna get married? I wanna get married. They drive me crazy. Now, I don't wanna wreck your Saturday night for you, Angie. You wanna go somewhere, you go ahead. I don't wanna go.

ANGIE. Boy, they drive me crazy too. My old lady, every word outta her mouth, when you gonna get married?
MARTY. My mother, boy, she drives me crazy.

[ANGIE *leans back in his seat, scowls at the paper-napkin container.* MARTY *returns to the sports page. For a moment a silence hangs between them. Then . . .*]

ANGIE. So what do you feel like doing tonight?
MARTY [*Without looking up*]. I don't know. What do you feel like doing?

[*They both just sit,* ANGIE *frowning at the napkin container,* MARTY *at the sports page.*

The camera slowly moves away from the booth, looks down the length of the bar, up the wall, past the clock—which reads ten to five—and over to the television screen, where the baseball game is still going on.

DISSOLVE SLOWLY TO:· *The television screen, now blank. The clock now reads a quarter to six.*

Back in the booth, MARTY *now sits alone. In front of him are three empty beer bottles and a beer glass, half filled. He is sitting there, his face expressionless, but his eyes troubled. Then he pushes himself slowly out of the booth and shuffles to the phone booth; he goes inside, closing the booth door carefully after him. For a moment* MARTY *just sits squatly. Then with some exertion—due to the cramped quarters—he contrives to get a small address book out of his rear pants pocket. He slowly flips through it, finds the page he wants, and studies it, scowling; then he takes a dime from the change he has just received, plunks it into the proper slot, waits for a dial tone . . . then carefully dials a number. . . . He waits. He is beginning to sweat a bit in the hot little booth, and his chest begins to rise and fall deeply.*]

MARTY [*With a vague pretense at good diction*]. Hello, is this Mary Feeney? . . . Could I please speak to Miss Mary Feeney? . . . Just tell her an old friend . . . [*He waits again. With his free hand he wipes the gathering sweat from his brow.*] . . . Oh, hello there, is this Mary Feeney? Hello there, this is Marty Pilletti. I wonder if you recall me . . . Well, I'm kind of a stocky guy. The last time we met was inna movies, the RKO Chester. You was with another girl, and I was with a friend of mine name Angie. This was about a month ago . . .

[*The girl apparently doesn't remember him. A sort of panic begins to seize* MARTY. *His voice rises a little.*]

The RKO Chester on Payne Boulevard.   You was sitting in front of us, and we was annoying you, and you got mad, and . . . I'm the fellow who works inna butcher shop . . . come on, you know who I am! . . . That's right, we went to Howard Johnson's and we had hamburgers. You hadda milk shake . . .   Yeah, that's right.   I'm the stocky one, the heavy-set fellow. . . .   Well, I'm glad you recall me, because I hadda swell time that night, and I was just wondering how everything was with you.   How's everything? . . .   That's swell . . . Yeah, well, I'll tell you why I called . . .   I was figuring on taking in a movie tonight, and I was wondering if you and your friend would care to see a movie tonight with me and my friend . . .   [*His eyes are closed now.*]   Yeah, tonight.   I know it's pretty late to call for a date, but I didn't know myself till . . .   Yeah, I know, well how about . . .   Yeah, I know, well maybe next Saturday night.   You free next Saturday night? . . .   Well, how about the Saturday after that? . . .   Yeah, I know . . .   Yeah . . .   Yeah . . .   Oh, I understand, I mean . . .

[*He just sits now, his eyes closed, not really listening.   After a moment he returns the receiver to its cradle and sits, his shoulders slack, his hands resting listlessly in the lap of his spotted white apron. . . .   Then he opens his eyes, straightens himself, pushes the booth door open, and advances out into the bar.   He perches on a stool across the bar from the* BARTENDER, *who looks up from his magazine*]

BARTENDER. I hear your kid brother got married last week, Marty.
MARTY [*Looking down at his hands on the bar*]. Yeah, it was a very nice affair.
BARTENDER. Well, Marty, when you gonna get married?

[MARTY *tenders the bartender a quick scowl, gets off his perch, and starts for the door—untying his apron as he goes.*]

MARTY. If my mother calls up, Lou, tell her I'm on my way home.

[DISSOLVE TO: *Marty's* MOTHER *and a young couple sitting around the table in the dining room of Marty's home.   The young couple—we will soon find out—are* THOMAS, *Marty's cousin, and his wife,* VIRGINIA.   *They have apparently just been telling the mother some sad news, and the three are sitting around frowning.*

The dining room is a crowded room filled with chairs and lamps, pictures and little statues, perhaps even a small grotto of little vigil lamps.   To the right of the dining room is the kitchen, old-fashioned, Italian, steaming, and overcrowded.   To the left of the dining room is the living room, furnished in same fashion as the dining room.   Just off the living room is

*a small bedroom, which is Marty's. This bedroom and the living room
have windows looking out on front. The dining room has windows looking out to the side alleyway. A stairway in the dining room leads to the
second floor.*

The MOTHER *is a round, dark, effusive little woman.*]

MOTHER [*After a pause*]. Well, Thomas, I knew sooner or later this was
gonna happen. I told Marty, I said: "Marty, you watch. There's
gonna be real trouble over there in your cousin Thomas' house."
Because your mother was here, Thomas, you know?

THOMAS. When was this, Aunt Theresa?

MOTHER. This was one, two, three days ago. Wednesday. Because I
went to the fruit shop on Wednesday, and I came home. And I
come arounna back, and there's your mother sitting onna steps onna
porch. And I said: "Catherine, my sister, wadda you doing here?"
And she look uppa me, and she beganna cry.

THOMAS [*To his wife*]. Wednesday. That was the day you threw the
milk bottle.

MOTHER. That's right. Because I said to her: "Catherine, watsa matter?"
And she said to me: "Theresa, my daughter-in-law, Virginia, she
just threw the milk bottle at me."

VIRGINIA. Well, you see what happen, Aunt Theresa . . .

MOTHER. I know, I know . . .

VIRGINIA. She comes inna kitchen, and she begins poking her head over
my shoulder here and poking her head over my shoulder there . . .

MOTHER. I know, I know . . .

VIRGINIA. And she begins complaining about this, and she begins complaining about that. And she got me so nervous, I spilled some
milk I was making for the baby. You see, I was making some food
for the baby, and . . .

MOTHER. So I said to her, "Catherine . . ."

VIRGINIA. So, she got me so nervous I spilled some milk. So she said:
"You're spilling the milk." She says: "Milk costs twenty-four cents
a bottle. Wadda you, a banker?" So I said: "Mama, leave me
alone, please. You're making me nervous. Go on in the other room
and turn on the television set." So then she began telling me how
I waste money, and how I can't cook, and how I'm raising my baby
all wrong, and she kept talking about these couple of drops of milk
I spilt, and I got so mad, I said: "Mama, you wanna see me really
spill some milk?" So I took the bottle and threw it against the door.
I didn't throw it at her. That's just something she made up. I
didn't throw it anywheres near her. Well of course, alla milk went

all over the floor. The whole twenty-four cents. Well, I was sorry right away, you know, but she ran outta the house.

[*Pause*]

MOTHER. Well, I don't know what you want me to do, Virginia. If you want me, I'll go talk to her tonight.

[THOMAS and VIRGINIA *suddenly frown and look down at their hands as if of one mind.*]

THOMAS. Well, I'll tell you, Aunt Theresa . . .
VIRGINIA. Lemme tell it, Tommy.
THOMAS. Okay.
VIRGINIA [*Leaning forward to the* MOTHER]. We want you to do a very big favor for us, Aunt Theresa.
MOTHER. Sure.
VIRGINIA. Aunt Theresa, you got this big house here. You got four bedrooms upstairs. I mean, you got this big house just for you and Marty. All your other kids are married and got their own homes. And I thought maybe Tommy's mother could come here and live with you and Marty.
MOTHER. Well . . .
VIRGINIA. She's miserable living with Tommy and me, and you're the only one that gets along with her. Because I called up Tommy's brother, Joe, and I said: "Joe, she's driving me crazy. Why don't you take her for a couple of years?" And he said: "Oh, no!" I know I sound like a terrible woman . . .
MOTHER. No, Virginia, I know how you feel. My husband, may God bless his memory, his mother, she lived with us for a long time, and I know how you feel.
VIRGINIA [*Practically on the verge of tears*]. I just can't stand it no more! Every minute of the day! Do this! Do that! I don't have ten minutes alone with my husband! We can't even have a fight! We don't have no privacy! Everybody's miserable in our house!
THOMAS. All right, Ginnie, don't get so excited.
MOTHER. She's right. She's right. Young husband and wife, they should have their own home. And my sister, Catherine, she's my sister, but I gotta admit, she's an old goat. And plenny-a times in my life I feel like throwing the milk bottle at her myself. And I tell you now, as far as I'm concerned, if Catherine wantsa come live here with me and Marty, it's all right with me.

[VIRGINIA *promptly bursts into tears.*]

THOMAS [*Not far from tears himself, lowers his face*]. That's very nice-a you, Aunt Theresa.

MOTHER. We gotta ask Marty, of course, because this is his house too. But he's gonna come home any minute now.

VIRGINIA [*Having mastered her tears*]. That's very nice-a you, Aunt Theresa.

MOTHER [*Rising*]. Now, you just sit here. I'm just gonna turn onna small fire under the food.   [*She exists into the kitchen.*]

VIRGINIA [*Calling after her*]. We gotta go right away because I promised the baby sitter we'd be home by six, and it's after six now . . .

[*She kind of fades out. A moment of silence. THOMAS takes out a cigarette and lights it.*]

THOMAS [*Calling to his aunt in the kitchen*]. How's Marty been lately, Aunt Theresa?

MOTHER [*Off in kitchen*]. Oh, he's fine. You know a nice girl he can marry? [*She comes back into the dining room, wiping her hands on a kitchen towel.*] I'm worried about him, you know? He's thirty-six years old, gonna be thirty-seven in January.

THOMAS. Oh, he'll get married, don't worry, Aunt Theresa.

MOTHER [*Sitting down again*]. Well, I don't know. You know a place where he can find a bride?

THOMAS. The Waverly Ballroom. That's a good place to meet girls, Aunt Theresa. That's a kind of big dance hall, Aunt Theresa. Every Saturday night, it's just loaded with girls. It's a nice place to go. You pay seventy-seven cents. It used to be seventy-seven cents. It must be about a buck and a half now. And you go in and you ask some girl to dance. That's how I met Virginia. Nice, respectable place to meet girls. You tell Marty, Aunt Theresa, you tell him: "Go to the Waverly Ballroom. It's loaded with tomatoes."

MOTHER [*Committing the line to memory*]. The Waverly Ballroom. It's loaded with tomatoes.

THOMAS. Right.

VIRGINIA. You tell him, go to the Waverly Ballroom.

[*There is the sound of a door being unlatched off through the kitchen. The MOTHER promptly rises.*]

MOTHER. He's here.

[*She hurries into the kitchen. At the porch entrance to the kitchen, MARTY has just come in. He is closing the door behind him. He carries his butcher's apron in a bundle under his arm.*]

MARTY. Hello, Ma.

[*She comes up to him, lowers her voice to a whisper.*]

MOTHER [*Whispers*]. Marty, Thomas and Virginia are here. They had another big fight with your Aunt Catherine. So they ask me, would it be all right if Catherine come to live with us. So I said, all right with me, but we have to ask you. Marty, she's a lonely old lady. Nobody wants her. Everybody's throwing her outta their house. . . .

MARTY. Sure, Ma, it's okay with me.

[*The* MOTHER's *face breaks into a fond smile. She reaches up and pats his cheek with genuine affection.*]

MOTHER. You gotta good heart. [*Turning and leading the way back to the dining room.* THOMAS *has risen.*] He says okay, it's all right Catherine comes here.

THOMAS. Oh, Marty, thanks a lot. That really takes a load offa my mind.

MARTY. Oh, we got plenny-a room here.

MOTHER. Sure! Sure! It's gonna be nice! It's gonna be nice! I'll come over tonight to your house, and I talk to Catherine, and you see, everything is gonna work out all right.

THOMAS. I just wanna thank you people again because the situation was just becoming impossible.

MOTHER. Siddown, Thomas, siddown. All right, Marty, siddown. . . .
[*She exists into the kitchen*]

[MARTY *has taken his seat at the head of the table and is waiting to be served.* THOMAS *takes a seat around the corner of the table from him and leans across to him.*]

THOMAS. You see, Marty, the kinda thing that's been happening in our house is Virginia was inna kitchen making some food for the baby. Well, my mother comes in, and she gets Virginia so nervous, she spills a couple-a drops . . .

VIRGINIA [*Tugging at her husband*]. Tommy, we gotta go. I promise the baby sitter six o'clock.

THOMAS [*Rising without interrupting his narrative*]. So she starts yelling at Virginia, waddaya spilling the milk for. So Virginia gets mad . . . [*His wife is slowly pulling him to the kitchen door.*] She says, "You wanna really see me spill milk?" So Virginia takes the bottle and she throws it against the wall. She's got a real Italian temper, my wife, you know that . . .

[*He has been tugged to the kitchen door by now.*]

VIRGINIA. Marty, I don't have to tell you how much we appreciate what your mother and you are doing for us.

THOMAS. All right, Marty, I'll see you some other time . . . I'll tell you all about it.

MARTY. I'll see you, Tommy.

[THOMAS *disappears into the kitchen after his wife.*]

VIRGINIA [*Off, calling*]. Good-by, Marty!

[*Close in on* MARTY, *sitting at table*]

MARTY. Good-by, Virginia! See you soon! [*He folds his hands on the table before him and waits to be served.*]

[*The* MOTHER *enters from the kitchen. She sets the meat plate down in front of him and herself takes a chair around the corner of the table from him.* MARTY *without a word takes up his knife and fork and attacks the mountain of food in front of him. His mother sits quietly, her hands a little nervous on the table before her, watching him eat. Then . . .*]

MOTHER. So what are you gonna do tonight, Marty?

MARTY. I don't know, Ma. I'm all knocked out. I may just hang arounna house.

[*The* MOTHER *nods a couple of times. There is a moment of silence. Then . . .*]

MOTHER. Why don't you go to the Waverly Ballroom?

[*This gives* MARTY *pause. He looks up.*]

MARTY. What?

MOTHER. I say, why don't you go to the Waverly Ballroom? It's loaded with tomatoes.

[MARTY *regards his mother for a moment.*]

MARTY. It's loaded with what?

MOTHER. Tomatoes.

MARTY [*Snorts*]. Ha! Who told you about the Waverly Ballroom?

MOTHER. Thomas, he told me it was a very nice place.

MARTY. Oh, Thomas. Ma, it's just a big dance hall, and that's all it is. I been there a hundred times. Loaded with tomatoes. Boy, you're funny, Ma.

MOTHER. Marty, I don't want you hang arounna house tonight. I want you to go take a shave and go out and dance.

MARTY. Ma, when are you gonna give up? You gotta bachelor on your hands. I ain't never gonna get married.

MOTHER. You gonna get married.

MARTY. Sooner or later, there comes a point in a man's life when he gotta face some facts, and one fact I gotta face is that whatever it is that women like, I ain't got it. I chased enough girls in my life. I went to enough dances. I got hurt enough. I don't wanna get hurt no more. I just called a girl this afternoon, and I got a real brush-off, boy. I figured I was past the point of being hurt, but that hurt. Some stupid woman who I didn't even wanna call up. She gave me the brush. That's the history of my life. I don't wanna go to the Waverly Ballroom because all that ever happened to me there was girls made me feel like I was a bug. I got feelings, you know. I had enough pain. No, thank you.

MOTHER. Marty . . .

MARTY. Ma, I'm gonna stay home and watch Sid Caesar.

MOTHER. You gonna die without a son.

MARTY. So I'll die without a son.

MOTHER. Put on your blue suit . . .

MARTY. Blue suit, gray suit, I'm still a fat little man. A fat little ugly man.

MOTHER. You not ugly.

MARTY [*His voice rising*]. I'm ugly . . . I'm ugly! . . . I'm UGLY!

MOTHER. Marty . . .

MARTY [*Crying aloud, more in anguish than in anger*]. Ma! Leave me alone! . . .

[*He stands abruptly, his face pained and drawn. He makes half-formed gestures to his mother, but he can't find words at the moment. He turns and marches a few paces away, turns to his mother again.*]

MARTY. Ma, waddaya want from me?! Waddaya want from me?! I'm miserable enough as it is! Leave me alone! I'll go to the Waverly Ballroom! I'll put onna blue suit and I'll go! And you know what I'm gonna get for my trouble? Heartache! A big night of heartache!

[*He sullenly marches back to his seat, sits down, picks up his fork, plunges it into the lasagna, and stuffs a mouthful into his mouth; he chews vigorously for a moment. It is impossible to remain angry for long. After a while he is shaking his head and muttering.*]

MARTY. Loaded with tomatoes . . . boy, that's rich . . .

[*He plunges his fork in again. Camera pulls slowly away from him and his mother, who is seated—watching him.*]

[*Fade Out*]

The Quest for Love   351

Act II

[FADE IN: *Exterior, three-story building.   Pan up to second floor . . . bright neon lights reading "Waverly Ballroom" . . .   The large, dirty windows are open; and the sound of a fair-to-middling swing band whooping it up comes out.*

DISSOLVE TO: *Interior, Waverly Ballroom—large dance floor crowded with jitterbugging couples, eight-piece combination hitting a loud kick. Ballroom is vaguely dark, made so by papier-mâché over the chandeliers to create alleged romantic effect.   The walls are lined with stags and waiting girls, singly and in small murmuring groups.   Noise and mumble and drone.*

DISSOLVE TO: *Live shot—a row of stags along a wall.   Camera is looking lengthwise down the row.   Camera dollies slowly past each face, each staring out at the dance floor, watching in his own manner of hungry eagerness.   Short, fat, tall, thin stags.   Some pretend diffidence.   Some exhibit patent hunger.*

Near the end of the line, we find MARTY *and* ANGIE, *freshly shaved and groomed.   They are leaning against the wall, smoking, watching their more fortunate brethren out on the floor.*]

ANGIE. Not a bad crowd tonight, you know?
MARTY. There was one nice-looking one there in a black dress and beads, but she was a little tall for me.
ANGIE [*Looking down past* MARTY *along the wall right into the camera*]. There's a nice-looking little short one for you right now.
MARTY [*Following his gaze*]. Where?
ANGIE. Down there.   That little one there.

[*The camera cuts about eight faces down, to where the girls are now standing.   Two are against the wall.   One is facing them, with her back to the dance floor.   This last is the one* ANGIE *has in mind.   She is a cute little kid, about twenty, and she has a bright smile on—as if the other two girls are just amusing her to death*]

MARTY. Yeah, she looks all right from here.
ANGIE. Well, go on over and ask her.   You don't hurry up, somebody else'll grab her.

[MARTY *scowls, shrugs.*]

MARTY. Okay, let's go.

[*They slouch along past the eight stags, a picture of nonchalant uncon-*

cern. *The three girls, aware of their approach, stiffen, and their chatter comes to a halt.* ANGIE *advances to one of the girls along the wall.*]

ANGIE. Waddaya say, you wanna dance?

[*The girl looks surprised—as if this were an extraordinary invitation to receive in this place—looks confounded at her two friends, shrugs, detaches herself from the group, moves to the outer fringe of the pack of dancers, raises her hand languidly to dancing position, and awaits* ANGIE *with ineffable boredom.* MARTY, *smiling shyly, addresses the* SHORT GIRL]

MARTY. Excuse me, would you care for this dance?

[*The* SHORT GIRL *gives* MARTY *a quick glance of appraisal, then looks quickly at her remaining friend.*]

SHORT GIRL [*Not unpleasantly*]. Sorry. I just don't feel like dancing just
  yet.
MARTY. Sure.

[*He turns and moves back past the eight stags, all of whom have covertly watched his attempt. He finds his old niche by the wall, leans there. A moment later he looks guardedly down to where the* SHORT GIRL *and her friend are. A young, dapper boy is approaching the* SHORT GIRL. *He asks her to dance. The* SHORT GIRL *smiles, excuses herself to her friend, and follows the boy out onto the floor.* MARTY *turns back to watching the dancers bleakly. A moment later he is aware that someone on his right is talking to him. . . . He turns his head. It is a* YOUNG MAN *of about twenty-eight.*]

MARTY. You say something to me?
YOUNG MAN. Yeah. I was just asking you if you was here stag or with
  a girl.
MARTY. I'm stag.
YOUNG MAN. Well, I'll tell you. I got stuck onna blind date with a dog,
  and I just picked up a nice chick, and I was wondering how I'm
  gonna get ridda the dog. Somebody to take her home, you know
  what I mean? I be glad to pay you five bucks if you take the dog
  home for me.
MARTY [*A little confused*]. What?
YOUNG MAN. I'll take you over, and I'll introduce you as an old army
  buddy of mine, and then I'll cut out. Because I got this chick waiting for me out by the hatcheck, and I'll pay you five bucks.
MARTY [*Stares at the* YOUNG MAN]. Are you kidding?
YOUNG MAN. No, I'm not kidding.
MARTY. You can't just walk off onna girl like that.

[*The* YOUNG MAN *grimaces impatiently and moves down the line of stags. . . .* MARTY *watches him, still a little shocked at the proposition. About two stags down, the* YOUNG MAN *broaches his plan to another* STAG. *This* STAG, *frowning and pursing his lips, seems more receptive to the idea. . . . The* YOUNG MAN *takes out a wallet and gives the* STAG *a five-dollar bill. The* STAG *detaches himself from the wall and, a little ill at ease, follows the* YOUNG MAN *back past* MARTY *and into the lounge.* MARTY *pauses a moment and then, concerned, walks to the archway that separates the lounge from the ballroom and looks in.*

The lounge is a narrow room with a bar and booths. In contrast to the ballroom, it is brightly lighted—causing MARTY *to squint.*

In the second booth from the archway sits a GIRL, *about twenty-eight. Despite the careful grooming that she has put into her cosmetics, she is blatantly plain. The* YOUNG MAN *and the* STAG *are standing, talking to her. She is looking up at the* YOUNG MAN, *her hands nervously gripping her Coca-Cola glass. We cannot hear what the* YOUNG MAN *is saying, but it is apparent that he is introducing his new-found army buddy and is going through some cock-and-bull story about being called away on an emergency. The* STAG *is presented as her escort-to-be, who will see to it that she gets home safely. The* GIRL *apparently is not taken in at all by this, though she is trying hard not to seem affected.*

She politely rejects the STAG'S *company and will get home by herself, thanks for asking anyway. The* YOUNG MAN *makes a few mild protestations, and then he and the* STAG *leave the booth and come back to the archway from where* MARTY *has been watching the scene. As they pass* MARTY, *we overhear a snatch of dialogue.*]

YOUNG MAN. . . . In that case, as long as she's going home alone, give me the five bucks back. . . .

STAG. . . . Look, Mac, you paid me five bucks. I was willing. It's my five bucks. . . .

[*They pass on.* MARTY *returns his attention to the* GIRL. *She is still sitting as she was, gripping and ungripping the glass of Coca-Cola in front of her. Her eyes are closed. Then, with a little nervous shake of her head, she gets out of the booth and stands—momentarily at a loss for what to do next. The open fire doors leading out onto the large fire escape catch her eye. She crosses to the fire escape, nervous, frowning, and disappears outside.*

MARTY *stares after her, then slowly shuffles to the open fire-escape doorway. It is a large fire escape, almost the size of a small balcony. The* GIRL *is standing by the railing, her back to the doorway, her head slunk*

354

on her bosom. For a moment MARTY *is unaware that she is crying. Then he notices the shivering tremors running through her body and the quivering shoulders. He moves a step onto the fire escape. He tries to think of something to say.*]

MARTY. Excuse me, Miss. Would you care to dance?

[*The* GIRL *slowly turns to him, her face streaked with tears, her lip trembling. Then, in one of those peculiar moments of simultaneous impulse, she lurches to* MARTY *with a sob, and* MARTY *takes her to him. For a moment they stand in an awkward embrace,* MARTY *a little embarrassed, looking out through the doors to the lounge, wondering if anybody is seeing them. Reaching back with one hand, he closes the fire doors, and then, replacing the hand around her shoulder, he stands stiffly, allowing her to cry on his chest.*

DISSOLVE TO: *Exterior, apartment door. The* MOTHER *is standing, in a black coat and a hat with a little feather, wating for her ring to be answered. The door opens.* VIRGINIA *stands framed in the doorway*]

VIRGINIA. Hello, Aunt Theresa, come in.

[*The* MOTHER *goes into the small foyer.* VIRGINIA *closes the door.*]

MOTHER [*In a low voice, as she pulls her coat off*]. Is Catherine here?
VIRGINIA [*Helps her off with coat, nods—also in a low voice*]. We didn't
    tell her nothing yet. We thought we'd leave it to you. We thought
    you'd put it like how you were lonely, and why don't she come to
    live with you. Because that way it looks like she's doing you a
    favor, insteada we're throwing her out, and it won't be so cruel on
    her. Thomas is downstairs with the neighbors . . . I'll go call him.
MOTHER. You go downstairs to the neighbors and stay there with Thomas.
VIRGINIA. Wouldn't it be better if we were here?
MOTHER. You go downstairs. I talk to Catherine alone. Otherwise, she's
    gonna start a fight with you.

[*A shrill, imperious woman's voice from an off-stage room suddenly breaks into the muttered conference in the foyer.*]

AUNT [*Off*]. Who's there?! Who's there?!

[*The* MOTHER *heads up the foyer to the living room, followed by* VIRGINIA, *holding the* MOTHER's *coat.*]

MOTHER [*Calls back*]. It's me, Catherine! How you feel?

[*At the end of the foyer, the two sisters meet. The* AUNT *is a spare, gaunt woman with a face carved out of granite. Tough, embittered, deeply hurt type of face*]

AUNT. Hey! What are you doing here?

MOTHER. I came to see you. [*The two sisters quickly embrace and release each other.*] How you feel?

AUNT. I gotta pain in my left side and my leg throbs like a drum.

MOTHER. I been getting pains in my shoulder.

AUNT. I got pains in my shoulder, too. I have a pain in my hip, and my right arm aches so much I can't sleep. It's a curse to be old. How you feel?

MOTHER. I feel fine.

AUNT. That's nice.

[*Now that the standard greetings are over,* AUNT CATHERINE *abruptly turns and goes back to her chair. It is obviously her chair. It is an old, heavy oaken chair with thick armrests. The rest of the apartment is furnished in what is known as "modern"—a piece from* House Beautiful *here, a piece from* Better Homes and Gardens *there.* AUNT CATHERINE *sits, erect and forbidding, in her chair. The* MOTHER *seats herself with a sigh in a neighboring chair.* VIRGINIA, *having hung the* MOTHER's *coat, now turns to the two older women. A pause*]

VIRGINIA. I'm going downstairs to the Cappacini's. I'll be up inna little while.

[AUNT CATHERINE *nods expressionlessly.* VIRGINIA *looks at her for a moment, then impulsively crosses to her mother-in-law.*]

VIRGINIA. You feel all right?

[*The old lady looks up warily, suspicious of this sudden solicitude.*]

AUNT. I'm all right.

[VIRGINIA *nods and goes off to the foyer. The two old sisters sit, unmoving, waiting for the door to close behind* VIRGINIA. *Then the* MOTHER *addresses herself to* AUNT CATHERINE]

MOTHER. We gotta post card from my son, Nickie, and his bride this morning. They're in Florida inna big hotel. Everything is very nice.

AUNT. That's nice.

MOTHER. Catherine, I want you come live with me in my house with Marty and me. In my house, you have your own room. You don't have to sleep onna couch inna living room like here. [*The* AUNT *looks slowly and directly at the* MOTHER.] Catherine, your son is married. He got his own home. Leave him in peace. He wants to be alone with his wife. They don't want no old lady sitting inna balcony. Come and live with me. We will cook in the kitchen and talk like when we were girls.   You are dear to me, and you are dear to Marty.   We are pleased for you to come.

AUNT. Did they come to see you?

MOTHER. Yes.

AUNT. Did my son Thomas come with her?

MOTHER. Your son Thomas was there.

AUNT. Did he also say he wishes to cast his mother from his house?

MOTHER. Catherine, don't make an opera outta this.   The three-a you anna baby live in three skinny rooms.   You are an old goat, and she has an Italian temper.   She is a good girl, but you drive her crazy.   Leave them alone.   They have their own life.

[*The old* AUNT *turns her head slowly and looks her sister square in the face.   Then she rises slowly from her chair.*]

AUNT [*Coldly*]. Get outta here.   This is my son's house.   This is where I live.   I am not to be cast out inna street like a newspaper.

[*The* MOTHER *likewise rises.   The two old women face each other directly.*]

MOTHER. Catherine, you are very dear to me.   We have cried many times together.   When my husband died, I would have gone insane if it were not for you.   I ask you to come to my house because I can make you happy.   Please come to my house.

[*The two sisters regard each other.   Then* AUNT CATHERINE *sits again in her oaken chair, and the* MOTHER *returns to her seat.   The hardened muscles in the old* AUNT's *face suddenly slacken, and she turns to her sister.*]

AUNT. Theresa, what shall become of me?

MOTHER. Catherine . . .

AUNT. It's gonna happen to you.   Mark it well.   These terrible years. I'm afraida look inna mirror.   I'm afraid I'm gonna see an old lady with white hair, like the old ladies inna park, little bundles inna black shawl, waiting for the coffin.   I'm fifty-six years old.   What am I to do with myself?   I have strength in my hands.   I wanna cook.   I wanna clean.   I wanna make dinner for my children.   I wanna be of use to somebody.   Am I an old dog to lie in fronta the fire till my eyes close?   These are terrible years, Theresa! Terrible years!

MOTHER. Catherine, my sister . . .

[*The old* AUNT *stares, distraught, at the* MOTHER.]

AUNT. It's gonna happen to you!   It's gonna happen to you!   What will

The Quest for Love   357

you do if Marty gets married?! What will you cook?! What happen to alla children tumbling in alla rooms?! Where is the noise?! It is a curse to be a widow! A curse! What will you do if Marty gets married?! What will you do?!

[*She stares at the* MOTHER—*her deep, gaunt eyes haggard and pained. The* MOTHER *stares back for a moment, then her own eyes close. The* AUNT *has hit home. The* AUNT *sinks back onto her chair, sitting stiffly, her arms on the thick armrests. The* MOTHER *sits hunched a little forward, her hands nervously folded in her lap.*]

AUNT [*Quietly*]. I will put my clothes inna bag and I will come to you tomorrow.

[*The camera slowly dollies back from the two somber sisters.*

SLOW FADE-OUT.

CUT TO *Close-up, intimate,* MARTY *and the* GIRL *dancing cheek to cheek. Occasionally the heads of other couples slowly waft across the camera view, temporarily blocking out view of* MARTY *and the* GIRL. *Camera stays with them as the slow dance carries them around the floor. Tender scene*]

GIRL. . . . The last time I was here the same sort of thing happened.
MARTY. Yeah?
GIRL. Well, not exactly the same thing. The last time I was up here about four months ago. Do you see that girl in the gray dress sitting over there?
MARTY. Yeah.
GIRL. That's where I sat. I sat there for an hour and a half without moving a muscle. Now and then, some fellow would sort of walk up to me and then change his mind. I just sat there, my hands in my lap. Well, about ten o'clock, a bunch of kids came in swaggering. They weren't more than seventeen, eighteen years old. Well, they swaggered down along the wall, leering at all the girls. I thought they were kind of cute . . . and as they passed me, I smiled at them. One of the kids looked at me and said: "Forget it, ugly, you ain't gotta chance." I burst out crying. I'm a big crier, you know.
MARTY. So am I.
GIRL. And another time when I was in college . . .
MARTY. I cry alla time. Any little thing. I can recognize pain a mile away. My brothers, my brother-in-laws, they're always telling me what a goodhearted guy I am. Well, you don't get goodhearted by accident. You get kicked around long enough you get to be a real

professor of pain. I know exactly how you feel. And I also want you to know I'm having a very good time with you now and really enjoying myself. So you see, you're not such a dog as you think you are.

GIRL. I'm having a very good time too.

MARTY. So there you are. So I guess I'm not such a dog as I think I am.

GIRL. You're a very nice guy, and I don't know why some girl hasn't grabbed you off long ago.

MARTY. I don't know either. I think I'm a very nice guy. I also think I'm a pretty smart guy in my own way.

GIRL. I think you are.

MARTY. I'll tell you some of my wisdom which I thunk up on those nights when I got stood up, and nights like that, and you walk home thinking: "Watsa matter with me? I can't be that ugly." Well, I figure, two people get married, and they gonna live together forty, fifty years. So it's just gotta be more than whether they're good-looking or not. My father was a real ugly man, but my mother adored him. She told me that she used to get so miserable sometimes, like everybody, you know? And she says my father always tried to understand. I used to see them sometimes when I was a kid, sitting in the living room, talking and talking, and I used to adore my old man because he was so kind. That's one of the most beautiful things I have in my life, the way my father and my mother were. And my father was a real ugly man. So it don't matter if you look like a gorilla. So you see, dogs like us, we ain't such dogs as we think we are.

[*They dance silently for a moment, cheeks pressed against each other. Close-ups of each face*]

GIRL. I'm twenty-nine years old. How old are you?

MARTY. Thirty-six.

[*They dance silently, closely. Occasionally the heads of other couples sway in front of the camera, blocking our view of* MARTY *and the* GIRL. *Slow, sweet dissolve.*

DISSOLVE TO: *Interior, kitchen,* MARTY's *home. Later that night. It is dark. Nobody is home. The rear porch door now opens, and the silhouettes of* MARTY *and the* GIRL *appear—blocking up the doorway.*]

MARTY. Wait a minute. Lemme find the light.

[*He finds the light. The kitchen is suddenly brightly lit. The two of them stand squinting to adjust to the sudden glare.*]

MARTY. I guess my mother ain't home yet. I figure my cousin Thomas and Virginia musta gone to the movies, so they won't get back till one o'clock, at least.

[*The* GIRL *has advanced into the kitchen, a little ill at ease, and is looking around.* MARTY *closes the porch door.*]

MARTY. This is the kitchen.
GIRL. Yes, I know.

[MARTY *leads the way into the dining room.*]

MARTY. Come on inna dining room. [*He turns on the light in there as he goes. The* GIRL *follows him in.*] Siddown, take off your coat. You want something to eat? We gotta whole halfa chicken left over from yesterday.
GIRL [*Perching tentatively on the edge of a chair*]. No, thank you. I don't think I should stay very long.
MARTY. Sure. Just take off your coat a minute.

[*He helps her off with her coat and stands for a moment behind her, looking down at her. Conscious of his scrutiny, she sits uncomfortably, her breasts rising and falling unevenly.* MARTY *takes her coat into the dark living room. The* GIRL *sits patiently, nervously.* MARTY *comes back, sits down on another chair. Awkward silence*]

MARTY. So I was telling you, my kid brother Nickie got married last Sunday . . . That was a very nice affair. And they had this statue of some woman, and they had whisky spouting outta her mouth. I never saw anything so grand in my life. [*The silence falls between them again.*] And watta meal. I'm a butcher, so I know a good hunka steak when I see one. That was choice filet, right off the toppa the chuck. A buck-eighty a pound. Of course, if you wanna cheaper cut, get rib steak. That gotta lotta waste on it, but it comes to about a buck and a quarter a pound, if it's trimmed. Listen, Clara, make yourself comfortable. You're all tense.
GIRL. Oh, I'm fine.
MARTY. You want me to take you home, I'll take you home.
GIRL. Maybe that would be a good idea.

[*She stands. He stands, frowning, a little angry—turns sullenly and goes back into the living room for her coat. She stands unhappily. He comes back and wordlessly starts to help her into her coat. He stands behind her, his hands on her shoulders. He suddenly seizes her, begins kissing her on the neck. Camera comes up quickly to intensely intimate close-up, nothing but the heads. The dialogue drops to quick, hushed whispers.*]

360

GIRL. No, Marty, please . . .

MARTY. I like you, I like you, I been telling you all night I like you . . .

GIRL. Marty . . .

MARTY. I just wanna kiss, that's all . . .

[*He tries to turn her face to him. She resists.*]

GIRL. No . . .

MARTY. Please . . .

GIRL. No . . .

MARTY. Please . . .

GIRL. Marty . . .

[*He suddenly releases her, turns away violently.*]

MARTY [*Crying out.*] All right! I'll take you home! All right! [*He marches a few angry paces away, deeply disturbed. Turns to her*] All I wanted was a lousy kiss! What am I, a leper or something?!

[*He turns and goes off into the living room to hide the flush of hot tears threatening to fill his eyes. The GIRL stands, herself on the verge of tears.*]

GIRL [*Mutters, more to herself than to him*]. I just didn't feel like it, that's all.

[*She moves slowly to the archway leading to the living room. MARTY is sitting on the couch, hands in his lap, looking straight ahead. The room is dark except for the overcast of the dining-room light reaching in. The GIRL goes to the couch, perches on the edge beside him. He doesn't look at her.*]

MARTY. Well, that's the history of my life. I'm a little, short, fat, ugly guy. Comes New Year's Eve, everybody starts arranging parties, I'm the guy they gotta dig up a date for. I'm old enough to know better. Let me get a packa cigarettes, and I'll take you home.

[*He starts to rise, but doesn't . . . sinks back onto the couch, looking straight ahead. The GIRL looks at him, her face peculiarly soft and compassionate.*]

GIRL. I'd like to see you again, very much. The reason I didn't let you kiss me was because I just didn't know how to handle the situation. You're the kindest man I ever met. The reason I tell you this is because I want to see you again very much. Maybe, I'm just so desperate to fall in love that I'm trying too hard. But I know that when you take me home, I'm going to just lie on my bed and think about you. I want very much to see you again.

[MARTY *stares down at his hands in his lap.*]

MARTY [*Without looking at her*]. Waddaya doing tomorrow night?
GIRL. Nothing.
MARTY. I'll call you up tomorrow morning. Maybe we'll go see a movie.
GIRL. I'd like that very much.
MARTY. The reason I can't be definite about it now is my Aunt Catherine
    is probably coming over tomorrow, and I may have to help out.
GIRL. I'll wait for your call.
MARTY. We better get started to your house because the buses only run
    about one an hour now.
GIRL. All right. [*She stands.*]
MARTY. I'll just get a packa cigarettes.

[*He goes into his bedroom. We can see him through the doorway, opening his bureau drawer and extracting a pack of cigarettes. He comes out
again and looks at the girl for the first time. They start to walk to the
dining room. In the archway, MARTY pauses, turns to the GIRL.*]

MARTY. Waddaya doing New Year's Eve?
GIRL. Nothing.

[*They quietly slip into each other's arms and kiss. Slowly their faces part,
and MARTY's head sinks down upon her shoulder. He is crying. His
shoulders shake slightly. The GIRL presses her cheek against the back of
his head. They stand . . . there is the sound of the rear porch door being
unlatched. They both start from their embrace. A moment later the
MOTHER's voice is heard off in the kitchen.*]

MOTHER. Hallo! Hallo, Marty? [*She comes into the dining room, stops
    at the sight of the GIRL.*] Hallo, Marty, when you come home?
MARTY. We just got here about fifteen minutes ago, Ma. Ma, I want you
    to meet Miss Clara Davis. She's a graduate of New York Uni-
    versity. She teaches history in Benjamin Franklin High School.

[*This seems to impress the MOTHER.*]

MOTHER. Siddown, siddown. You want some chicken? We got some
    chicken in the icebox.
GIRL. No, Mrs. Pilletti, we were just going home. Thank you very much
    anyway.
MOTHER. Well, siddown a minute. I just come inna house. I'll take off
    my coat. Siddown a minute. [*She pulls her coat off.*]
MARTY. How'd you come home, Ma? Thomas give you a ride?

[*The MOTHER nods.*]

MOTHER. Oh, it's a sad business, a sad business.

[*She sits down on a dining-room chair, holding her coat in her lap. She turns to the* GIRL, *who likewise sits.*]

MOTHER. My sister Catherine, she don't get along with her daughter-in-law, so she's gonna come live with us.

MARTY. Oh, she's coming, eh, Ma?

MOTHER. Oh, sure. [*To the* GIRL] It's a very sad thing. A woman, fifty-six years old, all her life, she had her own home. Now, she's just an old lady, sleeping on her daughter-in-law's couch. It's a curse to be a mother, I tell you. Your children grow up and then what is left for you to do? What is a mother's life but her children? It is a very cruel thing when your son has no place for you in his home.

GIRL. Couldn't she find some sort of hobby to fill out her time?

MOTHER. Hobby! What can she do? She cooks and she cleans. You gotta have a house to clean. You gotta have children to cook for. These are terrible years for a woman, the terrible years.

GIRL. You mustn't feel too harshly against her daughter-in-law. She also wants to have a house to clean and a family to cook for.

[*The* MOTHER *darts a quick, sharp look at the* GIRL—*then looks back to her hands, which are beginning to twist nervously.*]

MOTHER. You don't think my sister Catherine should live in her daughter-in-law's house?

GIRL. Well, I don't know the people, of course, but, as a rule, I don't think a mother-in-law should live with a young couple.

MOTHER. Where do you think a mother-in-law should go?

GIRL. I don't think a mother should depend so much upon her children for her rewards in life.

MOTHER. That's what it says in the book in New York University. You wait till you are a mother. It don't work out that way.

GIRL. Well, it's silly for me to argue about it. I don't know the people involved.

MARTY. Ma, I'm gonna take her home now. It's getting late, and the buses only run about one an hour.

MOTHER [*Standing*]. Sure.

[*The* GIRL *stands.*]

GIRL. It was very nice meeting you, Mrs. Pilletti. I hope I'll see you again.

MOTHER. Sure.

[MARTY *and the girl move to the kitchen.*]

MARTY. All right, Ma. I'll be back in about an hour.

MOTHER. Sure.

GIRL. Good night, Mrs. Pilletti.

MOTHER. Good night.

[MARTY *and the* GIRL *exit into the kitchen. The* MOTHER *stands, expressionless, by her chair watching them go. She remains standing rigidly even after the porch door can be heard being opened and shut. The camera moves up to a close-up of the* MOTHER. *Her eyes are wide. She is staring straight ahead. There is fear in her eyes.*]

[*Fade Out*]

ACT III

[FADE IN *Film—close-up of church bells clanging away. Pan down church to see typical Sunday morning, people going up the steps of a church and entering. It is a beautiful June morning.*

DISSOLVE TO *Interior, Marty's bedroom—sun fairly streaming through the curtains.* MARTY *is standing in front of his bureau, slipping his arms into a clean white shirt. He is freshly shaved and groomed. Through the doorway of his bedroom we can see the* MOTHER *in the dining room, in coat and hat, all set to go to Mass, taking the last breakfast plates away and carrying them into the kitchen. The camera moves across the living room into the dining room. The* MOTHER *comes out of the kitchen with a paper napkin and begins crumbing the table.*

There is a knock on the rear porch door. The MOTHER *leaves her crumbing and goes into the kitchen. Camera goes with her. She opens the rear door to admit* AUNT CATHERINE, *holding a worn old European carpetbag. The* AUNT *starts to go deeper into the kitchen, but the* MOTHER *stays her with her hand.*]

MOTHER [*In low, conspiratorial voice*]. Hey, I come home from your house last night, Marty was here with a girl.

AUNT. Who?

MOTHER. Marty.

AUNT. Your son Marty?

MOTHER. Well, what Marty you think is gonna be here in this house with a girl?

AUNT. Were the lights on?

MOTHER. Oh, sure. [*Frowns suddenly at her sister*] The girl is a college graduate.

364

AUNT. They're the worst. College girls are one step from the streets. They smoke like men inna saloon.

[*The* AUNT *puts her carpetbag down and sits on one of the wooden kitchen chairs. The* MOTHER *sits on another.*]

MOTHER. That's the first time Marty ever brought a girl to this house. She seems like a nice girl. I think he has a feeling for this girl.

[*At this moment a burst of spirited whistling emanates from* MARTY'S *bedroom.*

CUT TO MARTY'S *bedroom—*MARTY *standing in front of his mirror, buttoning his shirt or adjusting his tie, whistling a gay tune.*

CUT BACK TO *The two sisters, both their faces turned in the direction of the whistling. The whistling abruptly stops. The two sisters look at each other. The* AUNT *shrugs.*]

MOTHER. He been whistling like that all morning.

[*The* AUNT *nods bleakly.*]

AUNT. He is bewitched. You will see. Today, tomorrow, inna week, he's gonna say to you: "Hey, Ma, it's no good being a single man. I'm tired running around." Then he's gonna say: "Hey, Ma, wadda we need this old house? Why don't we sell this old house, move into a nicer parta town? A nice little apartment?"

MOTHER. I don't sell this house, I tell you that. This is my husband's house, and I had six children in this house.

AUNT. You will see. A couple-a months, you gonna be an old lady, sleeping onna couch in your daughter-in-law's house.

MOTHER. Catherine, you are a blanket of gloom. Wherever you go, the rain follows. Some day, you gonna smile, and we gonna declare a holiday.

[*Another burst of spirited whistling comes from* MARTY, *off. It comes closer, and* MARTY *now enters in splendid spirits, whistling away. He is slipping into his jacket*]

MARTY [*Ebulliently*]. Hello, Aunt Catherine! How are you? You going to Mass with us?

AUNT. I was at Mass two hours ago.

MARTY. Well, make yourself at home. The refrigerator is loaded with food. Go upstairs, take any room you want. It's beautiful outside, ain't it?

AUNT. There's a chill. Watch out, you catch a good cold and pneumonia.

MOTHER. My sister Catherine, she can't even admit it's a beautiful day.

[MARTY—*now at the sink, getting himself a glass of water—is examining a piece of plastic that has fallen from the ceiling.*]

MARTY [*Examining the chunk of plaster in his palm*]. Boy, this place is really coming to pieces. [*Turns to* MOTHER] You know, Ma, I think, sometime we oughtta sell this place. The plumbing is rusty —everything. I'm gonna have to replaster that whole ceiling now. I think we oughtta get a little apartment somewhere's in a nicer parta town. . . . You all set, Ma?
MOTHER. I'm all set.

[*She starts for the porch door. She slowly turns and looks at* MARTY, *and then at* AUNT CATHERINE—*who returns her look.* MOTHER *and* MARTY *exit.*

DISSOLVE TO *Church. The* MOTHER *comes out of the doors and down a few steps to where* MARTY *is standing, enjoying the clearness of the June morning*]

MOTHER. In a couple-a minutes nine o'clock Mass is gonna start—in a couple-a minutes . . . [*To passersby off*] hallo, hallo . . . [*To* MARTY] Well, that was a nice girl last night, Marty. That was a nice girl.
MARTY. Yeah.
MOTHER. She wasn't a very good-looking girl, but she look like a nice girl. I said, she wasn't a very good-looking girl, not very pretty.
MARTY. I heard you, Ma.
MOTHER. She look a little old for you, about thirty-five, forty years old?
MARTY. She's twenny-nine, Ma.
MOTHER. She's more than twenny-nine years old, Marty. That's what she tells you. She looks thirty-five, forty. She didn't look Italian to me. I said, is she an Italian girl?
MARTY. I don't know. I don't think so.
MOTHER. She don't look like Italian to me. What kinda family she come from? There was something about her I don't like. It seems funny, the first time you meet her she comes to your empty house alone. These college girls, they all one step from the streets.

[MARTY *turns, frowning, to his* MOTHER.]

MARTY. What are you talkin' about? She's a nice girl.
MOTHER. I don't like her.
MARTY. You don't like her? You only met her for two minutes.
MOTHER. Don't bring her to the house no more.
MARTY. What didn't you like about her?

MOTHER. I don't know! She don't look like Italian to me, plenty nice Italian girls around.

MARTY. Well, let's not get into a fight about it, Ma. I just met the girl. I probably won't see her again.   [MARTY *leaves frame.*]

MOTHER. Eh, I'm no better than my sister Catherine.

[DISSOLVE TO *Interior, the bar . . . about an hour later. The after-Mass crowd is there, about six men ranging from twenty to forty. A couple of women in the booths. One woman is holding a glass of beer in one hand and is gently rocking a baby carriage with the other.*

Sitting in the booth of Act I are ANGIE *and three other fellows, ages twenty, thirty-two, and forty. One of the fellows, aged thirty-two, is giving a critical résumé of a recent work of literature by Mickey Spillane*]

CRITIC. . . . So the whole book winds up, Mike Hammer, he's inna room there with this doll. So he says: "You rat, you are the murderer." So she begins to con him, you know? She tells him how she loves him. And then Bam! He shoots her in the stomach. So she's laying there, gasping for breath, and she says: "How could you do that?" And he says: "It was easy."

TWENTY-YEAR-OLD. Boy, that Mickey Spillane. Boy, he can write.

ANGIE [*Leaning out of the booth and looking down the length of the bar, says with some irritation*]. What's keeping Marty?

CRITIC. What I like about Mickey Spillane is he knows how to handle women. In one book, he picks up a tomato who gets hit with a car, and she throws a pass at him. And then he meets two beautiful twins, and they throw passes at him. And then he meets some beautiful society leader, and she throws a pass at him, and . . .

TWENTY-YEAR-OLD. Boy, that Mickey Spillane, he sure can write . . .

ANGIE [*Looking out, down the bar again*]. I don't know watsa matter with Marty.

FORTY-YEAR-OLD. Boy, Angie, what would you do if Marty ever died? You'd die right with him. A couple-a old bachelors hanging to each other like barnacles. There's Marty now.

[ANGIE *leans out of the booth.*]

ANGIE [*Calling out*]. Hello, Marty, where you been?

CUT TO *front end of the bar.* MARTY *has just come in. He waves back to* ANGIE, *acknowledges another hello from a man by the bar, goes over to the bar, and gets the bartender's attention.*]

MARTY. Hello, Lou, gimme change of a half and put a dime in it for a telephone call.

[*The* BARTENDER *takes the half dollar, reaches into his apron pocket for the change.*]

BARTENDER. I hear you was at the Waverly Ballroom last night.
MARTY. Yeah. Angie tell you?
BARTENDER [*Picking out change from palm full of silver*]. Yeah, I hear you really got stuck with a dog.

[MARTY *looks at him.*]

MARTY. She wasn't so bad.
BARTENDER [*Extending the change*]. Angie says she was a real scrawny-looking thing. Well, you can't have good luck alla time.

[MARTY *takes the change slowly and frowns down at it. He moves down the bar and would make for the telephone booth, but* ANGIE *hails him from the booth.*]

ANGIE. Who you gonna call, Marty?
MARTY. I was gonna call that girl from last night, take her to a movie tonight.
ANGIE. Are you kidding?
MARTY. She was a nice girl. I kinda liked her.
ANGIE [*Indicating the spot in the booth vacated by the* FORTY-YEAR-OLD]. Siddown. You can call her later.

[MARTY *pauses, frowning, and then shuffles to the booth where* ANGIE *and the other two sit. The* CRITIC *moves over for* MARTY. *There is an exchange of hellos.*]

TWENTY-YEAR-OLD. I gotta girl, she's always asking me to marry her. So I look at that face, and I say to myself: "Could I stand looking at that face for the resta my life?"
CRITIC. Hey, Marty, you ever read a book called *I, the Jury*, by Mickey Spillane?
MARTY. No.
ANGIE. Listen, Marty, I gotta good place for us to go tonight. The kid here, he says, he was downna bazaar at Our Lady of Angels last night and . . .
MARTY. I don't feel like going to the bazaar, Angie. I thought I'd take this girl to a movie.
ANGIE. Boy, you really musta made out good last night.
MARTY. We just talked.
ANGIE. Boy, she must be some talker. She musta been about fifty years old.
CRITIC. I always figger a guy oughtta marry a girl who's twenny years

younger than he is, so that when he's forty, his wife is a real nice-looking doll.

TWENTY-YEAR-OLD. That means he'd have to marry the girl when she was one year old.

CRITIC. I never thoughta that.

MARTY. I didn't think she was so bad-looking.

ANGIE. She musta kept you inna shadows all night.

CRITIC. Marty, you don't wanna hang around with dogs. It gives you a bad reputation.

ANGIE. Marty, let's go downna bazaar.

MARTY. I told this dog I was gonna call her today.

ANGIE. Brush her.

[MARTY *looks questioningly at* ANGIE.]

MARTY. You didn't like her at all?

ANGIE. A nothing. A real nothing.

[MARTY *looks down at the dime he has been nervously turning between two fingers and then, frowning, he slips it into his jacket pocket. He lowers his face and looks down, scowling at his thoughts. Around him, the voices clip along.*]

CRITIC. What's playing on Fordham Road? I think there's a good picture in the Loew's Paradise.

ANGIE. Let's go down to Forty-second Street and walk around. We're sure to wind up with something.

[*Slowly* MARTY *begins to look up again. He looks from face to face as each speaks.*]

CRITIC. I'll never forgive La Guardia for cutting burlesque outta New York City.

TWENTY-YEAR-OLD. There's burlesque over in Union City. Let's go to Union City. . . .

ANGIE. Ah, they're always crowded on Sunday night.

CRITIC. So wadda you figure on doing tonight, Angie?

ANGIE. I don't know. Wadda you figure on doing?

CRITIC. I don't know. [*Turns to the* TWENTY-YEAR-OLD] Wadda you figure on doing?

[*The* TWENTY-YEAR-OLD *shrugs.*]

Suddenly MARTY *brings his fist down on the booth table with a crash. The others turn, startled, toward him.* MARTY *rises in his seat.*]

MARTY. "What are you doing tonight?" "I don't know, what are you doing?" Burlesque! Loew's Paradise! Miserable and lonely! Miserable and lonely and stupid! What am I, crazy or something?! I got something good! What am I hanging around with you guys for?!

[*He has said this in tones so loud that it attracts the attention of everyone in the bar. A little embarrassed,* MARTY *turns and moves quickly to the phone booth, pausing outside the door to find his dime again.* ANGIE *is out of his seat immediately and hurries after him.*]

ANGIE [*A little shocked at* MARTY's *outburst*]. Watsa matter with you?
MARTY [*In a low, intense voice*]. You don't like her. My mother don't like her. She's a dog, and I'm a fat, ugly little man. All I know is I had a good time last night. I'm gonna have a good time tonight. If we have enough good times together, I'm going down on my knees and beg that girl to marry me. If we make a party again this New Year's, I gotta date for the party. You don't like her, that's too bad. [*He moves into the booth, sits, turns again to* ANGIE, *smiles.*] When you gonna get married, Angie? You're thirty-four years old. All your kid brothers are married. You oughtta be ashamed of yourself.

[*Still smiling at his private joke, he puts the dime into the slot and then— with a determined finger—he begins to dial.*]

[*Fade Out*]

ACKNOWLEDGMENTS

"A & P": Copyright © 1962 by John Updike. From *Pigeon Feathers and Other Stories*, by John Updike. Reprinted by permission of Alfred A. Knopf, Inc. Originally appeared in *The New Yorker*.

"anyone lived in a pretty how town": Copyright, 1940, by E. E. Cummings; renewed, 1968, by Marion Morehouse Cummings. Reprinted from *Poems* 1923–1954 by E. E. Cummings by permission of Harcourt Brace Jovanovich, Inc.

"Ariadne": Thomas Merton, *Selected Poems*. Copyright 1946 by New Directions Publishing Corporation. Reprinted by permission of New Directions Publishing Corporation.

"To an Athlete Dying Young": From "A Shropshire Lad"—Authorised Edition—from *The Collected Poems of A. E. Housman*. Copyright 1939, 1940, © 1959 by Holt, Rinehart and Winston, Inc. Copyright © 1967, 1968 by Robert E. Symons. Reprinted by permission of Holt, Rinehart and Winston, Inc.

"Autumn Begins in Martin's Ferry, Ohio": Copyright © 1962 by James Wright. Reprinted from *The Branch Will Not Break*, by James Wright, by permission of Wesleyan University Press.

"The Ballad of Sue Ellen Westerfield": By Robert Hayden from *Selected Poems*. Copyright © 1966 by Robert Hayden. Reprinted by permission of October House Inc.

"Base Details": From *Collected Poems* by Siegfried Sassoon. Copyright 1918 by E. P. Dutton & Co., renewed 1946 by Siegfried Sassoon. Reprinted by permission of The Viking Press, Inc.

"Buddies": by Giovanni Verga from *The She-Wolf and Other Stories,* trans. by Giovanni Cecchetti. Originally published by the University of California Press, reprinted by permission of The Regents of the University of California.

"Buffalo Bill's": Copyright, 1923, 1951, by E. E. Cummings. Reprinted from his volume *Poems* 1923–1954 by permission of Harcourt Brace Jovanovich, Inc.

"Christmas Eve Under Hooker's Statue": From *Lord Weary's Castle*, copyright, 1944, 1946, by Robert Lowell. Reprinted by permission of Harcourt Brace Jovanovich, Inc.

"Crossing the Frontier": From *Collected Poems* 1930–1965 by A. D. Hope. Copyright 1963, 1966 in all countries of the International Copyright Union by A. D. Hope. All rights reserved. Reprinted by permission of The Viking Press, Inc.

"David": From *Poems* 1930–1960 by Josephine Miles. Reprinted by permission of the Indiana University Press.

"David and Goliath": By Don Geiger. Reprinted by permission of *The Western Humanities Review*.

"The Death of the Ball Turret Gunner": Reprinted with the permission of Farrar, Straus & Giroux, Inc. from *The Complete Poems* by Randall Jarrell, copyright © 1945, 1948, 1969 by Mrs. Randall Jarrell.

"The Death of a Soldier": Copyright 1923, renewed 1951 by Wallace Stevens. From *The Collected Poems of Wallace Stevens*. Reprinted by permission of Alfred A. Knopf, Inc.

"The Devil in the Dark": From a *Star Trek* script by Gene L. Coon. Reprinted by permission of Paramount Pictures.

"Disabled": Wilfred Owen, *Collected Poems*. Copyright Chatto & Windus, Ltd. 1946, © 1963. Reprinted by permission of New Directions Publishing Corporation.

"Dulce et Decorum Est": Wilfred Owen, *Collected Poems*. Copyright Chatto & Windus, Ltd. 1946, © 1963. Reprinted by permission of New Directions Publishing Corporation.

BIBLIOGRAPHY

Allen, John Alexander, ed.:   *Hero's Way,* Prentice-Hall, 1971.
Boorstin, Daniel: *Image: Or, What Happened to the American Dream,* Atheneum, 1962.
Brombert, Victor, ed.:   *Hero in Literature,* Fawcett, 1969.
Campbell, Joseph: *The Hero with a Thousand Faces,* Meridian, 1956.
Carlyle, Thomas: *On Heroes, Hero-Worship, and the Heroic in History,* University of Nebraska, 1966.
Daiches, David: "The Possibilities of Heroism," *American Scholar,* Winter, 1955–1956.
Drotning, Phillip: *Black Heroes in Our Nation's History,* Cowles, 1969.
Feiffer, Jules: *The Great Comic Book Heroes,* Dial, 1965.
Fishwick, Marshall: *Hero, American Style,* McKay, 1969.
Frye, Northrop: *Anatomy of Criticism: Four Essays,* Atheneum, 1966.
Galloway, David: *The Absurd Hero in American Fiction: Updike, Styron, Bellow, Salinger,* University of Texas Press, 1969.
Graves, Robert: *The White Goddess, a Historical Grammar of Poetic Myth,* Noonday, 1966.
Grella, George: "James Bond: Culture Hero," *New Republic,* May 30, 1964.
Gross, Theodore: *The Heroic Ideal in American Literature,* Free Press, 1971.
Harmon, Jim: *The Great Radio Heroes,* Doubleday, 1967.
Heilbrun, C.:   "The Woman As Hero," *Texas Quarterly,* Winter, 1965.
Hook, Sidney: *The Hero in History: A Study in Limitations & Possibility,* Beacon, 1955.
Kern, E.:   "The Modern Hero: Phoenix Or Ashes?", *Comparative Literature,* Fall, 1958.
Lubin, Harold, ed.:   *Heroes and Anti-Heroes,* Chandler, 1968.
Moorman, Charles: *Kings and Captains: Variations on a Heroic Theme,* University of Kentucky.
Norman, Dorothy: *The Hero: Myth, Image & Symbol,* World, 1969.
Pickett, Roy: *The Theme of the Hero,* Wm. C. Brown, 1969.
Lord Raglan: *The Hero: A Study in Tradition, Myth and Drama,* Vintage, 1956.
Rollin, Roger: "Beowulf to Batman: The Epic Hero and Pop Culture," *College English,* February, 1970.
Schlesinger, Arthur M., Jr.:   "The Decline of Heroes," *Saturday Evening Post,* November 1, 1958.
Steckmesser, Kent L.:   *The Western Hero in History and Legend,* University of Oklahoma Press, 1967.
Warshow, Robert: *The Immediate Experience,* Doubleday, 1962.
Wecter, Dixon: *The Hero in America,* University of Michigan, 1963.
Yolen, Will and Kenneth S. Giniger, eds.:   *Heroes for Our Times,* Stackpole, 1968.